The critics praise
CHAYYM ZELDIS

"The author has a profound grasp of his materials. He presents a landscape that is compelling, bitter, and utterly believable."

—*The New York Times*

"Zeldis calls on us to luxuriate in the pleasures of old-fashioned brilliant narrative."

—*The Los Angeles Times*

"His writing has a magical quality."

—*Henry Miller*

"His knowledge of history is as amazing as his skill in using it."

—*Elie Wiesel*

"A Middle Eastern Romeo and Juliet . . . all the characters are sensitively drawn."

—*Publishers Weekly*

A FORBIDDEN LOVE

CHAYYM ZELDIS

BERKLEY BOOKS, NEW YORK

A FORBIDDEN LOVE

A Berkley Book/published by arrangement with
the author

PRINTING HISTORY
Berkley edition/November 1983

ISBN: 0-425-06739-4

A BERKLEY BOOK® TM 757,375
Berkley Books are published by The Berkley Publishing Group,
200 Madison Avenue, New York, NY 10016.
The name "BERKLEY" and the stylized "B" with design are trademarks
belonging to Berkley Publishing Corporation.

PRINTED IN THE UNITED STATES OF AMERICA

To Hope and Jodi—whose hearts were open

*For helping to make this book possible,
I thank my wife, Nina, whose compass never
failed me; and my editor, Mel Parker, whose
support was constant.*

As a lily among thorns, so is my love...
—Song of Songs

1982

Somewhere in the Negev, Israel

THE SUN WAS SINKING, setting fire to the forest of the sky.

Lieutenant-Colonel Uri Arnon climbed out of the dust-whitened jeep and walked slowly and deliberately up to the top of the rise. Alone on the ridge, he stared over the expanse of the red-shimmering sand into the far distance—into the vast, raw wilderness of the Sinai, from which, in April of that year, the Israelis had completely withdrawn. He stood there for several long moments, hands on hips, motionless, solitary, staring off into space. There were thoughts in his mind, and suddenly he felt the need to remember. . . .

He saw the faces of Arie and D'vora, his father and mother. They were smiling, both of them, but their eyes were filled with the kind of pain that never goes away. Then he saw the faces of Mahmoud and S'ad, Layleh's parents. A shadow fell across them and they vanished. Then he saw Layleh and himself. They were both young, not yet eighteen, sitting in their own private "grotto," their secret refuge out behind the big double house with the spacious backyard divided by the hedge on the outskirts of Jerusalem. . . .

Layleh was overcome—as she often was—by the fear that their relationship might end in nothing. Although that night she did not say explicitly, "I am Layleh Malek, the Arab girl, and you are Uri Arnon, the Jew," that was what she meant.

Lieutenant-Colonel Uri Arnon shivered. The scene faded. Suddenly and all but involuntarily, his arms dropped to his sides and his eyes filled with tears. Out of the raw wilderness of his heart, Layleh's voice spoke to him. *"Il el abed*—forever, Uri?" it said sweetly in Arabic.

Uri could not help himself. *"L'olam, yakirati*—forever, darling," he answered aloud in Hebrew.

1948

Saint-Michel, France
The Transit Camp

DUSK.

Beyond the high, rough-textured stone wall that snaked its way erratically around the chateau's grounds, the treetops swayed fitfully in sudden, sharp gusts of breeze that had sprung up from the sea. Over the trees' supple boughs the sky was losing the last, lonely sandbars of mauve and indigo and scarlet and gold; and farther to the west, the crests of the hills that encircled the cove like guardian sentries were blurring in the failing light and would in a matter of minutes be lost in darkness.

It was the time—neither of day nor of night; neither of this world nor of some other—that D'vora loved best. Life—not only her own existence but all life—seemed to hover like some fragile and yet indestructible bubble, filled with infinite longing and infinite satisfaction. D'vora knew, of course, that her feeling was sheer illusion; nevertheless, she persisted in indulging herself in the fantasy of being with her husband again, and whenever possible slipped away from her office and stood alone on the westward balcony of the crumbling chateau to welcome the twilight and dream her harmless, momentary dream.

The wind, rising with renewed resolution as if to bend D'vora as it bent the upper branches of the trees, tugged at the pale blond locks of her hair and lifted the corners of her open-necked khaki shirt. The long, elegantly tapered fingers of her hands gripped the rail of the balcony. Her lips, just parting, formed the three syllables of a name: "Arie..."

She could say the name Arie easily, casually, even dispassionately in conversation during the rest of the hours of the day and night, but at those times it had nothing to do with the real image of the person which she kept securely shut in the chamber of her heart: only in her secret twilight interludes would she

4

silently invoke his presence. Her lips opened and, like the shining bubble of the moment itself, the beloved name appeared and the man was sheltered in her arms: *"Arie..."*

D'vora shivered. Darkness. The stone wall had faded and the trees were gone. The hills that guarded the cove, out of which the ships with their human cargoes set out for the waiting coasts of Israel, had been swallowed up by the night. Even the neat rows of tents which fanned out from the edge of the sandy chateau courtyard to the dusty, excrement-pocked path along the base of the wall that the sentries walked, were no longer to be seen. Darkness. Darkness and a breeze that had become a chest-thumping wind carrying the dissipated scent of spoiled citrus and the mingled smells of invisible sea and impending rain. Darkness and the immigrants beginning to gather on the cinders of the chateau's northern yard to wait for the clanging of the tire rim that served the Saint-Michel transit camp as mealtime bell.

Suddenly, D'vora stiffened. She had within herself a certain sense that warned her of another's presence, even though she could neither see nor hear the newcomer. Actually, she had possessed this ability for as long as she could remember, from the earliest days of her childhood in Germany, and had come to call it her survival sense. She withdrew her hands from the balcony rail and turned.

"Ah, Dr. Arnon," said the thick, studiedly ironic voice to D'vora. "I thought I'd surprise you, but you've turned the tables—as usual!" The voice forced itself into laughter and added, "Nobody puts anything over on you, Dr. Arnon—I should have learned that by now."

D'vora shrugged. Though she could not in the new-fallen darkness see the face of the tall, big-boned, rough-voiced man who stood as solid as a hunk of granite in the doorway to the balcony, she could picture clearly in her mind the look of mingled disdain and amusement that was surely on his features. "Big Ed," as he was called in the camp, even by people who pronounced the words *Beeg Ett*, was an American ex-Marine, a veteran of the entire, arduous, bloody Pacific campaign of World War II, who was in charge of training—and, more often, of disciplining—the American military recruits during the time they were quartered in the French transit camp, awaiting pas-

sage to Israel, along with the immigrants whose lives they
would be called upon to defend. The peculiar look of truculent
merriment that D'vora imagined on the face of the former
Marine sergeant had been an inveterate topic of discussion in
the camp. "Like Adam was the Original Sinner," he was fond
of informing his motley charges, "I was the Original Sergeant—the guy they patterned all the other damn sergeants in
the Marine Corps after; so you better look out for me—even
when I'm sleeping, I'm more alert than you bastards are awake!"
Some people—probably the naive and the innocent—said that
the bellicose irony was a cover behind which the real Ed Markowitz hid, while others—most probably the cynics—claimed
that Ed's cover was the lid over a cesspool; still another group,
including D'vora herself, had never committed themselves to
a position.

"I hate like hell to disturb your meditations, Dr. Arnon,
but——"

D'vora interrupted. "I know, Ed—but *we've got a war
going on*. Isn't that what you were going to say?"

"You took the words right out of my mouth, Dr. Arnon! I
see that you know me very well——"

"How can I help?"

The huge mass of a man sighed. "I've got a sick man—or
sick *almost* man—in my third platoon. Tent number nineteen,
south quad. Name's Aronson."

"Can he come to the infirmary?"

The Original Sergeant guffawed. "If he could *crawl* to the
infirmary, Dr. Arnon, would I be here now?"

D'vora smiled. "You've got a good point there, Ed," she
said. "What seems to be the trouble?"

"Fever. Very high. Chills. Puking his guts up."

"I'll see him now."

"Good," growled Ed: "Let me take you over to the tent—
though from the smell, you could probably find it yourself."

———————

Aronson, Arnold H. . . .

Aronson, thought D'vora, staring down at the chart. *Ben-
Aharon,* "son of Aaron." What did the *H* stand for? Harold?

Henry? Hubert? It was unlikely, D'vora thought, given the tendency of Jews to assimilate, that it stood for Hillel....

Born 1926. Brooklyn, U.S.A....

As though to iron out the questions in her mind, D'vora smoothed down the chart. And what exactly, she wondered, had brought Arnold H. Aronson from the borough of Brooklyn in the United States, in the late August of 1948, to the transit camp of Saint-Michel outside of Marseille in southern France? What had pulled him from the safety of America toward the cauldron of slaughter that boiled over in the newly declared state of Israel? What magnet had drawn him into a conflict which American Jews generally regarded, in tremulous silence, from a distance? Why was Aronson, Arnold H., age twenty-two, *here?*

D'vora shook her head and picked up her pen. It was dry, and with some annoyance she had to refill it from a bottle whose cap resisted her efforts to get it off. She wrote briskly, in a large, loose handwriting that Arie had always, laughingly, called dinosaur tracks, of Arnold H. Aronson's diagnosed influenza and then filed the chart away. For a moment, she sat staring at the rusting steel cabinet into which the chart had unceremoniously gone; she knew that most probably it would never be seen again by her eyes. And yet, even as she turned her gaze away, she knew that she would remember the pale-faced, glassy-eyed image of the warrior Aronson from Brooklyn. That, as Arie would so often say, was his wife D'vora's nature.

A single unshaded bulb dangled on a cord from the high ceiling, bathing D'vora's desk in a harsh white cone of light but leaving the far corners of the enormous room in shadow. There was a small framed photograph of Arie on one corner of the desk. It had been taken a couple of years ago in Tiberias, just after their marriage, and showed her husband in khakis and sporting the thick black mustache he had cultivated in his late teens, though later, for some unfathomable reason, he had shaved it off just prior to her departure. D'vora glanced at it momentarily and then, after locking her desk drawer, rose and left her office.

She went hurriedly down a flight of dimly lit stairs whose worn and chipped marble surfaces sent echoes of her footsteps careening off the ghostly walls, and on the first-floor landing

ran into Menashe, the camp director, who was just coming out
of his office.

Menashe smiled and put a hand on her shoulder. "D'vora,"
he said, "Ed was looking for you a while ago——"

"Yes, I know. He found me."

"Anything wrong?"

"One of his men is sick."

"Serious?"

"Flu. A high fever and the usual symptoms." D'vora's eyes
narrowed. "Why do you ask?"

Menashe squeezed her shoulder. "The *Pan York*'s in the
harbor. She arrived late this afternoon."

"When will she leave?"

"As soon as she takes on supplies—tomorrow night, most
probably. Will he be able to go?"

D'vora shrugged. "Perhaps. I'll see how he is in the morning."

Menashe nodded. "And the rest of the population—how do
we stand?"

"We have one case of possible appendicitis, a child who
fractured his leg yesterday and theoretically shouldn't be moved
yet, and a woman who may go into labor at any time. Then
there is the usual batch of chronically ill who, if they've made
it this far, will certainly go on. All told, give or take a dozen
or so who may complain of exhaustion and remain for the next
boat, we can clear the camp completely."

"Splendid!" exclaimed Menashe. "You're far and away the
best doctor we've ever had here!"

"It's the power of my faith," said D'vora.

"Of course. . . ."

"No, but I mean it!"

Menashe laughed. "Whatever you say, D'vora." He dropped
his hand from her shoulder. "How about supper?"

"I thought you'd never ask," said D'vora.

————

The huge, lofty-ceilinged room that served as the camp's dining
hall faced the north. D'vora imagined that it had once, decades

ago, been a glittering, chandelier-studded, tapestry-draped salon in which the local aristocracy gathered on chill winter nights and drowsy summer evenings for splendid masked balls and impeccably proper receptions. But its gigantic windows had long ago been boarded up against the vagaries of the weather, and its barnlike walls had been whitewashed to cover over the mildew and rot. Over the entrance door, square black characters that had recently been repainted to enforce their impact proclaimed ONE PEOPLE, ONE LANGUAGE—SPEAK HEBREW! while high on the rear wall, words written by Theodore Herzl appeared: ZIONISM IS THE SABBATH OF MY LIFE. From the long, closely spaced rows of unpainted wooden tables and benches, which accommodated five hundred immigrants at a sitting, an unbroken cacophony of rattling tin dishes, scraping utensils, scuffling shoes, and buzzing voices rose into the air. While some of the members of camp's staff complained perennially to their tablemates about the unearthly din, D'vora always said that the sounds were music to her ears.

D'vora was moody and silent during the meal; attempts on the part of her colleagues to engage her in conversation or banter were met that night with blank looks, little jerks of her shoulders, a general sullenness. When someone irritatedly said, "You're not yourself tonight, D'vora," she gave him a savage look. She did not intend to offend, but she could not help herself. The time before an immigrant ship left for Israel was, as best as she could express it to herself, a sort of holy period. It made her feel somewhat as she had as a little girl in Berlin when her parents took her with them to the crowded, brilliantly lit synagogue. Though, as she well knew, she was incapable of restraining herself from feeling this way, the gentle rebuffs she dealt out to the others made her feel a little guilty—perhaps, she thought, it would have been better for her to eat alone in her office or come into the dining hall after the last shift had finished.

As the last bitter black dregs of the liquid which, as the camp staffers were fond of saying, "tried and failed miserably to pass as coffee" were being sipped and slurped from half a thousand tin cups, Menashe rose. D'vora looked up at him. He was a short, squat, powerfully muscled man in his late thirties, with thick, curly dark hair, jet-black eyes, and swarthy skin, who had come to what was then the British Mandate of Palestine in his teens from "among the oppressed Jews of Damascus," as he said, "on foot . . . over the mountains." Now he said nothing but simply stood and raised one hand and in almost no time obtained the silence he wanted from his audience. Such were the strength and authority of his bearing.

"Achim v'achot," he began in Hebrew and then, switching to the Yiddish that the vast majority of immigrants would understand, continued: "Brothers and sisters, I am happy to tell you that . . ." Then his right hand reached over his broad chest and set itself against his heart. His eyes shone and he went on: ". . . that the time all of you have been waiting and hoping and longing for—against all odds and despite all doubts and in the face of all obstacles—has at last arrived. The God of Israel, whatever relationship you have with Him and whatever He means to you, has answered your prayers. He Who first called to our ancestors in days of old has kindled the fire of courage and determination in the sons and daughters of the renascent State of Israel; and they have sent the ship to bring you home." He paused and, struggling to keep his voice from foundering in the tide of emotion that shook him, declared: "Home . . . from the four corners of the earth where you were unwelcome and unwanted; home from the alien countries in which you were despised and discarded. This afternoon, the ship arrived—*your* ship, brothers and sisters. At this very moment, she lies at anchor in a cove not far from our camp. And tomorrow, dear brothers and sisters, you will board her and set sail for *your* land, for *your own* soil, where you will be loved. . . ."

He stopped and leaned forward, then pulled a handkerchief from a trouser pocket and wiped the gleaming studs of sweat from his dark forehead, the hollows of his cheeks, the knot of his chin, and the strong curve of his neck. And then, grasping the handkerchief in a hairy-knuckled fist, he repeated the message in French and then again in Arabic—deliberately, unhurryingly, with exacting and painstaking care, so that no word might lose even an iota of its meaning and force. At length, covered again with perspiration that he did not bother to remove, he cried out, *"Shalom*—peace!" and was finished.

D'vora stared up at him. She swallowed and then turned her eyes toward the people whom he had addressed—toward

the unwanted and the unwelcome of the earth. The faces, bathed
in the harsh, uncompromising glare of naked bulbs and kerosene lamps, were a blur as flat and white as the walls. Sometimes, when on the eve of a ship's departure, Menashe made
such a speech, his audience cheered wildly and clapped and
stamped their feet and hugged one another or even hugged
themselves as if for the first time in their lives they felt they
were real. One time, D'vora remembered, a white-haired old
Jew from a small town in Poland, who—wounded only su-
perficially in the nape of his neck by a German bullet—had
crawled out from under a pile of corpses and lived to make his
way across the graveyard of Europe and then down to the
south of France, leaped up onto one of the front tables and in
a thin, uncannily beautiful voice that issued from his wizened
throat chanted: "'*B'shuv Adonai et shivat Tzion, hayyinu
k'chol'mim*—When the Lord returned us unto Zion, we were
like unto dreamers. . . .'" The crowd had snatched his frail and
writhing body up and borne it around the vast chamber of the
dining hall like a skiff on a raging river until the poor fellow
had fainted out of excitement, and the women, believing he
was dead on the very threshold of the Promised Land, had
begun to shriek and pull at their hair and were quieted only by
the most strenuous efforts of the staff.

But tonight, for some inexplicable reason, it was different.
Nobody in the room moved and nobody uttered a sound; it was
as if a sorcerer's pass had frozen the throng. Menashe had
nothing more to say. He and D'vora and the others at the staff
table—even the most cynical among them—could only stare
in amazement and wait for something—they had no idea what—
to happen. Several moments more of the glacierlike silence
and immobility elapsed, and still there was nothing. Then,
D'vora saw, a man at the very rear of the room, directly under
Herzl's legend on the back wall, stood up. Immediately he was
joined by his neighbor to the right, and then a woman at a
center table rose, and then suddenly—with earthquake ra-
pidity—the entire crowd was on its feet. D'vora knew now what
was coming, and even before she could get up, it did. "Hatikvah," the anthem of Jewish hope, burst simultaneously, like a
long-pent-up stroke of thunder, from five hundred throats inside
the dining hall and from the throbbing throats of countless

hundreds more in the trampled dust of the chateau's north yard, where a large crowd had gathered to hear Menashe's speech over the public address system.

D'vora had heard the words and plaintive melody of the song a thousand times before, even in Germany, before she had come to Palestine in 1938 when she was just eighteen. The song was as familiar to her as the whispers and caresses of her beloved Arie. But even as the glance or touch of her lover-husband awakened the spark of love that united them, so did the anthem stir her deepest emotions. She did not believe blindly in the love of nation, but she trusted implicitly, with all her being, in her nation of love. She who had herself been an immigrant a decade before, fleeing, while the escape hatches were still open, the horrors that had cut off the lives of her family, sang now with these new immigrants, passing effort-lessly through the open gates of the song into their pain and sorrow and desolation and mounting with them the well-worn steps of these feelings to some higher, healing realm of comfort and hope.

Once, during the early days of her medical practice, when a patient had died unexpectedly and she had been crushed by the loss, Arie had taken her chin into his hand and lifted her head and gazed into her tear-blurred eyes and said softly: "Sin-cere grief is prayer; and prayer, dear D'vora, is a pledge to live life better—with more compassion and understanding and with the honest recognition that no matter who we are or what we feel, or how much power we think we have, death in the end seals every exit and cancels everything out. So that, darling D'vora, we must make each instant of life count. . . ." She remembered the scene exactly now, down to every minute detail—even the lock of hair that had fallen across Arie's forehead as he stood with her in blazing summer sunlight on the brilliant white flagstones of the walk in front of the hospital on Mount Scopus.

His words came back to her now and added fervor to her singing. And then, her body shaken like the treetops she had seen from the balcony outside her office at dusk, D'vora wept. She wept openly, unashamedly—even with a fierce pride. There were those, the so-called "hardened" ones, among the members of the transit camp's staff and immigrants alike, who, no matter what happened, would never cry. Not so with D'vora.

———————

There were no stars in the sky over Saint-Michel. Perhaps, under the cover of the heavy clouds that had rolled in from the sea, the stars had all sped furtively toward the rust-hulled immigrant ship that lay at nervous anchor in the black waters of the cove, and managed to stow themselves away for the journey to Israel that would begin on the morrow. The wind had died down somewhat, leaving the exhausted trees to doze peacefully in the darkness, but the smell of impending rain was keener in the air; it would certainly fall before the light of morning. Through the massive, ornately grillworked front gates of the transit camp—where once splendidly groomed horses and fancy carriages with footmen and, later on, gleaming automobiles driven by chauffeurs had come to be received by the chateau's liveried servants—a fleet of gruff-engined trucks had entered and now lumbered along a dirt road to the storehouse at the rear of the kitchen to load supplies for the *Pan York*. On her way to the south quad, D'vora saw them and rejoiced.

After supper, D'vora had attended a staff meeting in Menashe's office and then gone to see her sickest patients. The case of possible appendicitis was turning out, fortunately, to be a false alarm—it was most likely a pulled muscle. The child with the fractured leg would all but certainly be able to leave on time—much to the relief and gratitude of his worried parents. And the pregnant woman's baby, for its own inscrutable and indisputable reasons, had decided that it was not yet ready to enter the world. Barring an emergency, D'vora was through for the night. Menashe had invited her to come to a staff *kumsitz*—a general and, it was hoped, good-natured get-together—after she was finished with her rounds, but D'vora had tactfully declined, pleading exhaustion. Actually, she wanted to go back to her office, which was also her room, and write a long-overdue letter to Arie that she would manage to give to one of the *Pan York*'s mates the next day. On a sudden impulse, though, she decided to look in on the ailing American she had examined before supper. From a medical point of view, it wasn't really necessary, but she wanted to see Ed Markowitz's "almost-man," Arnold H. Aronson, anyway. The urge was inexplicable, but she felt it nonetheless; somehow it brought to mind an experience with Arie that happened just some weeks after they were married.

She had called the *Sochnut Yehudit*, the quasi-governmental agency representing Palestine's Jews, where Arie worked, to tell him she would be late. "How late, D'vora?" he asked.

"Say seven, eight at the most."

When, toward dawn, she entered their tiny apartment, she found her new husband waiting up for her. Wordlessly, they fell into each other's arms and soon made love. But D'vora seemed distant and distracted. Only after it was over did Arie say, "What happened, D'vora?"

"I sat up with a patient—a young girl who stepped on a land mine last week and lost a leg."

"Why didn't you sedate her?" Arie asked.

"Because . . . because I felt she needed the human contact."

"I see," said Arie. "But then why didn't you call me again?"

"To tell you the truth, Arie, I almost forgot you existed!" There was a silence and then she said, "Can you understand that? I mean . . . for the moment, I forgot about everything."

Arie nodded.

"But why didn't *you* phone the hospital?"

A slowly evolving smile lit Arie's tanned features. "D'vora, do you know what the Talmud says about physicians?"

She shook her head.

"The Talmud says 'A doctor is a doctor by the authority of God.'" He kissed her and then whispered softly: "Well, D'vora, according to that definition, God must have personally dispatched an angel to bring you your degree."

D'vora's mind skipped from that experience to others in which she had been unexpectedly late in coming home and Arie had been understanding. "You're a born healer," Arie often told her. And that was true. The urge—almost the necessity—to heal, to repair what was damaged and broken in human beings by the cruel vagaries of life and perhaps the greater cruelty of men, had always been a part of her nature. She had been that way as a child in the 1920s and as an adolescent in the '30s in Germany. She had always looked after injured dogs and cats, and once, as a small girl in Berlin, kept a pigeon with a shattered wing in her room and nursed it back to health. Even as a child, she had dreamed of one day being a doctor, and her parents had encouraged her.

Though they had not accompanied her to Palestine in 1938, they had provided her with the necessary funds to study medicine at the Hebrew University in Jerusalem. Now, at twenty-eight, she *was* a doctor, "more intent," as Arie often said, "on healing than ever." Arie understood D'vora's need; and he understood the consequences.

But at the outset, he seemed not to have understood her need to go to the transit camp in Saint-Michel. "There's more than enough to do here in Israel," he had told her. "Why must you go to France?"

It had not been easy to tell him—she had hedged. "They've asked me to serve in Saint-Michel," she said, "and I feel I *have to*. That's all."

"There are other doctors in Israel, D'vora. Why . . . *you?*"

Telling him forced her to speak openly of all of the old wounds—of the grimness and pain of her years growing up under the rise of the Nazis; of the stubbornness and blindness of her parents in their tragic belief that the Nazi era would swiftly pass; of the sadness of her departure from her own family and friends at the age of eighteen; of the ensuing flames of the Holocaust that had engulfed everyone and everything she had left behind. She had, of course, told Arie these things before, but now—given no choice—she unbolted these locked closets of her memory and recounted them again. And then she had said: "The remnants—the pitiful remnants—of our people are coming out of the ashes . . . are coming home. Something deep, very deep inside me says that I must . . . meet them at the threshold. I will have a special understanding for them, a special way with them. Can you understand that, Arie? It's difficult . . . almost impossible to explain, but——"

"I . . . understand," said Arie.

"Do you? Do you really?"

He took her in his arms. "I shall miss you, D'vora——"

"And I shall miss you, darling. More than I can ever say . . ."

———————

"*Doctor* Arnon!"

She turned quickly. On the path behind her was the tall

figure of Big Ed Markowitz. An Aussie hat—always his favorite—with turned-up brim-flap and worn leather chin strap
dangling to his Adam's apple, was perched on his head. His
khaki shirt was open to midchest, and the square handle of a
revolver—he referred to it constantly as the "faithful .45" that
had paved his way across the Pacific—jutted from a polished
holster bulging at his right hip. He was wearing paratrooper
boots and had a cigarette tucked snugly behind one of his ears,
and over one shoulder he carried a heavily loaded burlap sack.

"Dr. Arnon," he boomed. "Come—that is, *please* come to our
party!"

D'vora smiled. "Whose party?"

"My men—that is, my 'almost-men'—and I are celebrating
the arrival and, more so, the imminent departure of the *Pan
York*. In their name, and as their commander, I invite you to
be present. There'll be food and drink, but most important of
all, good spirit!" The Original Sergeant grinned. "Will you
come?"

"Thanks, Ed, but I can't." D'vora shrugged. "As a matter
of fact, I've already turned down one party tonight."

"Is that so? Who invited you before I did?"

"Menashe."

Big Ed guffawed. "Menashe! That's ridiculous! How can
you compare Menashe Halabi to Big Ed Markowitz? It's like
comparing a bedbug to a butterfly! Only a fool—which I know
you are not, Dr. Arnon—would put the two invitations in the
same category."

"I'm sorry, Ed, really. . . ."

The look of irony on Ed's coarse, weatherbeaten features
suddenly and surprisingly vanished. When he spoke again, his
voice softened, so that it was all but unrecognizable. "Listen,
D'vora," he said, "all kidding aside, I know you're a busy
doctor and a tired lady, but I really want you to be with us—
even for a little while. It's a special night, and, well, with you
there . . . it'll be even more special."

"Ed——"

"You see," said Ed, shifting the weight of the sack on his
shoulder, "this is my last night at Saint-Michel."

"Your last night here? What do you mean?"

"My replacement," said Ed quietly, "is coming down from

Paris tomorrow. I'm leaving on the *Pan York* with the men."
He cleared his throat. "It seems they're expecting some sort
of desperate push by the Arabs soon and, well, they want me
in Israel." His eyes shone. "What else can I say . . . except that
it's about time for me——"

"I—we'll all miss you, Ed."

"Sure, you will," Ed sighed. "Will you come to our party,
D'vora?"

"I wouldn't miss it for the world."

Between the last of the south quad's conical, green-gray field
tents—almost two thousand of the identical tents surrounded
the chateau—and the encircling stone wall, the men of *Mit-
nadvei Chutz la-Aretz*, the Overseas Volunteers Unit under Big
Ed Markowitz's direct command, had, after meticulously
combing the camp grounds from end to end, heaped up fallen
tree branches, dry brushwood, bits of broken packing crates,
scraps of long-ago discarded furniture—whatever they could
scrounge and physically bear away—and built an impressive
pyre. That done, they had ranged themselves, nearly a hundred
and fifty of them, in a wide semicircle that faced inward toward
the chateau. Ed and D'vora found them that way, strangely
silent, almost like anxious children awaiting their teacher on
the first day of school. But Ed, as he murmured to D'vora,
was not a man to lose time, which people squandered shame-
lessly, as if they would never run out of it. At once, he set the
burlap sack down on the earth and bellowed out: "Okay, men,
let's go!"

The sound of his gruff, self-assured voice was all that was
needed to break the tension. Instantly, a beefy-faced fellow in
ill-fitting khakis jumped to his feet and doused kerosene over
the pyre from a large tin can. Beside him, another volunteer
lit a paper torch and then flung it onto the wood. Within seconds, a roaring bonfire blazed up, laying uneven tongues of
yellow-orange light over the clearing and sending a steady
stream of sparks into the starless sky. A hoarse, prolonged
cheer leaped from the open mouths of the volunteers as, caught

between shifting waves of firelight and darkness, they rose to begin their celebration.

D'vora had one—or half of one—drink of Scotch, which Ed served her somewhat apologetically because it was warm, since there was no ice to be had at Saint-Michel. D'vora took tiny sips of her drink, without much enthusiasm but with a strong sense of obligation. She toasted *"L'chayyim*—to life!" with Ed, who beamed from ear to ear, and then with a steady succession of volunteers who emerged a little uncertainly out of the swirling, laughing, chanting, stomping crowd to resolutely touch and knock their battered tin cups against hers. Then, a little self-consciously at first but gradually with more ease, she shook hands with a long, uneven, jostling line of young men in a strange and motley assortment of army and old army clothing. Some were diffident and uneasy, averting their glances and mumbling almost inaudibly in English and broken Hebrew; others were bold and all but brazen, thrusting their hands out belligerently and shouting out their salutations. But each and every one of them, D'vora sensed, was eager for the comfort of a woman's eyes and hungry for the healing contact he supposed to be in the touch of a woman's flesh.

These, D'vora thought, were Big Ed's "almost-men" who would soon be called on to reach for the resources of their young manhood. He had, for hours on end, put them through the doll-like rigors of close-order drill with rickety wooden rifles in the dry, fuming dust of the chateau's south yard, which he had claimed exclusively as his own, inviolable parade ground, working them into sweat-soaked, scarlet-faced marionettes in the blazing heat of the August sun. He had trotted them, in ragged, puffing files, along the footprint-pocked path that followed every crazy zigzag and erratic turn of the chateau's grimy, urine-stained outer wall. He had led them, howling and whooping like savages, through the camp's copses of crooked pines and yellow-needled firs. He had coached them endlessly and relentlessly in boxing and wrestling and jujitsu. He had compelled them, with ruthless insistence, to shimmy up ropes, scale crumbling stone walls, vault over half-splintered sawhorses, and crawl on their bellies until their nostrils and mouths and eyes and pores filled with particles of the earth they slithered on. He had driven them ferociously through interminable programs of calisthenics and exercises until a goodly number of them had passed out and been dragged aside to the dispassionate shade of eucalyptus trees. Finally, he had raged and ranted and lectured and pontificated and cajoled and threatened and blasted them to hell and raised them redemptively to the heaven of his approval.

But now, D'vora thought with a pang, the games—rough-and-tumble but always, at the core, good-natured—were over. Over for the eager-eyed, buoyant-spirited recruits; over for the ex-Marine sergeant, Big Ed. The frolic and harmless froth of war play would turn, in short order, to the naked reality of war. The warm, well-wishing hands that sought her soft woman's hand in the frenzy and merriment of firelight and drink and banter would squeeze real triggers and fling live grenades and clutch the air for release from pain. The eyes that shyly or arrogantly or seductively probed her tender woman's eyes in the coziness and safety of the fire-mottled darkness would peer through cold metal sights and shut against suffering that would scar the retinas of memory forever. There was nothing D'vora could do for these supple-hearted young lads except give them the fleeting caress of her trembling fingers. There was nothing Dr. D'vora Arnon could say to them except *"Shalom aleichem*—peace be with you!"

At length, it was over. The party turned inward on itself, and D'vora was once again, as was fitting, an outsider, a spectator standing beyond the circumference of an intimate circle. An iron-muscled hand clasped her shoulder and she turned. Ed was standing beside her. His face, burnished by flame-red beads of sweat, was lit by a broad smile; his Aussie hat was rammed back over an unruly mop of matted hair; he held a half-filled cup in one hand and a half-empty bottle in the other. "D'voritchka!" he boomed. "Can I pour you some more?"

She shook her head.

"Are you sure?" He lifted the bottle and sent the Scotch inside it swirling. "There's plenty more where this came from, so don't be bashful!"

"No thanks, Ed. I've had enough." She wet her lips with her tongue. "I've got to be going. . . ."

"Going? So soon? But . . . the party's just begun! We're just warming up, D'vora. Wait till you see what comes next!"

D'vora smiled. "Thanks again, Ed, for inviting me. I really have to go now."

"I see . . ." said Ed. He grimaced and slurped from his cup. "Well," he murmured, "if it has to be, it has to be. That's life, I suppose."

"It's a wonderful party, Ed."

"It is . . . it is! Why, it's everything a party should be, and then some!"

"And they are wonderful men, Ed."

Big Ed shook his head. *"Almost men,* Dr. Arnon! Remember that: they are almost-men!"

D'vora steadied her voice. "No, Ed," she said softly. "They are *men.*"

The Original Sergeant's gaze swept out over the leaping flames of the bonfire, through the brilliant whitish cascade of sparks that went whooshing up into the spongy blackness of the sky, into the shadowy mass of cavorting bodies. A thoughtful, sober look came over the thick features of his cast-iron face. He was silent for a moment and then he said hoarsely: "Well, well, Dr. Arnon, perhaps you are right. Perhaps you have seen something that I have not . . . perhaps they really *are* men."

D'vora held out a hand. "Ed . . ."

But the big ex-Marine ignored it. Instead, he reached out and grasped both her shoulders and then leaned forward and with sandpapery lips kissed her cheek. "How do they say it in Hebrew, Dr. Arnon? *Yi-hi-yeh tov . . .*"

"That's the way they say it in Hebrew, Ed," whispered D'vora. *"Yihiyeh tov*—it will be good. . . ."

———

In the damp darkness of the tent—there was sure to be rain before morning, she thought again—D'vora groped in the upper compartment of the upright orange crate for matches. She found them at length, then removed the glass cover of the kerosene lamp and, after she had lit the wick, replaced it. A haze of soft yellow light fanned up against the seamed, sagging canvas of the roof. She turned and walked back to the narrow cot to the right of the entranceway. Arnold H. Aronson groaned, rolled over onto his back, and stared up at her with uncomprehending eyes. "Where . . . where am I?" he stammered.

"You're in your tent—number nineteen in the south quad," said D'vora softly.

"My . . . tent?"

"You're in Saint-Michel—the transit camp."

Gradually, the puzzled look faded from Aronson's drawn, flushed face. "Ah, yes! Of course. I remember." He managed a weak smile. "It must be the fever. . . ." He paused and swallowed and then said, half-apologetically: "For a moment, when I first opened my eyes, I thought——" His voice broke off.

"Thought what?"

Aronson's parched lips formed a sheepish grin. "I thought I was . . . back home . . . in my bedroom. And . . ."

"Go on."

"I thought that . . . you were my mother! But it was just for an instant—a split-second . . ."

After a moment, D'vora said: "I'm Dr. Arnon, the camp physician. You can call me D'vora."

"Sure," said Aronson, "I've seen you around. I remember your face now." He sighed. "I don't know what's the matter with me. Everything's confused. . . ."

"You have the flu, my dear Mr. Aronson. But don't worry about it—you're going to be fine." D'vora laughed. "You'll see, in a day or so you'll be *meiyah achuz*—one hundred percent. I gave you enough penicillin for an elephant!"

On a nail in the tent's center pole hung a canteen in a cloth case. D'vora got it and unscrewed the cap and set it to Aronson's mouth. When he had finished, D'vora returned the canteen to its place. Walking back to Aronson's cot, she said, "Would you mind if . . . I asked you a personal question?"

"We're *chaverim*, D'vora—comrades. Ask me anything you want."

"Why are you going to Israel to fight?"

The young man's feverish eyes turned away, toward a dark corner of the tent. He was silent.

"If you feel you can't answer," said D'vora, "it's all right. I'll understand."

The eyes, burning like the flames of the bonfire in the clearing D'vora had just left, swept back and gazed unflinchingly up at her face. Aronson hesitated for yet another moment and then said in a low voice: "To tell you the truth, I never really thought about it very much; never bothered to figure it out in so many words. I just felt I *had* to go! I suppose . . . it's like the way somebody feels when he decides to get married . . . or to have a child. It's really beyond what people call a logical decision; it's something deep inside—almost a command." On the green-black folds of the army blanket, Aronson's long, pale fingers locked together; his eyes shone with even greater intensity. "I'm a Jew, right?" he exclaimed with a sudden, almost savage force. "The Nazis butchered us in Europe, and the world twiddled its thumbs and looked the other way as if nothing were happening! And then . . . the Arabs attacked us and said they would push us into the sea, and nobody gave a damn! How—how could I *not* go to Israel?" He shrugged. "Does that . . . answer your question?"

D'vora nodded. "Yes," she said in a whisper. "Yes, it does."

Aronson raised himself on an elbow and looked around the silent tent at the empty cots. "Where . . . is everybody?" he asked.

"They're all at a party. In the clearing below the south quad. I've just come from there."

"At a party? What kind of party?"

D'vora shook her head. "It's a party," she said, "to celebrate the last night in Saint-Michel. You see, the ship's in—the *Pan York*. She leaves tomorrow for Israel."

With a violent start, Aronson sat up. He was naked to the waist, and his frail, elongated, gaunt-ribbed torso, with its flat, almost concave chest, knobby shoulders, and pathetic display of limp, overfine hair, was covered with sweat. "Doctor Arn— D'vora!" he blurted out: "I—I'm going with them, aren't I!? I won't—be left behind, will I?"

"I think you will be going, Aronson. I'll come to see you first thing in the morning, and——"

Aronson's white-fingered hands curled into fists. "But you don't understand: I must go—*I must go with them!*"

D'vora reached out and took his clenched hands and gently eased him back down. "Don't worry, Mr. Aronson," she said with quiet, deliberate authority. "I understand."

With well-trained, unerring fingers, D'vora reached a hand to the right and turned the oversized switch to light the single, shadeless bulb that dangled, as on a noose, in the center of her office-room. She stood where she was in the wide doorway, drained for the moment of even the slight store of energy it required for her to take another step and turn and close the door. "This isn't me," her mind said, "and this won't do." But her body, utterly spent and unwilling to make even a modest concession, said: "This is you, Dr. Arnon; and this will have to do." So she remained standing exactly where she was, exhausted and inert, staring numbly at the naked light bulb until her mind forced her weary limbs to yield. She drew a deep breath and stepped into the room and pulled the heavy door shut, and wished all the while that she were asleep.

Against the near wall, directly across the room from her desk, were a cot and a small chest of drawers. She seated herself on the cot and, bending forward with an effort, unlaced her dusty shoes and kicked them off. Then, forcing every movement of her fingers, she began unbuttoning her khaki shirt. Her body kept murmuring, *Sleep . . . sleep,* and she was more than inclined to give her body its rightful due. But at the same time her mind told her inflexibly that there was something she must do. It was odd, this war between her mind and her body; absurdly, it made her feel as if she were caught in the middle— in a no-man's land. She removed her shirt and got out of her khaki skirt and took a worn, faded blue bathrobe that Arie had bought for her down from its hook. She slipped into the robe and, feeling somewhat relaxed at last, she remembered at once that she owed her husband a letter and had to get it done despite her fatigue.

At her desk, under the glare of the single bulb, she unlocked the center drawer and took out a clean white sheet of paper and Arie's last letter, which for the sixth or seventh time she reread. Then, leaning slightly forward, she began to write.

Saint-Michel
August 28, 1948

Dearest Arie,

I know that this letter should have been written long ago—please forgive me for the lapse, but my schedule has been nothing short of hectic. I don't mean to complain, but there is so much to do here and, as might be expected, we are perennially short-staffed. One of the nurses broke an arm and another decided that she had to return to Israel no matter what, so additional burdens have found their unerring ways to my shoulders. The days begin early, and before I turn around I am back in my office-room in the chateau and half-asleep. Please don't be annoyed or offended by this latest period of silence. Know, always, that my thoughts are constantly of you. There is scarcely a night that passes without my dreaming that I am in your arms.

Darling, I have some wonderful news! Last night, just after I had switched off the light and stretched out to sleep, I felt—for the very first time—the stirrings of our child! I cannot describe the powerful feelings of awe and wonder and love that came over me when this new life saw fit to announce itself.

Somehow, and I don't know why, it's nothing that's rational or logical . . . I have the distinct, unshakable feeling that our first child will be a girl. If this comes true, I would like to name her Ilana, after your father, Yitzchak, who, with oaklike strength, was the proud head of your family. Ilana, then, it seems to me, would be the perfect choice. The two of us, I know, would do everything possible to help our Ilana grow and thrive and spread her beautiful branches.

Do you realize, my darling, that it is fully four months since we have seen each other? Sometimes it seems like but a moment ago that we parted; it seems like only yesterday that we sat at a tiny, white-clothed table in the little café on the slope of Mount Carmel. I can smell the roses on the garden trellises and hear the whistles from the Haifa harbor and taste the red wine that you said tasted like the wine your grandfather made in Rishon le-Zion. At other times, though, I feel that we have been separated for a decade! I am fearful that I cannot really recall your face . . . or the sound of your voice . . . or the touch of your fingers . . . or what it's like to make love with you. I can look at your photographs and I can squeeze an unending stream of memories from my mind—but it is impossible for me to recapture the real you or the marvelous reality of our life together. Don't laugh at me, Arie, but there are times when I begin to doubt that we were ever together. And then there are times, far worse, when I believe we were indeed together but despair that we will ever be united again!

Make no mistake about it, though—I do not regret even for an instant that I came to Saint-Michel. If the choice to come were offered to me again, this very moment, I should decide now exactly as I decided then. I have written often and much about the immigrants who spend several weeks or months here on their way to Israel, but nothing I have ever written or ever will write can possibly convey the sense of worth I feel because I am, in some small way, a part of this awesome migration. Nor can it remotely describe what happened to these people in Nazi Europe or how they feel about going "home," to Eretz Yisrael—the Land of Israel. In the future, I'm sure, many will write and speak about what these people experienced in the death camps and at the hands of the Germans. But most of it—however well intentioned and however sincere—will remain on the surface of their experience; little of it will penetrate, even to the slightest degree, the depth of the horror; and none of it, I am absolutely certain, will ever reach the bottom. All that I, or any of us here, can do is to assist the flow of survivors to the only real sanctuary that awaits them.

I have decided, dearest Arie, that I am a very strange— even a demented—person. Although I know, and have known now for years, that it is impossible, I keep hoping nevertheless that I will one day meet my parents or my brother. It is a verified and indisputable fact—you and I ourselves, with our own eyes, have seen the evidence; we know the location and manner and almost the dates of their deaths in the crematoria. And yet—and I tremble as I write these words—I keep walking down the paths between the tents, gazing at the faces in the dining hall, waiting at the front gate when the trucks unload, watching as the new arrivals

*set down their shabby bundles and battered suitcases
. . . thinking that at any moment, any second I may set eyes
on a beloved face. It is foolish; it is futile; it is crazy; I
realize all this! But who can blame me?*

*So, my dearest husband, you have my letter . . . and my
deepest love . . . and the love of our wakening child. I am
aware that my words may reach you at the front. May the
strength of the love and, yes, adoration I feel for you shield
you from all harm! I long to hold you and be held by you;
and I pray that this wish may be realized. Now that this
letter has been written, my darling, I shall sleep well and
safely.*

Yours,
D'vora

Exhausted by her day's work in Saint-Michel, D'vora fell asleep
at once. But soon she had a strange and terrifying dream. In
it, there was a knock at the door—a steady, persistent, nagging
knock that rolled off the landing and descended the shabby
marble staircase and returned as a hollow, ominous echo. D'vora
did not want to hear it; she wanted no part of it; she wanted
desperately to sleep. *Let me sleep,* a voice inside her cried out.
Please let me sleep and dream of Arie. . . .

But the knock was even louder, more determined.

With a helpless sigh, she opened her eyes and sat up. The
shutters over the balcony door were shut tight and the cavernous
room was pitch-black. "Just a minute," she called out with
some annoyance, "I'm coming—I'll be right there." And, as
she threw back the thin cover and drew her robe over her naked
body, she added: "For heaven's sake, stop that banging!"

In the dream, Big Ed Markowitz was standing in the dim
light of the hallway. He was flushed and sweating; his khaki
shirt was out and unbuttoned, and he was barefoot. "I'm sorry
to disturb you at this time of night, D'vora," he rasped, "but
something's happened to my boy, Aronson——"

"What's the matter, Ed?"

"I don't really know. But something's wrong and I think
it's serious. Please hurry."

D'vora bent and snatched up the little black bag that always stood on the tile floor at the foot of her cot. "Let's go," she said.

The August night had turned sultry. A strange, oppressive heat, like the metal lid of a cauldron, pressed down from the opaque sky. Oddly enough, there was a moon now, a thin, insubstantial wafer of a moon that looked as if it might crumble into bits at any instant. D'vora stared up at it and was repelled. "It's diseased," she murmured involuntarily.

"What's that?" said Ed.

D'vora shook her head. "Nothing," she said. "It was just a hasty diagnosis. Don't pay any attention to it."

They hurried around the huge, shadowy bulk of the chateau to the south side. A crowd of immigrants, huddled together like sheep, had collected on the cinder path and barred their way. D'vora was puzzled. "What are they doing here?" she asked.

Ed shrugged. "I dunno. Word travels fast around this place— like fire through straw." He glared at the crowd. "Out of the way," he commanded gruffly. "Let us by!"

The crowd parted, but a bony hand suddenly reached out and took hold of D'vora's sleeve. With surprise and irritation, she turned and saw a little gray-haired man in familiar, be-draggled immigrant's clothing with a terrible scar that zig-zagged across his entire face. She had seen him around the camp on a number of occasions—one could not view his coun-tenance and forget it—and found out from Menashe that a German bayonet had made the gash. "Doctor," he muttered in a reedy voice. "Will the patient live?"

"Let go," said D'vora, pulling away. "I've got to hurry."

The man hung stubbornly to her robe. "But . . . will he live, Doctor?" he persisted.

"I can't say until I see him."

"It would be a pity if he died, Doctor."

D'vora shuddered, and Big Ed reached out and broke the man's grip. "Come on, D'vora," he snapped.

The two of them entered the south quad, but for some unaccountable reason the going was maddeningly slow. The cinders seemed to suck at their feet, and they had to exert tremendous effort to make progress. "Where is the tent?" D'vora asked.

Ed rubbed his glistening face against the shoulder of his shirt. "It should be over here, on the right," he said. "Or else it's on the left. . . ." A look of confusion and consternation distorted his squarish face. "Or maybe . . . it's in the next row. . . ."

"Don't you know?" exploded D'vora.

"Of course, I know," growled Ed. "What the hell do you think I am—a rookie?" He tore savagely at a tent flap. "An old Marine like me never gets lost!"

In mounting desperation, they moved from row to row. But each cone-peaked, gray-green tent into which they peered only revealed the same tableau: orange crates atop which lightless kerosene lamps stood, hanging canteens and mess kits, heaped-up duffel bags and neatly stacked footlockers, and soldiers-to-be, sound asleep beneath their regulation blankets. Despite herself, D'vora shivered. "Ed," she said hoarsely. "We'll never get to him in time!"

Big Ed replied through clenched teeth: "We will, D'vora—we *must!*"

Suddenly, just ahead of them, there was a faint moan. Ed sprinted forward and D'vora followed. The tent, which was the last one in the very last row, was empty of everything but a single cot from which the blanket had fallen. On the sweat-soaked sheet which had pulled away at its corners from the lumpy straw mattress was the skinny, naked body of the young recruit from Brooklyn. In the sickly cast of the moonlight that poured in through the open flap, the unclothed flesh looked like wax.

"Aronson——" began Ed.

"Ben-Aharon . . . call me Ben-Aharon. . . ."

"Aronson, the doctor's here. You're going to be okay, you little bastard! She told me so herself."

D'vora stepped forward and took out her stethoscope. "Ed's right," she said. "You're going to be perfectly fine, Ben-Aharon. You're going to sail on the *Pan York* tomorrow with all the rest—just as I told you this evening."

A long, waxen arm reached up, and thin, tapering fingers clutched D'vora's wrist and held it with surprising strength. Ben-Aharon, as he wanted to be called, struggled for breath and then said haltingly, "You . . . can't . . . hide the truth from me. I'm not . . . a child. I know that . . . I'm going to die. . . ."

Ed struck the fist of one hand into the palm of the other. "Aronson, you're delirious! Let the doctor examine you."

"No . . . I'm not delirious at all. And no examination . . . will help. Nothing . . . can help me . . . now. I'm . . . going to die . . . and nothing can change that. . . ."

D'vora trembled. "Ben-Aharon, please let me——"

Ed pointed a finger at her. "You're wasting your breath, dammit!" he bellowed. "He doesn't know what he's saying— he's out of his mind! Just give him a shot and get it over with!"

A strange, fragile smile hovered on Ben-Aharon's lips. "Don't quarrel over me," he said in a half-whisper. "It's too late for that now. Just write my folks . . . please . . . and tell them I was thinking of them. I wasn't . . . a very good son—but I am trying very hard . . . to be a good Jew. . . ." He paused for a moment to catch his breath and then continued: "And . . . promise me, the both of you, promise me that I'll sail on the *Pan York* tomorrow. I'll be dead and in my coffin . . . but that doesn't mean I can't go home. . . ."

"The kid is raving mad!" roared Ed.

"Listen to me, Ben-Aharon," said D'vora, twisting her hand free of the trembling fingers, "I——"

The long arm fell, trailing its fingers on the tent's earthen floor and Ben-Aharon's eyes filled with murky sightlessness; his frail body lay motionless. D'vora bent over him and, though she knew at once it was futile, went through the necessary routine. Slowly, she stood up and stepped back. "Ed," she said huskily, "he's gone."

"I don't understand——"

A sudden noise at the entrance to the tent made them both turn. It was the man with the ragged scar across his face they had met on the path. Behind him, crowding close, were other shadowy faces. In his tremulous, flute-thin voice, the man said: "We know he's dead."

"Listen here," barked Ed, "I——"

But the man ignored him. "We've come to wash the body," he said, "and to stand vigil over the corpse." His little frame bent slightly and he moved into the tent. "Begging your pardon, Doctor," he said with an odd little bow of his head, "but your turn is over; it's *our* turn now."

D'vora could no longer restrain herself and began to weep

openly. Grim-faced, Big Ed took her by the elbow and steered her through the crowd of immigrants out of the tent. "Get hold of yourself, D'vora," he ordered, but it didn't help.

As they neared the chateau, Menashe Halabi came running toward them. Big Ed shook his head. "Aronson's dead," he mumbled. "We don't know how it happened. He seemed to be getting better and then, like a bolt out of the blue, he took a turn for the worse. I got D'vora, but——"

Menashe paid no attention to what he said. Instead, the camp director spoke directly to D'vora. "Listen to me," he said hoarsely.

D'vora stared at him.

"Something terrible has happened," he blurted out. "Your child is gone!"

"My . . . *child?*"

"Your little girl, Ilana—she's gone! While you were away with Ed, the Germans took her! We don't know how they got into the camp, but one of the sentries spotted them leaving——"

"Menashe, my child hasn't been born yet!"

Menashe's voice ripped from his throat. "Ed, get your men up at once! I'll issue the rifles. The Germans were heading north—they can't be far."

"But Menashe, I'm only five months pregnant! I haven't given birth yet."

Big Ed was already running. "We'll be at the gate, Menashe," he called back over his shoulder. "Make sure that the guns are there!"

D'vora began to scream. . . .

————————

With a violent start, D'vora awakened. For several moments, she lay under the blanket, not moving a muscle. Even the sound of her own breathing frightened her. Then, with a shudder, she sat up and half-turned and reached under her pillow for her flashlight and flicked it on. Its cold white beam speared through the darkness, illuminating a section of her desk. With chattering teeth, she rose from the cot and went forward. On the desk, just in front of Arie's photograph, lay the letter she had written to him before retiring. It was in an unsealed envelope. She seated herself on the desk chair and drew the letter out and, in the glare of the flashlight, reread it. Then she uncapped her pen and steadied her hand and wrote:

> *P.S. Arie, I love you so very much—more than I can ever tell you.*

She put the pen in its place, slipped the letter into its envelope, and, moistening her lips with her tongue, sealed the envelope. Then she got to her feet and went to the balcony door and opened the shutters. The sky over the hills was cut viciously by a long, jagged blade of lightning. A low roll of thunder, which seemed to shake the world from end to end, followed. And then, as if whispering softly, the rain began to fall.

D'vora stood for a long time in the doorway of the balcony, staring out and listening. Flash after flash of blue-white lightning paled the sky, showing her the breastlike curves of the hills, the glistening crests of the trees, the moldering stone wall that encircled the camp, the gleaming, identical peaks of the tents in their symmetrical rows, the dark cinder paths, the rain-soaked dust of the chateau yard below her. She heard the steady, murmuring fall of the rain, at once tumultuous and calm. At last, she felt peaceful and in control of herself. With a sigh, she closed the shutters and with the flashlight guided herself back across the huge room to the cot.

But before she stretched herself out to sleep once again, she ran her hands over her naked breasts and then down to the silken swell of her belly. "Ilana..." she murmured aloud. "Ilana... my darling child. Nobody will ever... take you away. *Ilana... I promise you that....*"

1948

Mount Scopus, Jerusalem

DUSK.

Looking westward from the compound in front of the building whose basement served as the besieged Israeli battalion's dining hall, Captain Arie Arnon stared from Mount Scopus into the distance. After its long trek over the cloudless sky, the sun was sinking. Beyond the high, drab-gray concrete wall, with its squat concrete sentry posts and massively sandbagged machine gun emplacements that divided Jerusalem in half, the sprawling, clean-avenued Jewish sector lay bathed in scarlet and gold. To the naked eye, everything looked toylike: toy buses and automobiles and houses and office buildings and synagogues and parks—a city that children at play, with an inexhaustible energy for detail and form, might fashion in a blaze of imagination on some endless, childhood afternoon.

Below Mount Scopus's commanding height, on the near side of the bisecting wall, the crowded, crazy-rooftopped houses that comprised the Old City—which had been captured in a fierce struggle by the better-armed forces of the Arab Legion—were already collecting deep shadows of mauve and indigo. Here and there in the intricate maze of severely angled and softly curved stone was the blood-red flash of a windowpane or the silvery-scarlet flash of metal.

Despite himself, Arie shivered. When the fighting was at a lull, which had been the case for the last several days, one would inevitably begin to imagine oneself leaving the enclave on Mount Scopus, descending to the Old City and passing in safety through its winding, pungent-smelling streets to the beloved and familiar avenues and boulevards of the western section of Jerusalem. How good it would be to reach *that* particular street, with its well-worn sidewalks and low terraces of tenderly pink Jerusalem stone and shady, dust-chastened firs and cypresses, until at last one stood in front of a graceful, supple-branched oak; and then to swing to the right and move down the carmine-hued flagstones, with their hollows and seams, into the shadowy, cool, fresh-smelling entrance of the modest apartment building.

And then, as in Arie's oft-repeated dreams, he would mount two flights of stone stairs, counting each step impatiently as he ascended, before arriving at the door with the now-tarnished brass plate that read ARIE AND D'VORA ARNON. And then he would pause for a fragmentary instant, step quickly to the door, and knock.

D'vora would open that door. Without sign or signal or spoken word, she would *know* that her husband had returned from the din and fury of war to the drowsy stillness of their street and the sheltering peace of their home. Framed by the doorway, she would stand in a simple housedress or in the robe he had bought her. Her pale blond hair, curling like a wreath of gold about her face, would be resting on her shoulder blades; her eyes would be wide open and shining with tears; her lips would be parted. For a moment, transfixed by the raw power of their emotions, they would stand and stare at each other, separated only by the threshold of the apartment. And then, daring at long last to believe in the reality of the meeting, they would fall into each other's arms...

With a tiny, all but inaudible cry of mingled hope and despair that involuntarily escaped his lips, Arie shook himself back into the present. He was staring, from the peak of the beleaguered enclave, at the glowing panorama of Jerusalem at sunset. The dome of radiance over the old and new sections of the city, the crystalline air in which, as in a glittering goblet, the last drops of ruby-gold light lingered, conveyed the impression of well-being and peace. But the Jews and the Arabs were locked in bloody conflict. Peace, Arie knew all too well, was no more than a phantom, a dangerous illusion.

Grimly, Arie turned his eyes away. He spotted Lieutenant Admoni on the path to the dining hall. "Yoskeh!" he called out.

Lieutenant Admoni halted in his tracks and waited for Arie to come over. "What can I do for you?" he said.

"Zamir spoke to me this morning," said Arie. "It seems there's a kid in your platoon who's having some problems. Zamir asked if I would talk to him, perhaps help him to straighten out. So . . ."

Admoni grimaced. "You mean the *Romani*—the little trouble-maker."

"I don't know his name."

Lieutenant Admoni grunted. "His name's Feldman, but I call him pain-in-the-ass. I've tried every which way to do something with him, but I'm up against a stone wall."

"Where is he stationed?"

"He's assigned to the Amphitheater—the left-flank post. You can't miss him: he's got red hair and freckles, and he always looks like he's about to bawl."

Arie nodded and then reached out and touched the other's shoulder. "Thanks for briefing me, Yoskeh. I'll visit him after supper and see what I can do."

Lieutenant Admoni shrugged. "Good luck," he said with a twisted smile. "You'll need it."

"We all do," said Arie.

Supper in the crowded, noisy basement dining hall was the usual drab affair. Some sixty tanned and dust-caked Israeli soldiers of the Mount Scopus enclave, in their ill-fitting, un-washed uniforms and wearing their battered British-issue En-field rifles slung over their shoulders, filled the stale air with stories and complaints that were by now, after long months of isolation, as tasteless and unappetizing as the food dished out by the sour-faced, irascible, incorrigibly cynical cook.

Amid the confused din of conversation and the rattling of utensils, Arie finished his meal and left. The sun had gone down. Like newly minted silver coins thrown at random onto a black velvet cloth, four or five evening stars gleamed with a pristine flame. Carried aloft on a current of air, the melan-choly wail of a jackal reached his ears.

Cutting through a copse of threadbare fir trees, he moved east and south. Where the path ended and the mountain began its steep drop to the ravine, a sentry challenged him. "It's me, soldier—Captain Arnon," he answered.

The soldier—a wispy-bearded Yemenite with a gaunt, craggy face that looked a thousand years old—knew him, but nonetheless demanded the password.

Arie gave it.

"Thank you, Captain Arnon," said the Yemenite. He grinned. "And have a good evening, *ya sidi!*"

"A good evening to you, Yirmiyahu!"

Below Arie now were the semicircular stone tiers of the Amphitheater's seats; at their bottom, bathed in pale starlight, was the curving crescent of the stage. Arie halted for a moment and gazed downward.

It was impossible for him to view the scene and not remember the times he and D'vora had been to performances together there. As young lovers and then as man and wife, they had heard the Israel Philharmonic send the music of Bach and Beethoven and Mozart *min ha-amakim—de profundis—*out over the stone and skull-littered emptiness of the ravine and through the incalculably vast void that began at Jerusalem's southeastern rim, and ran all the way to the bitter salt waves of the Dead Sea. Hand in hand in the slowly lengthening shadows of late afternoon, or in silver light pouring from the moon, they had seen the plays of Sophocles, Shakespeare, and Shaw. The Amphitheater, like the Einstein Mathematics Building and the Physics Complex and the National Library, were among the facilities of the Hebrew University which, together with the Hadassah hospital buildings, dotted the Jewish sector of Mount Scopus.

But Arie restrained the flow of memory and hurriedly—as if to make up for his "lapse"—descended the chipped and bullet-nicked stairs of the mountainside auditorium. Another sentry stepped—like some actor left over from bygone days— out from the shadows of the stage.

Arie gave the password.

The sentry nodded.

"Is Feldman here?"

Pointing a finger, the sentry said, "He's in his bunk."

Arie crossed the stage and entered the square stone structure at its left extremity. He went down a steep flight of stairs and halted at the bottom. The chamber, whose single window was shut off by a steel shutter, was dark and foul-smelling.

"Feldman?"

There was a slight sound—a whisper or perhaps an inadvertent sigh. Arie waited until his eyes became accustomed to the darkness and he was able to make out, against the far wall, a cot which supported a dark shape. "Okay," said Arie, moving forward, "I see you now."

The dark shape lifted itself into a sitting position.

"I'm Captain Arnon, deputy commander of the enclave. You can call me Arie. How are you this evening, Feldman?"

There was no answer.

Arie remained silent for a moment; then he said, "What is your given name, Feldman?"

A strained, high-pitched voice that seemed not as yet to have found its manhood, said haltingly, "Ya'akov—but they . . . call me Yankel."

"Can I sit down, Yankel?"

"Yes, of course. Forgive me."

Arie seated himself on the edge of the cot. He could just make out the other's face now: it was a small, cramped-featured, ferretlike face, with elfin ears and sharp nose and pointy chin and tiny, close-set eyes that looked like buttons or beads; the lips, drawn tightly back like rubber bands over small, evenly formed teeth, were thin and pale. "Well, Yankel," said Arie, "have you had supper yet this evening?"

"No, I haven't."

"Why not?"

"I—I guess . . . I'm just not very hungry."

"Don't you know that it's not a good idea to miss meals, Yankel? A soldier has to eat in order to keep up his strength."

The thin, high-pitched voice quavered: "Begging your pardon, Captain Arie, but, well, I'm . . . not a soldier."

"Who says you're not a soldier, Yankel?"

"Well, everybody says it: the men in the platoon . . . and some of the men in the other platoons as well. Even . . . Lieutenant Admoni says so."

Arie was silent; then he said, "How about you?"

"Me?"

"Yes, Yankel. What do *you* say? Do you think you're a soldier?"

Yankel cleared his throat. "The truth, Captain Arie?"

"Yes, Yankel, the truth."

"It will . . . go no further?"

"It will never leave this room."

Yankel sighed. "Well, Captain Arie," he said in a voice that was scarcely above a whisper, "I really . . . don't know."

"You don't know?"

Yankel shook his head. "No, Captain Arie, honestly, I don't. Sometimes, I think that I *might be* . . . and then at other times I think that I'm not a soldier . . . and that I'll never be one."

"What makes you doubt yourself, Yankel?"

The other's slight body twisted on the cot; he drew a deep breath and said hoarsely: "I doubt myself, Captain Arie, because . . . I'm afraid."

"Afraid of what?"

"Afraid of being blown to bits by a shell! Afraid of being hit by a bullet and bleeding to death on the field!" Yankel's voice rose to a shrill pitch. "And I'm afraid of being taken prisoner by the Arabs, Captain Arie! I know what they do: *cut off ears and fingers and pull out tongues and——*" He stopped suddenly, as if some invisible hand had seized his throat and choked off his voice, and he doubled over and began to shake with silent sobs.

Arie reached out and grasped a bony shoulder and dug his fingers into the convulsed flesh and waited.

At length, the spasm subsided and, still choked, Yankel's muffled voice slid through the fingers that covered his face. "I'm . . . sorry."

"There's nothing to be sorry about," said Arie softly.

The other's bitter laughter exploded in the chamber. "Of course, there is!" murmured Yankel. "You see, I'm *not* a soldier, Captain Arie—*I'm a coward.*"

Now it was Arie's turn to laugh, but the laughter was gentle and accepting. "You're not a coward, Yankel Feldman," he said. "You're just human."

"Sure, sure."

"We're all human, Yankel, and we're all afraid. Being a soldier means conquering that fear so that we can fight and defend ourselves." Arie's fingers gripped the other's shoulder even more tightly than before. "Nobody is born a soldier, and every soldier is afraid sometimes. Remember that, Yankel."

"You ... are afraid sometimes, Captain Arie?"

"Yes, Yankel. Sometimes I am very much afraid."

The other sat up. "And how do you conquer that fear, Captain Arie?"

Arie thought for a moment and then said quietly, "Well, Yankel, I think about what I have to lose if I don't."

The other said nothing.

Arie dropped his hand and rose. "How about coming up to supper now, Yankel?"

"Supper?" The other sighed and then said: "Yes, I will have supper, Captain Arie. In just a few moments ..."

"Good!" Arie patted the frail shoulder and rose. "Well, soldier," he said, "I'll be seeing you around. Come and talk to me any time."

"Thank you, Captain Arie. I will."

Arie was lying on the cot in his little room. He was thinking about D'vora, and a particular, haunting memory came to mind.

He was standing in front of the large, clean-lined hospital building on Mount Scopus. He knew very well how the hospital was now: its outer walls were gouged by artillery and mortar shells and pockmarked by countless bullets; its walks were cracked and overrun with grass; its lawns were charred and its gardens thick tangles of weeds and defiant nettles; its windows were shattered; its interior was no more than a mute maze of deserted rooms whose patients had long ago been evacuated to the western sector of Jerusalem. It was nothing but a shell— a hospital for ghosts.

But as he remembered it, the hospital was perfectly intact, a gleaming structure of immaculate white stone and flawless glass. The late afternoon sun softened the severity of its walls. Blowing in from the west, a gentle breeze stirred the branches of the acacias and mimosas and slender-trunked poplars that surrounded it, and nudged the flowers in the gardens. On the walks, the snow-white garments of doctors and nurses mingled with the gray and brown work clothes of visitors.

He glanced at his watch. It was just two minutes to five, and he could expect D'vora to come out of the front door at any instant. Nevertheless, he was terribly impatient, and despite his resolve and much to his chagrin, he began to pace the flagstones. Up and down the broad plaza he went, half-expecting some stranger to stop him and ask how long his wife had been in labor. Abruptly, he halted and looked at his watch again. It was now exactly five o'clock. A pretty young nurse and two people in street clothes—a man and a woman—came out of the front door. Where was D'vora? Would she be delayed? How long would he have to wait for her?

Suddenly, he spied her familiar, unmistakable form. She was just inside the hospital's front door, in the spacious lobby. It was silly, he knew—he felt like an adolescent, but there was nothing he could do to control the urge—he ran forward. He reached her just as she came out onto the walk and swept her into his arms. "D'vora," he murmured, "D'vora, my darling, how good it is to see you... how wonderful it is to hold you in my arms...."

She kissed him and laughed. "Dearest Arie! Have you been waiting long? I'm sorry that I'm a bit late, but Dr. Shainbaum got hold of me on the second floor just as I was leaving. He's an incredible surgeon and a brilliant supervisor, but a compulsive talker! I knew that you'd be impatient, but I just couldn't manage to escape him." Her eyes clouded. "Are you angry with me?"

"Of course not."

Arm in arm, they began to walk. The sun threw a web of pale gold fire around D'vora's hair; it flashed on her eyelids and shone on her smooth, tanned flesh.

D'vora spoke animatedly of her day's work—of doctors and patients and diagnostic breakthroughs and confounded hopes and stubborn riddles that demanded greater knowledge and perseverance—and Arie listened. He listened faithfully to each word and concentrated with rapt attention on each thought, but above all else he heard his young wife's soul: it came to him with sweet, distinct, rhythmical clarity.

"Why are you looking at me that way, Arie?"

"Looking at you what way?"

"I don't really know. But..." Her voice trailed off.

"No, no—don't dismiss it. Try to tell me how I'm looking at you."

She smiled. "It almost seems as if... as if..."

"As if what, D'vora?"

"As if . . . you're looking . . . *into* me."

"That's exactly it. I'm looking into you."

"Arie——"

"But I *am,* D'vora. I'm looking into your soul."

She laughed.

"You can laugh all you want," he said affectionately. "But I'm quite serious."

She stared at him. "Well," she mused, "if, indeed, you are looking into my soul, what do you see?"

Arie halted and held her close to him and said softly: "I see, my darling D'vora, a plain bathed in sunlight and purple shadow, teeming with life . . . a deep, endless green forest whispering with secrets . . . a little cabin, with its windows new-lit, at the end of a long road in the dusk . . . a mysterious glen with a brook running through it. I see a . . . universe." He paused and then, steadying his voice with effort, went on: "And it's always new, my dearest wife—as if I'm seeing it for the first time."

They kissed—long and hard and with a passion that seemed at once as old as all the days and years of their lives and as fresh as the moment. And when, at length, they drew apart, Arie said: "D'vora, I'd like to take you to a house now. It's an old, beautiful place, with a big, shady backyard that's divided by a high hedge." He paused for a moment, staring into the distance, and then went on. "At work, yesterday, I was driving around Jerusalem in the jeep and I happened to see it, and I was so taken with it that I stopped and looked around. And——"

"And what?"

"And I thought . . . well, I thought that if we could possibly swing it, we might buy it. You're pregnant now, and we're certainly going to need more room . . . and there's really no point in waiting . . . and so I made a few inquiries, and I think we can do it! One side of the place has already been sold, but the other side is still up for sale, and the owner says that——"

"That we can afford it!"

Arie squeezed her arms. "Precisely. With a little maneuvering here and a bit of manipulation there, we can buy the place."

"Arie!"

"Are you happy, darling?"

"Happy? I'm ecstatic! I can't wait to see it!"

———————————

Suddenly a knock at the door ended Arie's reverie.

"Come in," he murmured.

A tall, stooping figure entered. Arie stared up at Major Zamir. The commander's eyes were dark-ringed and his cheeks overrun with bristling gray-tinged stubble. Behind him, the unshaded kerosene lamp threw his shadow across the wall and up onto the ceiling of the little room. Arie sat up at once. "What is it, Yochanan?"

Zamir rubbed his chin. "Petrushka reports that his sentries have detected movement on the northern flank."

"They usually do," said Arie, containing a yawn. "Begging the major's pardon, but Petrushka encourages it."

The commander nodded soberly. "I know, I know," he drawled in his heavy voice. "But tonight we can't take chances. We've just had a radio report that a convoy with weapons and ammunition is coming through enemy lines. I wouldn't want anything to interfere with their safe passage."

"Of course not."

Zamir scratched at the thick mop of his hair. "I'd like you to take three or four men out, Arie, and see what's doing."

Arie smiled wryly and bent forward to put on his shoes. "*I'd* like Lieutenant Petrushka to take them out," he said.

The major clucked his tongue. "Now, now, Aritchka, surely you realize that even *three* Lieutenant Petrushkas don't equal *one* Captain Arnon."

Arie finished lacing his shoes and stood up. "A peculiar arithmetic," he said with a grimace.

Major Zamir's lips were smiling, but his dark, thoughtful eyes were sober. "A commander's arithmetic," he said quietly, "by which his men live or die."

Arie's webbed belt and holstered revolver were lying atop the rickety little chest of drawers beside his cot. He passed in front of the other man and snatched up the belt and fastened it about his waist. "If you have no objections, Yochanan, I'll pick my men from Avivi's platoon; on the whole, they're a more seasoned bunch."

"As you wish, Arie."

Arie glanced at his watch. "It's 0105 now: we'll leave at 0130."

"Right," said Major Zamir. He sighed and put out a hand. "Good luck, Areleh," he murmured.

Arie pressed the outstretched hand and remembered, as always with the first touch of the large, work-hardened fingers, that it was the hand of a good, solid, earth-loving farmer which—because of the enemy's designs—had been turned from plowshare to sword. He walked out of the tiny top-floor room, went quickly down the stairs, and left the black thick-walled hulk of the Einstein building.

Arie had picked four men from Lieutenant Avivi's platoon: Amnon Peled, a tousle-haired young sabra with piercing blue eyes and a ready, infectious smile that belied his seriousness and competence; Musa—or Moshe—Zaritsky, a squat, powerfully built fellow who had come from Yugoslavia in his teens; Micha Zalmanovich, a reticent, taut-faced man in his midforties who had seen combat in the Warsaw Ghetto and with the partisans in the forests of Poland; and Ovadiah Malachi, a plucky, sharp-tongued Yemenite who was the best marksman in the Mount Scopus unit. Swiftly, he led them out of the machine gun emplacement westward along the deep trench that ran along the northern flank of the mountain.

Up over the pale white rocks and chalky dust of the trench's lip they went. The mountain sloped gradually down for perhaps a couple of hundred meters to a narrow path worn soft by the feet of countless patrols. When they reached that point, Arie motioned his men down and waited. To the northwest was the black hump of a hill on which the darkened houses of Isfiya sat; to the southeast, across the emptiness of the ravine and the summer-dry bed of the wadi, were the far slope of Mount Scopus and the Arab Legion camp tucked away in its pine woods. Now and then came the dispirited barking of a village dog and the mocking wail of a jackal in answer—nothing more. Crouched on the pulverized earth of the path, Arie and his men peered into the darkness and listened.

At length, Arie raised a hand and rose. The men, trying their best not to trip or dislodge stones, followed him down the plunging slope. They moved steadily, without stopping, to within fifty meters of a shadowy mass. Arie signaled the men down once again and turned. "Amnon," he whispered.

Grinning, the lean sabra crept forward.

"See what's doing."

At once, Peled was gone.

Without thought, almost casually—as if he were taking a handkerchief out of a pocket—Arie drew his revolver from his holster and cocked it. He had lost sight of Peled's slithering body but had an unimpeded view of the dark mass. A minute went by—then another—and another. A little refrain, set to the tune of a popular song that one dislikes intensely but somehow cannot—like stale chewing gum—get rid of, popped into his mind: *Peled, take care . . . Peled, take good care. . . .* Four more minutes passed, and then a fifth—and then he heard the scraping, slipping sound of a body hugging the mountainside.

Peled's round, dimpled face loomed up. "Clean as a whistle," he murmured, smiling broadly.

"Are you sure?"

"As sure as I am that you are Captain Arnon."

Arie nodded and moved the men down the slope to the clump of tall, flat-bladed cacti. Motionless and in silence, the five men squatted in dense shadow. Musa Zaritsky's heavy-lidded eyes seemed half-closed, and his gray-barreled sten gun, anchored on a thigh, stood upright like a spear. Micha Zalmanovich, his gray head bent low, hugged his sten gun to his chest like the child he might well have lost in Warsaw. The gnomelike Yemenite, Ovadiah Malachi, who filled the furnace of his speech with the fire of biblical phrases, noiselessly drummed his thin fingers over the stock of the weatherworn Enfield he habitually referred to as *barak*—"lightning." And Peled picked aimlessly at his teeth with a spit of dry grass he had plucked from the hide of the mountain. Every once in a while, Arie glanced at his men, and despite himself, the insane scrap of music that he could not evict from his mind returned, this time with a slight variation of the lyrics: *Chaverim, take care . . . chaverim, take good care. . . .* And then, struggling to dismiss the refrain, he swung his eyes outward.

Suddenly, a hand touched his shoulder.

He swung his head sharply. Peled's white teeth flashed. "There," the sabra snapped.

Arie craned his neck. "I don't——"

Peled pointed directly downward. "Keep looking."

At that instant, Arie saw. Downward, directly below them, in the stony bed of the wadi: shadows. One...two...three of them raced forward—and then another four or five. Where the wadi forked, they swung to the left into the hollow between the enclave and Isfiya. Arie turned to Peled, who, clutching a long-barreled pistol which he had taken in battle several months ago and from which he was never parted, was just behind him. "They're probably out to ambush one of our patrols. What do you say, Amnon?"

"Probably."

"But they may very well, as Zamir says, run into the convoy."

"Let's get them."

Arie shook his head. "Not here," he whispered. "We don't have enough cover, and they have too good a chance to get away." His body was already in motion. "I've got a hunch," he went on. "I think I know where they're headed."

Peled's mouth fell open. "Of course!" he hissed. "The *chirbeh*—the ruin."

Arie's arm set the men moving. As was the custom in the Israel Defense Forces, he led the column himself. Next came Zaritsky, breathing hard, thrusting his muscular body along like a bear. After him, bending low as he had bent in the sewers of Warsaw in his escape from the rubble of the ghetto, came Zalmanovich. Next in line was the agile-footed Malachi, noiselessly mouthing the words of a Yemenite song or perhaps a snatch of the Psalms of David. And bringing up the rear, his amiable baby face lit by a grin, came Amnon Peled with his long-barreled pistol.

At length, on a line that reached almost directly over the ravine to the hill on which the houses of Isfiya clustered, Arie stopped them. Though he was certain that he had arrived at the correct point for their descent, he took a long, hard, careful look. War was no game of chess; it afforded no second chances or return matches. Either one made the right move at the right time, or one paid the price in blood and bone. He craned his neck and strained to see. At the very bottom of Isfiya's hill, lying like a sunken wreck on the floor of an ocean, was his immediate objective: the *chirbeh*—a tumbledown Arab ruin that had once, long ago, been the domicile of an outcast or madman or disgruntled recluse who had sickened of the society of his fellow men.

Now, thought Arie, *let's hope we make it before they do*.

The *chirbeh* stank of excrement and mildew. Beneath these odors was the smell of putrescence: some living creature— perhaps a rat or wild dog or jackal—had died among the debris and managed, even in death, to revenge itself on the world by befouling the air. The *chirbeh* had no roof: years ago, a victim of the weather or of human scavengers bent on taking what they could bear away and possibly use, or perhaps of its own weariness, it collapsed and mingled its stone and mud and mortar with the rubble of the half-collapsed walls. Thus, the men, whom Arie had quickly assigned to their posts, were able to gaze up at will to the same vast, star-sprinkled vault of sky that arched over their enemies.

For a time, there was nothing untoward or unnatural. The dogs and donkeys of Isfiya uttered their plaintive protests, and from the distance the jackals launched their long-drawn ululations into the darkness. To the east, the pebbles of the wadi bed gleamed. Ovadiah Malachi's lips drew back, and his mouth formed the silent words *They're coming.* . . .

Arie had heard as well. His hunch or instinct or guess— whatever one wanted to call it—had been accurate: he had cast the dice of decision and the right number had come up. The four men and their commander stiffened. Crouching behind his shield of rocks, Arie slid his tongue along his dry lips and then held his breath. For the merest, fractional instant of time, D'vora's tender, serene-eyed countenance appeared before him, but by an enormous effort of will he banished it. He knew it might be the last such vision he ever saw. Wedded solely now to the mechanical, clocklike workings of the event in process, he leaned forward over his barricade.

He saw the first of the Arab Legionnaires come around the bend of the mountain and down the faintly shining wadi floor. The second man came into view—and then the third and fourth. Arie counted twelve in all. They came closer. Their guns were superior: semiautomatic rifles and even a pair of Bren guns. He knew that his own firepower was no match for theirs and that everything depended on surprise. Swiftly, he drew a grenade from one of his side pouches and reached over to tap Zaritsky, who did the same and then made contact with Zalmanovich. In an instant, there were five grenades wrapped in taut fingers, primed and ready to go on his signal.

Now the column of Legionnaires was halted, squatting motionlessly on the pebbles of the wadi floor. And now the scouts were out—a pair of them. Hunched over like stalking animals, they came forward, thrusting the antennalike barrels of their guns into the night. Meter by meter, they moved toward the *chirbeh*. It was enormously difficult to see them advancing and to hold back, and yet, strangely enough, it was ridiculously simple. Everyone knew his part, and it required only the commander's gesture to set the lethal drama in motion.

The Arab scouts were almost upon them now, perhaps fifteen meters or so from the *chirbeh*. They were men with bull necks and cork-blackened faces. Arie let them advance in crouching positions, another five or six meters, then, at once, he lifted his left hand with the grenade and sighted with the pistol in his right. Two simultaneously fired shots—one from his own revolver and one from Peled's long-barreled pistol— streaked out. Almost at the same moment, the two Arab scouts spun around and collapsed. One of them unleashed a piercing, inhuman cry—the cry, at once of uttermost protest and complete surrender, of a man acknowledging his long-avoided and long-dreaded death. The other fell with the same, blood-curdling scream frozen in his faltering heart. Then, as one, five grenades went up and out, arching far into the wadi until five flashes that rolled into a single, flame-fingered explosion ripped into the night. The fugue of sound, ricocheting from the near slope of Isfiya to the far, wooded slope of Mount Scopus, echoed like thunder in the ravine.

Arie rose to his feet. Gently, longingly, his mind whispered, *I love you, darling D'vora,* but his mouth cried out hoarsely: "*Acharai*—after me!"

He clambered over the *chirbeh* stone, firing as he went. Beside him, in a loose, uneven line at whose extreme right flank was Peled, went his men, filling the air with bullets.

Ahead, a tangle of frantic shouts veered crazily into the air. As stray bursts of fire slashed back at them, Arie signaled his men down. Once again their grenades looped forward, and as the crashing explosions merged, they reloaded. Through the confused din, a single hoped-for command barked in Arabic reached Arie's ears: *"Retreat!"*

Savagely, his thighs propelled him up and forward. *"Chevrah!"* he screamèd: *"After me—they're running!"*

Once again, the ragged line of Israelis charged, seeding the wadi with their slugs. As they raced, the night seemed to burst open. From the ghostly pinnacle of Augusta Victoria down the mountainside to the nethermost fringes of the dense pine wood, a barrage of fire lashed out: rifles, Brens, heavy machine guns, and mortars sent their projectiles smashing into the ravine. From Isfiya, a lighter and more sporadic crossfire descended. Arie sent his men to the ground on their bellies. And then, as if in vehement answer, the enclave on Jewish Mount Scopus opened up. *"Aysh chofshi!*—fire at will!" Arie shouted. And when he saw that the last of the Arab column had disappeared from the wadi, he called out: *"Hafsik aysh!*—hold your fire!"

For a time, there was nothing to do except cling to the breast of Mother Earth and wait. Arie and the men could only stay where they were and hug the slowly chilling stones beneath their warm bodies and keep breathing. But that, Arie knew, was a lot. Each breath that he and his men breathed was precious—a gift that might at any instant be snatched from them forever. Several times over, exploding shells ruptured the wadi floor. Once, when he looked backward, he saw the weather-softened stones of the *chirbeh* leap up and go streaking for the stars.

The Israelis waited, pressing themselves to a hardened rind of earth that, while it would support them, would never give its shelter to them unless they were gone from the earth and never would return to it again. They waited, together and yet each alone, to face the terrible but inescapable question of living or dying, while above them the bullets whined and whistled and moaned and the shells screamed.

At length, the Arab barrages from Augusta Victoria and Isfiya and the pathetic, outgunned counterbarrages from the Israeli enclave diminished. Arie knew it was time to go. They had to go before darkness was gone. He lifted himself into crouching position and turned. "Zaritsky," he called out.

"*Ha-m'fakayd,*" said Yugoslavo's thick voice.

"Zalmanovich."

"Here," answered the veteran of the Warsaw Ghetto.

"Malachi."

There was no reply.

"*Malachi, Ovadiah.*"

Peled's voice came back to him. "Arie . . . he's hit."

The commander scrambled to the right.

Peled's face seemed twisted out of shape. In a trembling voice, a strained, almost unrecognizable voice, he said, "Arie . . . he's hurt."

The Yemenite was lying on his stomach. Carefully, Arie turned the wiry body over. Malachi's delicate-boned face was dead-white. Great blisters of sweat sat like islands on his skin. From his lips, a string of drool stretched out and dropped. He opened his eyes. "*Ya* Captain Arnon . . ." he murmured. "I've been stung."

"Take it easy, Malachi. You're going to be okay."

The Yemenite tried vainly to smile. "If . . . God wills it . . ." he whispered.

Arie's fingers tore the dust-caked battle jacket and soaked shirt front away. A sickly-sweetish smell—at once familiar and alien—entered his nostrils. He bent his head and saw blood in the smashed basin of the Yemenite's chest.

"*Ya* Captain Arnon," Malachi muttered hoarsely. "What . . . do you see?"

"Just take it easy, Ovadiah—don't talk."

"If you see death, *ya* Captain, don't . . . trouble yourself to worry. I'm . . . not afraid."

"We're going to get you back to the enclave, Ovadiah, and you'll be fine."

"If God says so," croaked the Yemenite. "But who can tell . . . what God will decide . . . ?"

Arie ripped the blood-soaked shirt and crumpled a wad into the open wound. He peeled off his battle jacket and ordered Zaritsky to do the same. Together, he and Zalmanovich tied the two jackets to the Yemenite's Enfield and Zaritsky's sten gun. Then they lifted Malachi's little body onto the rude stretcher.

The wounded man groaned. "*Ai...ai...ai...*" he whispered haltingly. "I think God is saying something to me...but I cannot make out...what it is...." He licked his cracked lips. "No matter," he went on. "If I can't understand it at the beginning...I will understand it...at the end."

"Let's go," snapped Arie.

The commander led the way. Behind him, Zaritsky bore the front end of the stretcher and Zalmanovich carried the back end. Peled was last. The four men and their stretcher-borne comrade traveled as swiftly as possible, moving past the debris of the *chirbeh* and up onto the flank of Israeli Mount Scopus. The Yemenite was bounced from side to side. But he did not complain—not a moan or cry issued from his lips. Instead, in a nasal, twangy voice that often broke but always seemed to recover itself, he sang, in the Yemenite manner, refrains of the Hebrew liturgy. "*Melekh...al kol ha-aretz,*" he intoned, "*m'kadaysh Yisrael*—He Who is King of all the world...sanctifies Israel!" And he chanted: "*Halleluya! Halleluya! Praised be the Lord!*" And then, as the men plodded upward, he murmured: "*Ya, chevrayah*...it wasn't the God of Israel whispering in my ear at all—it was the Angel of Death," and shuddered and closed his eyes.

The guns of Isfiya were still now, and only an occasional burst from Augusta Victoria striking the Israeli enclave disturbed the spending night. Arie led his men hurriedly up the last stretch of the mountain's flank. "*Easy,*" he called out over a shoulder. "*Easy with the stretcher!*"

Major Zamir was waiting in Lieutenant Petrushkin's machine gun emplacement. Just behind him, huddled over his field set, a signal corpsman was repeating instructions to the men in the trenches and bunkers. The stretcher bearers were replaced by two men from Petrushka's command, and Arie barked: "Get him to the infirmary—quick!"

The major touched his arm. "How bad, Arie?"

"Bad." Arie drew a sleeve across his perspiring face. "How did it go up here, Yochanan?"

The commander tugged at an ear. "Not badly, Aritchka. Plenty of external damage, but no casualties, thank God. Everybody was dug in and prepared for the fireworks."

"And the convoy?"

"Headquarters radioed us—they turned back. They'll have

to try another time." Zamir cleared his throat. "Listen," he murmured, "about the Yemenite—do you think he'll pull through?"

Arie shrugged. "As Malachi himself would put it," he said wearily, "only God will decide."

———————

Arie buried his face in his hands.

For a long time he remained that way, with his cupped fingers that smelled of earth and Ovadiah Malachi's blood sheltering his face from the world as his body hunched forward on the wooden bench. Following a will of its own, his mind drifted back to the days of his childhood and youth on a *moshav* that his parents had helped to establish in the early twenties. He remembered the smile that never failed to appear on his father's leathery, sun-blackened face, even in the darkest times. And he remembered the line that his father always quoted from the Book of Proverbs and the determined tone of the man's voice when he spoke it: *Ayzehu gibbor: ha-kovaysh et rucho*— Who is the strong one: the man who conquers his own spirit! And he remembered his father's comment that "nobody is fearless; it is, quite simply, that the strong man overcomes his fear." He saw before him once again the green-gold stacks of hay in the newly mown fields, gleaming in the light of early morning, and the flashing scythe blades as they cut through plots of alfalfa and clover, and he saw ripening corn and neat rows of citrus trees and the herd of milk cows ambling homeward in the wine-red dust of late afternoon sunlight.

And he saw his mother, with her rumpled hair and careworn face, setting portions of simple, fresh farm food on the table in their immaculately clean kitchen. And once again he heard his mother's soft, warm voice saying, "Eat hearty and enjoy God's good food, and grow strong and become a good man and a good Jew!" And then it seemed to him, though it was absurd, that he felt the touch of her loving fingers fall gently on his hair. Shaken by the reality of the caress, he dropped his hands from his face and looked up.

Lieutenant Raphael Avivi was staring down at him. It was he who had touched Arie's head.

"Raphi."

Avivi was a well-built, good-looking fellow in his mid-twenties, with wavy blond hair, hazel eyes, and a ruddy complexion. "Areleh," he said with warmth. "How are you?"

Arie shrugged. "So-so," he replied. "As you know, we managed to get a few of them—but, unfortunately, not enough."

Avivi nodded. "However many of them you get, there are always more. That's a sad fact of life, *chabibi*." Avivi was silent for a moment; then he jerked his head toward the metal door. "Is there any word on the Yemenite?"

Arie shook his head.

Avivi said nothing. He stood for a while, staring blankly at the metal door, and then asked: "Mind if I sit down?"

"Of course not." Arie rubbed his temples. He hesitated for a moment and then said, "Malachi was wounded while we were charging, but he never let on; he just kept going! He's a real man, Raphi."

"The best!" Avivi sighed. "When I told him that you wanted him with you on the mission, he said, 'If Captain Arnon hadn't asked for me, Lieutenant, I should have volunteered—I should have *made* him take me along!' Then I said, 'Watch out for yourself, Ovadiah,' and he answered, 'Don't worry, *ya chabibi;* dead or alive, I am in God's hands.'"

Arie swallowed. "There was nothing I could do for him on the field, Raphi, so——" Abruptly, Arie broke off and both officers looked toward the metal door.

On creaking hinges, the door swung open and a broad-shouldered, heavyset, balding man wearing steel-framed glasses entered the antechamber. He was clad in a long, bloodstained operating gown and still had on his rubber gloves and mask. Catching sight of Arie and Avivi, he halted and then slowly reached up and pulled the mask from his mouth.

Captain Arnon and Lieutenant Avivi were on their feet.

"Dr. Rabinowitz," said Arie hoarsely. "How is he?"

The doctor's black eyes focused on the two officers. Absently, he touched the fingers of his right hand to his sweat-blotched forehead. Then he cleared his throat and in a thick voice said: *"Hu halach*—he's gone."

With his back against the wooden shoring of the bunker wall, Arie lowered his head and wrote:

> *My darling D'vora,*
>
> *I hope this letter finds you in good health and in good spirits.*
>
> *I haven't had any word from you in some time and assume that it's due to a combination of your heavy schedule of responsibilities and the vagaries of the mails.*
>
> *I am well and in good spirits—especially when I think of you. I can't, of course, tell you where I am, but I can say that everything is quiet—one might even forget at times that there's a war on. In fact, we hear repeated talk about another ceasefire.*
>
> *Last night I was thinking about how I met you one day after work and told you about the house we want to buy. Do you remember how I described the place and how excited you were?*
>
> *How I wish we already lived there! One of the things that keeps me going, my darling, is the belief that someday soon we will be together again. I think of you constantly, D'vora, and I love you always . . . and I look forward with all my heart and soul to peace and to our reunion.*
>
> *Keep well, darling, and write to me whenever you can. Maybe the mail will get through.*
>
> *With all my love,*
>
> > *Arie*

Arie began to fold the letter, but then, on second thought, he smoothed it out again and wrote:

> *P.S. I've been thinking about what we might name our child. If it's a boy, I'd like to call him Ilan. And if it's a girl, we could call her Ilana. What do you think? Please let me know.*

When Arie looked up again, he saw that Major Zamir had come over and, arms folded across his chest, was gazing down at him. "Areleh," said the major, "you look exhausted. Why don't you try to get some sleep?"

Arie sighed. "I've tried," he said slowly. "But it doesn't help."

1948

Jerusalem

DAWN.

Mahmoud Malek had made several attempts to doze off
again, but it seemed to him that the harder he tried, the less
successful he was. Sometime after midnight—actually, about
two-thirty in the morning, because he had looked at his watch—
he had been awakened by a series of tremendous explosions
coming from the direction of Mount Scopus. His young wife,
S'ad, had awakened as well and, her lithe body trembling with
fear, sought the protection of his arms. Though he knew that
the words he spoke—"No harm will befall you, my dearest
wife; all will be well!"—were mere ritual words, formula phrases
reserved for just such occasions, his fierce, impassioned hugs
and tender kisses did manage to calm her down somewhat.
Then, bidding her to stay where she was in bed, he had risen
and on bare feet traversed the smooth, cool tiles of the floor
to the window. Prying back the shutter just a crack with care—
as if somehow that innocuous act might expose him and S'ad
to danger—he had peered out.

To the north, where the twin heights of Mount Scopus rose
above the city of Jerusalem, ferocious flashes of flame robbed
the night sky of its color. Like raw welts, long lines of incen-
diary fire streaked this way and that. Artillery pieces and mortars, machine guns and rifles, sent their lethal sounds crashing
down over the now-sleepless rooftops of the houses in deaf-
ening barrages. The troops of the Arab Legion on the slope of
Augusta Victoria had opened up and the soldiers in the Israeli
enclave on the other slope, just over the Old City, were an-

swering. Flash after flash blinded Mahmoud's eyes, lingering on his retinas. And sometimes a tremor, coming down from the mutual bombardment like a seizure of the earth itself, shook the walls of the bedroom as if it would topple the house.

Transfixed, standing barefoot on the tiles in his pajamas, his right hand frozen on the shutter, he remained at the window and watched the duel. It was silly, Mahmoud knew—utterly pointless and without meaning—and yet somehow, for some reason, he could not tear himself away. Back and forth went the artillery and mortar shells and the machine gun and rifle bullets. It seemed to Mahmoud that at any instant all of the ammunition in the world would have to be consumed—but still the firing went on. Inadvertently, he murmured aloud: "If all of the bullets and shells on earth were used up, this would stop! But I'm wrong; *even if all the ammunition on earth were spent, men would make more!*"

Faintly, from the bed, S'ad's voice came to him: "What's that, Mahmoud? What did you say?"

He started. "Nothing," he hastened to reply. "Nothing at all. I just said that all will be well."

"Mahmoud——"

"Don't worry, S'ad . . . please don't be afraid. Nothing will happen to us. The firing will stop soon—it has to stop soon."

He remained at the window for perhaps an hour or more, but then S'ad, unable to contain herself any longer, began to weep, and he let the shutter fall forward into place and turned and went back to their bed. His wife was trying valiantly to hide her distress from him and had buried her head in her pillow in a vain attempt to stifle her sobs. He knew she wanted desperately to control herself, to show him that she was calm and unafraid, and he was moved by her effort. Quickly, he slipped into the bed and gently lifted her face. Her large, dark eyes were wide with fear and brimming with tears that had stained her cheeks and were touching her lips; thick locks of her black hair were matted over her forehead. Softly, so as to convey the boundless serenity and warmth that their love brought him, he kissed her eyelids and wet cheeks and took her into his arms. "There, there," he whispered. "I'm here now. I will protect you. I won't let anything hurt you. Trust me, my darling, and try to relax." Her body, at first stiff and inert, began

to loosen up. A violent spasm of trembling seized her limbs
and through her broken, half-choked sobs, she murmured ab-
jectly: "I'm . . . sorry, Mahmoud . . . I'm terribly sorry. I didn't
mean to upset you." He held her more tightly to him and
repeated his words of solace again and again, though he knew
very well that they were meaningless if anything should happen.
But they soothed her. She trusted him, wholeheartedly, de-
voutly, beyond the pale of reason, as indeed he trusted her.
And after a time her body stopped shaking and she was quiet.
He did his best to ignore the unrelenting thunder rolling down
from Mount Scopus and compelled his mind to concentrate on
her desperate, touching neediness and keep her calm. Though
there was absolutely nothing he could do about the savage
barrages that crashed back and forth between the Israeli enclave
and the Jordanians on Augusta Victoria, there was much he
could do for his wife. Struggling to keep control of himself,
he kissed and caressed S'ad and at length felt her moist, burning
lips against his.

He responded and then, in a sudden, wild burst of desire,
their bodies locked together in a frenzied embrace of love. He
forgot the bullets and shells and shrapnel whining through the
night air over Mount Scopus; the searing, razor-edged bursts
of light that ignited the northern skyline of Jerusalem. Instead,
he sank into the comfort and reassurance of physical bliss.
S'ad's firm, pointed breasts bore into his chest; her round,
swelling belly ground against his; her legs wrapped around his
thighs. "Mahmoud!" she cried out, with urgency and abandon,
"hold me closer, my darling, hold me closer!"

He kissed her ears and face and mouth and neck and drew
her taut nipples out and stroked her calves and gripped her
writhing buttocks and uttered the words of endearment and
longing and satisfaction that he and she alike wanted to hear.
Sometimes, he lifted himself to arm's length and gazed down
at her with mingled awe and gratitude. Free and flowing, her
tresses of long, dark hair lay wreathed over the white pillow
behind her head, and farther down were her straining breasts
and delicate navel and the compact, darkly gleaming wedge of
her pubic hair. Staring up at him with unabashed, adoring eyes,
she would call out, "I love you, Mahmoud; I love to have you
in me!" And he would answer, "I love you, my dearest S'ad!"

and fall again, as some shipwrecked sailor in a raging sea, upon the safe raft of her body.

The strength and ardor of their caresses intensified. The mysterious, compelling gravity that draws man and woman together increased its pull as the intimate, mutually paced rhythm of their lovemaking grew more rapid. The words of encouragement and devotion and praise they spoke rang out against the bedroom walls and seemed to linger in the darkness. Mahmoud arched his well-muscled body up for what he knew would be the last time. Below him, he saw the consummately sculpted point at which their conjoined figures met in the naked surrender and possession of the act of love. With a groan of ecstasy and relief, he thrust himself down and fully forward between the curves of his wife's waiting thighs. A long, throbbing spasm seemed to pull him out of himself and into the sheathe of flesh of the woman he loved. He felt neither the fierce lock of her arms about his waist nor the cut of her teeth that drove into his neck. He heard neither the sounds that leaped in a shuddering release from her lips, nor the words of gratified love that escaped his own.

For a long time they lay, silently and motionlessly, in each other's arms. Two hearts were beating, but the lovers felt the beat of only one. A delicious limpness made their limbs feel like liquid. They breathed each other's breath and smelled each other's smell and sensed, with haunting clarity, each other's repletion. At length, S'ad's lips parted and she whispered, "I love you, my darling—I love you very much." And then, sighing, she murmured drowsily, "My Mahmoud . . . my husband."

Mahmoud heard her soft, peaceful, regular breathing. Her eyes were closed and her mouth was smiling serenely. Cautiously, so as not to disturb her sleep, Mahmoud disengaged his limbs from hers and moved himself off and away from her inert body. He lay quietly on his back beside his wife and listened. From the warring heights of Mount Scopus, the exchange of gunfire had diminished. Only occasional, sporadic bursts of rifles and machine guns and the isolated thump of exploding mortar and artillery shells echoed down over the darkened buildings of Jerusalem. He reckoned that the duel would soon taper off.

Suddenly, Mahmoud felt his wife's hand on his shoulder. He started. "S'ad . . . I thought you were asleep."

S'ad drew closer to her husband. "But why are you awake, Mahmoud?"

Mahmoud hesitated for a moment; then he said, "I—I've been thinking about . . . a publication . . . a journal."

S'ad was surprised. "What sort of a publication will this be?" she asked.

Her husband smiled, and when he spoke his voice was warm and vibrant. "I have . . . been considering this for a long time," he said. "A . . . *Journal of Peace*. In this journal, I—and others who feel as I do—will write about how peace may be achieved. What do you think of the idea, S'ad?"

"It's a beautiful idea, Mahmoud—one that only a man like you could have." S'ad sighed. "But . . ."

"But what?" said Mahmoud anxiously.

"But there are so many dark forces among the Arabs, my husband; so many forces against peace—surely, you know that as well, Mahmoud."

"I do, but the knowledge does not deter me; if anything, it makes the need for such a journal even greater."

"Mahmoud——"

"Yes, S'ad."

"Perhaps . . . now is not the time, my husband. Perhaps you should wait a while. Perhaps, with the passing of years, the climate will change for the better."

Now Mahmoud sighed. He understood his wife's fear that there might be reprisals against him for the launching of such a journal and reached out to stroke her hair and comfort her. "Don't worry, my darling," he murmured. "No harm will befall us. I, Mahmoud, am your protector and defender. The *Journal of Peace* will bring only good."

"Mahmoud——"

"We'll discuss the matter again some other time. Go back to sleep now, S'ad."

S'ad kissed her husband and turned over. She pretended to sleep once again so that Mahmoud could continue with his thoughts and plans for his journal.

Mahmoud wanted desperately to sleep. He tried, but he could not. The lovemaking had relaxed his body, but his mind—

perversely and insistently—was tense.. He closed his eyes and attempted to force his mind into peaceful channels of thought, but his efforts were in vain. Again and again he saw the fitful flashes of man-made lightning on the Mount Scopus skyline. Over and over, he heard the growling, virulent claps of man-made thunder. With all his heart, he wanted not to think of the war. But the war, like a succubus, would not leave his heart or mind alone.

At length, more awake than ever, he decided to abandon his strained and fruitless attempts and give up. He shifted his body and allowed his eyes to roam aimlessly around the room. The luminous dial of the clock on the dresser said four-forty. In the fragile silence that had fallen on Jerusalem with the cessation of the bombardment on Mount Scopus, its ticking seemed overloud. With a curious sense of unreality, a sense almost of not belonging to the world, he stared up at the white expanse of the ceiling.

Some thought Mahmoud Malek was a queer sort of person, a nonconformist, an iconoclast—an oddity, in fact. His father would say: "He is a deep one, our Mahmoud, and who can say where his impenetrable nature will lead him in life or where he will end?" Mahmoud's mother, with just the faintest hint of a smile at the corners of her expressive lips, would answer: "Don't worry about Mahmoud, my husband: where and how he will end is in God's hands—and our son's."

Abdullah Malek, Mahmoud's father, had died three years ago, just after the end of the Second World War; his mother, who had grieved inconsolably—who had, in fact, declared openly on more than one occasion that she did not wish to be consoled—had followed him, as she put it, "to wherever God had seen fit to take him" less than a year later. Thus, at the age of twenty-five Mahmoud had lost both parents.

Abdullah, a portly, cherub-faced man with dark, keen eyes in which shrewdness and humor mingled in twinkling glances, had been a successful and wealthy merchant whose diverse interests and complicated enterprises had taken him from city to city throughout the Middle East. He had lived with his wife alternately in Baghdad, Damascus, and Beirut and then taken up residence in Cairo, where his son, Mahmoud, was born. Then, when Mahmoud was twenty, the Malek family had come to settle in *Al-Kods*—the Holy City of Jerusalem.

Their Jerusalem house, which Abdullah ordered to be built while the family still resided in Egypt, had taken fully three years to complete. It stood on an extensive plot of land that had been planted with flower gardens and fruit trees. Fashioned by sun-blackened masons of pink and carmine Jerusalem stone, the house, with its balconies that faced all four points of the compass and arched windows and trellised walks and enormous roof patio, was situated in the Sheich Jarrach neighborhood, beyond the Old City. Here, amid the roses and brilliant rose-purple blooms of the climbing bougainvillea and delicate, conch-pink petals of oleander and burgeoning saplings, Mahmoud's father, who had by now retired, and his mother, gray-haired and bespectacled, prepared to spend the rest of their days.

Abdullah smoked his hookah and read his books and news-papers. He had always, as long as his son could remember, been a voracious reader. His wife was with him constantly, responding to his conversation with patience and sagacity and sharing his excursions into silence. She would sit opposite him in the gracious warmth of the well-appointed living room or on the expansive, freshly cut sward of the hedge-enclosed rear garden, patiently embroidering and knowing just when to lift her eyes and meet his with a look of love.

It was the firm bond of devotion between husband and wife that was the mainstay and inspiration of young Mahmoud's life. He knew what his father meant when Abdullah said, "Every day, I marry your mother all over again." It was the motif that coursed, like a river of joy and trust and illumination, through Mahmoud's childhood and young manhood in Cairo.

Abdullah and his wife saw to it that their only son had an excellent education. He attended grammar and secondary schools in Cairo. Excelling in all of his subjects, Mahmoud finished secondary school at the age of sixteen. Some of his classmates, older than he, had decided to embark on military careers and urged him to do so as well. But he refused. When his parents discussed the matter with him, he told them that that was the last thing he wanted to do with his life.

Thus, young Mahmoud entered the university. Like his father, he read avidly and with enormous curiosity, but he was not burdened with the exigencies of his father's business enterprises. When his schoolwork was completed, he hurried to the isolation of his room and his bursting bookshelves. He loved nature and friends, but literature was the magnet that drew him to it with the strongest force. It was no wonder that he elected literature as his main pursuit.

As a child, he had always written poems and sketches and stories. Shut away in his room or in a favorite corner of the small garden at the rear of the house in which they lived, or even in the living room, he would draw a scrap of paper from a pocket or from his father's desk and begin to set down the words that gyrated inside his skull.

Mahmoud Malek understood, in the days of his awakening manhood at the university in Cairo, that at the heart of a writer's quest was, as he put it, "the advancement of man." He could not blind himself to the suffering and degradation he saw every day amid the squalor of Cairo. Cairo, as he then wrote, was "a cesspool that stank to the high heavens." And Egypt, the land in which he had been born, was "a chancre-ridden patient awaiting its ever-distant cure."

The poverty and squalor and numbing resignation that were rampant among millions of his countrymen, Mahmoud felt, cried out for attention and alleviation. On occasion he traveled with Abdullah on business trips in Egypt and throughout the Middle East. Everywhere he went, he saw disease, misery, appalling ignorance, and benightedness—the grinding, horrendous, marginal existence of human beings who were, as he had once read in English, *"bowed by the weight of centuries."* He tried to discuss with his father what he had seen and experienced, but Abdullah, though essentially a good man, would only shrug and answer, "My son, what you see so clearly and say so poignantly are true. These same, crushing stones have been on these same crushed backs for hundreds upon hundreds of years. But what is there to do about it, my Mahmoud? Who will lift the monumental stones from the bent backs? One man will cry out here and another there, my grieving son, but the desert winds will always sweep their words back into the bowels of the earth!"

Mahmoud listened to his father's lament and sensed the pain in his heart. But though he loved and admired and respected his father—even understood his disillusionment—he could not accept the answers he had given him. He discussed the matter with his fellow-students, but usually they cut him off, declaring that society was none of their affair. Some gave Mahmoud the same dispirited answers that Abdullah always gave him, and some murmured of revolutions in the making.

Nonetheless, Mahmoud could not accept these answers. He believed in his duty to effect change and in what he called "the true renaissance of man, which can only come through peaceful and persistent evolution." In an essay he wrote during his second year at the university, he said: *I believe firmly and with wholehearted conviction in the rebirth and the resurgence of the Arab world. But it cannot and will not come about by the use of force—by tyrannical directives and edicts from a military government. Nobody can dictate human "progress." Nobody can command rejuvenation. Like water entering a parched field, the urge for human advancement must trickle slowly and thoroughly into the lives of our people. We must create for ourselves a cadre of dedicated teachers who will understand and absorb and instruct. Their students must, in turn, become teachers devoted to the same task. Teaching must beget learning; learning must beget teaching. Then we in the Arab world will experience the only human "revolution" that is enduring: the "revolution" of individual human effort and individual human redemption!*

Mahmoud expected reactions of apathy and disagreement, but in no way had he been prepared for the extent and severity of the negative responses, and he had to struggle against despair. He had never had a large circle of friends, but even the small group shrank. He found himself shunned; at times he caught the sneers and obscene gestures that were half-meant to be seen by him. But even though the isolation and the contempt pained him, they did not divert him from his views. If anything, they made him feel more strongly that he was right. Stubbornly, then, he kept developing his ideas and continued his writing. He did not neglect his studies, but he considered them ancillary to the main purpose of his life: writing the truth as he experienced it.

So Mahmoud Malek persisted in his beliefs, but he changed his tactics. He no longer showed his writings in public, and he stopped speaking about them openly. He limited his confidences to his parents and to a single constant friend by the name of Ahmed.

Two years Mahmoud's senior, Ahmed was a tall, spindly-limbed fellow with a narrow, sallow-skinned, pockmarked face and bright, eager eyes that blinked nervously behind the thick lenses of his glasses; he alone could be shown the secret writings. One evening, in the privacy of Mahmoud's room, when Ahmed finished reading a newly composed poem by his friend called "Arabs, Awaken," in which the author had likened Arab society to a bedridden man who, out of "disgusting self-pity," will do nothing to rid himself of his "filthy ailment," Ahmed looked up and said with conviction: "You are correct in what you perceive, my dear Mahmoud—and you state your case with a powerful metaphor! We Arabs cry out continually that we are victims. We bemoan our miserable state. We point to our festering sores and beg for help. But we are our *own* victims, and we ignore the *self-help* that would rid us of the plagues which hold us inert."

Mahmoud nodded vigorously. "Exactly, Ahmed. You have understood what I am driving at!"

Ahmed smiled. "I understand," he said. "And I agree."

Mahmoud leaned forward. "Listen," he said with agitation, "and I will tell you something that sums up the Arab situation. As you know, my father travels a lot on business. One time, after he returned from a long trip, he related what he had heard from a business associate in Jaffa: 'The nations of the West are bent on romanticizing the Arabs; they call the Arab people, "sons of the desert." But the bitter truth is, my dear friend, that the Arabs are *fathers* of the desert: wherever they go, desert follows!'"

To no one except Ahmed did Mahmoud reveal the motivation of his "lonely journey," as he called it. *I live in an isolated chasm,* he wrote during his third year at the university, *where there is no one to help me with my thoughts or steady my groping hands or guide my stumbling feet—where there is not even so much as the merest echo to sing me to sleep or comfort me in sorrow. But though I wander endlessly and, at times, I feel, aimlessly, and though I fall again and again and must with my own strength rise to my feet, and though my separation from others is often overwhelming, and though I burn with fevers of frustration and doubt and, occasionally, self-pity, I do not despair! There is some vital, unconquerable, invigorating human force within me that nourishes and sustains me and keeps me searching for the exit I must one day find. And if the minds and hearts and souls of other men are shut off from me, I can always reach deep into myself for this strength; and joyfully, I can reach over the barriers that surround me so forbiddingly by reading the words of men whose voices I find in harmony with the deepest yearnings and most noble longings of my essence.*

Mahmoud Malek sighed and for the hundredth time twisted his body on the mattress. S'ad, lying on her stomach now with an arm thrown out to one side, was serenely asleep. It did his heart good to know that even if she was shut away from him by her dreams, she was at peace. There was no one in the world, he felt, as deserving of comfort as the devoted and innocent young woman beside him. He reached out to touch the smooth hollow of her back but, fearing to disturb her, withdrew his fingertips. His body, abandoned long ago by the delicious calm of lovemaking, was tense and rigid. His mind, unable to surrender itself to the shadowy arms of sleep, seemed to cringe from the waking world, but it had nowhere to go. From the yard outside the window of the bedroom, the exuberant chirping of birds in the grass and on the branches of the trees filtered into his ringing ears. The calls of birds lighting on dewy grass and brushing gently through dewy leaves, he thought, had replaced the roaring of the guns on Mount Scopus. But for how long? He gritted his teeth. *How he loved the infinite delights of peace! How he loathed the endless horrors of war!*

Suddenly, he started violently.

There was a dull, thudding sound.

Were the guns starting up again? He held his breath, his mind whirling, like a carousel gone berserk, with a single, fixed fantasy: to leap up from his bed and run outside to cry out in a voice that all Arab-held Jerusalem and all the Arab world would hear: *I, Mahmoud Malek, son of Abdullah and*

*Alima Malek, naked and unarmed and unafraid, call upon you
to stop! Stop the maiming and the carnage and the slaughter!*

But then the sound came again, and Mahmoud realized that
it was someone at the back door.

But in these times and at this hour—*who?*

S'ad stirred and her lips murmured dreamily, but she did
not waken. Mahmoud threw on a robe and, wrapping the belt
around his waist, hurried out of the bedroom, down the hallway,
and through the kitchen. At the rear door, on which the knocking stubbornly persisted, he halted and then, with a trembling
hand, slid the latch from the peephole and peered through it
onto the back porch.

A chill went down his spine. In soiled khaki clothes and
dirt-caked shoes, unshaven and with hair in which burrs and
bits of twig were tangled, was Fawzi al-Najari, S'ad's older
brother. His eyes, which kept shifting from the door to the
yard, were ringed in purple-black and bloodshot. His right arm,
in the sleeve of his bloodied shirt, hung limply to one side.

Involuntarily, Mahmoud retreated a step. Essentially as good-
and warm-natured as his father, he was receptive to the goodness in other human beings until their behavior proved them
unworthy of his trust. But he had always, almost from the first
time he had set eyes on the man, distrusted the intentions of
Fawzi, whom he considered wily and deceptive. It was clear
that S'ad's brother was in some sort of trouble, but instinctively—despite the wish to believe otherwise—Mahmoud had
the feeling that the trouble, no matter what it was, was deserved. Still, with a sinking, disquieted heart, he did not see
how he could turn the wounded man away. For several long
and agonizing moments, feeling his mouth go dry and his legs
go weak and the cold sweat erupt on his forehead and cheeks
and neck, he stood and silently debated the conflict. Something
deep inside him told him not to open the door under any circumstance. And yet, with tortuous insistence, he kept hearing
his young wife's dismayed voice. *But how could you have let
him go, my husband? How could a merciful man like you turn
my own flesh and blood away from our door?* Of course, there
was always the possibility that S'ad would never know. If Fawzi
were not admitted, he might succumb to his wound and——

Mahmoud did allow himself to finish the thought. With an

enormous effort of will, he stemmed the revulsion that rose in him like a tide, and stepped forward and unbolted the door. Shoving his stunned brother-in-law aside with a sharp butt of his good shoulder, Fawzi burst into the kitchen and barked: "Lock the door again—*quickly!*"

Numbly, Mahmoud obeyed.

Clutching his wounded arm and grimacing with pain, Fawzi lowered himself slowly onto a chair. "It took you long enough to answer," he said harshly, fixing his narrow, yellowish eyes on his brother-in-law: "I might have died out there, you know."

"I was . . . in the bedroom, Fawzi. I didn't hear the knocking at first."

The other grunted. Glancing down at his blood-soaked sleeve, he said, "I've got a scratch here on my arm that needs some attending to. Get me some antiseptic, Mahmoud, and something to bandage it with."

"How did it happen?"

Fawzi's thick lips twisted into a derisive sneer. "What the devil is the difference *how* it happened? I'm hurt—and that's all you need to know! Just get me what I asked for, dammit, and be quick about it before I bleed to death!"

"Fawzi!"

Both men looked toward the inner doorway of the kitchen, where, clad in a long nightdress, S'ad stood. Fawzi, who had half-risen in alarm, sank back onto his chair. Mahmoud took a single step toward his wife, but stopped abruptly.

Pale-faced and breathing harshly, S'ad steadied herself by gripping the frame of the door. "Fawzi," she murmured. "How . . . when did you——"

Her brother interrupted her with a heavy, bludgeonlike voice. "I just got into the house this minute," he said, "but I stood outside knocking at the door for an endless time! Your husband——" Wincing, he checked himself. "All that doesn't matter," he snapped. He pointed to his limp right arm. "I'm hurt," he said, suddenly softening the tone of his voice. "I need your help, my sister."

Mahmoud roused himself. "I'll get the iodine, S'ad," he said, "and some bandage. Stay here with your brother and I'll be right back."

In the thick, sickly-looking glow of the overhead bathroom

bulb, Mahmoud caught sight of his face in the medicine chest mirror. Haunted-eyed and pinch-mouthed and bloodlessly wan, it looked like the face of a stranger—a stranger not from a foreign land, Mahmoud thought, but from another planet. Nervously, he rummaged in the cabinet for the supplies he required. He found the brown bottle of iodine readily enough and then the roll of bandage, but it was only a small one and would never do to bind Fawzi's wound, and so he hurried to the linen closet in the hallway and got a clean white towel from the shelf and tore it into strips. When he returned to the kitchen, he saw that S'ad was cutting away the wounded man's right sleeve. With a sharp intake of breath, she murmured, "It—it's an ugly gash, Fawzi! I——"

Her brother's eyes rolled up at her. "There . . . there," he said in an unctuous tone that was meant to calm S'ad down. "Don't fret over me! We shall do what we have to do, my little sister, and everything will be fine." His eyes, like little lizard tails, flicked over to the figure of his brother-in-law. "Hey, Mahmoud," he snapped. "Don't stand there and gape at your poor, crippled guest. Come over here and fix me up!" As if to make light of the order, he sent a burst of forced laughter echoing from the kitchen walls. And then, as Mahmoud came forward, he smiled up at his sister and added, "What a splendid nurse your husband makes, S'ad! I shall be certain to recommend him to the medical authorities for a citation of excellence!"

Mahmoud said nothing. His initial anxiety had been replaced by dispassionate, almost clinical calm. There was a gashed arm to be sterilized and bound. He set aside the fact that the arm belonged to Fawzi al-Najari and left off thinking about how his brother-in-law had come to be injured and what he was doing in Jerusalem, and instead concentrated on the task. Deftly, he washed the wound with water that S'ad had boiled in the kettle, and sterilized it with the iodine and then layered it over with gauze bandage, over which he tied the strips of white towel. Stepping back, he said: "There, it's done."

"So it is," said Fawzi, drawing his left hand over the black stubble that bristled on his chin. "My compliments!" Then he dropped his hand and reached into his shirt and drew out a single, bent cigarette, which he inserted between his lips.

Glancing over at S'ad, he murmured, "Get me a light, little sister, will you?"

But it was Mahmoud who went quickly to the stove and got the box of matches from the shelf at its side and then, with movements as precise as those he employed to dress the wound, lit Fawzi's cigarette. It came as a sudden awareness to Mahmoud—although the feeling was undoubtedly a long-standing one—that he resented the condescending tone of his brother-in-law's voice when he addressed S'ad, and the domineering, almost contemptuous look in the man's eyes. It required no small effort of will for Mahmoud to control the bitterness and anger that rose up in him, but for his wife's sake he did so.

Fawzi leaned back in the chair and slowly inhaled. Gray-blue smoke trickled from his hairy nostrils, and when he withdrew the cigarette from his lips, it curled in a thick, indolent little cloud from his mouth. For several moments, he sat in silence, the heavy lids drooping over his half-shut eyes, and gave himself over to the enjoyment of smoking. Then, with a jerk of his powerful shoulders, he roused himself and said, "My dear kinsmen, forgive me for being so forward, but I haven't, unfortunately, had a meal in some time, and I'm ravenous."

"Of course!" S'ad blurted out. "Forgive *me*, brother, for not asking you sooner—it's just that I couldn't really think of anything else but your wound!"

Fawzi waved the cigarette and smiled amiably. "No need to apologize, S'ad," he said. "I understand that it's not an everyday occurrence for a wounded man to appear in your kitchen."

S'ad hurried to the stove. "I'll make you something right away, Fawzi," she said.

Her brother nodded. "And there's another thing," he drawled slowly. "I shall need to take advantage of your very gracious hospitality for a little while, at least until this evening. And perhaps, kind people, until tomorrow night. But you must not—I implore you both—put yourselves out for me in any way. I shall be as quiet as a fieldmouse in its hole and not disturb you. Just continue with your routines as usual, and I'll rest up. And when the right time comes, I'll leave, eternally grateful for the help and sanctuary with which you provide me."

Mahmoud cleared his throat. "Don't you want to have a doctor look at your arm, Fawzi? I think the wound needs stitching——"

S'ad's brother stared at him without speaking.

"I can drive you over to the infirmary—it's not more than five minutes away."

"Honestly, Fawzi," said S'ad, breaking eggs into a frying pan, "it's no trouble at all! Mahmoud will be happy to do it—and I'll certainly feel better knowing you've had proper medical attention."

Fawzi ignored his sister's words and continued to stare with icy rigidity at his brother-in-law. He drew on his cigarette and then, removing it from between his lips with a savage snap, said, "Thank you, dear Mahmoud, for your solicitous concern, but there is no reason in the world for me to visit an infirmary or see a doctor. I'm perfectly fine just as I am." His eyes darted over to S'ad by the stove, on whose front burner the eggs in the pan had begun to sizzle, and then back to her husband. "All I want and all that I require are some food and some rest. Everything else, I assure you, will take care of itself in good time. I repeat: you, Mahmoud, and my sister must pay absolutely no attention to me; as far as the Malek household is concerned, I am not a guest, not even a visitor—I am nothing more than, so to speak, a passing ghost." He paused and for an instant reflected, as if to make sure he was choosing exactly the words he wanted to use. Then, raising his half-smoked cigarette to the level of his eyes, he pointed it directly at his brother-in-law. "One thing more," he said in a measured tone. "No one—neither friend nor neighbor nor acquaintance nor casual passer-by—must know that I am in this house. And when I have gone, it must be as if I have never been here. Is that perfectly clear?"

Mahmoud swallowed. "I don't understand."

The veins in Fawzi's temples bulged. "I am not asking you to *understand*," he said coldly. "I am telling you what *must be!*"

Despite himself, Mahmoud's voice rose. "Listen here, Fawzi," he said rapidly. "We'd better get things straight between us right now. Don't think for a moment that you can barge into my home and begin giving me orders! I'm not your

servant, and I'm not your pawn! Don't presume to tell me what
I can and cannot——"

"Mahmoud!" cried out S'ad. "Fawzi! Stop it, the both of
you, this minute!"

Fawzi silenced his sister with a venomous look. Then, twisting on his chair, he returned his gaze to her red-faced husband.

"It is impossible—you must believe me when I tell you
this—for me to explain just now, but one day you will know
all; and you will, dear fellow—I promise you—be glad and
proud that you granted my wish on faith." Fawzi halted and
wet his dry lips with his tongue and then reached over to touch
the crude bandage on his right arm. "I am wounded, as you
see, my gracious brother-in-law, but the wound is not grave.
Because of your goodness, I will be restored to full health.
But—and I say this in all seriousness, Mahmoud—if you
should choose, out of false pride or irritation or whim, to
discuss my visit with anyone on this earth but S'ad, I may
suffer terrible and irreparable harm." A melancholy smile struggled onto Fawzi's lips. "My appeal is closed," he said re-
signedly. "I rest my case with your wise judgment, Mahmoud."
And, as if the weight of his burden were too much for him to
bear, he bowed his head.

Mahmoud stood in silence. As before, when he had discovered it was Fawzi knocking at the door, he felt torn and
uneasy—except that now the conflict within him had become
acute, and the uneasiness had turned to anxious dismay. He
had listened patiently and with care to every word that his
brother-in-law had uttered, but the speech—insidious in its
formulation and cloying in its tone—had, rather than allaying
his fears and uncertainties, only served to increase his discomfort. Somehow, there was an implicit threat in Fawzi's utterances and behavior. The appeal for mercy—designed by its
inventor, quite obviously, to be pathetic and disarming—was,
so Mahmoud felt, nothing more than a thinly veiled warning.
For how, if his brother-in-law were made out to be the cause
of Fawzi's downfall, could Mahmoud ignore or escape the
backwash of guilt and grief that must surely engulf his wife?
And how, even if Fawzi were to avoid the "terrible and irreparable harm" of which he had spoken, was Mahmoud to believe
that his wife's brother would not exact some punishing retri-

bution? Mahmoud had known Fawzi al-Najari for almost four years and found him to be a harsh, uncompromising, and at once outspoken and devious man, given to dark, impenetrable moods and sudden impulses of violence. In the Galilean village where S'ad's family lived, he had a splendid house and land and considerable wealth, but—for his own undivulged and unchallenged reasons—spent little time in the actual, day-to-day management of his domestic affairs, which he entrusted to, as he phrased it with a cynical smile, a "myrmidon cousin." Even S'ad, who seldom had a bad or even critical word for anyone, said that her older brother was more feared than respected and more obeyed than loved by the villagers and even by his late wife and his son. But, as she told her husband candidly, she was bound to Fawzi by a sense of common origin and by the strength of family loyalty.

In truth, Mahmoud was always sorry to see Fawzi—whenever it was possible, he avoided the man. This morning, he wished that, as he phrased it in his mind, the intruder had never shown up. Now that he was in the house, Mahmoud wished passionately that he would depart and never come back. But, as he realized with pain and despair, all the wishes in the world could not change the reality. Fawzi was there and he would not leave until he was ready to go. To argue or dispute or quarrel with the man was foolish: it would not alter the fact of his domineering presence, and it would only disturb S'ad. Trying to discover Fawzi's motives or purposes was a lost cause; attempting to persuade the man rationally was futile. There was nothing to do except to dampen his brother-in-law's violent nature by seeming to cater to his wishes.

Mahmoud saw that S'ad was staring at him. Her eyes were large with hurt and apprehension. A lock of her dark hair had fallen across her forehead, and on her lower lip, where she had bitten it, there was a spot of bright red blood. The eggs in the pan on the stove had long ago fried and the water in the kettle was boiling with a furious hiss of steam, but she made no move to serve her brother his food. Mahmoud felt his heart constrict. He wanted to enfold her in his arms and tell her gently that everything was going to be all right, but his body seemed strangely paralyzed. He made an effort to collect himself and, trying to smile, said to his brother-in-law: "Fawzi, if you don't wish to see a doctor, don't see one. If you want to remain in this house for a time, you may stay with us——"

Fawzi lifted his head. The smile on his lips was a prisoner there—it did not reach his yellow eyes. "I know I can count on you, Mahmoud," he said.

———— · ————

In the distance to the east, beyond the lichenous stone wall at the rear of the yard, the mountains had lost their color, the soft, chastened color of late afternoon that gave them their substance and shape, and would soon be obscured by fast-falling evening. The calls of the birds, which had filled the yard and surrounded the tile-roofed stone house by day like some endlessly repeated but always new theme song, were fading in tiny, ever more subdued, poignant wisps of sound. From the direction of the Old City, which S'ad could not see, the flat, heavily cadenced, plaintive cry of a muezzin's prayer, coming from the circular balcony of some rough-stoned minaret, seemed—long after it was actually gone—to linger in her ears. In the hushed, sultry, spent air, the smell of sun-blasted grass and dying rose blossoms was overpowering.

Against the yard's south wall, midway between the house and the back boundary, was a low bench built of rust- and amber-colored slabs of stone. It was there that S'ad liked to sit and wait, as her husband once said to her, "for the cathedral of evening to be lit by the tapers of the stars." On occasion, Mahmoud sat with her—the bench was just large enough for the two of them; it had, as Mahmoud liked to remark, been made for lovers such as they. But most often S'ad occupied the seat alone, during the times that her husband was away or busy writing in his study—especially at day's end. To the east, as she sat with her back pressed to the now-familiar curves of the wall and her bare feet thrust into the crude-textured blades of grass, were Jordan and the distant mountains. To the west was the large house, one side of which she and Mahmoud had lived in for nearly a year. And to the north, directly opposite her, was the high, densely branched hedge that divided the spacious yard in two.

The other side of the house, the side beyond the dividing hedge, was empty—it had been untenanted from the first day she and Mahmoud had moved in and, most probably, for months or even years before that. Sometimes, as she sat, S'ad found herself staring fixedly at the hedge, over which she could see only the roof of the other, vacant half of the house. Occasionally, when she wearied of sitting, she would get up and cross the grass and stand at the hedge and peer through. Actually, there wasn't much to see: shuttered windows from which the sun had peeled the paint; a back porch, identical with her own, except that the flagstones of the floor were cracked and sprouting unruly grass; the same yard as the one on her side, but for the burnt and neglected lawn and the unpruned trees and flower gardens that had gone woefully to seed. That and, aside from the scampering lizards and ever-present, ever-hopeful sparrows and raucous starlings and solitary, plodding tortoises, nothing more.

Sometimes, after returning to the bench from what she liked to call an excursion to the hedge, S'ad would indulge herself in speculating about what kind of people might move into the uninhabited half-house. Almost invariably, in her fantasies, she would reject the notion of a grown or even half-grown family and picture for herself a young couple, about the same ages as she and Mahmoud and somewhat like themselves in tastes and interests. Often she would get so caught up in her daydreams that when Mahmoud, having finished writing for the moment, came out of the house he could rouse her from thought only by actually sitting down beside her on the bench. More often than not, the direction of her eyes and the look on her face announced like trumpets, as he would laughingly observe, what she was thinking about, and he would say to her with a broad grin: "Well, dearest wife, please tell your curious husband who our new neighbors are! Are they young or old? Do they have children? Do they have dogs . . . cats . . . canaries . . . pigeons? Do they play any musical instrument—perhaps a flute or a drum? Do they like to read—or play chess? Aren't they ever going to paint the doors and windows . . . and weed the gardens . . . and prune the trees? And what about that horrible back porch . . . and the broken section of wall to the rear . . . and the roof tiles that are missing? When do they intend to repair all of that? And what about the lawns? And what are their favorite foods? And do they like cinema?" And, with a pause to catch his breath and a sly, adoring wink, he would take S'ad's blushing cheeks between his hands and kiss her mouth and then whisper, "Ah, and there's one more thing, a detail actually, but still and all: are they Arabs or Jews?"

The two-family house with the hedge that divided the two backyards down at the end of the winding Jerusalem street was situated at the western edge of an open, untenanted area that, with the outbreak of hostilities in 1948, had become a stretch of no-man's land, separating the Israeli and Jordanian armies. In consonance with his vision of peace between the Arabs and the Jews, Mahmoud Malek had sold the house that his father, Abdullah, had built in the Arab quarter of Sheich Jarrach after the death of his parents and moved there late in 1946. S'ad had come from her uncle's house in the Old City to join him there soon after she and Mahmoud were married.

Just before the Arab armies attacked and the war broke out, a young couple—much like the couples that peopled S'ad's imagination—had indeed come to inspect the vacant side of the house. Through her front window, S'ad had seen their battered jeep drive up and watched the two of them get out and, hand in hand, go up the front walk. Mahmoud was in his study, writing, and in the stillness of the house, S'ad thought she could hear the newcomers next door. Giving in without protest or embarrassment to her excitement and curiosity, she had hurried into the backyard and seated herself on the bench. Fifteen minutes or so later, the young man and his wife came out of the kitchen door onto the back porch. The man was tall and curly-haired and even-featured and had an unlit pipe between his teeth. The woman, who was younger than her husband by perhaps a year or two, had long blond hair and was wearing a white medical jacket. The afternoon, late in April, was a glorious one. A bright, benevolently warm sun shone down from the translucent blue sky of Jerusalem, upon whose brilliant-stoned rooftops the gently moving clouds cast soft gray shadows. Still holding hands, the couple slowly traversed the yard on their side of the hedge. They looked here and there, touching this bush and that tree, and once the man knelt and picked up a small clod of earth from one of the garden plots and crumbled it between his fingers. They spoke often, but so softly that S'ad could catch none of their words. At the rear wall, there was a stunted but somehow surviving almond tree, and it was in full blossom. The couple halted in front of the tree and, arrested by the striking pearl-white beauty of the almond petals, continued to stare at it. Then, at the same instant, as if some secret voice had whispered simultaneously to each, the man and the woman turned to each other and embraced.

A strange and inexplicable feeling came over S'ad at that moment, and mysteriously, it kept coming back to her every time she went into the backyard for weeks afterward. She wanted *that* couple to move into the house next door. And then, without thinking about it, S'ad suddenly defied her shyness—which Mahmoud always said was just a cover for the boldness and daring that he insisted were at the core of her nature—and ran across the yard to the spot where the hedge intersected the rear wall. The embrace, which was tender and confiding, in front of the splendor of the blooming almond tree, lasted for several moments, and then the couple, smiling warmly and gazing into each other's eyes, broke reluctantly apart. Still standing where they were, they spoke softly for a time in Hebrew, most of which S'ad was able to understand, about the tree and about the breathtaking view beyond the wall and about the spaciousness of the yard and about the repairs that were needed and finally about the possibility of their moving in. Pressed to the hedge, S'ad listened to what the man and the woman said to each other without the slightest shame or guilt. She did not at all feel that she was eavesdropping, but oddly enough—as she later told Mahmoud—she had the feeling that she was a silent partner in the conversation. When the couple turned from the tree and started, now arm in arm, back toward the house, she walked, as she described the experience to her delighted husband, with them, step by step, on her side of the hedge.

"Did they notice you?" Mahmoud asked.

S'ad shook her head. "No," she replied. "They were too engrossed in their discussion of the yard and the house, and much too preoccupied with themselves."

"Would you have been embarrassed if they had seen you?"

S'ad shook her head again and smiled. "No," she said, "not

in the least!" Then, with a gleam in her eyes, she added, "As a matter of fact, if they *had* seen me, I——" But she flushed and did not finish the sentence.

Mahmoud took her hands in his. "Go on," he urged. "Say what you were going to say."

His wife cleared her throat. "If—if they had seen me," she said with emotion, "I should have invited them in for tea—and then urged them to be our neighbors."

"Just like that, eh, S'ad?"

"Just like that, Mahmoud. They seem to be a lovely couple."

Mahmoud laughed warmly and pressed his wife's hands. "And so," he said, "what were their names?"

"I don't know their last name, but hers was D'vora and his was Arie."

"Hmmmm," said Mahmoud. "I see." He was silent for a moment, and then the intense, dreamy look that S'ad loved to see came onto his face. "Well, well," he mused aloud. "So perhaps one day soon Arie and D'vora will live next door to Mahmoud and S'ad. How does that sound to you?"

"Beautiful," she whispered. "It sounds beautiful."

———————

By now evening had come, like an expected and always welcome visitor, to Jerusalem. The house was a shadowy mass—it looked like the hulk of a ship riding at anchor. The hedge was black and seemed constantly to be changing its shape. The yard, except for the fireflies exploding here and there into blue-green pinpoints of light, was shrouded in darkness. Above S'ad's head, the first stars of evening glittered in the sky. Mahmoud was in his study. Fawzi was asleep, as he had been the whole day long, in the guest room. S'ad was seated on her little stone bench, alone with her thoughts.

Remembering the visit of D'vora and Arie and the discussion with Mahmoud that followed it saddened S'ad. That glowing April afternoon, with its lazily drifting sun and mildly blue sky and miniature clouds, had seemingly been filled with so much hope and promise. The young couple in front of the flowering almond tree on the other side of the hedge had seemed so incredibly *near*. On that day, only short months ago if one reckoned strictly by the calendar, the future, like some generous host, had opened its welcoming arms and life had seemed bountiful and rich.

But then, in the month of May, everything had turned topsy-turvy. The guns had begun firing and the tanks, like invading metal locusts, had begun rumbling across the borders, and the helmeted soldiers had begun moving forward with their blood-hungry bayonets thrust before them. Where, S'ad wondered, were D'vora and Arie now? Were they wounded or maimed or even—on the very threshold of lives that were just starting—already buried beneath the earth? Would they ever return to this house and move their belongings in and mend what was broken and care for what had been for so long neglected and live their lives fully and peacefully and rewardingly as loving husband and wife? And if they did manage to survive and to return, would there even be a house and a hedge and yard still intact?

The war, thought S'ad bitterly, had plunged everything into chaos; it had shattered all plans; it had dampened all hopes. There was nothing one could do in a war but live day by day, minute by minute, since human existence was no more than a tenuous bridge that might at any instant collapse and hurl the persons on it into a hideous void. This day and, thus far, this evening, the sirens and the guns were silent; *but who could say for how long?*

To escape the cutting edge of the war, S'ad often turned her thoughts to the past. To someone in limbo or in trouble, the past could be a refuge. Like a prospector intent upon finding a treasure he is certain is there, one could sift through its soil with the sieve of memory and find glittering grains of comfort and solace. As a traveler who retraces his steps on the long road he has journeyed to the point from which he began his trek, she liked to return in her mind to the village in the Galilee where she had been born. The village was high up, on the top of a hill surrounded by other hills. Mahmoud, not long after he had visited the place for the first time, had said to her that it rubbed its shoulders against the sky. In the distance, to the east, were, in Mahmoud's words, the big brothers of the hills—the mountains. And to the west—its presence, although it could not be seen, always felt—was the sea. "The colors of the Galilee," S'ad once told Mahmoud, "are blue and green, but especially green." And it was true. Over the rhythmical, endlessly repeated curving crests of the hills arched the vast blue vault of the sky. In summer it was an incandescent blue that the fiery hammer of the sun, striking blow after blow without remorse and without surcease, all but ground to white powder. In the fall it was a vibrant, electric blue into whose shifting currents of air flocks of starlings flew. In winter it changed to a moody, unpredictable blue, tinged with hues of purple and gray and often filled with towering haystack clouds that, opening amid cracks of thunder and white forks of lightning, disgorged torrential rains. And in the spring it was the mild, unruffled, half-dreaming blue of a lake. And below the sky's blueness was the green of Galilee's earth. Not ubiquitous, all-embracing green—there were too many barren, stone-hided hills for that—but green in the earthen terraces on the slopes and green in the parceled garden plots and green in the steep wadis after the rains: the sharp, intense, breathtaking green of growth from the soil.

Once, when they were returning to Jerusalem from a visit to S'ad's village, Mahmoud said suddenly: "Do you know, S'ad, that *you* are green?"

S'ad shook her head. "Mahmoud, what are you saying? I don't understand."

Mahmoud gazed intently at her. "I'm quite serious, S'ad." And then, smoothing her puzzled forehead with his fingertips, he explained. "The color you like best, the color you're always talking about, is green. And suddenly, today, I knew the reason why! It's because, as I just told you, *you're green*. Why, you're like a tender green blade of grass growing up out of flinty soil. You're like a green sapling, tender and resilient and, in spite of all odds, bent on reaching the heavens!" He held his wife's chin gently in his fingers and went on: "You're natural and filled with the sap of life and pliant: you're green, my darling, and I love you!"

S'ad's eyes were moist. She put her hand on his.

Mahmoud turned for a moment and looked back through the window of the bus and saw once again, receding as in a dream, the now-tiny houses of S'ad's hilltop village. Then he twisted around once more to her and, with a sigh, said, "Do you know that as a young man, I visited this territory with my father? And do you know that I must have passed your village on this very same road? And do you know that, like you, I was impressed by every patch of green I saw—even the tiniest bit?"

S'ad reflected. "Actually," she mused, "there isn't that much green. Perhaps that's why we value it so."

Mahmoud nodded. "I'm sure that's the reason," he said slowly. "Do you realize, S'ad, that it's the Jews who are bringing green back to this land." Mahmoud's eyes had a faraway look in them. "This land was all but empty when the Jews began coming back," he said. "And when they did, S'ad, the Arabs began pouring in."

"The Arabs were attracted by the green—is that it?"

"Exactly, S'ad. The more the Jews plowed and tilled and irrigated, the more the Arabs were attracted. The Jews were magnets, S'ad—even as a boy I could see that." Mahmoud's smile mingled pleasure and pain. "But I've never really been able to talk about this to anyone. My parents—even my best friend in Cairo, Ahmed—didn't want to understand. They refused to believe that Jews and Arabs could ever live in peace. But you, dear S'ad——"

"But I what, Mahmoud?"

"But you . . . are different: open to experience . . . open to life!"

S'ad was silent for a moment. Then she said, "We are two of a kind, you and I, Mahmoud."

"Yes. Two of a kind," he murmured, holding her hand.

S'ad's life in the Galilee village had not been an easy one. There were seven children in her family: three boys and four girls. Fawzi was the eldest. There was beauty in her life, beauty

that captivated and sustained her and that she knew she would
remember always. The sky and the rolling hills and the sheep
and the goats and the trees that blossomed and bore fruit and
the crops that lifted themselves up out of the rocky soil and
reached toward the sun. There were summer days of profound,
awesome silence when the Galilee seemed like a raft drifting
aimlessly in some endless current of time; autumn nights when
the wind howled and seemed to shake the tenuously fastened
stars and one could smell the distant sea; winter evenings that
were bitingly cold, when S'ad huddled with her brothers and
sisters before the flames that leaped up in the soot-blackened
stone hearth; and spring afternoons when the blood-red anem-
ones and delicate purple irises carpeted the hill slopes and all
the world seemed to be singing a song of praise.

But there was also the back-breaking, interminable round
of chores that stretched from sunrise to sunset and then, with
relentless tyranny, began once again when the new day arrived.
There were monotonous, nagging weariness and bone-grinding
exhaustion. But worst of all, there was loneliness. Minutes and
hours and days and weeks of stultifying, draining, unbearable
loneliness that sometimes, when S'ad felt that she had reached
the uttermost limit of her endurance, made her want to die.

Mahmoud was right when he said that she was different.
Something inside her—she did not know what it was, but she
knew it was there—set her apart. Something—she knew not
why—stamped her life with a peculiar seal. Some compelling
voice—though she realized it was within her—seemed to call
her from afar. Her father and her mother, though they were
relatively young, withered before her eyes under the crushing
burden of unrelieved toil. When S'ad was seven, her father
became ill and for the next few years was often bedridden. His
eyes clouded; his skin grew sallow, drawing tautly, like the
skin of a drum, over his bones; his limbs became sticklike and
feeble; his voice faltered; and his mind, like a parchment-dry
leaf that the wind catches and blows here and there at will,
wandered. When S'ad was ten, she came home one autumn
evening to find that he was dead.

Fawzi, the eldest sibling, became head of the al-Najari family. S'ad's father had been stern, but not without a reserve of
kindness and compassion. Fawzi, on the other hand, was an

absolute despot—inflexible, punitive, wholly in love with and unqualifiedly jealous of the prerogatives of his power. Always capricious and often sadistic, he ruled the now-fatherless brood with an iron hand and took pleasure in the humiliation which he recklessly inflicted on the others. The villagers, almost without exception—people who had admired and respected S'ad's father—detested and, so far as it was possible, avoided Fawzi. As a village wag, who had himself been "burned" by Fawzi in a cunning swindle, once said, and as the villagers and those from neighboring villages from then on repeated: "Even the scorpions run from Fawzi al-Najari!"

One of Fawzi's favorite scapegoats was S'ad. With unerring instinct, he sensed her fiercely independent mind, her passion for justice, her capacity for human empathy, her appreciation of beauty in nature and in people. Sensing all of these, he attacked her wherever and whenever she was open and vulnerable. Constantly and calculatedly, he showered her with criticism which she was not permitted to refute. He blamed her when she was innocent and allowed her no defense. Her altruism and innocence annoyed him. S'ad, more than any of the others, was the special target of his perverse fury, and he never lost an opportunity to castigate her or sometimes even do her outright harm.

S'ad could not strike back at him—because of her position in the family and, more telling even than that, because of her nature. As she said to herself so many times over in her suffering and in her solitude: *I cannot hit back at my brother Fawzi because I know who he is . . . and, more to the point, I know who I am!* Thus, she took his abuse in silence and with a patience so formidable that it sometimes astonished even her. To Fawzi, whose actions derived from spitefulness, his sister's unrevengeful behavior was further proof of what he considered her aloofness and recalcitrance. Once, in a burst of wrath, he bellowed at her: "You think by your muteness and by your disgusting holier-than-thou haughtiness that you will escape me, do you, S'ad? Well, you are wrong, little sister, you are sadly mistaken!"

The suffering inflicted on her by her brother bruised S'ad, and the harshness and barrenness of her life in the hilltop village took their toll, but they did not break her spirit. S'ad had long ago, even as a young child, decided that she was quite alone, and the world around her confirmed her view, thrusting her ever deeper into herself. But the wasteland outside her put her in touch with an inner oasis and, in the face of all that oppressed and tormented her, she flourished. No one, she felt—not Fawzi, not a dozen like him—could dim her vision or tarnish her dreams. Hauling water from the well or guiding the sheep in from remote hillside pasture or picking olives from gnarled, silver-rinded trees that had survived the ravages of droughts and hailstorms and pests, she dreamed of some other world to which she must—and would one day—escape. The very solitude of nature itself seemed to have a voice that whispered to her not to despair. The mothlike stars, majestic clouds, and tender, jeweled drops of dew underfoot were her friends. Though Fawzi scorned her and her other brothers and sisters mocked her, and even the villagers, taking their cue from the members of her own family, taunted and teased her, she redeemed herself by persisting in the unshakable belief that some time in the future redemption must come to her. The supreme lesson of life, she concluded, was endurance.

And redemption did come. An uncle—her dead father's brother—visited the village. Hassan Ali, the uncle, was a man in his mid-fifties who had lost his beloved wife to an outbreak of cholera and his only daughter to a stray bullet fired by a British soldier, one of the hundred-thousand-member military force occupying the territory of Palestine under the League of Nations mandate. A jeweler of some means who lived and had a shop in Jerusalem's Old City, he was—though embittered by tragedy and made distraught by his loneliness—a man of heart and sensitivity. S'ad, who was nearly fourteen at the time of his visit, captured his fancy and, on an impulse that, as he said, sprang from his parched and wizened soul, he proposed to Fawzi, the head of the village family, that his niece come to live with him.

Fawzi, though he detested S'ad and was eager to be rid of her, saw his chance to benefit. He could—as he realized in a flash of malevolent insight—kill two birds with one stone by disposing of his irksome sister and making a handsome profit at the same time. Thus, he protested vigorously that as a laborer she was worth her weight in gold. With a well-placed tremor in his skillfully controlled voice, he told Hassan Ali that S'ad could do the work of two men and, besides that, was clever with her hands and could sew and embroider as well—and that her loss would be a damaging loss of income and, in addition, a devastating family loss. S'ad's uncle stroked his gray beard patiently and, not at all taken in by his nephew's wiles but willing, nevertheless, to play the game, said, "And does she also cook, Fawzi?"

"Cook?" echoed Fawzi, pretending to be astonished and even a trifle offended by the question. "Why, each meal that my versatile little sister prepares is a banquet! If you doubt me, good uncle, ask her mother or her admiring brothers and sisters."

With consummately feigned innocence, the wise and knowing Hassan Ali murmured: "Then she is worth a lot, your praiseworthy sister S'ad."

Fawzi spread his open palms. "An incalculable amount, dear uncle," he boomed. "Why, one is fairly staggered when one begins to contemplate it!"

"Doubtless, then," countered Hassan Ali, "she is beyond the reach of a poor jeweler from Jerusalem." And with a dejected sigh, he went on: "Ah, well, taking S'ad home to live with me was but a well-meant wish. In truth, dear Fawzi, you are absolutely correct: I could never pay you what S'ad is worth." Hassan Ali drew up his shoulders in a hopeless shrug. "Forgive me for wasting your precious time and energy."

Fawzi's face paled. He knew instinctively that the shrewd and nimble-minded jeweler had maneuvered him to the wall and that there was nothing to do but backtrack. "Wait a moment, Uncle," he cried out, scarcely troubling himself to mask his alarm, "wait *just* a moment! There's no reason in the world for us to give up so easily at this point. Two, as you so aptly say, men of experience can state their positions in extreme and then retreat. Why, the meaning of life itself is . . . negotiation."

Hassan Ali clucked his tongue. "I don't know," he muttered. "Such a prize as S'ad . . . for a man of my insignificant means? It doesn't seem possible."

Fawzi was frantic. Judging his uncle by the image of himself, he was not at all certain that the jeweler did not mean to teach him a lesson by abandoning his proposal. "Come, come,

Uncle," he said unctuously, letting the words slip out of his mouth like cards from a deck, "let us not succumb to a despair that might be—that is, in fact—momentary! As the villagers in these parts say: 'Behind the gloomy clouds, sits the smiling sun, coyly waiting to be coaxed out!' That's a good motto, Uncle, is it not? Something to take back to Jerusalem with you, eh?" And, drawing a sleeve across his sweating face, Fawzi continued hurriedly. "Let's talk, Uncle, let's talk the night away if it's necessary! I have time and you have time. Surely, when we've thrashed things out at length, we can come to an agreement."

"Well, Fawzi, perhaps anything *is* possible in this old world."

"Not perhaps, Uncle! *Certainly!* Be optimistic! I *know* we can agree."

So, like *shach-mat*—the ancient game of chess invented by the Persians—the discussion went on. Fawzi moved and Hassan Ali countered. And, in the end, a deal was struck. The jeweler handed over to his nephew the sum that they at length agreed upon—ironically, it was the sum that Hassan Ali had in his mind intended to pay at the outset—and S'ad's departure was arranged.

Fawzi was more than pleased with the result of the bargaining, and for his part, Hassan Ali, though he shrewdly took pains not to reveal his feelings, was jubilant. He would have willingly paid almost any price within reason to bring his niece into his household and thereby assuage the isolation and grief that gnawed at his heart. S'ad's sensitivity, earnestness, and glowing human warmth had been apparent to him from the very first moment he set eyes on the girl. *As a man and as a jeweler*—so he said to himself with a wry, inward smile—*who should know a real gem better than I?*

It was on a morning late in fall that S'ad took leave of the village in western Galilee in which she had been born. Though the sky was crowded with big, swollen gray clouds, the sun somehow managed to break through them and mantle the gentle, rolling hills with serene light. S'ad's spirit rejoiced. She found it fitting that the sun should shine benignly on the day that, as she phrased it in her mind, she was set free. Dutifully, but with the real feeling that was so integrally a part of her nature and set her apart from the others, she bade farewell to her brothers and sisters. One by one, she embraced them and wished them, with sincerity and ardor, good hopes and good lives and told them that she would come back to visit them whenever possible. When she held her mother's fragile, work- and care-worn body in her arms, she wept. Gently but firmly, Hassan Ali grasped her shoulder and told her that it was time to go.

Outside, as S'ad and her uncle, their belongings neatly stacked on the trampled earth of the yard, waited for a neighbor's wagon to come and take them to the road below, Fawzi approached and said to her in a low voice: "Sister, if at times I may have been too harsh with you——"

"There is no need——" began S'ad.

But Fawzi interrupted her and adamantly pursued his point. "If sometimes I seemed to mistreat you, please know that I meant you no harm. Life, as you will better come to know in the days and years ahead, is harsh and unsparing. Since the death of our beloved father, I have been burdened heavily and have often been unable to deal with certain delicate matters in the manner they deserve. But believe me, little sister, that I have always acted, even in moments of impatience and pique, in the very best interests of our family. My chastisements and my strict discipline were intended only to benefit us all." A stiff smile that seemed uncomfortable with itself wrenched Fawzi's lips from their characteristic grimness. "Go with Hassan Ali in peace, little sister," he said. "Obey him in all matters and serve him according to his wishes. And he, being the fine man he is, will surely reward you."

The jeweler's business took him from the hilltop village first to the port of Haifa. For the first time in her young life, S'ad gazed at the sea. From the steeply plunging flank of Mount Carmel's sprawling bulk, she saw below her the vast, glittering crescent of the bay that stretched all the way to Acre, shimmering beneath the cloud-swept sky like some magical fairy city. And beyond the magnificent blue cup of the bay was the open sea that stretched, like a light-spangled plain, to the distant horizon. She felt giddy and buoyant and joyous and carefree, almost weightless, as if she were nothing more than a bubble that at any instant might be snatched up by an impish, frolicsome wind and borne far out over the bay, dotted with tiny boats at anchor.

What a world is out there! a voice inside her cried with triumphant release. *What a wide and warm and loving and wondrous world is out there waiting for me, just as I always knew that it must be!* It was the world, S'ad sensed, as she gazed in awe and delight outward from the mountain slope, that she had glimpsed—even in the darkest times of her sorrows and isolation—in the mirror of her soul. And, deeply moved by the view of the enormous and welcoming outer world's beauty, she began to weep. It was silly, she thought, and she had not intended to do any such thing, but she could not restrain herself. Hassan Ali, who had just concluded his business inside a large jewelry store, emerged to find her frantically, and unsuccessfully, trying to stem the tears that coursed down her ruddy cheeks. All too familiar himself with the pain of pent-up emotions, he did not rebuke his niece but understood her joy at once. "That's it," he murmured huskily, patting her shoulder with a hand he could not keep from trembling. "Cry all you want! Don't be ashamed, my dear—let the tears flow as they will. It eases the heart."

S'ad soon threw herself into her new life with a hungry eagerness. Her uncle installed her in a little room that, incredibly, was *hers alone*. It had been his daughter's room, and he said that now, since she would be like a daughter to him, it was seemly that she should live in it. Astonished and a little overwhelmed by the coziness and privacy of the chamber, she scarcely closed her eyes the first night she spent in it.

In the snug little house itself, which had been somewhat neglected by her uncle after his losses, she cleaned and swept and tidied up and scrubbed, and soon established what her uncle admiringly termed a harmonious order that would draw the praise of any mistress of any household. Her uncle took her through the narrow, twisting, pungent-smelling streets of the Old City and showed her the various markets and their amazing produce. Thereafter, carrying wicker baskets on her arms, she did the shopping, choosing the fruits and vegetables and fish and meats with singular concern and counting out the money, mil by mil, to pay for her purchases with painstaking care. She prepared the meals for her uncle and herself with pride and skill and served them almost with an air of reverence. Delighted with what he ate, Hassan Ali would often interrupt his lunch or dinner to cry out, with the regularity of the refrain of a song: "Wonderful, little S'ad! Excellent! Truly superb! Well, I must say that Fawzi didn't err or exaggerate when he told me what a good cook you were: every meal is indeed a feast!" And, patting his stomach and rolling his eyes, he would add: "I'm full. I will burst if I consume one drop more . . . but I cannot stop! I must go on!"

Sometimes, in the afternoon, after she had finished her household chores, S'ad would help her uncle in his tiny jewelry store crowded with shelves. How she loved to see the rings and bracelets and pendants and filigreed silver earrings that were as delicately fine-spun as shimmering spider webs. How she loved to see the gems, varicolored and of subtle hues, that seemed to wink at her from their settings like mysterious eyes. How she loved the textures of the metals and the stones and the soft, comforting semidarkness of the shop and the smell that arose from the tiles of the floor after she had scrubbed it, and the pristine look of the gleaming glass showcases when she had finished cleaning them with a porous sponge and drying them with a cloth, and the sight of her uncle, his eyepiece set firmly in place, bent with complete, absorbed attention over his work. The jewelry store, which was on a corridorlike, stone-paved street just around the corner from where she lived with her uncle, bewitched and enthralled her; it was another new world.

Once, when the day's work was ended and her uncle had finished stowing away the most precious pieces in the squat little safe under the counter at the rear of the store and they had gone outside and Hassan Ali had turned the key in the lock and pulled the heavy metal shutter down and padlocked that as well, she touched his arm and, drawing a deep breath, said: "Uncle——"

Hassan Ali had already pocketed his keys and turned to stride down the street toward home, but the tone of his young niece's voice arrested him. Looking around and, to reassure S'ad and prompt her to speak openly, smiling gently, he said, "What is it, my dear?"

"I don't quite know how to say it, Uncle. . . ."

"Try, S'ad! Give your heart the free rein it must have, and the rest will follow."

His niece cleared her throat. "It—it's just that there is some-times so much beauty in the world. It's in the shop . . . it's in the streets . . . it's in the sky and on the earth . . . it's in our little home! Uncle, it's *everywhere*—if only one opens one's eyes to see!"

Hassan Ali was so moved by S'ad's shining eyes and the candor in her voice that for a moment he could not speak. Then, swallowing, he reached out and took her hand in his and said, "You are blessed, my child, in that which you perceive. There are those who live to be four and five times your age, and yet see little or even nothing at all of what this world has to offer. God is great; and in His generosity, He fills the earth with bounty and with beauty! How good it is to know that you are aware of His precious gifts."

Hassan Ali scarcely slept a wink that night. He lay twisting and tossing on his bed, turning his tousled head on the pillow. He had brought his niece from the hilltop village in western Galilee home to Jerusalem with him for the human company that he had sensed, on first meeting, she would give him. He had reckoned, quite correctly, that she would fill the intolerable void of his loneliness. But what she gave him, he realized, was turning out to be far more. There was, it was more and more obvious to him with each day that passed, a richness and depth of spirit in the young girl that exceeded his fondest hopes. He gave to her, as his part of the bargain, shelter and sustenance and—so he thought—the pitiably small measure of good feel-ing that he was able to fan up from among the embers of his grief-numbed heart.

That night, following their conversation in front of his jew-elry shop on the thin, stone ribbon of the Old City street, he resolved that he would teach his niece from the Galilee to read and to write. It was clear to him that this new world, as S'ad herself might put it, would be one in which, like a blazing meteor, she soared through boundless skies. He knew that to teach her would be to break with old and calcified tradition, but he did not care. Behind his staid exterior and unassuming manners and careful formality, there was a hidden Hassan Ali who believed with firm conviction that every man—no matter

what the rest of his fellow creatures said or how they behaved—
must measure the dimensions of his own soul and choose the
path along which it should go. He wondered, as he pulled the
rumpled sheet up about his shoulders and buried his bleary-
eyed face in his creased pillow, why he had not thought of his
plan before this night. And he exulted that, despite the delay,
he had finally made the decision. Happily, his weary mind and
exhausted body were able to relax at long last, and he fell at
once asleep.

The very next day—for he was a man who, once he had
chosen a course of action, liked to put it into execution immediately—Hassan Ali began teaching his niece the alphabet.
S'ad was, as he had fully expected, enormously enthusiastic
and wonderfully receptive. She made rapid progress, and the
lessons, given always at a regular hour after supper, took on
a profound, almost sacred significance for both teacher and
pupil. For Hassan Ali, they came to be the catalytic agent that
returned love to his once achingly empty heart. For S'ad, as
she learned to read and write, they opened boundless horizons.
One evening, when the lesson was done and the book she had
been reading aloud from was closed, S'ad, with a look of
enchantment on her face, murmured, "Uncle, I think I must
be dreaming. . . ." And Hassan Ali, beaming as he patted her
cheek, replied, "No, dear child—you are coming awake!"

So the years went by, strengthening and deepening the bonds
of affection and trust between the girl from the hilltop village
and the jeweler in Jerusalem's Old City. Hassan Ali knew in
his heart and S'ad knew in hers that they had drawn very close
and were like father and daughter. From time to time, S'ad
made the trip back to the western Galilee and her family there.
And once in a while, Fawzi al-Najari, now more prosperous
and more haughty than ever, paid a visit to Jerusalem. The
blood kinship was still there, but S'ad, by now an attractive
and accomplished young woman, felt remote from the place
and people she had left both in spirit and in outlook. When
Hassan Ali fell suddenly and seriously ill, she devoted herself
to nursing him with loving care. And when, because of his
failed health, he sold the little jewelry shop he had owned for
decades, she went to work in the coffeehouse on the campus
of the Hebrew University on Mount Scopus. It was there that

she met and fell in love with Mahmoud Malek, who was a student at the time.

———————

"S'ad . . ."

Startled from her reverie, she looked up and saw her husband standing before the bench. "I'm sorry," she murmured. "I was so lost in thought that I didn't hear you coming."

"That's all right, darling," said Mahmoud. He reached out and gently touched her hair.

S'ad hesitated; then she said: "Is something wrong, Mahmoud? You look . . ." Her voice trailed off.

Mahmoud cleared his throat. "Fawzi's gone," he said.

"Gone? But when?"

Mahmoud shook his head. "I don't really know when he left. I was in my study writing, as you know. Just a few minutes ago, I went into the guest room to see if he needed anything— and it was empty!"

"Did he leave a note?"

"Nothing, S'ad—nothing at all. He just disappeared."

S'ad rose. "He's my brother," she said, "and I realize that it's probably a terrible thing to say, but . . . I find that I'm relieved. I think that he is more oppressive than ever. Do you understand?"

Mahmoud nodded slowly. For a moment, he stared at his wife in silence; then he said, "S'ad . . ."

"What is it, Mahmoud? Tell me what's troubling you, please."

"S'ad . . . Fawzi had a revolver."

"Are you certain?"

Mahmoud sighed. "I'm absolutely certain," he said. "He had the gun tucked into his belt, under his shirt. A button had come unfastened—I caught a glimpse of the revolver when he first came into the kitchen. I didn't want to alarm you by telling you, but more than that, I had no idea what Fawzi might do if I confronted him with the fact. So I kept still."

"What does it mean, Mahmoud?"

Her husband shook his head. "I can't say, S'ad. Anything

is possible. But there's one thing that's certain: Fawzi is up to no good. I've had that feeling for a long time, but I haven't wanted to hurt you—or perhaps I simply lacked the courage to speak. The gun confirms my worst fears." He bit his lip. "S'ad . . ."

"Yes, my husband."

"Fawzi . . . may be involved . . . with saboteurs."

S'ad's body trembled. "It's all so terrifying," she murmured, "so . . . inhuman."

As if to shut out the pain of what he saw so clearly, Mahmoud closed his eyes. "That is exactly the right word, S'ad," he muttered, more to himself than to his wife. *"Inhuman."*

Abruptly, there was a silence between the two. Like swimmers far out at sea who are suddenly separated by powerful waves, husband and wife seemed lost to each other. From the blackness of no-man's land beyond the rear wall of the yard, an owl hooted mournfully and then, as arbitrarily as it had begun, left off. Mahmoud opened his eyes and stared at S'ad. Clearing his throat, he said quietly: "S'ad, no matter what my feelings are toward your brother, I don't have any real proof to condemn him. He's badly wounded, and he shouldn't have left the house. He may need help."

"What should we do, Mahmoud?"

"I'm going to try and find him, S'ad. It's our responsibility."

"Mahmoud——"

Mahmoud's eyes narrowed. "I don't like your brother's politics," he said slowly. "Nevertheless," he continued, "he is your kin, your own flesh and blood. Therefore, like Fawzi or not, I feel that I must do something. He had a serious wound. He really isn't in any condition to go wandering around."

S'ad shivered. "Mahmoud," she said huskily, "Fawzi is my brother and he *is* hurt . . . and may be in trouble. But I don't want you to endanger yourself. If anything were to happen to you——" She lifted a hand. "If anything were to happen to you, Mahmoud——"

Mahmoud caught her delicate hand. "It won't, S'ad," he said. "Don't be afraid."

S'ad seemed uncertain. She hesitated for a moment and then said, "If you say so, Mahmoud." She forced a smile onto her lips. "All right," she said as firmly as she could. "Go, then— go look for Fawzi."

"He can't have gone far. I'll take the car and drive to the main road. I should be back within half an hour or so." He kissed S'ad lightly on her cheek and turned to go.

But she caught his arm. "Mahmoud," she said. "The cur- few——"

"I'll be all right, darling! Don't worry."

"Be careful, Mahmoud!"

"See you in a while," he called out over his shoulder.

He sprinted down the yard and through the narrow pas- sageway between the left side of the house and the outer stone wall. She followed him at a slower pace. "Take care!" she called out again, but he either did not hear her or did not want to answer. As she reached the gravel drive, he was backing the car out. Slowly, she walked across the front lawn and onto the porch. Holding the wrought-iron rail, she stood quietly and watched. If Fawzi had left their house only a little while ago, she knew, Mahmoud would have some chance of finding him. Otherwise, the effort would be in vain. Though she was con- cerned about her brother's wound, a part of her had wanted to discourage her husband from leaving. But she was certain the arguments she marshaled would have proved futile in the face of Mahmoud's determination to go. Mahmoud always did what he felt he had to do; that was his way in life.

She saw the dim slits of the car's headlights gleam like cat's eyes, and then the vehicle straightened out and sped off down the street and within a moment or so rounded the first bend and was lost from sight. The whining of the motor sounded ever more faintly in S'ad's ears, but still she did not move from her place on the front porch. It was ridiculous, even infantile, but something—she did not know what—kept her rooted where she was. Like moths in dizzying flight, strange and disconcerting thoughts swirled through her mind. For a moment, she felt hollow and unreal. Then, with a determined effort, she got hold of herself and turned to go into the house.

Suddenly, there was a savage, violent explosion that twisted her body around like a top. Out of the corner of an eye, she saw a blinding tongue of flame leap up into the night, igniting the branches and densely packed needles of three or four of the cypresses that lined the street leading from her house to the main road.

"Mahmoud!" she screamed, stretching forth her arms into the fire-stained darkness. *"My Mahmoud!"*

1960

Jerusalem

DAWN.

Ilana Arnon had been up for some time, even before the first fine lines of light had appeared at the shutters of her bedroom window. It was silly—absurd, actually; she had no reason to be awake for a good hour and a half yet, and even that rising hour gave her more than enough time to get to school and be among the first to arrive, but she was awake nevertheless. She was tired and resented not being asleep and could have, without a doubt, dozed off again, but she was afraid to close her eyes again and try. A terrifying nightmare—in which she had been captured by Arab marauders and was being tortured to reveal information which she could not convince her captors she did not have, although it was the truth—had seized her sleeping mind and made it cry out for release. Even after she broke the power of the horrible dream, it took her a long while to fully realize and accept the fact that she was safe in her own bed in her own room. But then, though she was calmer, there was nothing to do. She did not want to be up at dawn, but she did not trust herself to fall asleep again and give the nightmare another chance to get at her. She was ashamed that she was so afraid. It did not at all suit her image of herself as an Israeli girl of twelve. On the other hand, she was honest enough and realistic enough to recognize and admit to the strength of the fear.

Lying on her back between the crisp, clean sheets and staring up at the freshly painted white ceiling of her pretty room, she wondered what had caused her to have the nightmare. Was it the fact that at about noon yesterday a Jordanian soldier had, from his concrete emplacement on the high wall that zigzagged through Jerusalem and divided the city into eastern and western sections, suddenly and without cause opened up with a burst of machine gun fire and murdered an Israeli passer-by? The evening edition of the paper her father always brought home from the Foreign Ministry had carried a front-page picture of the slain man's body lying in the bloodied street and surrounded by grief-stricken onlookers. She had not been able to get the scene out of her mind all that night. There would, she knew, be popular outrage and outcry and official protests, but nothing would ever bring the dead man back to life. He had been cut down while innocently crossing a city street, preoccupied by an errand or on his way to lunch, haphazardly struck by a hail of bullets, and had gasped out the last, fleeting moments of his life on the sun-scoured pavement. She had not read the article—only the caption under the photograph, which had turned her stomach and made her avert her eyes. After supper, in the living room, when little Uri was not present, her parents, Arie and D'vora, had begun a discussion of the incident, and she had left at once.

Or, she thought as she lay stiffly on the mattress, with her eyes wide open and fixed on the smooth expanse of ceiling, was it the story she had heard yesterday morning at school that had made her fall prey to the bad dream? One of the boys in her class had a visiting uncle who lived on a *moshav* in Gush Tel-Mond, an area between the city of Natanya to the north and Tel Aviv to the south. This uncle related to his nephew's family of how Arab *fedayeen*—infiltrators—from the notorious *meshulash,* or triangular area, that jutted, as Israelis often put it, "like a thorn" from Jordan into the heartland of the country, had slipped across the border by night and attacked two citrus grove workers. The Arabs had murdered their ambushed victims with knives and cut off their ears and noses. Ilana, with a stubbornness born of desperation, had insisted that the story could not possibly be true. "Even Arabs cannot be that cruel!" she had cried out, though she knew her outcry was sure to bring ridicule. But in her heart, she knew very well her classmate's uncle had not lied. From the Gaza Strip and from the jagged and all but indefensible *meshulash,* the Arab *fedayeen* set forth like locusts in a plague; they waited only for nightfall to hide their murderous movements. Of course, the Israelis stood guard—every city and town and village and settlement had its watchmen—but the nights were dark and long, especially in wintertime, and the Arabs were many. Every ugly and forbidding story of death and mutilation and plunder and destruction added cumulatively to the effect of what had happened before. And the stories went on and on—there never seemed to be an end to them.

Ilana shivered and turned her eyes to the near wall on the other side of which little Uri, her brother of five, had his room. She wondered, did he have nightmares as she did? He was just a small child, and the family tried its best to keep the terrible stories from him. But, as she knew, the truth, like fine grains of sand, had an insidious way of slipping through the sieve of silence. In Israel even the little children realized what was going on and, more than that, that *they were not, despite their innocence and fragility, immune from the dangers that threatened the country*. One could glimpse the truth in their eyes and tell it from the games they played and see it in the pictures they drew, and sometimes sense it in their sullen and impenetrable silences. Almost from the day he was born, a child in Israel began absorbing, like radioactive dust, the knowledge that the country was at cruel and constant and unremitting war.

One day, not long ago, Ilana had been in the backyard with Uri when suddenly, without warning, her little brother had pulled at her skirt. With mingled annoyance and amusement, Ilana asked, "What is it, Uri?"

He looked up at her. "Why do we need so many soldiers in Israel, Ilana? *Please*, Ilana. Why must we have so many soldiers?"

His strained voice and the urgency in his eyes made it impossible for Ilana to put him off. She chewed at the eraser of her pencil and thought for a moment and then said, "Well, Uri, you see ... we need the soldiers ... to keep us safe."

Uri was silent; then he said: "Why do the Arabs hate us, Ilana?"

His sister stared at him. "Why ... do they hate us?"

"Yes, Ilana—why?"

His sister put her pencil down on the composition book that lay open on her lap. She seemed to lack the breath to speak. There was a wound in her heart, and the question had opened it up. She wanted to send Uri away, to say, "I'm really too busy now" or "Go and play" or "Ask your father," but she knew it wasn't possible. Staring directly into her brother's pained and puzzled eyes, she murmured: "It's hard to say, Uri. I really . . . don't know. . . ."

Uri was adamant. "But you *must* know, Ilana!" he protested. "You're almost in high school and you know how to play the piano and—and you know so many things! Can't you tell me the answer?"

Ilana reached out and ran her fingers through her little brother's curly black hair. "I wish I could, Uri." She sighed. "But I can't. I don't know why the Arabs hate us. Perhaps . . . perhaps they don't even know why themselves."

Uri's fingers curled into fists; his eyes flashed. "Maybe," he said, "maybe they just like to hate!"

Ilana shrugged helplessly. "Maybe," she said.

Uri nodded and turned and walked away; but after taking a few steps, he suddenly halted and faced his sister again. "Ilana," he called out, "I'm glad we have so many soldiers to keep us safe, aren't you?"

"Yes, Uri," she replied, averting her eyes that had begun to fill with fear.

Ilana rolled over and gazed across the bedroom. On the wall directly opposite her bed, above her desk, was a painting she had done last summer at camp. It showed a small, white-walled cottage with red-shuttered windows and a bright red door. The cottage was surrounded by thick banks of brilliantly hued flowers, and from its yellow straw-thatched roof a stone chimney sent up blue smoke. On the right, its banks lined with willows, was a fish pond. On the left there was a grape arbor that sheltered a little white bench. The painting's background was a patchwork of green- and brown- and beige-colored fields that stretched to a distant range of purple-blue mountains: and over all, suspended between sky and earth, a luminous rainbow gleamed. There was a delicate, ethereal quality about the painting—as if the artist had struggled to evoke the sense of some unearthly beauty that lay beneath the surface of earthly "reality"—and Ilana had received a good deal of praise for her accomplishment. Many of her fellow campers and a number of counselors had suggested that she pursue painting seriously. Though she liked the painting and was grateful for the compliments it brought her—in actuality, she had been somewhat astonished by its warm reception—Ilana's major and passionate interest was in music.

She had been playing the piano for as long as she could remember—D'vora sometimes said laughingly that her daughter must have listened to music in the womb—and planned a career for herself as a concert artist. Even her paintings—the one on the bedroom wall and the others that she occasionally did—were expressions of what she called her musical feelings. The rustic scene she had done at camp was in fact, as she confided to her friends, based on one of the themes of a Mozart sonata. As did few things in life, music brought her respite from what she considered to be the harshness of the world.

Both Arie and D'vora, but especially her mother, who had also studied music as a child in Berlin, encouraged her and took great pleasure in her development and accomplishments. Once, when she and her parents had come home after a performance she had given in the auditorium of the local school and Arie had gone to bed and she and her mother were left alone in the quiet living room, D'vora suddenly grasped her daughter's thin shoulders and said huskily, "Do you know, Ilana, that I always hoped that one of my children would be a musician?"

"Always, Mother?"

D'vora nodded solemnly. "Always, Ilana—even before you were born." And with a distant look in her eyes, she smiled and went on: "As I've told you many times, I was pregnant with you in a transit camp where I had volunteered to work——"

"In Saint-Michel, wasn't it, Mother?"

"Yes, in Saint-Michel. There was ... so much horror about me at the time: in the eyes and faces and bodies of those who had survived the death camps. And the War of Independence was being fought in Israel—so many of the people I knew and cared for were being wounded and killed. Your father and I— we were newlyweds, actually—were separated; and, of course,

Arie was at the front. There was so much to oppress and discourage me, and so little to sustain me. One of the few escapes I had was music. Somehow—I don't even rightly remember how at this point, but I know that it seemed like a miracle at the time—I got hold of a battered old phonograph and some records, which I played, at all hours of the day and night, over and over and over again. And sometimes—usually in the early hours of the morning, before the first light appeared—I used to put my hands on my round, swollen belly and say: 'Little child, are you listening with me? Can you hear the beautiful music? Someday, little child, you will be out in the world, and beautiful music will surround you and lighten your burden and help you to find your way as a human being. Perhaps . . . perhaps you will even play it . . . and I, your mother, will listen and remember this time!'" Then D'vora drew her daughter closer and hugged her with all her strength, and in a voice that trembled said: "And now, dear Ilana, that day has arrived! I am remembering."

"Mother . . . don't cry."

"It's all right, Ilana."

"Please, Mother——"

"I'm fine, Ilana. Honestly, I am."

Now, as Ilana gazed at her painting, which she called in her mind, *The Rainbow Cottage*, the theme of the Mozart sonata trickled into her mind and then, like a flood, seemed to pour over her. She could hear the notes—crystalline-clear and majestic and hauntingly sad and yet in a strange way supremely triumphant, as if the very expression of the sadness somehow dissolved it—and she could feel them tingling and vibrating on her sensitive fingertips. She was much calmer now. The nightmare seemed to be fading away, losing its power over her. From beyond the shuttered window, where the tenuous light had turned to solid bright strips, the sound of the excited birds outside in the yard flowed serenely in to her.

Gradually, she was able to relax. The spring day would be brilliant and beautiful. The almond tree in the backyard, which

was her favorite and near which she liked to sit and dream and
compose little melodies, would be in full bloom, dropping its
creamy-white petals on the newly cut grass. Her friends and
fellow students and teachers would welcome her in school. No
Arab bullets would fly from the gray concrete wall that divided
Jerusalem. No *fedayeen* would strike. Nobody would step on
a land mine. All would be well and peaceful. How did she
know? How could she be certain? It was simple: *the music told
her so and the music did not lie*. People hedged and were
evasive and lied; *but the music was always unequivocal and
truthful*. She glanced over at the clock on her dresser. It was
just twenty minutes past five. The alarm was set for six, so
she still had time to sleep. With a yawn she pulled the sheet
up over her fragile shoulders and closed her eyes. She seemed
to be sitting in the shade of the grape arbor, next to the thatched-
roof cottage. High above her, in the gleaming sky, the rainbow
arched from one end of the land of Israel to the other: it showered multicolored notes of music, like butterfly wings, down
upon her.

The kitchen was flooded with soft morning light. In her pale
blue bathrobe, over whose shoulders her long blond hair lay
in thick tresses, D'vora went to the stove and turned on the
flame under the kettle. Arie was still shaving in the bathroom.
Ilana was dressing for school in her room. Little Uri was still
asleep and dreaming, without a doubt, of the treehouse he and
his father had begun to build the afternoon before. D'vora still
had a little time to herself before breakfast, and she was glad.
The day at the hospital would be long and hard, and the family
would occupy her evening. Arie had some financial matters he
wanted to talk over, and Ilana would want help with her homework and advice about a piece she was preparing for a concert
next month, and Uri would want to play. The few precious
moments alone with herself would help her to endure the storms
that were sure to be ahead.

She seated herself in her chair at the kitchen table and,
resting her cheek on her hand, let her mind drift freely. For

some inexplicable reason, she thought of Saint-Michel again and of her last day there. She remembered how Menashe, the camp director—a man who was always calm and unruffled—had been extremely nervous that day. He had barged into her office-room a dozen times during the morning and asked her a hundred questions and pestered her with countless trivial matters until, reaching the limit of her patience, she had turned to him and said, "Menashe, what in the world is the matter with you? You're driving me crazy!"

It was as if the outburst had drenched him with ice water and at once, almost in midsentence, he left off speaking and fidgeting and stared at her. "D'vora——" he began after a moment.

"What *is* it, Menashe? I don't understand you today. You're acting——"

"I'm acting not like myself—is that it?"

D'vora smiled. "That's exactly it, Menashe!"

The camp director shrugged. "I know . . . I know," he muttered apologetically. "You're absolutely right—I won't deny it! Something's bothering me and, for the life of me, I can't say what it is." Abruptly, he stopped and stared at D'vora fixedly, as if she might vanish if he were to take his eyes off her, and then with a sigh that shook his powerful torso, said: "Forgive me, my dear D'vora, but actually I *do* know what's wrong: it's that you're leaving tonight on the *Pan Crescent*." A sheepish, forlorn smile came to his lips. He coughed and cleared his throat and went on: "I realize that I'm behaving like a child, or a fool, but I simply cannot help myself! The truth is, Dr. Arnon, that I . . . shall miss you terribly."

"And I shall miss you very much as well," D'vora said. Then she took his hand and added: "And if you say just one more word on the subject, Menashkeh, I shall burst into tears!"

And they both laughed.

That dark November night in 1948, she had indeed left Saint-Michel and the rows of cone-peaked tents and the chateau, and traveled in one of the twenty trucks of the convoy southeast to the cove where, shrouded in a chill, thin blanket of softly falling drizzle, the *Pan Crescent* lay at anchor, awaiting the arrival of her immigrant cargo. Menashe went with her and bade her farewell at the gangplank. "Give my best to Arie," he said.

"And please keep in touch!" He nodded at the curve of her belly. "And let me know if it's Ilan or Ilana."

"I will ... I will, Menashkeh. I promise."

Then, amid the hoarse shouts and the nervous exclamations and the bewildered murmurs and cries of the infants and children and the ubiquitous, impassioned singsong of prayer and the raucous blare of the ship's public address system, she had waved to him from the deck, and he, standing among the tarpaulin-covered trucks and wrapped in cold November drizzle, had waved back. "Good-bye, Menashe," she called, though she knew her voice would not be heard. *"Shalom!"* And he, knowing as well that his words would be lost in the din, had called back.

The *Pan Crescent,* an old, dilapidated, rusty-hulled freighter whose dark and musty holds had, like beehives, been sectioned off with rough wooden planking on which the immigrants slept and ate and huddled together for warmth, set sail an hour or so later, drawing away from the black, sullen coast of southern France and steaming steadily, like an overworked beast of burden, out to open sea. D'vora remembered the long and tedious days of the week-long journey across the Mediterranean and the weary, care-marked faces of the immigrants as they conversed with each other and sank into their private reveries and ate their rationed food and drank their rationed mouthfuls of water and gazed anxiously over the rails at the sea for signs of intercepting vessels, even though the British blockade had ended. They peered with puzzlement down into the gloomy holds in which—though they could scarcely believe it—they lived. And she remembered the wild and dreamlike and fiercely exultant looks on their faces when, battered and wheezing but steadfast and unfaltering, the *Pan Crescent* sailed into Haifa Bay. What a moment of human triumph that was! The freighter's whistle blasted its arrival call again and again into the air and was answered by the welcoming whistles of launches. "Hatikvah" sounded over the ship's public address system. The immigrants, crowded in one dense human mass to the shoreward rail, sang and wept and swept handkerchiefs back and forth like banners and cried out, *"Baruch atah Adonai eloheinu Melech Haolam she-hecheyanu v'ki'yemanu v'higiyanu laz'-man hazeh*—Blessed art Thou, O Lord our God, who hath kept

us alive and sustained us and enabled us to reach this time!"
And on the dock, standing in front of tin-roofed sheds, dozens
of Israelis who had proclaimed this soil the Land of Israel and
were defending that audacious proclamation with their lives,
cheered and waved back. And she remembered how scores and
scores of the new arrivals, having descended the gangplank,
fell upon their knees and with tear-filled eyes kissed the gray
concrete of the pier beneath which lay the holy earth of their
yearned-for home.

Faithful to her promise, she did write to Menashe. She wrote
to tell him that the child she had been pregnant with in Saint-
Michel had been born a girl and that she and Arie had indeed
named the baby Ilana. She wrote to inform him that she and
Arie had, as they had dreamed of doing, bought the house—
or "half-house," as she phrased it in the letter—on the fringe
of no-man's land in Jerusalem and that the family had moved
from the little apartment on the shady street in the western
section of the city to its "new and beautiful" home. Menashe,
for his part, wrote back faithfully and promised to visit them
and "see the new sabra" when his mission at Saint-Michel was
completed and he returned to Israel. Somehow—though Israel
was a tiny country, a mere splinter of land, as Arie always put
it—Menashe never did get to see his friends the Arnons. Something inevitably seemed to come up and ruin the plans.

Menashe went on another mission, this time to Aden in
1949, to help fly the beleaguered Yemenites back to the land
of their forefathers. Then Arie was sent out of the country on
Foreign Ministry business, and D'vora and Ilana traveled with
him. For one reason or another, the promised meeting never
took place. And then, in 1956, during the Sinai Campaign,
Menashe fell in battle. The Arnons were not even able to attend
his funeral. Arie was away at the front, and D'vora could not
be spared from the hospital.

Aronson—the "warrior from Brooklyn" who had been ill
with the flu in Saint-Michel—was dead, too. He had been
killed in battle early in 1949, D'vora learned, and, according
to his wishes, had been buried in a Jerusalem cemetery. D'vora
had visited his grave several times and had written to his parents, who never answered her letter. And Ed Markowitz, "the
sergeant's sergeant," had been killed as well. He had—so Arie

reported to his wife—interposed himself between the enemy and his retreating men, and by his action saved an entire platoon from destruction.

So many dead, D'vora thought. There was a whole population of dead men in Israel, she realized. But in some way they seemed to live on—in the memories of those who lived on and in the steady influx of Jewish immigrants from all parts of the world and in the flowering of the land. Every Jew who had fallen in the defense of Israel seemed stubbornly and defiantly to cling to life, because, D'vora thought, it was for life he had died. She confided this thought to her husband one day, and Arie told her that he agreed. "How one dies makes a difference," he said. "Life has a way of recognizing those who loved it."

"D'vora," said Arie.

Startled, his wife looked up. "I didn't hear you come into the kitchen," she murmured.

"I know you didn't. What were you thinking about?"

D'vora shrugged and nervously drew the belt of her robe more tightly around her waist. "About—well, about the past."

"Recent or remote?"

D'vora waved a hand and rose from her chair. "Both," she replied.

Her husband's eyes narrowed. He understood by the look in her eyes that she did not wish to talk about her thoughts, and so he nodded at the stove. "Kettle's boiling," he murmured.

"So it is, dear. I'll make you coffee."

"Sit down again," Arie said with a smile. "Let me make it for the both of us!"

She did sit again while he busied himself at the stove, but then she got up again and began to prepare breakfast. When she saw that Arie was glancing over at her, she said with a tight smile: "I'm sorry, darling, but I simply can't sit still any longer."

"Is something bothering you, D'vora?"

His wife hesitated for a moment and then slowly nodded.

"Want to tell me about it?"

"It's Ilana—she was so upset last evening. I tried to talk to her before supper, but I couldn't get a word out of her. After supper she went directly to the piano. When she finished practicing I made another attempt—I thought I'd use her performance as a means of breaking the ice. But it didn't work: she went right off to her room. When I looked in on her later, she was already asleep."

Arie put the steaming cups of coffee down on the table. "I'm sorry," he said. "I was so preoccupied with the Foreign Office last night that I didn't notice a thing. By the time I was through, you had gone to bed. Do you know what was troubling her?"

D'vora sighed. "I think I know," she said slowly. "It was the man whom the Jordanians killed from the wall."

Arie's face darkened. "The usual, eh?"

D'vora winced. "The *usual*," she repeated: "Even the way you put it is horrifying. Because it *is* the usual: the usual murdering and maiming and crippling!" She drew the collar of her robe tightly to her neck and shuddered. "They exterminated us in Germany and in Europe, and now they're trying to exterminate us in Israel! Finally we have a parcel of land which we can call our own and in which we want to live in peace, but they won't leave us alone!"

Arie was silent.

"Arie," his wife went on, "I'm a human being and a Jew and an Israeli, and so, naturally, I feel the pain—as we all do. But in addition, I'm a physician. Every day, day after day, I see the results of this campaign of terror against us. I try to repair the destruction that is thrust upon innocent bodies. It's my calling . . . and it's my duty. But sometimes, Arie, I am overwhelmed with bitterness and despair! I try to extricate the despondency from my heart, to force it from my mind: but it's not always possible. Cruelly and without warning, the dead are robbed of life and the wounded of health! And those around them are stunned and shocked and scarred—even our children!" D'vora's voice, powered by a force that shook her body, trembled. "It's no wonder Ilana is so disturbed! It's no surprise, either, that she doesn't want to speak to me—or to anyone—about the pain that must be inside her! What am I—or what

are you or anyone else in the world—going to say to her? Can
we explain what is happening? Can we assure her that the terror
won't touch us—or her? Can we give her the certainty that all
will be well? Arie," she continued in a voice that rose shrilly,
"can we——" But she was unable to complete the sentence.

Her husband left the table and went to her and took her into
his arms. "D'vora, D'vora . . ." he murmured, kissing her forehead and hair and hugging her shivering body close to his own.
"D'vora, my darling."

D'vora pressed her face into his shoulder. "Arie," she muttered through stifled sobs, "you can't explain it to me either!
You mean well, but you can't explain it . . . or make the hurt
go away."

"I love you, D'vora."

"Yes, yes, Arie, you love me—I know it. And I love you,
more dearly than ever—I know that, too. We love each other
and our children and our people and our land, and we love
life—but it's not enough!"

Her husband rocked her like an infant in his arms. "D'vora,"
he whispered gently, "there are no words to explain what has
happened and what is happening to us. There are no theories
to explain it. I can't erase the pain. I can't relieve you or anyone
else of our burden." He paused for a moment to regain his
breath and then, still rocking her, continued: "All I can do is
to ask you to go on." He cleared his throat. "There is a song
that the pioneers used to sing in the thirties; one doesn't hear
it much these days. *Al s'fod, al b'chot: avod, avod!*—Don't
mourn, don't weep: work, work! That's all anyone can do! We
have to work. We have to go on!" He kissed his wife's cheeks
and then, drawing back and lifting D'vora's face, her tear-
salted mouth. "Courage isn't something that's injected into a
person at birth—a person has to learn it anew each day."

"Arie——"

"Does that make sense to you, D'vora?"

"Arie, I——"

"Does that help you a little, D'vora?"

"Arie, I—don't know how I—should go on without you."

Her husband forced himself to smile. "Why should you go
on without me, darling? We shall always be together, you and
I."

"Always?"

"Always, D'vora."

Slowly, D'vora grew calmer. Arie handed her a handkerchief, and she dried her eyes and blew her nose. There was a strange look on her face—the look of someone who has returned to familiar ground from a distant place. "I—I'm sorry," she murmured, crumpling up the handkerchief and thrusting it into a pocket of her robe.

"There's nothing to be sorry about."

By the time Ilana came into the cheerful, sun-splotched kitchen, breakfast was on the table—orange juice and hardboiled eggs and cottage cheese and cucumber, tomato, and scallion salad and rolls and a piping-hot urn of coffee—and D'vora and Arie were in their places. Behind the screen of an open window, framed by gauzy-white curtains as if it were an actor on a miniature stage, a sparrow hopped on the sill and flooded the room with delicate chirping. Through the crack under the rear screen door, a little lizard slid onto the spotless tile floor and then, in a sudden change of mind, darted out again onto the back porch. Ilana, her hair done in two tightly twisted braids that were wound around her head and wearing freshly ironed khaki shirt and shorts, sat down in her place. "Good morning, Abba," she said.

"Good morning, Ilana," replied Arie.

"Good morning, Imma."

"Good morning, darling," replied D'vora. "I hope you slept well."

Ilana reached for her orange juice. "I was exhausted last night, so I slept like—like a turnip!"

They all laughed.

"Did you wake Uri up?" asked D'vora.

"I did, Imma. He said he'd be right down."

Arie glanced at his watch. "I'll give the little imp two more minutes," he murmured with a smile. "And if he isn't here by then, I'll go up myself and get him! He likes to dawdle, you know—yesterday, he was almost late to school."

The sparrow on the sill chirped loudly, as if to signal its departure, and then flew off into the bright spring sunlight. The Arnons continued eating their breakfast. After a time, Arie looked at his watch again and then, snatching his napkin from

his lap and depositing it on the table, got up from his chair
and went to look for his son.

Uri was in the backyard.

There were two best times to be in the yard: in the cool
early morning, when the grass was wet with dew and the spider
webs sparkled while the birds, bent on finding their breakfast
worms and insects, went flying down from the branches of the
trees and hopped fitfully across the lawn; and in the evening,
when the spongelike shadows came creeping out from the stone
walls and the huge, high hedge, the crickets sang in a friendly
chorus, and the flowers all seemed to sigh with relief in the
breath of coming coolness with which gentle breezes filled the
air.

After Ilana had wakened him, Uri had hastened to dress
himself. He had quickly pulled on a pair of shorts and slipped
into a shirt and dashed barefoot downstairs—not bothering
even to thrust his feet into his sandals. Cleverly, so as to avoid
his parents in the kitchen, he had slipped out the front door
and scurried around the side of the house to the backyard. All
night long, so it seemed to him, he had dreamed about the
treehouse that he and his father had begun to build the day
before. In his dreams the treehouse—completely finished and
furnished with splendid furniture made of cane and rush that
grew on the banks of a mighty, mud-watered river in which
enormous crocodiles slithered and gigantic rhinoceroses wal-
lowed and lumpy hippopotamuses swam—was in the midst of
an African jungle, and from its lofty and safe height he had
looked down on the wild animals that prowled below. In reality,
the few planks that Arie had nailed together were in the branches
of the oak tree that stood almost in the center of his yard,
midway between the rear stone wall and the back porch of the
house. That was the reason Uri had hurried so: he wanted to
see—he *had to* see—what he had dreamed about.

Up in the oak tree, the sparrows and a robin or two flitted
to and fro, jostling the leaves and scattering down the last drops
of vanishing dew. Uri gazed upward. There were the new

planks of white pine—the floor of the house. Next, with Uri helping him, Arie would put up the walls. After that, his father would build the roof. And finally there would be a ladder of two-by-fours, neatly sawed to size and set in their proper places. Then the treehouse would be finished—*and it would be his!* Arie had promised him a little mattress and a chair, and then he would be able to climb the ladder and from his sheltered perch see far into the distance. He would, with ease, be able to see over the rear stone wall into the empty nettle- and cactus-spotted expanse that belonged to neither the Israelis nor the Arabs—he knew that was the reason why the grownups called it "no-man's land"—and all the way to the twin heights of Har ha-Tzofim, Mount Scopus, where the Israelis and the Jordanians sat looking at each other across a deep ravine; over the red-tiled roof of the house into the western section of Jerusalem; and southward into the emptiness at the bottom of which lay the Dead Sea, which his parents always talked about and which they promised one day to show him.

Uri's heart rejoiced. He could scarcely keep himself from crying out—only the fact that he would be discovered restrained him from giving vent to what he felt. He would be able to borrow his father's army binoculars—he was certain Arie would give him permission—and see everything he wanted to look at close-up: trees and rocks and houses and cars and people going about their daily rounds. And if he were to notice anything suspicious, anything that didn't look just right—such as Arab soldiers with bayoneted-rifles creeping closer on their bellies—he would be able to cry out from his vantage point and sound the alarm! How surprised and dismayed the Arabs would be to find out that they had been discovered by a child! How proud the Jews would be to know that somebody so small had so much foresight and courage! And when he was not on lookout duty—even a soldier in the army had periods when he was not on guard—he could relax and rest and eat the guavas and grapes and bananas he would bring up with him, and he could read his books and perhaps even curl up snugly on his mattress and doze off and dream of the marvels of Africa and Asia and Australia and America. How truly wonderful it would be when the plank floor would have its walls and its roof and the ladder was fixed in place and the treehouse was finished and given over to its owner! If only it were already so; *if only it were so this very minute!*

Suddenly, Uri heard a noise.

His first thought was that someone had seen him from the kitchen window. But it wasn't so. He looked and saw with his own eyes that it was empty. There was only a sparrow on the sill, a little gray-brown bird that—seemingly startled by his sudden turn and glance—flew off and out of the yard. He was relieved. But what was the noise? Were the Arabs coming already, before he had his treehouse and could stand guard? The Arabs, he knew, didn't believe in being fair, and anything was possible with them. Motionless at the foot of the oak tree, with his heart pounding in his breast, he strained to hear. The noise came again: it was high-pitched and delicate and tinkly— it didn't sound at all like Arab soldiers or spies. It sounded like somebody singing. And it came from the direction of the hedge.

Cautiously, he left his place and moved across the yard, putting each bare foot carefully down in the grass as if he were walking in one of the minefields his father was always talking about. He had on several occasions while riding in the jeep with Arie seen the little tin signs hanging from strands of barbed wire with their red triangles and the words SACCANAH: MOK' SHIM—DANGER: MINES! A grasshopper landed on his left knee and, impatiently, he shook it off. Farther on, a darning needle— which Uri's friends, though he did not believe them, always said would sew up your lips if it got angry—whizzed past his face. Noiselessly, he continued until he reached the thick, high hedge. Now, he could hear the sound that had disturbed him very clearly. It was the little girl next door, and she was singing a song.

For a moment, he did nothing but listen. The girl had a pretty voice, and the melody she sang was pleasant—it sounded like a lullaby. But why would a lullaby be sung in the morning? The song had words, too, but Uri could not catch all of them. Besides, they were in Arabic, and though both of his parents spoke the language, they hadn't taught him much yet. He wanted to know Arabic; that was the way you could question Arab spies and infiltrators when you caught them.

The song went on, and it both charmed and intrigued Uri.

Most probably, the little girl who was singing thought that nobody was listening, but that wasn't true. He wondered if she would stop if she knew that he was there, behind the hedge that divided their yards. Then, as he crouched on the grass, a curious desire came over him: he wanted to see the singer. He knew, of course, what she looked like, but he had little or nothing to do with her, just as Arie and D'vora had little or nothing to do with her parents. Sometimes the neighbors said "Good morning" or "Good evening" or "How are you feeling?" or "Have a nice day," but never much more. The two houses and the two yards were side by side, but their occupants might just as well have lived on different continents. All of his and Ilana's and their parents' friends were Jewish. The Maleks next door didn't seem to have any friends—they seemed always to be by themselves. Mahmoud Malek had been hurt—Arie said that long ago, in 1948, a mine had exploded and crippled him— and he sat in a wheelchair. He read a lot—often in his yard— but sometimes you could hear him talking to his daughter, whose name was Layleh. S'ad, his wife, was pretty—her long hair was as dark as D'vora's was blond—and she liked to play with Layleh. Often, you could hear them whispering and laughing for hours on end. And Layleh looked like her mother, with long black hair and large, dark eyes and a ready smile. But she had no brother or sister and was frequently by herself in the yard.

It was a strange and puzzling situation for Uri. He knew that Jews and Arabs sometimes lived together—his father had told him stories about their living together for years and years in the Old City before the War of Independence. And he had seen Arabs in Tel Aviv and Haifa and in the western section of Jerusalem when he traveled with his parents. But he also knew that the Arabs and the Jews were constantly at war. That meant, so Uri reckoned, that there were peaceful Arabs just as there were warlike Arabs. The Maleks obviously belonged to the peaceful group. Then why, Uri wondered, didn't the two families mix? Why didn't they visit each other? Why didn't he play with the little Arab girl behind the hedge? On occasion, he had posed these questions to his parents, but they had been "too busy" or otherwise evasive, and so he had never gotten any real answers. Ilana, as well, had not been of much help.

Once, when he pressed her hard, she had become annoyed and turned on him and snapped, "That's just the way it is, Uri. Maybe you'll understand someday—and maybe you won't. Don't bother me with questions like that anymore!" And so Uri hadn't. But he continued to wonder.

Now, lured by the beauty of the song and overwhelmed by his curiosity, Uri moved still closer to the hedge. He lifted his hands and, as quietly as possible, parted the springy, green-leafed branches. Then he thrust his face forward. A little spider—no bigger than a dot, actually—scampered over his wrist and away from him. He pushed the branches aside still more. And then, holding his breath—as if the slightest sound might shatter the spell and make everything disappear—he peered through the latticework of the foliage and saw into the neighboring yard.

The little girl named Layleh was sitting on the grass not far from an azalea bush. She was bending slightly forward, her hair hanging in glossy tresses that shone softly in the morning light, intent on the doll she was cradling in her thin arms. As she gently rocked the doll, she crooned the song that had first attracted Uri's attention. Now he understood: the lullaby was for Layleh's imagined baby, which she was putting to sleep! Uri smiled. The scene before him was so filled with gentle warmth and earnest serenity that he could not take his eyes from it. It charmed him so completely that he forgot everything else—that he had stolen out of the house without his parents' knowledge and come into the yard; that he had yet to eat breakfast and put on his sandals and take his satchel and go to his school, the *gan*. Even the wonderful treehouse that was at long last on its way to being built faded from his mind. At the moment, so he felt, he wanted nothing more than the dazzling, almost unreal vision of the little girl on the next-door lawn and the sweet lilting of her doll's lullaby. Time flew by, but he no longer had the slightest notion of time, and so, frozen at the hedge, with his face pressed into its resilient branches and bright green leaves, he continued to gaze and to listen. Then, sounding a last crystalline note, Layleh's voice faded away and was heard no more. With intense concentration, she bent over the doll. A solemn and satisfied expression appeared on her delicate features. That, Uri realized, could have only one meaning: the "child" in her arms was asleep. He held his breath. What would she do now?

As if somehow Layleh had heard his question and was giving him her answer, she rose. Hugging the doll to her breast, she looked around her yard and then began slowly to move in the direction of her house. Setting one bare foot after the other in the still-wet grass, she walked with graceful ease. Uri watched every movement of her lithe body. He watched her face, too, and saw how when a dragonfly drew near—perhaps it was the same one that had been in his yard before—she pursed her lips and halted to let it fly harmlessly past her. It was clear to him that she was leaving the yard; the "baby" needed to be put to bed in its crib. But a feeling of sadness suddenly came over him. It surprised him totally and he was at a loss to explain it, and that bothered him, too, because he usually liked to figure things out. The little girl, making steady progress, had almost reached her back porch. In another moment or so she would step onto it and then disappear through her kitchen door. He realized with a pang that he did not want her to be gone.

But she was on her back porch now. He saw her bare feet glide over the flagstones and heard the faint, whisperlike slapping they made. The kitchen door was only a meter or so away, its metal knob glistening in the intensifying sunlight.

Abruptly, casting away all doubt and hesitation, he made his decision. His mouth opened and he called out a single, unfamiliar word: "Layleh!"

She turned.

Like a hawk, he watched her eyes. The look in them told him clearly that though she was surprised, she was not alarmed. She stood motionless where she was on her porch, staring, puzzled and earnest, at the hedge.

"Uri?"

Dimly, as from a vast distance, Uri heard his name being called. It was his father's voice.

Somewhere behind him a door slammed, and Uri heard that, too, but he did not—or did not care to—realize its significance.

"Uri! So there you are!"

Layleh's gaze held him fast as, he knew, his own kept her frozen in her place. But already—despite his desperation and his stubborn determination, she was drawing back. The expression in her eyes had altered—it was one of consternation and even of alarm.

There were footsteps behind him—the heavy footsteps of his father.

"Uri! Come here this instant!"

He turned.

Arie, with a stern look on his clean-shaven face, was walking quickly toward him. "Uri, what are you doing in the yard?"

Uri moved away from the hedge. When he gained enough self-possession to speak, he told the truth—or at least part of it: "I came out . . . to see the treehouse," he said.

Arie frowned. "But it's late! And you haven't eaten breakfast yet—the whole family's waiting for you at the table." He glanced at his watch. "At this rate, you won't get to the *gan* on time. Your teacher will be annoyed—you know you almost weren't on time yesterday—and I can't blame her."

"I'm sorry, Abba."

Arie shook his head. "Sorry won't do, my friend! Come in to breakfast at once—and don't let this happen again! Do you understand?"

"I understand, Abba."

Arie shrugged. "I hope so," he said.

Uri glanced over at the hedge and then followed his father into the kitchen. The expression on his mother's face was severe, but her eyes were smiling. "Sit down and eat your food," she said quietly. "And be quick about it."

Uri began his breakfast dutifully. Out of the corner of an eye, he saw Ilana get up from the table and leave the kitchen to get her satchel of schoolbooks. Shortly after, Arie tossed his napkin onto the table and went out of the room to make his final preparations for work. Uri saw that his mother, standing by the sink, was watching him, but he did not meet her glance. After several moments of silence, she asked: "Well, son, how do you like the treehouse?"

He was so absorbed in thinking about Layleh and the meeting through the hedge that he did not hear the question, and she had to repeat it. Without looking up at her, he replied, "I like it very much, Imma—it will be beautiful when it's finished! It will be the best treehouse in all of Jerusalem—and maybe in the whole world!"

She smiled. "I'm glad that you're so pleased, Uri," she said.

Uri swallowed and cleared his throat and said, "I'm going to spend a lot of time in it, Imma—I'm going to keep a look out for Arab infiltrators and spies . . . and then no one will ever be able to sneak up on us."

He saw his mother's face darken, but she said nothing, and so, lapsing back into his thoughts about Layleh, he kept on eating in silence. But when he finished, the question that he had asked so many times before to which he had never received a satisfactory answer suddenly came to his lips, and he felt that he had no choice but to ask it again. Lifting his eyes to his mother's, he burst out impetuously: "Mother—why don't we ever have anything to do with the family next door?"

Now, it was D'vora who was preoccupied with her own thoughts, and Uri had to ask her a second time.

She seemed taken aback and did not answer at once. Then, almost hesitantly, as if she were loath to get into the subject, she said, "What makes you ask something like that out of the blue?"

Uri shrugged. "I don't know, Imma. But why do we act like strangers to each other?"

"Uri, I myself don't know why. The Maleks have made it clear that they wish to be isolated from us. We have respected their wish."

With a battered briefcase in one hand and an unlit pipe between his teeth, Arie appeared in the kitchen doorway. He pulled the pipe from his mouth and said firmly, "Young man, you have exactly one minute to go upstairs and put your sandals on and get your things for the *gan* and meet me in the driveway! Otherwise, you're going to be in big trouble! Understand?"

Uri understood very well and lost no time in obeying his father's command. But as he raced out of the house toward the jeep waiting for him in the driveway, calling out a hasty farewell to his mother as he went, he made up his mind that no matter what, he was going to get the true answer to his question— even if he had to get it from Layleh.

———

S'ad was in the big bedroom when she heard the kitchen door suddenly creak open and then slam shut and the rapid patter of Layleh's feet on the tiles of the floor. For an instant, panic gripped her. Why was Layleh running? What if something terrible had happened to her daughter? What if she had been stung by a scorpion or bitten by a snake or—— She did not finish the numbing thought but threw the pillow she had been fluffing up down onto the bed and rushed to see just what had occurred.

Layleh had just that moment come into her cheerful little room. She was clasping her doll to her breast and looked flushed and breathless but quite unharmed. When she caught sight of her mother, the gentle smile of affection that was so much a part of her nature came onto her lips. "Hello, Umm," she whispered. And then, raising a finger in warning to her face, she added sternly: "Mustn't speak too loudly, Umm, the baby's asleep."

S'ad nodded knowingly. It took her several moments to calm herself and regain her composure. And then, in accordance with her daughter's injunction, she whispered, "Are you all right, Layleh dear? You rushed into the house. It scared me."

"I'm fine, Umm," Layleh whispered. With a sigh she carried the doll to a tiny crib that stood at the foot of her bed and set it down on the little mattress inside and covered it with a pink, lace-edged blanket that S'ad had herself made and given to the child. Then, with a silent kiss blown downward, she turned and went over to her mother and, slipping her diminutive hand into S'ad's big one, whispered hurriedly: "Let's go into another room, Umm, so we won't wake the baby!"

"Of course, darling," S'ad whispered, squeezing her daughter's fingers and leading her into the big bedroom. Gazing down at the child, she said, "You came back into the house so suddenly, Layleh. Tell me, did something happen in the yard?"

Layleh shook her head. "Nothing, Umm. I just wanted to come in—that's all." She blinked. "The baby wanted to be in her crib."

"I see . . ." S'ad said. Reassured now, she was able to laugh. "And what would you like to do now that your baby's safely sleeping in her crib? Would you like to help Mommy do the housework? Or look at the pictures in a book? Or, in just a little while, help Mommy prepare the food for supper?"

Layleh's brow knitted. "I don't think I'd like to do any of those things, Umm."

"Then what?"

Layleh scratched her head and thought for a moment; then she said forcefully: "I'd like to draw, Umm! Is that all right?"

"That's just fine, darling."

S'ad helped her daughter to bring crayons and paper from Layleh's room—the two of them tiptoed carefully past the "baby's" crib—and arrange them on the kitchen table. Then, seated on the special chair that had been built to make it possible for her to sit at the table like the grownups, Layleh began to draw. S'ad had intended to return at once to her housework, but something arrested her and she halted and turned and gazed back at her little daughter. With a look of intense preoccupation on her face, Layleh was bent over a white expanse of paper over which she had begun to move a pale green crayon. Through the window above the sink, the sun—now ascending the blue Jerusalem sky—poured a broad shaft of light, igniting the child's ebony hair and turning her delicate arms to gold. S'ad's heart swelled with love—but contracted with pain as well. She wished that Hassan Ali, the kind and wise uncle who had been responsible for her move from the Galilee village to *Al-Kods,* the Holy City, were alive to see the glowing vision that her eyes beheld with such affection and reverence. In her mind she saw him beam and stroke his beard and heard him murmur softly: *What a child . . . ah, what a beautiful child—what grace, what charm, what innocence radiate from her being! In truth, I tell you that she is—like the mother who bore her—a gem for all the world to look upon and admire! Cherish her, gentle S'ad, and hold her dear . . . and she will light the darkest corners of your life. . . .*

Hassan Ali, Hassan Ali—to remember his blessed name brought tears to S'ad's eyes. He had lived to see her marry Mahmoud and to rejoice, but he had not lived long enough to see their child born. When his illness attacked him again, sinking his eyes into their sockets and wasting his noble features and turning his body into a skeletonlike collection of bones, S'ad and her husband had taken him to the hospital in the western section of Jerusalem—he had come to live with them in this very house before the outbreak of war in 1948, "abandoning," as he always used to say, the little house in which he had been born in the Old City—and he had the best care. For a time, it appeared that he would survive and, as he was wont to say, "totter down the dusty, twisting, but warmly lit corridors of old age." But suddenly he had taken a turn for the worse. The doctors tried everything possible. S'ad and Mahmoud kept a constant vigil in the hospital waiting room, but the generous and compassionate jeweler slipped slowly and irreversibly away. S'ad prayed ardently and devotedly for her uncle's recovery, and Mahmoud comforted her and tried to encourage her hopes, but Hassan Ali's life, like an oil lamp that is running out of fuel, got fainter and fainter.

The end came on a stormy day in December. In the early afternoon, a cold, crystal-dropped rain fell splashing into the streets and gurgling down the gutters. Hassan Ali was lucid, and S'ad and Mahmoud were summoned to his bedside. Calling upon whatever strength remained with him, the jeweler reached out and took his niece's warm fingers into the bony clutch of wasted hand. "The time . . . has come," he murmured huskily, fighting to ensure that each hard-earned word would be heard and understood. "But . . . I am not dismayed that I must go. In truth, I am . . . weary of the burden of existence . . . and entirely willing to set it down." He paused to gain the breath he needed and then went on: "S'ad," he said in a voice that was no more than the shadow of a whisper, "you entered my life as a niece . . . a stranger almost . . . and became the daughter . . . of my soul. You weep now at the recognition of my approaching death . . . and that is understandable . . . I do not chide or condemn you for this natural reaction. But after I am gone . . . your joy must exceed your sorrow . . . for you will realize and know . . . that you took me from the living tomb of desolation . . . into the warm and sunny courtyard of life. Your heart will be glad, my daughter . . . for you made Hassan Ali's heart glad . . ." And turning his clouding eyes—into which the light of Jerusalem had soaked—on Mahmoud, he whispered, "Prize my daughter greatly, young man; honor her . . . and protect her with all your strength. Give her understanding and patience . . . and the sweet milk of friendship. And give her children, and . . . of this I am sure as I am sure of the nearing hour of my death . . . she will reward you beyond your wildest dreams and fondest expectations."

And, so saying, Hassan Ali turned his face to the window that was wet with the shining drops of Jerusalem's winter rain and closed his failing eyes and departed from the earth.

———————

S'ad roused herself from her daydream and dried her eyes on the backs of her hands and, with a last, lingering glance at the child sitting at the table drawing, turned and went down the hallway. Mahmoud's study was situated just before the living room, and the door was ajar. She meant to go on and finish her cleaning but, after a moment's hesitation, she nudged the unclosed door gently and peered into the room. Her husband was not at his book- and paper-littered desk. Instead, he was sitting in his wheelchair, staring outward through the open-shuttered window, southward toward the distant hills of Judea. He was totally lost in thought and completely unaware of her observing eyes. The sight was a familiar one; he often sat that way, preoccupied and alone, for hours on end. Since the fateful evening in 1948 when he had gone in search of her brother Fawzi and his car had struck the land mine and his legs had been shattered in the explosion, this isolated, all but impenetrable absorption that went on for prolonged stretches of the day had become for him almost a way of life.

S'ad remembered that night. It disturbed her dreams, almost making her wish that she would not fall asleep, and intruded, like a violent, unwelcome but obdurately persistent guest, into her wakeful hours. She had always to be ready—at any moment of any day—for this ghastly, indestructible fragment of her memory, but despite all the will in the world, she was never prepared for the damage it did. Over and over again, she was compelled to watch—as if some cruel and unrelenting operator slipped the same imperishable length of film into the projector of her mind—the terrible scene that had so disjointed and dislocated their lives. Time after time she was forced to see herself running from the porch across the front lawn and hurtling—she did not know how, by what stamina or what power of will—through the darkness up the twisting street and around the bend into the hellfire of the burning cypresses and flame-engulfed car. When she got there, there was already a circle of people—Jews who lived on the same street, in similar stone-walled, red-roofed houses—standing around the overturned vehicle. Two of them had dragged the limp and mangled body of her husband out onto the pavement. On the main road, a siren shrieked, its wail growing louder with every passing instant. To the right, from their flame-lit lawns, shadowy figures turned hoses upward into the burning branches above them.

S'ad had lunged forward and, tearing herself free of restraining hands, knelt at her husband's side. She saw his face—contorted and blackened almost beyond recognition—and his outflung arms and blood-spattered torso and then, with final horror, the tatters of his pants over the shreds of his legs. *"He's dead!"* she screamed: *"I know he's dead!"* and then someone—a fire-edged shadow—knelt down beside her and threw an arm around her shoulders, and she remembered thinking—and that memory never left her but it stayed, embedded, like a white-hot needle in her mind always—*It is the Angel of Death who is at my side! He has taken Mahmoud and now he will take me! And I am glad!* And, kneeling on the rough pavement of the street in her husband's blood, she opened her mouth to say, *Welcome, Death—let us go quickly so that Mahmoud will not be without me for long*—and fainted.

Mahmoud recovered, however, in the same hospital in Ein Kerem where Hassan Ali had died. S'ad was with him as much as possible. She scarcely broke her vigil to eat or sleep. Her husband was so thin—almost emaciated—so very pale, so still-lying, so taciturn: so unlike her Mahmoud. But he was alive, and that was what mattered. At his bedside, she talked, though he rarely responded. She read to him from books and magazines and newspapers, though he scarcely seemed to notice. More often, as time went by, she just sat in silence and, whenever he allowed it, took his hand in hers. She knew that she loved him, that she loved him more than ever. And she knew that he loved her in return. She knew that they were man and wife, but she did not know what their relationship would be like in the future.

At long last the day arrived when he could leave the hospital. She was overjoyed to take him home—she had dreamed of the moment since the night the ambulance had taken him from the blood-soaked pavement of the street, and almost of nothing else—but she was also apprehensive. What would he be like in the house? Would he write again? Would he talk to her, as in the past, openly and freely, sharing the innermost recesses of his consciousness with her and confiding the deepest of his secrets? Would he laugh once more? How she loved and treasured his sharp wit and good-natured humor! Would he press her to him and make love to her as he had in the past? A part of her hoped for the best and trusted that it would be. Another part of her, which she could neither banish nor ignore, feared the worst. There was nothing for her to do except, as was so often the case in life, wait and see. . . .

At first her husband was much as he had been in the Ein Kerem hospital. He acknowledged her presence, but did not really respond to it. He listened passively to what she read to him, but seldom made a comment and did not read himself. He looked around him and saw the familiar and beloved sights, but seemed somehow unable or unwilling to admit to himself that he had indeed 'come home. With careful and loving restraint, so as not to prod him or push him too hard, S'ad spoke to him about his feelings. Initially, though, her attempts met with tough, cold, almost disdainful silence.

But one evening, when spring came, he surprised her by initiating a conversation. They had just finished their supper and were out in the backyard. She was sitting on "her" low stone bench, and he was seated in his wheelchair. The last scarlet and purple cloud-islands had faded from the sky. A gentle breeze, which seemed to sing as it surged, glided through the deepening dusk, rippling in unseen wavelets against the trees and the shrubs. Mahmoud stirred in his chair and murmured suddenly: "S'ad . . ."

His tone was firm, yet gentle and loving, and a chill ran down his wife's spine and she shivered. It was so long a time since she had heard him pronounce her name that way. "Yes, darling," she answered, leaning forward in expectation.

He cleared his throat and then, hesitantly but with a determined effort, went on: "S'ad," he said, "I have been far from you . . . very far——"

"Mahmoud, I know . . ."

But he shook his head impatiently and she left off speaking. "No, no," he protested, "you may think you know, but you don't, really. No one who has not been where I was can ever know . . . how far I was. You see, on the night my car hit the mine . . . and my legs were shattered . . . I made a journey—a terrible journey to the border. Not the border of Israel and Jordan nor the border of Israel and Syria nor the border of Israel and Egypt, but the border between life and death. And the border was like a tightrope—and I, Mahmoud, good and evil, pure and sullied, winsome and ugly, stood on that terrifying tightrope and swayed, first toward one side and then toward the other, first toward life and then toward death . . . for what seemed an eternity." Mahmoud paused, perhaps to regain his breath or perhaps to reflect, and though in the feathery, newly fallen darkness she could not actually see it, his wife sensed that he shuddered. And then, with a sigh, he continued: "And as I swayed, I thought: *I must not fall onto the side of death, because that will be final;* and it seemed to me that never before had I actually understood the meaning of the word *final*. Of course, I wanted to live, but the effort it required for me not to topple over into the realm of death seemed to me so great and so demanding that I almost gave up. A strange— even an unnatural—reaction, you might think. But you see, at the time I felt somehow that simply to prolong my own personal, intimate, solitary life was, well—was *not enough*. Weary—so weary—with my suffering, I was ready, even willing, to yield . . . to blot myself out of this wretched world forever." Mahmoud lifted a hand whose ghostly shape seemed, like some lost creature, to flounder in the darkness. "And then," he went on, "and then, my dearest friend, I thought of you! I saw your face before me . . . and your shining eyes. I heard the tender sound of your voice. What you said to me then I do not know, but it didn't matter. *Your loving presence,* as it were, sufficed. And I knew at once, dearest S'ad, that if I had not the strength to live for myself, I must continue to live because *you* wished me to. And it was, my darling, as if your strength and your steadfastness and your will were infused into me. And so I refused to succumb. And so, my loving wife, I struggled on."

Mahmoud sighed and sank back in his chair. For several moments, husband and wife sat without speaking. The gentle, whisper-filled silence of the spring evening enveloped them.

Then S'ad said, slowly and with an almost intoxicating sense of gratitude and relief: "Mahmoud, my own true friend, at last——" But her voice failed her and she could say no more.

"At last what?" asked her husband.

Still, S'ad could say nothing.

"S'ad . . . speak to me."

"At last, Mahmoud, you have returned." She leaned forward on the little bench and reached out and took his trembling hand. "I have waited so long for this moment—so very long."

As if S'ad's words, through no fault of their own, had struck him, her husband turned his face away. When he spoke, his voice seemed tight and edged with bitterness. "If you say so, S'ad," he murmured.

"But it's true, Mahmoud—I wouldn't say it if it weren't true! You have been far away from me, in a place where I could not—though, heaven knows, I wished to—join you. I waited and waited, but you wouldn't—or couldn't—come back. And now, this evening, in this yard, you *have* returned."

Mahmoud shrugged. "I'm not sure," he said.

"But it's a start."

Mahmoud did not answer.

"It's a start, my husband, and you will go on! I want you to go on, and you want to—and you will; I know you will!"

Mahmoud twisted his body in the wheelchair. "Perhaps . . ."

S'ad pressed his hand. "The accident is behind you, my husband. You have survived it and you are alive and well! And 1948 is gone—the guns aren't firing across Mount Scopus any longer: surely, there will never be another war in this land again! And spring has come and we are together, you and I, and life is before us, beckoning and calling exultantly for us to rejoice and be glad! You will read again and you will write and perhaps begin the journal that you have dreamed of for so long! And I will be at your side—more than ever. And one day, even, Mahmoud——" But here she paused.

"One day what, S'ad?"

S'ad steadied her voice. "One day, Mahmoud," she said, "we will have a child."

"A child? You want to bring a child into *this* world?"

"Yes, Mahmoud—I do!"

Her husband said nothing, but slowly—almost stealthily—

he withdrew his hand from hers. Then, with a harsh laugh that jarred his wife, he mur. .red: "A child, is it? New flesh into a world that blows flesh to bits! I don't know why people insist on having children: either they are uncaring or blind or recklessly foolish—or else they are simply biological slaves."

"Mahmoud——"

But her husband lifted a hand. "Please, S'ad," he said, with an almost desperate weariness, "let's not talk about it anymore right now. Perhaps another time."

S'ad bowed her head. There was silence again, but this time she felt lost in it, as if she might not ever find her husband again, or even herself. With effort, she discarded the feeling and tried to calm herself. At length, when she had regained her composure, she looked up. Something had changed in the yard. Through the high, wall-like hedge that divided their property from the property next door, a square of lighted window showed. Almost uncomprehendingly, she stared at it for an instant. Then she realized that their neighbors were home.

Mahmoud stirred. It was obvious that he, too, was staring at the window, for he said, "The Arnons are in their kitchen."

S'ad nodded. "Yes, darling. They always get home at about this time."

Her husband cleared his throat. "They've been over to see us several times since I came back from Ein Kerem, haven't they?"

"Yes, they have, Mahmoud. They're very nice people— and they've tried to be as helpful as possible. D'vora's a doctor, you know. She——"

"We don't need them," Mahmoud interrupted gruffly.

"What's that?"

Mahmoud's voice lashed out like a whip: *"We don't need them,"* he repeated. "We don't need anyone. We'll make out just fine on our own."

S'ad was stung. She wanted to speak; to tell her husband how wrong she thought he was; to tell him how long she had waited for the time when they would have neighbors; to make him understand how generous and understanding the Arnons had been and what a good relationship she believed the two young families could have—but the words and phrases that her mind offered for the task seemed weak and inadequate. So she decided to say nothing. Perhaps, as Mahmoud had suggested before when she had mentioned having a child, they would discuss it at some other time, when he felt more well disposed. Perhaps, as he had told her with an uncharacteristic brusqueness, he had indeed not fully returned to her. She sat on the bench and waited a little, and then at length got to her feet and said: "Shall we go inside now, Mahmoud? It's getting chilly out here in the yard."

For answer, he swung his wheelchair toward the house.

———————

Throughout the years following Mahmoud's accident in 1948, the problems between husband and wife had never been because of material things: the money from the sale of the house in Sheich Jarrach and the considerable inheritance left to Mahmoud by his father, Abdullah, had provided for all of their physical needs. And these funds would continue to do so until, as Mahmoud put it, they "emptied the unrefillable coffers of life." The source of the tension in the Malek household lay elsewhere—in Mahmoud's truculent bitterness.

Now, as S'ad stared at her husband through the partially open door of his study, she thought that she did not know which of them had been right that spring evening in 1949 about Mahmoud's "return" from the place he had been—and perhaps, she realized, she would never really know. On the one hand, he was still embittered. He was still given over to lengthy periods of isolation during which, like a prisoner in a straitjacket, he seemed to have no contact—"no touch," she once said to him—with the world around him. He still would have nothing to do with the Arnons, whom he often said he respected, but—as he hastened unfailingly to add, as if S'ad might somehow forget it—"from afar." He still wanted no close friendships, which he considered to be entangling and draining. Since, as he observed, they inevitably led nowhere, they were scarcely worth the trouble and energy that one had to invest in them.

Instead, Mahmoud spent most of his time reading—confining himself almost exclusively to literature and scholarly books and journals. He rarely read newspapers and magazines. To him, they were saturated with blood and violence and insanity.

And he wrote—never sending what he put down on paper out for publication and rarely showing it even to his wife, but keeping it, as he sarcastically remarked from time to time, like a miser, locked away in his voluminous files—but nevertheless he wrote again. And he spoke to her—not as extensively as before, because, as he said acidulously, he needed time to speak to no one, not even himself, and perhaps not as openly and as freely as when they had courted and first been married—but nevertheless he spoke to her again. And he made love to her— not with the same uninhibited passion and unrestrained abandon as of old—but nevertheless he made love to her again. And, of course, they now had a child, born four years ago, in 1956, the year, as he could not help himself from pointing out, of the Sinai Campaign—the war that had come to Israel despite his wife's belief that the 1948 war would be surely the last war in the land.

S'ad thought much and often about the birth of their child. She realized that it reflected and symbolized, in a way that nothing else did, the conflict that was—and perhaps always would be—between her and her husband. It had taken him some six years to accede to what he initially considered her irrational wish to have a baby.

She remembered another evening in 1949 when, driven by an urge which she had felt powerless to resist, she had brought it up again. But her husband had instantly and adamantly rejected her proposal.

"Into *this* world," he asked her, gripping the arms of his wheelchair, "into this garbage dump . . . this cesspool . . . this abattoir . . . you wish to bring a new life?"

S'ad trembled. "Mahmoud . . ." she began, but in apprehensive uncertainty, her voice trailed off.

"Speak," demanded her husband, "go ahead and speak to me. Say what you have to say—I won't devour you!"

"Mahmoud, you yourself——"

"I myself what? Go on—tell me."

"You yourself . . . are guilty."

Mahmoud looked perplexed. "Guilty, you say? Guilty of what? Explain yourself!"

S'ad leaned forward. "Guilty," she said in a low, tense voice that seemed to spurt from her lips like a jet of steam, *"of the very crime which you so deplore!"*

Her husband was taken aback. His pale cheeks reddened, and he stared at her uncomprehendingly.

S'ad's eyes met his unwaveringly. She hesitated for a moment before speaking. She felt fear—fear that what she would say might hurt her husband—but she felt even more strongly the fear of what might happen to herself and to what was between the both of them if she were to remain silent. Wetting her dry lips with her tongue, she said slowly: "When we worked together in the jewelry store in the Old City, Hassan Ali always used to say to me: 'Remember, S'ad, that for true understanding to exist between two people, one must speak with love ... and the other must listen with love!' Therefore, Mahmoud, my husband, I dare to say to you—with all of my love as your wife—that *you yourself* are guilty of the inhumanity which causes you such anger and such despair. Nothing could be further from your nature, dear Mahmoud, than violence or brutality or ruthlessness or lust for power. And yet, I think, in some dark and insidious way you are—by your withdrawal and isolation from those around you, from life itself—turning off the faucet of human feeling in yourself!" S'ad lifted a soft, white, delicately motioning hand. "Especially," she said huskily, "when you speak about not wanting to have a child."

Mahmoud winced; his face darkened. "S'ad," he said hurriedly, "I didn't mean to hurt you—please believe me when I say that." He gestured lamely. "Perhaps I spoke too harshly, too bluntly; perhaps I should have chosen my words more carefully."

S'ad shook her head slowly. A gentle, half-wistful, half-ironic smile crossed her lips and then vanished instantly, as if it had never really intended itself to be seen. "No, no," she said, "it's much better for both of us that you told me what you truly feel. And it's not how you said it, Mahmoud, but *what* you said that's so disturbing! Mahmoud, I know, as you do, that the world is evil and cruel. But I know, as well, if I don't shut off the humanity inside me, that it is good and compassionate!"

Mahmoud closed his eyes and touched a finger to each lid.

For several moments, he sat that way in silence, as if a statue had taken his place in the wheelchair.

"Did you understand me, Mahmoud?"

He nodded. "I understood very well, S'ad. But——"

"But what?"

"But I cannot accept what you say."

"You do not agree that you have, in some ways, cut off your humanity?"

"I do not agree."

"And you don't wish to have a child?"

"I do not wish to have a child."

S'ad's voice trembled: "Do you think . . . that you will ever change those views?"

Mahmoud grimaced. *"Ever* is a word I no longer like to use," he said dryly. "All I can do now is live each day as it comes."

His wife cleared her throat. "Mahmoud . . ." she began hesitantly.

"Yes?"

"You have heard me, Mahmoud, but——"

"But?"

"But you have not understood me," said his wife, brushing away the tears that she could not keep from falling.

———•◦•———

Now, years later, those tears still fell. Not for herself, but for that part of her husband which had not—and which most probably, she saw now with the passing of the years, never would—come back. And that, more than anything else she could determine, was the truth of it. A part of Mahmoud was with her as she had known him before the explosion of the mine. Another part of him was in a place where—given all the love and perception in the world on her part—she could not follow him.

Now Mahmoud read selectively, wrote secretly, and sometimes talked about, but never made an actual move toward, establishing the *Journal of Peace* that had once been among the most passionate of his dreams. He made love cautiously, almost painstakingly, as if he feared to overturn some precariously balanced skiff of emotion. And despite his protests and arguments and bouts of despondency and fits of silence and moodiness, he had fathered a child at last—a little girl by the name of Layleh whom he came to adore.

But nonetheless those tears still fell—and they were falling now as S'ad stood in the doorway and, unobserved herself, gazed at the unmoving figure in the wheelchair. They were tears that fell in sorrow—familiar, always expected and wholly unrewarding tears. But they were also tears of relief—the relief that had begun, tentatively and then with steadily greater assurance, to come to S'ad after the birth of her daughter. Layleh had brought comfort directly; that was a natural by-product of motherhood. She had also softened what S'ad thought of as Mahmoud's granite stance and, as his wife was not afraid of saying to his face, made him more human again. For the child named Layleh, S'ad was, as a mother, eternally and unutterably grateful. For the daughter called Layleh, S'ad was, as a wife concerned with her husband's well-being, totally indebted and beyond any hope whatsoever of repayment. When Mahmoud was with Layleh—the child whom it had taken him six years, as he sometimes himself rather sheepishly and abashedly said, to admit into the world—it seemed to S'ad that, more than any other time, he emerged from the shadows of pity for himself and disdain for others.

Eventually, he became freer in his movements and with his gestures. He smiled often and sometimes even laughed aloud, boisterously and raucously. He read stories from children's books and even declaimed, from what he called animated memory, little tales and poems that he himself had learned as a child in Cairo. Despite the fact that he claimed to have the voice of a frog with a very sore throat, he sang songs to and with his daughter. In the backyard, he pointed out all of the different birds and insects and trees and flowers and—sometimes until Layleh blinked her eyes and yawned—rhapsodized about nature's wonders. In her room, he involved himself in her games and with her toys, which he unfailingly repaired when they were broken. At the table, when she ate, he discoursed charmingly and even—on occasion, when he forgot himself and got carried away by his own enthusiasm—with flamboyance about food and its preparation and crops and agriculture in distant and exotic parts of the world. Father and daughter were good together: they met "soul to soul," as S'ad happily said to herself, and meshed and stimulated each other's imaginations and provoked each other's merriment and soothed each other's overt and hidden hurts. Even Mahmoud had to confess openly—though with grudging peevishness—that he was more awake and more alive in Layleh's presence. But of course, being Mahmoud-after-the-explosion, he could not let such a statement stand without proper qualification. Thus, with an impatient nod of his head and a certain pinched grimness about his lips, he hastened to add: "She is my little friend and you, S'ad, are my big friend, and the two of you quite suffice. I don't need, nor do I wish to need, anyone else." And though the child was—and knew very well she was—special and had special privileges, she, like her mother, was never permitted in Mahmoud's study. That was an unwritten and untransgressed law in the house.

Now, given the necessary release that her tears afforded, S'ad grasped the doorknob and slowly, with regret but with a resignation born of long years of experience, pulled the door toward her. Mahmoud, by his own severe and unimpeachable desire, had to be within the circle of forbidding fire which he himself had ignited—to be alone with his doubts and his fears and his terrors and with his forlorn, deserted dreams. He had not noticed her watching him. He was not aware that she was shutting him off from her view. That was the Mahmoud she could never reach.

The door clicked softly shut. She glanced down at her wrist-watch and was amazed to see that nearly half an hour had gone by. Hurriedly, she turned and went back down the hallway to the kitchen. Mantled in brilliant morning sunlight, Layleh was sitting quietly in her place at the table, drawing. At the sound of her mother's familiar step, she looked up. "Umm," she murmured in her lilting voice. "Hello . . ."

"Hello, darling! How have you been?"

"I've been just fine, Umm. I'm drawing a beautiful picture."

"May I see it, Layleh?"

Layleh smiled. "Of course you may, Umm—it's for you and for Abu anyway."

"Hold it up, then, please."

Layleh nodded vigorously. "I will," she said forcefully, putting down her crayon.

S'ad stood and watched as two little hands deftly lifted the crayoned sheet of paper and held it up for inspection. S'ad saw a great patch of yellow-green—the largest single block of color, by far, in the entire picture—divided vertically, almost evenly, in two by a dark green-blue stripe. On the left side of the stripe was a balloonlike smiling face with short, spiky hair. On the right was another floating, round face with even a broader smile and long, flowing hair. Above everything, at the very top of the picture, a bright yellow sun carelessly flung down its cheerful rays. Layleh rattled the paper impatiently. "Do you like it, Umm? Do you like my picture?"

"I do, Layleh . . . yes, I like it very much."

Layleh laid the paper down on the table again and then looked thoughtfully at her mother. "I have to put the name of the picture on it," she murmured.

S'ad smiled. "Have you thought of the name?" she asked.

Layleh's dark eyes shone and her face grew solemn, and then in a hushed voice, as if she were saying something very mysterious and yet despite that—with effort—communicable, whispered: "It's called *Magic Morning*, Umm."

"What a splendid name, Layleh! Does it have anything to do with something that happened this morning . . . or some other morning? Or with people that I know? Or . . . ?"

But S'ad's voice trailed off. It was clear to her that Layleh had no interest whatsoever in saying any more on the subject. Indeed, with a light-hearted, almost casual shrug of her frail shoulders, the little girl turned away from her mother and picked up a crayon from the table. Then, bending over in rapt absorption, she began working on the letters—her father had taught her the alphabet only some weeks ago—that spelled out the title of her picture.

D'vora left the hospital early. The opportunity came her way, and she did not hesitate to take it. One of the surgeons who lived not far from her dropped her off. Flushed with pleasure and excitement, she burst into the house, calling out: "Surprise, everyone! I'm home!"

But nobody was there. The house was deserted and unnaturally still, and somehow it unnerved D'vora to be in it alone. She went out of the kitchen and into the yard.

Gentle afternoon sunlight was pouring like sluggish honey over the oak and almond trees, the flowerbeds, the rear stone wall, and the thick-leafed hedge. Being outside in the fragrant, warmed, drowsy air relaxed her immediately and, with a sigh of relief, she stooped and removed her shoes and began to wander aimlessly over the grass.

Suddenly, she halted. A flash of color glinting through the dividing hedge had caught her attention. She hesitated for a moment, but then made a decision and walked swiftly to the hedge and peered through its branches. S'ad was standing there, almost opposite her, in the other yard. The Malek woman's thick black hair was tied behind her back, resting on the bright green-and-white print of her dress. Once more, D'vora hesitated. And once more, she came to an instant decision. Clearing her throat, she called out: "Mrs. Malek! Mrs. Malek, may I speak with you?"

The other woman looked surprised, even startled, but there was also the gleam of satisfaction in her eyes.

Putting her knowledge of Arabic to good use, D'vora lost no time and continued: "Would—would you like to come over and have a cup of tea with me?"

S'ad's eyes gleamed with open and unabashed pleasure. She took an unhesitating step forward and opened her mouth to speak. D'vora was certain—as certain as she had ever been of anything—that the other would accept her invitation.

But then another voice spoke up: the voice of Mahmoud Malek from his wheelchair beneath the grape arbor. "S'ad!" he demanded.

S'ad said, "Excuse me," and, flushing, turned and went to her husband. D'vora could hear their turbulent, intertangled voices, but she could not make out what they were saying to each other. She stood where she was and moved her bare feet in the grass and brushed a fly from her face and waited uncomfortably.

At length, S'ad came back, dragging her nimble feet, to the

other side of the hedge. She looked weary and embarrassed and avoided D'vora's eyes. "I cannot visit you now, Mrs. Arnon," she said softly. "Thank you—thank you very much for your kind invitation." Her voice trembled. "Another time, perhaps..."

———————

At supper, in the cozy, brightly lit Arnon dining room, Arie talked about his day at the Foreign Office and D'vora described what had happened on the ward and Ilana discussed her day in school and the sonata she was preparing for her forthcoming concert. Uri, listening only half-heartedly, remained silent and concentrated, to the best of his ability, on eating his food. When they finished eating, his father said to him, "How about us working on the treehouse for a little while, *chabibi?* We can rig up a light on the back porch——"

Uri shook his head. "Thanks, Abba, but not tonight."

"Are you certain, Uri?"

His son nodded. "Not tonight, Abba. Let's do it tomorrow night."

"Is something wrong?" asked D'vora.

"No," muttered Uri. "I just don't feel like it, that's all."

Ilana grimaced. "He had a hard day at the *gan,*" she said with a wry smile.

And they all laughed—even Uri.

About half an hour later, when Arie was busy with some work he had brought home in his briefcase from the office and D'vora was engrossed in helping Ilana with her Biology, Uri left his room and, without being observed, slipped out of the house and into the backyard. The moon had not yet come up and he could not see clearly, but he sensed that someone was in the yard next door. On bare feet, he sped across the cool grass to the hedge—to the exact spot where he had encountered Layleh that morning. He was happy when he discovered that he was right: there was a shadowy form standing just beyond the high barrier of branches and leaves, seemingly waiting for him to appear. With eager hands, he parted the branches and whispered: *"I'm here...."*

The little girl said something in Arabic which he did not quite understand, but it didn't matter—he knew by the warm tone of her voice that she was glad to meet him again.

The little girl was then silent for a moment. Abruptly, she stooped and lifted something from the grass on her side of the yard: it was a large sheet of drawing paper. Uri craned his neck—the hedge branches jabbed against his forehead and cheeks and poked at his eyes—and squinted to see more clearly. "Closer," he called out. "Put it closer to the hedge so I can see."

Instinctively, Layleh thrust the sheet of paper forward.

Uri pushed his face farther into the hedge and tried to make out what the little girl had drawn. Despite his effort, the as-yet-moonless evening allowed him to see only vague, amorphous shapes. But it really didn't matter; something inside him told him that Layleh had drawn a picture of the two of them. He drew a deep breath and in a trembling voice murmured: *"Yofi*—it's beautiful!"

"Yofi?" echoed Layleh's bell-like voice.

"Yofi . . . yofi . . . yofi . . ." repeated Uri, laughing each time he said the word.

"Yofi," Layleh repeated still again in a quiet, reflective voice that seemed to say that the word was at once strange and familiar to her. After a pause, she said three words in Arabic, pronouncing them slowly and distinctly: *"Sabach el-fadida."*

Uri did not understand, but it was clear to him that she wanted him to remember what she said. *"Od pa'am,"* he murmured—"Say the words again."

She did, and he repeated them aloud for her and saw that she nodded in approbation.

Suddenly, from the lighted Malek kitchen, a voice rang out across the yard—it was S'ad.

"Layleh," Uri whispered urgently.

But she was already gone—he saw her shadow-form streaking over the lawn and then he saw it silhouetted in the yellow square of her kitchen doorway and then it vanished from sight. The sound of the slammed kitchen door faded away in the still air of the spring evening. Uri let the branches of the hedge spring back into place and turned and went into his own house.

Arie was in the little office he had built for himself off the master bedroom. In the glare of an overhead bulb, he was bent over a sheaf of papers on his desk, smoking his pipe and glancing at the pages one by one. Uri stood watching him for a while and then, becoming impatient, said: "Abba."

His father looked up, more surprised than annoyed. "Uri?"

"I'm sorry to disturb you, Abba."

"It's all right, Uri—I've worked on this report too long as it is."

Uri cleared his throat. "Can you tell me . . . what three Arabic words mean?"

"I don't see why not. Go ahead—say them."

Uri spoke them slowly and distinctly, as Layleh had taught him: "*sabach el-fadida.*"

Arie nodded. "They mean 'magic morning.'" He leaned back in his chair and pulled the pipe from his mouth. "Where in the world did you hear them?" he asked.

His son shrugged. "Oh, somewhere around . . ." he muttered. And with a smile of thanks, he turned on his heel and left the room.

———————

In the lamp-lit living room of the Malek house, Layleh was sitting on the rose-colored rug—her favorite, she said, because it looked like a flower—at the foot of Mahmoud's wheelchair. Looking up at her father, she pleaded: "One more story—please, just one more story."

Mahmoud tried to put a stern look on his face. "Well, young lady, I don't really know if I should. I'm sure it's past your bedtime—and your mother will be angry with me."

"No, she won't! No, she won't!"

"Say what you will, my daughter, but I know your mother."

"Please, Abu—I *know* that just one more story can't hurt!"

"Well . . ."

"Please, oh, *please!*"

Mahmoud felt his features relax, and he was compelled despite himself to smile. "All right," he said with a sigh, "you're very persuasive, and you've convinced me. But then, when I'm finished, I want no more stalling. You're to go straight up to your room and jump into bed."

"I will, I will! As soon as you finish the story!"

Mahmoud closed his eyes and leaned back in his chair. "It seems," he began, in the singsong voice which he reserved for such occasions, "that once upon a time, there were——"

"Long ago—was it long ago?" Layleh put in.

"Yes," said Mahmoud, "it was very long ago, such a long time ago that the world had scarcely been created." He paused and gently rubbed his forehead. "Now, let's see," he murmured, "where was I?"

"There were . . ." Layleh interjected at once.

"Ah, yes—there were two little elves who lived on two little islands in the middle of a vast blue ocean. . . ."

"Far from Jerusalem—was the ocean far from Jerusalem?"

"Yes, Layleh, it was very far from Jerusalem. One would have to travel to that ocean on a donkey."

"Or on a camel?"

"Yes, on a donkey or a camel, for certain! And these elves did not lack for anything—neither shelter nor clothing nor food—and they had wonderful, kind parents who loved them very much. And so they were very happy little elves, except——"

"Except what? Tell me what!"

"Except, Layleh, for the fact that they had no one to play with——"

"No sisters and no brothers?"

Mahmoud shook his head. "No," he said dreamily, "they had no sisters and no brothers . . . and not even any friends. Because——"

"Because what?"

"Because, Layleh, there was only one family to an island. And the islands, as I told you, were very remote. And no one ever came to them because they were so far away."

"Not even by ship?"

"Not even by ship and not even by airplane! And so the elves were lonely and sad."

"And then what happened to them? How did they get to be happy?"

Mahmoud lifted a hand. "Patience, Layleh, and I'll tell you." He let his hand fall and went on: "Now, it seems that at one point—and one point only—these two islands came very near to each other. So near, indeed, that if you stood at that point, you could see clearly from island to island."

"Just as we can see each other—is that it?"

"Yes, exactly, that's exactly the way it was, Layleh. And so one fine day——"

"In the morning—was it in the morning?"

"As a matter of fact, Layleh, it *was* in the morning. Just before breakfast. And so on that particular day, it happened that *both* of the little elves were strolling by that point at the very same time——"

"And they *saw* each other—is that what happened?"

"Yes, Layleh, that is precisely what happened. Across the narrow strip of blue water that separated the two islands, they found themselves looking into each other's eyes."

Like lapping waves, Mahmoud's dreamily intoned words went on—but his daughter had stopped listening. The tale that her father, with closed eyes and softly spun sentences, was telling her could not help reminding her of the meetings at the hedge with Uri. And suddenly, without the slightest warning, she had an urge to interrupt her father and tell him *her* story. For an instant the desire was so strong and so tempting that she reached out to touch his fingers on the armrest of the wheelchair and stop him from talking so that she could confide her secret. But just before she made contact with his, she pulled her own hand back. Some instinctive feeling told her that no one in the world, not even her own mother or father, must know about the boy on the other side of the hedge, the boy who had suddenly, like one of the elves her father had been telling her about, appeared.

Mahmoud had opened his eyes. He was leaning forward in his wheelchair and staring at her. "Layleh!"

"Huh?"

"Layleh, you haven't been listening at all, have you?"

Flustered, she shook her head.

"Don't you want to hear the end of it tonight? Are you too sleepy?"

Layleh felt relieved. Her father was giving her the opportunity she wanted. Rubbing her eyes with her knuckles, she said softly, "Could you finish it tomorrow night?"

Mahmoud reached down and gently patted his daughter's dark hair. "Of course, I can finish it tomorrow night, dear. Run along to bed now."

She rose and stood by his chair, and he tilted his cheek

downward, and she kissed it and then scurried out of the room.

"Sweet dreams!" he called after her.

She scarcely heard him because there was another story whirling in her head.

---·-···--·---

And so the secret and mysterious relationship, begun one mild spring morning through the new-leafed hedge that divided the two Jerusalem backyards, continued and progressed.

The two children found themselves rising early—after dreaming the night long of rising early—and stealing out in the slate-grayness of dawn to brief meetings at the hedge. At twilight, when the blood-orange globe of the sun sank down, they were again at the hedge, breaking the clear, rain-chilled stillness of evening. They spoke without reservation or inhibition, picking up—with rapacious swiftness, like birds seizing upon kernels of grain—words and phrases of their kindred tongues: Uri learned *bukreh* for "morning" and *waled* for "boy" and *hon* for "here." Layleh learned *erev* for "evening" and *yaldah* for "girl" and *sham* for "there"—and so it went. But beyond the circle of spoken language, which widened meeting by meeting, there was the spacious and variegated and subtle realm of gestures and facial movements and expressions of the eyes. Nothing—however minute and howsoever slight—that one did was lost to the other. Everything, whether spoken or unuttered, that passed between the two of them was regarded as significant and so was noticed, recorded, and stored. The two of them were, from their very first encounter, strangely and unaccountably but indisputably familiar with each other, attuned one to the other and—ever more deeply and faithfully as the days and weeks and months went by—pledged to the strengthening of the bond between them.

They talked—sometimes they even sang songs that they knew and loved. They gestured cunningly and inventively— sometimes they moved their entire bodies and seemed to dance. They exchanged knowing and mysterious glances—sometimes they peered into each other's eyes as if therein, and nowhere else in the world, was lodged the solution to the riddle of human attraction. They showed each other pictures that they had drawn in pencil and crayon and done in watercolors and paints—Uri brought what he had done in the *gan* and Layleh brought what she had done on the table in her kitchen and in her room. On occasion they brought each other gifts which were thereafter concealed and treasured. Uri presented a little amber-and-black-shelled tortoise he had found behind the almond tree—he had spied it from his treehouse, which Arie had finished, even putting red-orange shingles on the sloping roof, early in the month of June. And he gave Layleh some of the highly prized seashells he had picked up on the white-sand beach at Herzlia when the family had vacationed there for a week in late August, and a shiny red-and-silver fire engine, ingeniously tooled in wood, which he had received as a gift from D'vora last year in December for Chanukah, the holiday which he loved best of all. Layleh, in turn, gave him a necklace strung with wooden beads and an intricately carved wooden spoon which she had received on her fourth birthday and a box of sweets that she had helped her mother make one rainy evening. The gifts were exchanged by using a forked stick and twine taken from Arie's toolshed.

One spring afternoon, Uri ran to his father's toolshed and rummaged about and found exactly what he wanted: a flat square of pine wood left over from the building of the treehouse. He hurried back to the hedge and deftly set a top spinning on the board. Through the newly budding branches of the hedge, Layleh's shining eyes were watching intently. Uri pointed at the whirling top. *"S'vivon!"* he shouted: *"S'vivon!"*

"S'vi-von . . ." Layleh repeated.

"Excellent!" Uri cried out. "Say it again, Layleh: *S'vivon!*"

"S'vivon!" Layleh called out exultantly.

The two of them kept watching as the top spun around and then, at length, wobbled unsteadily and toppled over on its side. Uri started forward to pick it up and set it going once more, but suddenly changed his mind. Instead, he spread out his arms and slowly began to turn his body. *"Ani s'vivon,"* he called out. "I am a top!"

At once, Layleh spread her arms and began to turn. *"Ani s'vivon,"* she cried.

Around and around the two friends went, shouting as they

increased their pace. With a burst of impetuous laughter, Layleh staggered dizzily and fell to the ground and, seconds later, Uri followed after. From each side of the hedge, their delirious laughter rose up and merged in the air above the barrier. At last, when the giggling stopped, Uri got up and grabbed the top. He pointed at it and then at Layleh and said: *"Zeh shelach!*—It's yours!"

Thus, whenever the weather permitted and whenever they could be managed, the meetings went on, each one of them in and of itself a precious gift. Magic mornings and magic evenings, magic moments of childhood rapture and entrancement that were, perhaps, when all is said and done, as real as or even more real than almost anything else they would ever experience.

1964

Jerusalem

OVER THE SWELTERING, heat-stupefied city of Jerusalem, in whose stifling, motionless air neither bird nor insect seemed bold or foolhardy enough to stir, the sky was heaped like a towering pile of blindingly white rocks which the sun was methodically sledging into mirrorlike slivers of light. It was mid-August and the sun was at the height of its arrogance and power, holding incontestable sway over the land of the Jews and over the ancient, hill-nestling capital of David, the psalmist and king. Automobiles seemed to drag themselves along the streets, fighting their way meter by meter through the maze of shimmering heat that boiled up from the pavement. Pedestrians sought the restricted comfort and coolness of their homes and offices and of the sidewalk cafés.

In his study, Mahmoud sat shirtless in his wheelchair, staring blankly at the window shuttered tightly against the almost blinding light. Later on, when the sun had dropped in the west and the heavy-sedimented, lessened light of late afternoon had begun to fill the sky, he would fling open the shutters and gaze out southward, toward what he called the "rim of the world"— the edge of the vast crater at whose bottom, like water left unboiled at the bottom of an enormous cauldron, lay the glazed, lifeless expanse of what the Jews named Yam ha-Melech— the Sea of Salt. For the present, however, the shuttered window would do—it would serve as well as anything else as a focal point for his unfocused eyes.

He knew that S'ad resented, and perhaps even feared, his "lapses," as she put it, when, according to her, he did nothing but sulk and mourn. She was always happy when he used the book-lined room to read or to write, but could not cope easily with the long periods in which he sat pouring the bitter and irreducible ashes of the past on his head. At first, after he had returned from the hospital in Ein Kerem and begun the practice, she had repressed her feelings and left him alone. Then came a period in which she had, unable to restrain herself any longer, reproached and rebuked him, touching off acrimonious quarrels that lasted for days on end. Finally, when she realized that she could not possibly get anywhere with her frontal confrontations, she had resigned herself to silent reprimand and grudging aloofness. Mahmoud was a sensitive man and a husband who loved his wife dearly and so understood her point of view—"as well as you do yourself," he told her on numerous occasions—but he could not, so he felt, help himself or discontinue his addiction to despair.

This blazing afternoon in August, when three-quarters of Jerusalem was dozing or wholly asleep, awaiting the setting of the sun and the respite of shadow and dusk, Mahmoud had been seated at his desk, going through old files: it was a custom he almost invariably followed after lunch. Today, whether by accident or hidden design, he did not know, his hand fell upon a file of old correspondence. Brushing a fly from his face, he dumped the contents of the cardboard drawer onto his desk. A veritable deluge of old letters tumbled helter-skelter out: letters from his university days in Cairo; letters that his father Abdullah had written to him while on business trips to all parts of the Middle East; postcards and rambling missives that former friends in Jerusalem had mailed to him from Europe and even from America; notes that his mother had, in her charming fashion, stuck in his briefcase or tucked into his books secretly at night or before he got up in the morning, so that he discovered them only later on during the day while he was studying on Mount Scopus; and drafts of letters and essays and poems that he, in turn, had sent to ex-comrades and acquaintances and literary colleagues.

As it happened, almost the first letter he had picked out of the file was one penned by Ahmed, the single companion and confidant of his youthful period of what he had once liked to call revolutionary idealism. The envelope, now yellowed and

frayed—which he had saved, he remembered clearly, out of
the wistful and somewhat ingenuous feeling that it, too, had
been written by his friend's hand and so was somehow a part
of the message—was postmarked Cairo and dated the fifth of
July 1955. Inside it was a severely creased letter whose shaky,
hastily dashed-off scrawl revealed the writer's profound agitation. The mere sight of the furiously scribbled page was
sufficient to bring back everything, virtually to the last detail,
that Ahmed had put down. Nevertheless, because he felt mysteriously obliged or perhaps simply because, once started, like
a man who impetuously leaps from a diving board without so
much as bothering to see if there is water in the pool below
him, he could not stop himself, Mahmoud read the letter again
from first word to last.

In short, staccato sentences, Ahmed informed his friend that
he had been conscripted into the Egyptian army of Colonel
Nasser.

The conscription notice, he wrote, *struck me a savage blow.
Not to the face or head or even to the body—but straight to
the soul!* And Ahmed went on to say: *I am devastated, shattered. All my dreams are empty husks; all my hopes chaff in
the wind. I have tried* everything *to overturn the decree, but
my most strenuous efforts have come to naught. All escape is
denied me. Unwillingly, but incontrovertibly, I must become
part and parcel of a repulsive fighting machine!* And he continued, with gloomy insistence: *There is little doubt—given
the war hysteria that prevails here—that one day, sooner or
later, Nasser will send us to fight. And there is less doubt—
so my grieving heart tells me—that I shall perish. And there
is no doubt whatsoever that my death shall be in vain!*

Drawn on by the force of a magnet more powerful than any
resistance he could muster, Mahmoud read it all, every single
word of the letter he already knew by heart, even down to the
postscript below the frantic signature that read: *Since there is
no direct communication with Israel, this letter is being sent
via my cousin Musa in Paris, whom I am instructing to transmit
it to you.*

There was only one more letter—actually, no more than a
fragmentary note—from Ahmed, also transmitted via Musa
from France. It was dated sometime in February 1956 and

related the fact that Ahmed had been sent to officers' training school and would, upon his graduation, command an infantry platoon. The note, set down in a cramped, obviously controlled hand on austere brown paper, was somewhere buried in the pile on Mahmoud's desk. But he had no need to search for it—he knew that one by heart as well. It ended by saying: *Despite the tumultuous beating of the drums and the strident blaring of the trumpets; despite the banners and the pomp and the glitter; despite the formidable weaponry and the frenetic pronouncements; despite all of the hoopla and bombast, I am— we are—nothing more than carrion in uniforms. Our lives have been reduced to dust. Our deaths will be less than the memory of dust. It pains me to have to write you this. But it would pain me more to keep silent.*

The next word about Ahmed came in the latter part of December 1956. It was a brief letter from Musa in Paris, informing Mahmoud that Ahmed had been killed in the Sinai, soon after the outbreak of hostilities in October of that year. Along with the note, Musa had enclosed a snapshot of his cousin which had been taken when Ahmed was on leave in Cairo in September and which he had asked Musa to forward to Jerusalem. On the back of the photograph Ahmed had written just four words: *I remember bygone days.* And he had signed it: *With admiration and affection . . . Ahmed.* Oddly and disturbingly enough, both Musa's note and the snapshot of Ahmed in the uniform of an Egyptian infantry officer were missing. Mahmoud had searched time and again, literally turning his study upside-down, but had never managed to locate them.

Staring at the shuttered window before him, Mahmoud lost track of time. Only the gradual diminution of the sunlight on the other side of the smooth wooden slats let him know, on some subliminal level, that there was such a thing as time at all. His mind wandered, haphazardly, chaotically. His thoughts—if they could properly be called thoughts—were vague and amorphous. Perhaps, so Mahmoud felt when he was lucid, they weren't thoughts at all, but rather some kind of prehistoric muck out of which thoughts might, under better circumstances, emerge. Feelings of bleakness, hopelessness, and lassitude possessed him during these trancelike periods. He was like a prisoner in a cramped and gloomy dungeon who does not know why he has been incarcerated or who it was that sentenced him or, worst of all, how long he must remain in his solitary cell.

Slowly, as if the room were an airtight chamber filling with murky water, the study grew darker. Mahmoud stirred. As abruptly as his mood of depression and lethargy had come upon him, it departed. He stared down at his lap and saw something—for the first, startling instant he did not know what—in it. With a growing sensation of pain—as one feels when, at length, anesthesia wears off—he realized that it was Ahmed's last letter to him. It was strange and eerie and grotesque: just below his eyes, on a scrap of cheap brown paper, were the words—the living voice, as it were—of his friend and intimate. But the man who had written them was no longer on earth. Mahmoud shuddered. He lifted the letter to eye level, not to read it yet again—there was no need for that—but simply to examine the queer, dark spots that had stained the paper and smudged the ink. The spots had not been there before, he was certain of that, and he was puzzled. Then he realized, with an impatient jerk of his shoulders, that they were tears—tears that had fallen from his own eyes. But he could not remember crying. It was as if, so he felt, someone else, some stranger that he had never met and perhaps would never meet had cried for him. Roughly, he spun the wheelchair around and propelled it across the study to his desk. He flung the letter onto the pile and then swept everything, pell-mell, into the cardboard file and, leaning forward, thrust the file into its place among the others. In his mind, an insane sentence insistently repeated itself over and over again, and despite his prodigious efforts he was powerless to check it: *The case is closed; the case is closed!* But, of course, he knew it wasn't and never would be.

With a sigh so loud in the stillness of the room that it sounded like a bomb, he rolled himself out of the study and down the hallway and to the kitchen. S'ad was standing by the stove preparing supper. She was so absorbed in her work that she did not know he was there, and for several moments, after his eyes had accustomed themselves to the light, he sat quietly and watched her with pleasure. How graceful she was! How finely feminine! How sensitive and thoughtful and expressive were her features! When, at length, she turned and caught sight of him unexpectedly, she was startled. "Mahmoud!"

He cleared his throat. "Hello, S'ad," he said. Then, after a second's hesitation, he added: "I'm back."

His wife's eyes were moist. She nodded slowly. "So you are," she murmured, "so you are. Welcome."

The two of them stared at each other in silence. As S'ad moved from the stove to the counter alongside the sink, Mahmoud asked, "Where's Layleh?"

His wife did not answer at once; then she said, "Layleh's in her room; she's been there . . . all afternoon."

"All afternoon? What was she doing?"

S'ad shrugged. "Nothing."

"Nothing at all?"

"Nothing at all—just lying on her bed and staring into space. I went up several times and tried in every which way to get her attention. I even asked her if she would like to help me prepare supper, which you know she enjoys—but she seemed a bit distant."

Mahmoud's face darkened. "S'ad, are you hiding something from me? Is—is she ill?"

His wife shook her head. "So far as I can tell, there's nothing physically wrong with her. I insisted on taking her temperature, and it was normal."

"Then what . . . ?"

"I don't know, Mahmoud. But it's got me worried. Actually, she's been like this off and on for several days. Honestly, I'm stymied."

Her husband's fingers drummed on the arms of the wheel-chair. "Tell her I want to see her," he said.

"Right now?"

"Right now, S'ad."

"Mahmoud——"

"Please, S'ad—go and tell her."

S'ad nodded and left the kitchen. But in a short while, she returned—without her daughter.

"Well?" said Mahmoud.

"She was asleep," his wife explained. "I was sure that you would not have wanted me to waken her."

"No, I wouldn't have." Mahmoud stroked his chin. "S'ad," he murmured in an anxious tone, "I don't like the looks of this at all. Frankly, I'm concerned."

"We could take her to the doctor and have her examined. What do you say?"

Mahmoud passed an unsteady hand over his furrowed brow. "Yes, yes," he said, "that's exactly what we'll do. We'll drive over to the clinic in Ein Kerem tomorrow morning bright and early."

S'ad cleared her throat. "The Arnons are away on vacation," she said. "They left almost a month ago. If they were at home, I'd knock at their door and ask D'vora what she thinks."

Mahmoud stared at his wife. "I don't think *that* would be necessary," he said crisply. "Certainly, it can wait until the morning——"

"Mahmoud, how stubborn and how foolish can you be?"

But her husband did not reply. With forceful movements of his arms and hands, he spun the wheelchair around and left the kitchen.

S'ad remained where she was. She knew there would be no point in following.

———————

When Layleh heard her mother's footsteps on the stairs, she closed her eyes and, lying perfectly motionless on her bed, pretended to be asleep. It was a device that she seldom employed—as a general rule, she hated tricks, which she considered dishonest—but there were times, she had decided after giving the matter much thought, when a little harmless subterfuge was in order. It made life easier and more bearable for everyone concerned. Breathing regularly, with her face turned toward the wall, she listened as her mother came into the room and stood, shifting her slippered feet, by the bed for a moment and then walked out and went down the hallway and the stairs. When she was quite certain that she was alone once again, she opened her eyes and sighed openly with relief.

The truth was that she did not wish to be disturbed by her mother or father or anyone. She was by nature a happy and exuberant child, filled with the avid curiosity and bubbling energy of her girlhood. But something strange and disconcerting had happened to her after Uri's departure with his family. She had expected to miss him, of course, but she was unprepared for the feelings that came over her after he was gone. She knew that she cared deeply for her friend next door, but she had never imagined that his absence would cause her such distress.

After a time, as Layleh had known would happen, her mother came upstairs again to "wake" her for supper. Dutifully, she sat up in bed and, rubbing her eyes for effect, slipped into her sandals and accompanied S'ad down to the kitchen. Though S'ad tried strenuously to create an animated mood, the meal was gloomy and, to Layleh, at least, interminable. Mahmoud was sullen, obviously out of sorts, and scarcely said a word. Layleh picked unenthusiastically at her food, shunting aside more than she ate. When at last the family was finished, she asked her father—trying to conceal the impatience in her voice—for permission to leave the table. But, with a significant stare, he detained her. "Do you feel ill, Layleh?" he asked.

She shook her head. "No, Abu, I feel fine."

"You've been keeping to yourself these past few days. Is something amiss?"

"No, no, Abu—there's nothing wrong."

"Nothing at all, Layleh?"

"Nothing at all, Abu."

"You mustn't be afraid to confide in us, you know. That's what parents are for."

"But I assure you, Abu, I'm perfectly all right!"

Mahmoud continued to stare at her.

Layleh cleared her throat. "May I be excused now, Abu?"

Her father shrugged. "Yes," he murmured wearily. "You may."

When she had gone from the table, S'ad said quietly: "Well, Mahmoud, what do you think?"

Her husband was silent. He removed his napkin from his lap and said, "Something *is* bothering the child—that's for certain. Have you any idea what it is?"

S'ad sighed. "None whatsoever."

"Well, we'll take her to Ein Kerem in the morning, as we agreed. Perhaps the doctor will shed some light on the mystery."

S'ad's eyes clouded. "Perhaps," she murmured. But she did not sound convinced.

Early the next day, in Mahmoud's hand-controlled car, they drove over to the clinic in Ein Kerem. Dr. Lowenstein, white-haired and soft-voiced and courtly, examined Layleh. When he finished, he said to S'ad in faultless Arabic: "I find nothing physically wrong with your daughter; she's a fine, healthy eight-year-old. But———"

S'ad leaned forward. "But what, Doctor?" she asked tensely.

"But she seems to lack spirit. Is she often this way?"

"No, no, Doctor—the reverse is true. She's always full of energy and life. It's just the last few days that she's been acting this way."

Dr. Lowenstein removed his metal-rimmed glasses and pressed two fingers to the bridge of his nose. "Don't be alarmed, Mrs. Malek," he said gently. "I'm sure that it's nothing serious and that this apathy will soon be a thing of the past." He picked up a pad from his desk and uncapped his pen. "In the meantime, I'll prescribe a tonic, which should help. Let me know in about a week how she's doing."

S'ad rose. "Thank you, Doctor."

The doctor smiled and handed her the prescription across his desk. "Everything will be fine," he said. "Everything will be just fine."

The rest of the family was unpacking, but Uri left his baggage just beyond the threshold of his room and slipped hurriedly down the stairs and out into the dimming sunlight of the back-yard. So far as he was concerned, unpacking could wait—he had something else, something of overriding importance to do, and nothing, he felt, must delay him. With scarcely a glance at the treehouse he had not seen in nearly a month, he dashed across the lawn and parted the branches of the hedge. His heart stood still. Would Layleh be there, or would he have to wait before he saw her?

He swallowed hard. Layleh was, indeed, in her yard. She was sitting on a little stool under the cover of the broad leaves of the grape arbor—just sitting there quietly, with her hands folded neatly, like delicate flowers, on her lap, doing nothing. She was as lovely as he had remembered her to be all the time he was away—no, he thought quickly, that wasn't true at all. She was, as incredible as it seemed, *even lovelier!* He wanted to call out to her, to let her know that he was there—but, as he saw to his disappointment, her father was there in the yard as well. Mahmoud was seated in his wheelchair, which was stationed just outside the arbor, reading a book. From time to time he glanced up and into the mottled shade of the arbor at his motionless daughter.

Uri squirmed. What was he to do? Should he leave and come back to the hedge later—or should he remain at the hedge and wait, hoping that Mahmoud would leave? Both choices seemed intolerable. But of the two, the latter seemed best. Gradually, he lowered his body until his weight rested on his heels and remained in his place. In his troubled mind, a single refrain began to repeat itself over and over: *"Mr. Malek, please go! Mr. Malek, please go away and let me speak to Layleh!"* He mumbled the words just under his breath, first in Hebrew and then in Arabic, with an urgent, almost hypnotic cadence, as if he were pronouncing some incantation that was bound, by the studious force of its repetition, to produce the hoped-for result.

Lost in the spell, he forgot about time. Slowly, without his taking notice, the sun slipped downward and the shadows of coming dusk lengthened. Suddenly, Mahmoud Malek snapped his book shut and turned the wheelchair in the direction of his house. He was going to leave! Propelled by its occupant's strong hands, the chair rolled noiselessly across the grass. Uri held his breath. But midway on the lawn, the chair stopped abruptly and Mahmoud turned his head and called to the girl sitting under the canopy of grape leaves. As if stirring from a dream, Layleh rose and started after her father.

She came closer and closer and Uri saw every detail of her face. She was almost directly opposite him now, but she was slipping away, drawn on an invisible string toward her house. *He would not—he could not—let it happen!* Swiftly, he stooped and from the soft earth at the base of the hedge snatched up a clod of earth. Stepping back, he flung it over the high, leafy barrier and watched it fall just at her bare feet.

She halted in her tracks.

Her features, which had been rigidly composed, registered a startled expression. But at once, a gleam of understanding and recognition lit her dark eyes. She turned her head and he saw that her parted lips trembled and her eyes grew moist. For a moment, she did nothing but stare fixedly at the hedge. Then, acting with unerring instinct, she called out to her father, who was negotiating his chair up the ramp to the back porch. "I'll be with you in a minute," Uri understood her to say.

With enormous restraint—Uri could see her body grow tense with the effort—she waited until Mahmoud had disappeared into the house. In a flash, she darted close to the hedge and parted its branches. *"Uri!"*

"Layleh!"

They had so much to say, but it seemed that they could not say any more: just the exchange of their names overpowered them.

For several long moments they stood facing each other, locked in the embrace of their eyes. Everything—so they both felt—seemed completely familiar and natural, as if they both knew, down to the most minute details, exactly what this re-union would be like. And yet everything seemed totally strange and unexpected, as if no amount of imagining could possibly have pictured the actual experience. It was Uri who managed to speak first. "Layleh," he murmured. "I . . . missed you."

The girl on the other side of the hedge did not reply. She seemed dazed, and yet she seemed raptly attentive.

"Layleh . . . I missed you so very much! I'm so glad to be back! You are my dearest friend."

"I missed you, too, Uri."

"I thought about you every day, Layleh."

"That's the way it was with me, Uri."

"Sometimes I wished I had never gone away at all." Uri swallowed. "I wished . . . they had left me behind."

Layleh heard him and smiled. "Uri," she said huskily. She hesitated but then, quite obviously unable to check her words, went on: "Uri, don't ever go away again—please."

"I won't! Layleh, I won't!"

Her face darkened—it seemed that what she had just said

startled her, and she murmured: "I didn't really mean that, Uri——"

He cut her off. "I won't go away again, Layleh," he said hoarsely: "I promise you."

The fear vanished and her eyes shone with pleasure. "Uri . . . Uri—it's so good to see you."

He laughed. Then he fumbled in his pocket. "Wait—wait just a minute, Layleh."

"What are you doing?"

"You'll see—just a second." He had something in his hand.

"What . . . is it?"

"Let me find the stick, Layleh." Impatiently, he searched at the base of the hedge. "It's here," he mumbled. "Just where I left it. Now," he cried out, "I'll tie it on and——"

She saw his fingers fly this way and that. "What is it?"

"There!"

The stick slid smoothly through the hedge, and Layleh's fingers seized its end. "Uri!"

"Do you like it, Layleh?"

Holding the bracelet in both of her hands, she was silent. Then she murmured softly: "It's *beautiful.*"

"You really like it?"

"Like it? *I love it!*"

"I got it in Holland."

"It's *so* beautiful."

"I couldn't wait to give it to you——"

"Oh, Uri——"

"Wear it well, Layleh."

"I shall wear it . . . always, Uri."

From the kitchen window of her house, S'ad's voice called. Layleh turned her head. "I'm coming, Umm," she cried out. Then she said to Uri: "I've got to go now, Uri—but I'll see you soon."

"Soon . . ." said Uri.

Layleh moved back from the hedge. But before she started away, she lifted her hands to her face and put her lips to the bracelet.

———— • ••• •

That night, in bed, S'ad turned to her husband and said softly, "Are you asleep, Mahmoud?"

He grunted.

"Mahmoud——"

"Yes?"

"I think that——" She hesitated.

"Go on, S'ad."

She drew a deep breath. "I think that from now on we are going to see a change in Layleh."

"A change?"

"A change for the better."

"How so, S'ad?"

"Well, you see, Mahmoud, the young man from next door has returned."

"Yes, I suppose he has. I heard their car drive up this afternoon. But I fail to see what that has to do with our daughter."

S'ad put her face closer to her husband's. "I was at the kitchen window, just after you came in from the yard," she said. "And I saw . . . our daughter . . . at the hedge . . . and——"

"And so?"

"She was talking to young Uri."

"Yes?"

"And for the first time—for the very first time since the Arnons left on their vacation, she looked and acted as if she had come alive."

"S'ad——"

"No, no, Mahmoud! I saw it—and I saw it *clearly*. Uri's absence was the illness . . . and Uri's return is the cure! *That* explains everything."

"Impossible!"

Slowly, S'ad shook her head. "True," she murmured. "Absolutely true!"

Her husband did not speak for a moment. Then, with a shrug of his shoulders, he said curtly: "Silliness!"

S'ad opened her mouth to reply but abruptly changed her mind. It was foolish to argue. Turning away from her husband, she closed her eyes. She was apprehensive about what she had seen through the kitchen window and, at the same time, she was relieved that the mystery of Layleh's perturbation had been solved. For the first time in weeks, she felt that she would be able to sleep soundly. "Good night, Mahmoud," she whispered.

Her husband was already snoring.

1965

---·⊰•⊱·---

Jerusalem

THE DOOR TO Mahmoud's study was closed.

It was a sign, S'ad knew, that he was writing—a sign that brought hope to her heart as few things in the world did. She always, except for a second or two of what she called in her mind "silent prayer," passed the closed door and never—no matter what the circumstance—disturbed what she viewed as the sanctity of the small, book-lined room's occupant. If there were any road, she felt, that would lead her embittered husband back to life, it was his writing.

But today—a grayish, cloud-swept October day whose off-and-on sun had a dull, metallic tint—she felt that she had no choice in the matter. Still, as she stood before the door, she hesitated—force of habit and the deep respect she had for Mahmoud's writing restrained her. But in the end, she remembered her purpose in being there. Fawzi, her older brother; Ibrahim, a younger brother; and a cousin, Abdul, were sitting in the living room. They had arrived unexpectedly nearly an hour ago and she did not feel she could keep them waiting any longer. Fawzi, in his ingratiating but insidiously forceful manner, kept pressing her to summon her husband with a tight smile that was meant ostensibly to put her at her ease but which somehow, she felt, had in it the kernel of implicit menace. Fawzi reiterated the urgency of the visit and admonished his sister for the untoward delay. At length, unwillingly but out of clear necessity, she had to yield. She raised a reluctant hand and knocked on the door of Mahmoud's study.

There was no answer; it was obvious that her husband was deeply absorbed. She felt guilty and embarrassed, but on the other hand, she felt that she could not return to Fawzi and the others without Mahmoud. And so, more loudly, she knocked once again.

Still, there was no answer.

"Mahmoud!" she called and knocked for the third time.

She heard a sigh and then she heard a desk drawer rasp roughly shut and then the faint whispering sound of wheelchair tires on the tile floor. For an instant, as she had when she was a small child in the Galilee, she felt blind panic and wanted to flee. But there was no escaping—she had to remain where she was and fulfill her purpose.

A moment later the study door swung open. With a puzzled, distraught expression on his face, Mahmoud stared up at her. S'ad knew that he wanted desperately to vent his annoyance, but she sensed with wifely intuition that he would restrain himself and was both pleased for herself and touched by his discomfort. With a gesture of helplessness—for which she was ashamed—she said: "Mahmoud, I . . ." But her voice trailed off.

"Go on, S'ad."

"Mahmoud, I'm terribly sorry to interrupt you this way, but——" Again, she was unable to continue.

"It's all right, S'ad," he reassured her. "I know that you wouldn't interrupt me without good reason. Please tell me what's wrong." His eyes clouded. "Is it Layleh? Has something happened to her?"

S'ad shook her head. "Mahmoud—we have visitors."

"Visitors?"

"They're in the living room, waiting to see you."

"But who?"

S'ad swallowed. "It's Fawzi, and my brother Ibrahim, and my cousin Abdul—I don't think you know him. They arrived an hour ago and they want to talk to you. I put them off as long as I decently could, but——"

Mahmoud's features grew rigid, almost freezing his face into a mask. He sat, silent and motionless, in his wheelchair with eyes that stared past his wife.

"Mahmoud, I'm sorry."

Her husband started. He saw the pain in S'ad's eyes and said with a sigh: "Don't blame yourself, S'ad—it's not your fault. I understand why you called me. It had to be done."

"I don't know what they want of us, Mahmoud." She turned her head and glanced down the hallway in the direction of the living room and then returned her attention to her husband. "Fawzi is obviously the spokesman. He kept pushing me to call you." Involuntarily, she lowered her voice: "He—he's so——"

"So aggressive," Mahmoud finished, "and so deceitful." His fingers drummed nervously on the armrests of the chair. "We've seen him perhaps two or three times in Jerusalem during the past dozen years," he mused, "and the visits have always seemed . . . obligatory, as if for his own obscure reasons he finds it somehow necessary to keep contact with us." He lifted a hand and gently rubbed his jaw. His eyes narrowed and he murmured, "I, too, wonder why he heads this 'delegation' to our home."

S'ad hesitated. Then, with sudden determination, she said, "Mahmoud, I can go back to the living room and tell Fawzi politely that you're ill—that you're not up to seeing anyone." She stepped forward over the threshold ˥f the study and, leaning over, grasped her husband's shoulders. "Go into the study, Mahmoud, and lock the door behind you—go ahead. I'll send Fawzi and the others away—I *will*—I know I can do it! I'll tell Fawzi not to come back! I'll tell him that we want nothing to do with him."

Mahmoud took her wrists. Squeezing them gently, he said: "You would . . . tell your brother Fawzi that?"

"I would, Mahmoud, and *I will!* Get into the study and lock the door and let me deal with him as I see fit."

"But he's your blood relative—and so are the others."

S'ad's voice trembled. "You, Mahmoud, and Layleh are everything to me! We belong to each other, and that reality is paramount in my life! Fawzi and the others in the Galilee are my blood ties, but——" She could not go on—indeed, she knew from the look in her husband's eyes that it was not necessary to go on.

Mahmoud kissed her forehead and sighed. For a moment, he said nothing and then, slowly shaking his head, he said: "No, S'ad, I cannot let you stand in my place. I cannot allow myself to . . . hide behind your skirts. I appreciate your loyalty and I am moved—moved deeply—by your wish to protect me. But Fawzi has come with his 'partners' to see me. If anyone sends him away from this house, it must be me." Tenderly, he caressed his wife's hair. "Don't worry, S'ad, I can deal with Fawzi's kind."

"Mahmoud——"

"Trust me, S'ad."

"I *do* trust you, Mahmoud! It's Fawzi——"

Her husband forced a smile. "Everything will be fine, S'ad," he said: "I promise you."

When the wheelchair rolled into the living room, the three visitors from the Galilee rose almost as one man. Mahmoud nodded, lifted a hand, and entered into the intricate ritual of salutation and greeting. Abdul, a squat, square-shouldered young man with a drooping black mustache and heavy-lidded eyes, was—partially because he was the youngest and, Mahmoud sensed, partially because of his ungiving nature—the most taciturn and deferential of the three. He seemed to squeeze his words through his tobacco-stained teeth. Ibrahim, lean and—despite his attempts to conceal the fact—shifty-eyed, with a long, jagged scar that marred one gaunt cheek, was well spoken but manifestly ill at ease, as if he feared that, given his readiness of tongue, he might say something beyond what he intended. And Fawzi, quite openly the leader of the triumvirate, was so lavishly effusive that it was painful for Mahmoud to listen. Nevertheless, as he put it in his mind, he fell easily "into the game."

S'ad, moving sedately, refilled the demitasse cups with the black, bitter, steaming brew she made in the kitchen and passed around sweets. Nodding with stilted exaggeration, the men sipped their coffee and ate with pronounced pleasure, smacking their lips and tossing their heads. Their talk, moving forward at a carefully measured pace, turned to weather and winter crops and livestock and market prices. With flashing eyes and controlled, drawling voice, Fawzi, like an orchestra conductor, led them cannily and with practiced skill through the ritual. It seemed that he would go on forever, but then, without warning, as if he had suddenly discovered that he was at the end of the score, he put down his cup and, amiably but firmly, said: "Dear Mahmoud, generous host. I trust that you will grant me a favor."

"Ask it, Fawzi. If it is within my power, I will try."

Fawzi smiled. "If it is not asking too much, I should like to have a few words with you—alone."

"Will my study be suitable?"

Fawzi glanced at S'ad's retreating figure. "Can we have privacy there?"

"Complete privacy, Fawzi. No one will disturb us."

"Excellent!" boomed S'ad's brother. He rose from his chair. "Let's go, then."

Mahmoud led the way in his wheelchair, and Fawzi followed.

When the study door was closed and Fawzi was seated on a stool opposite the desk, Mahmoud cleared his throat and said: "Now, then, what's on your mind?"

There was a moment of silence during which S'ad's brother fiddled with the fringes of his kaffiyeh, more to unnerve his host, Mahmoud felt, than anything else. Releasing the cloth from his thick, beringed fingers abruptly, he said, "Dear Mahmoud, it must be obvious to you that I have not come to Jerusalem with my companions to pay you a social call. While it is always my deep and abiding pleasure to visit with you and with my adored sister, there is—as you have surely realized by this time—another purpose." He sighed.

Mahmoud lifted a hand. "You don't have to beat around the bush with me, Fawzi. I am certain that you are here for a specific reason. Just get to the point."

S'ad's brother uttered a hoarse little laugh. "Splendid!" he drawled. "I will do exactly that—it will save us both valuable time and energy." On his broad lap, his fingers found each other and laced themselves together. "You see," he went on, clipping his words as he spoke them, "it's like this. We need someone in Jerusalem—someone we can trust and rely on completely—someone who is, shall we say, untainted by the past and wholly above suspicion—someone who will work with us and aid us in the hour of need." He cracked his knuckles. "When a list of the, so to speak, possible candidates was drawn up, your name, dear brother-in-law, appeared at its head."

Mahmoud leaned forward in his chair. "Just a moment, Fawzi," he said quickly, "don't gallop so fast—I'm not following you at all. Whom do you refer to when you say 'we,' and exactly what kind of 'help' do you want and precisely what sort of 'list' is this of 'candidates untainted by the past' and 'above suspicion'? You have, indeed, as you said you would, gotten directly to the point. But the point is vague—even obscure. Explain yourself, please."

Without answering, S'ad's brother reached deliberately into a pocket. "Do you mind if I smoke?" he said affably.

"As you wish. But——"

Fawzi drew out a cigarette from its package. *"Sh'woyah..."* he murmured, almost absently. "Patience, my dear Mahmoud." He set the cigarette between his lips and unhurriedly lit it. Spewing out the smoke in a grayish-white cloud, he said in a tight, grimly altered voice: "Come, come, dear brother-in-law, certainly a man of your perspicacity and experience, a man who hails from the great Arab capital of Cairo and has lived all these years in Al-Kods, cannot be so utterly ignorant of my meaning."

Mahmoud stiffened. Struggling not to betray his irritation, he said softly, "Fawzi, you must forgive my bluntness, but I didn't ask for philosophy. I asked for an explanation. What is wanted of me—and by whom—and why?"

Fawzi waved the cigarette. "Incredible!" he muttered. "Not to be believed!"

Mahmoud reared back. "I want an explanation—clear and concise," he said.

The other's face darkened, but he did not speak. For a moment, staring fixedly at his brother-in-law, he puffed on his cigarette. With narrowed eyes, he said: "Mahmoud, Mahmoud...don't you know that we are at war?"

"At war? Who's at war? What are you talking about?"

Fawzi let a tiny, thin whistle escape from his lips. When it had gone, he said throatily: "Why, we Arabs are at war with the Jews, of course! How can you sit here in Jerusalem, in Al-Kods, under the very shadow of Jewish guns, and tell me that you have no knowledge of that fact? Where do you exist, my brother-in-law, on the earth...or on the moon!? Every Arab child in this city and in this land and in the Middle East knows that fact! And you want to look in my eyes, Mahmoud, and tell me you do not?"

Mahmoud's lips were dry. He wanted to speak, but the words rushed into his mind and collided with each other. Desperately, he battled to make order out of the chaos. But even, at length, after he had managed to calm himself down somewhat, all he could say was: "So that's it, Fawzi; so *that's* what you are driving at. I *thought* so! I thought so from the very onset, but against my better judgment, I tried to deny it." With difficulty, Mahmoud swallowed and went on: "And—now—" he stammered, "now that—your cards are on the table—I see clearly that—that my first perception was correct."

"My 'cards'?" echoed Fawzi. "You call them my *'cards'?*"

"Yes, Fawzi: your ugly, cheater's cards! That's what I call them!"

The other paled. "Retract!" he said, pointing the cigarette like a weapon at Mahmoud. "Apologize!"

"I will do neither!"

"You *must!*"

"Never!"

"You have insulted me, Mahmoud!"

"Insulted *you?*" Mahmoud said, throwing his arms up in dismay. "But, Fawzi, you—you are besmirching my home! You——" But suddenly, struck by what he realized in a flash of despairing insight was the utter futility of the exchange of invective, he broke off and bit his lip. He was silent for a moment, meeting his brother-in-law's withering look with an expression of naked pain in his eyes. And then, subjecting his voice to an iron discipline, he said slowly: "Listen, Fawzi, there is no use in our quarreling. I know now what it is that you propose, and I can never—I repeat, *never*—accept it. So..."

It cost the other no small effort to pry his thick lips, in whose corners spots of spittle were forming, into a smile. But he did so nevertheless. Lifting his open-palmed hands in a gesture of reconciliation to the man in the wheelchair, he said in an emotion-clogged voice: "Dear brother-in-law, gracious host, fellow Arab: For kinsmen and brothers in Islam to wrangle is senseless and shameful." His cigarette had gone out, but he made no move to relight it. In a lowered, almost hushed tone,

he went on speaking: "Do not close your mind—and the magnanimous heart that I know, from experience, you have—to
my proposal . . . until, at least, you have heard me out in full.
Allow me, dear Mahmoud, the privilege and the courtesy of
presenting my case——"

"Fawzi——"

But the other overrode him. "Mahmoud," he said, thrusting
out his words with rapid forcefulness, "we Arab patriots are
on the move! Surely, you cannot be totally oblivious of that
fact. Again and again, our *fedayeen* strike at the Jews, sowing
terror and destruction as the farmer sows grain! From Gaza in
the south and from the 'triangle' in the east, our raiders move
stealthily among the Jews, inflicting pain and chaos and death!
We soldiers of Islam are spinning a web, Mahmoud, a web of
steel and fire . . . of which I am a part! But here in Jerusalem
there is a break in the web. Israeli security has torn the strands
apart." Fawzi paused to sigh and then went on: "That, in essence, is why I have come to see you." As if someone had
oiled it, his voice grew softer. It began to purr. "You, Mahmoud, are in a perfect position to repair the shattered network.
You are clean, beyond the slightest suspicion—uncontami-
nated, as it were. Nobody in his wildest dreams would ever
think to connect you with our struggle. Your blemishless record
and"—Fawzi rolled his eyes—"and forgive me for saying it
so bluntly, but the reality cannot be denied, your *condition*
place you, my dear brother-in-law, in a special and, indeed,
enviable situation to come to our aid." Fawzi's bull neck thrust
forward, and with an almost theatrical flourish he placed one
hand on his breast. "Mahmoud, say what you will, but I sense—
I perceive—I *know* that in your deepest heart of hearts you are
an Arab patriot who, though distant in the past for his own,
perhaps sincere but wholly misguided reasons, cannot remain
aloof from the tide—no, from the *flood*—of Islam! Take up
the banner, Mahmoud! And take up the sword! We need you
and we want you—and you must answer our call!"

"Fawzi——"

The other crumpled his burnt-out cigarette into his closing
palm and raised the fist. "Have you heard, Mahmoud? You
must! We are pressing you into service, Mahmoud! We are
conscripting you!"

There was a long, leaden moment in which the two men

stared at each other fixedly in a silence that each seemed loath
to break. Gripping the arms of his wheelchair with a strength
that turned his knuckles white, Mahmoud said: "No!"

"Mahmoud!"

S'ad's husband shook his head. "I said *no*, Fawzi," he
declared through clenched teeth, *"and no it stands!* I have never
in my life been a servant or a lackey or a slave—or a conscript!
And as long as I live, I shall never be!" His eyes flashed and
his next words flew pointedly from his mouth like arrows: "Did
you hear me, Fawzi?"

S'ad's brother's face grew red and purple. A flow of yellow-
white spittle foamed across his lips. He lifted his powerful
body from the stool. "Mahmoud," he said in a low, brutal
growl, "in the name and on the blood of the Arab patriots, I
warn you . . ."

Mahmoud trembled, but his voice was firm. "An Arab patriot, Fawzi—a true Arab patriot—dreams of peace. And he
works to bring it about."

"Do not disregard the warning, Mahmoud. Do not slough
it off lightly! Things . . . happen to those who do not take us
seriously . . . who turn away from us in disdain."

"Fawzi, get out."

"Ugly things, Mahmoud!" Fawzi snorted. "We have learned
well to deal with traitors."

"Fawzi, get out of my house."

———————

Having summoned reinforcements from the west, the clouds
had won the day and covered the Arnon and Malek yards with
dull gray shadow—the special, heavy, silver-tinted shadow of
approaching winter. The wind was rising steadily, daring every
now and then—as if testing its strength against the strength of
man—to blow in brazen, fitful gusts that sent long-dead leaves,
like restless ghosts, flying eerily through the air. It was not yet
November, but already the promise of rain and hail—and perhaps even tenuous, whirling, wet flakes of snow—was man-
ifest.

On one side of the wind-stirred hedge, a ten-year-old boy

crouched, oblivious to all but the pressing business at hand. Uri wore a knitted brown pullover and long trousers, patched at the knees where they had been worn to shreds by kneeling. On the other side of the hedge, nine-year-old Layleh was clad in a dress, so long that it reached to her ankles, and a button-down sweater—it was pink, the color she loved best—that her mother had made.

What went on in their respective houses; what was happening in the dim-stoned, cloud-roofed city of Jerusalem; what was occurring in the land of Israel; whatever the events that were transpiring in the spinning world of man called earth: all of this was remote from the boy and the girl—it was beyond the charmed circle that the two, friends and companions now for several years, had by common consent drawn in time and space. For the moment—seeing and hearing and thinking about nothing else—they were concentrating with all of their energy and imagination and zest on a pair of dolls that Layleh had fashioned out of rags and cotton stuffing and twine in the private sanctum of her room. One doll was male, with blue shorts and white shirt and a tight-fitting pale-blue hat that sat jauntily, like an inverted soup bowl, on its head. The second was female, with flowing, long hair made of white string dyed black, and a long white smock embroidered neatly with loops of red thread. Layleh had held the pair of dolls up proudly and shown them to Uri through the bare branches of the hedge. He had applauded them lustily and at length. But now, being Uri, he wanted to see them up close, and so his friend, being Layleh, was busily binding them with raffia to the forked stick which served the two children as a faithful messenger through the thick leaves of the hedge.

Uri, to show his prized and often-talked-about "maturity," wanted to be patient. But Layleh's progress was not sufficiently rapid for him and so—despite his resolve to remain calm—he could not refrain from calling out: "Hurry, Layleh—do it more quickly, will you? It's getting dark already!"

"But I'm going as fast as I can, Uri."

"It's not fast enough, I'm afraid! You must do it more quickly."

"I'm hurrying, Uri," she said breathlessly, making her fingers fly. "In just another second, it will be done."

And then it *was* done!

Layleh uttered a little cry of victory and, with painstaking care, so as not to damage or tear the dolls or poke—heaven forbid!—one of their shiny button-eyes out, passed the stick through the tangle of branches. Both of the children held their breath throughout the delicate operation, and then, at long last, Uri had the dolls safely in his hands! *"I have them!"* he said.

"Be careful, Uri."

"Don't worry, Layleh, I will."

The girl pressed closer to the bare hedge, while the boy knelt on the cold, browned grass, silently inspecting Layleh's handiwork.

"How . . . do you like them, Uri?"

Without looking up, he whistled. Then, holding the dolls, he raised his eyes and, softly but distinctly, murmured: "They're beautiful."

"Thank you," whispered Layleh. She hesitated for a moment and in a gentle, trembling voice, said, "Uri . . ."

"Yes?"

"Do you know . . . who they are?"

Kneeling on the cold-grassed earth, Uri did not reply. He smiled, and a mischievous light—which Layleh in the gray dullness of the spending afternoon failed to see—shone from his eyes. She waited anxiously, but still he did not answer. Then, controlling the merriment he felt from bubbling up into his voice, he said, "I really don't know, Layleh."

"Uri, think, think hard!"

He shook his head. "I'm sorry, Layleh, but——"

"Can't you guess, Uri?"

He forced himself to frown. "I can try. . . ."

"Well, then, *try!*"

Once again, Uri was silent. He stared at the dolls. With a deep sigh, he murmured, "Are they real people, Layleh, or are they from a fairy tale?"

"Uri," she murmured faintly, "they're *real* people." She stared at the ground. "Can't you guess who?"

The disappointment in her voice and the dejected look on her face pained him and he felt that he could no longer go on with the pretense. "Layleh," he said.

"Yes?"

"Layleh, look at me."

She raised her eyes.

"Layleh, forgive me for hurting you—I was only pretend-ing, jesting with you." Uri swallowed. "I . . . *do* know who they are."

She flushed. "You *do?* Honestly?"

Uri nodded. "They are," he said solemnly, "you and I."

Layleh clasped her hands together. "Exactly so!" she whis-pered with mingled excitement and pleasure.

"Yafeh m'od," said Uri. "They are beautifully made, and it was a beautiful idea to make them."

Layleh hesitated for a moment. Then she said softly, "I made them because we are such good friends, Uri. Once, when I was almost finished, my mother came into my room and saw them and said, 'Layleh, how pretty! Let me look at them!' And she held them in her hands and said, 'Who are they? Do they have names?' And I answered, 'Umm, they are good friends, very good friends. And they have names, but their names are secret.' And she smiled and said, 'Secret even from me, daugh-ter?' And I replied, 'Secret from everyone in the world, Umm— even from you.'"

"And then what did she say, Layleh?"

"Nothing, Uri. She laughed. Then she gave me back the dolls and went out of the room." Layleh reflected for a moment. Then she said slowly, "I didn't lie to my mother, Uri: the dolls *are* close friends . . . and their names are secret from everyone else. So I told the truth."

"Yes," said Uri, "you certainly did tell the truth. *We* are very dear friends. Why," he added with a wink, "we even speak each other's language now."

They both laughed.

Then Uri said: "Layleh, do you think your mother knows?"

"Knows . . . about us?"

"Yes, about us."

Layleh shrugged. "My father doesn't."

"But does your mother?"

"Perhaps."

"Has she . . . ever said anything?"

Layleh shook her head. "No. Except——"

"Except what?"

"Except sometimes she looks at me."

"Looks at you how?"

"I don't know . . . in a strange way, I suppose. It usually happens when I tell her I'm going into the yard. She stares at me and——"

"And what?"

"And nothing. She just stares and nods. It's—I don't know— it's as if she wants to say something, but then she holds herself back." Layleh was silent. Then she said, "How about your parents, Uri?"

He shook his head. "I can't really say," he muttered. "They're both so busy—Abba in the Foreign Office and Imma at the hospital. But sometimes, when she's around and I'm about to go into the yard, my mother also gives me a strange look. As if——"

"As if what?"

"As if she thinks something is going on." Uri cleared his throat. "But Ilana," he said thoughtfully. "Now, *she's* a different story."

"How so?"

"I don't exactly know, Layleh. But she's always asking questions."

"Like what, Uri?"

"Like 'How is it that you know so much Arabic, Uri?' She's asked me that a few times."

"How can your sister tell that you know so much Arabic, Uri?"

Uri sighed. "I asked Ilana that myself."

"And what did she answer?"

"She said, 'I hear you speaking Arabic in your room, Uri— I hear you speaking aloud almost every time I pass your door.'"

"Do you, Uri?"

"Yes. I always try to practice what you've taught me, Layleh."

"You've never told her that, though, have you?"

Uri snorted. "No! You know that we are a secret."

"Then what *do* you tell your sister?"

Uri hesitated. Almost shyly, he replied: "I tell her that I'm practicing Arabic because I want to be in the Foreign Office like my father when I grow up."

Layleh caught her breath. "Uri," she exclaimed, "that's—" But she did not finish the sentence.

"A lie?" said Uri.

"Well, not exactly a lie, since there isn't any other way of protecting our secret."

"But I *do* want to be in the Foreign Office!" Uri protested.

And once again, they both laughed together.

Holding the dolls up, Uri said, "Layleh, what do you want to do with them?"

She did not reply at once. Then she said: "I thought that . . . you would keep the girl . . . and I would keep the boy."

"Hmmmm . . ."

"Is that all right, Uri?"

"I have another idea."

"What is it, Uri?"

"Suppose—that is, if you agree, Layleh—we keep them both in the treehouse."

"In the treehouse?"

"Yes, Layleh. That way . . . they can live together."

"I see. . . ."

There was a nervous edge to Uri's voice when he spoke. "Well, Layleh," he said, "what do you think of my idea?"

"I think," she murmured, "that . . . it's a wonderful idea."

"You do?"

"I really do."

"Then I'll put them in their home."

"When?"

Uri smiled. *"Right now!"* he said.

Layleh clapped her hands. "Then do it quickly, Uri," she urged, "before one of us has to go in!"

Swiftly, Uri's fingers untied the raffia that bound the dolls to the stick. Then he rose and ran over to the oak tree. From her side of the hedge, Layleh watched him climb up the ladder, holding the dolls to his chest with one hand, and disappear into the treehouse. A moment later he reappeared. He waved to her from his perch and then, in a flash, scurried down the ladder and was back at the hedge. "Layleh," he said breathlessly. "Layleh . . ."

"Yes?"

"You should see them! They're happy!"

"They are?"

"They're so happy to live together, Layleh—and they always will be!"

"Oh, Uri!"

From the Arnon kitchen, D'vora's voice called.

Uri touched the hedge. "I've got to go now, Layleh," he said: "*Shalom.*"

"*Salaam,* Uri—go in peace."

She watched as he sped across his yard and vanished from sight through his kitchen door. Then she turned from the hedge and started for her own house. Halfway across the lawn she halted. Three dark figures slipped—one after the other, like shadows—onto her back porch. Her mother's figure, framed by the kitchen doorway, appeared. She did not know what to make of the scene, but she was afraid. The strange and foreboding tableau lasted for but an instant and then broke up. The three men rushed down the length of her yard and, without taking the slightest notice of her, disappeared over the stone wall at the rear. She saw them silhouetted for a second in no-man's land and then—as if into thin air—they were gone.

Layleh ran with all the speed she could muster toward her house. "Umm," she cried out in terror. "Umm!"

Almost imperceptibly, the gray October afternoon melted into twilight. The chill which had been in the air all day long had, like a knife blade, sharpened to cold, and the wind now blew with steady, blustering force. At the point where the main road intersected with the narrow little street that wound its way down to the Arnon house, the command car screeched to a halt. The driver—a young, red-bearded soldier with a broad, easy smile and sober blue eyes—faced the lone passenger who sat next to him and said, "Are you sure you don't want me to turn in, Major Arnon?"

Arie shook his head. "This is perfectly fine, Yossi; I assure you."

"It's no trouble at all to take you to your front door."

Arie reached back and picked up his knapsack. He smiled.

"As a matter of fact, I'd rather walk," he said. "It will give me a chance to 'decompress.'"

The driver nodded. "I know what you mean," he murmured. Extending his hand, he said, "Well, *shalom* for now. Until we see each other again, take care of yourself."

Arie took the young, strong hand and shook it firmly. "You, too, Yossi. *L'hitraot*—until we meet again!"

The command car sped off, and Arie, his dusty knapsack slung over one shoulder, started down the street. He walked at a steady, measured pace, but unhurriedly, looking around him at the quiet, tree-lined street and at the peaceful houses that, behind their winter-gray lawns, were beginning to display lighted windows. Walking calmly toward his home and the family that waited for him within it, after a month of reserve army duty, gave him a queer, almost unreal feeling. He had come from four weeks of reserve maneuvers in the Negev— Israel's southern pie-slice of semiarid wilderness. From rough, strident, exhaustive preparation for war . . . back to the tranquil, sheltered, blessed society that hoped and prayed that war would never come.

What he had said to the driver Yossi, was correct: a reservist returning home from maneuvers needed time to "decompress"—one could not possibly make the transition from war to peace without a period of adjustment. And so he walked, trying to shed the role of Major Arnon, combat infantry officer, a role that had taken over his life for a month, and assume the role of Arie Arnon, member of the Israel Foreign Office, husband to D'vora and father to Ilana and Uri; trying to see what now, since his absence, looked strange, as familiar as it had been before he left; trying—with an almost pathetic desperation—to get used to a serene and unmilitary winter's evening in an outlying section of Jerusalem.

His casual remark to his driver about decompression had made it sound easy, almost routine. But it wasn't. Sometimes, as he walked down the twisting street, it seemed to him, uncannily, that there were fellow soldiers walking with him in step: "Major" Zamir—somehow, in Arie's mind, he would always call him that—with whom he had served in 1948 on Mount Scopus and once again in 1956 in the push for the Suez and who now—though he would forever be a stoop-shoul-

dered, slow-spoken, gentle-mannered farmer—was actually a
lieutenant-colonel; lieutenants Avivi and Admoni—now cap-
tains and now both married—who were still in his unit; Lieutenant Petrushka, who had never had the chance to be promoted
or—though he had been engaged—to be married since he had
fallen during the first day of battle in the Sinai Campaign;
Amnon Peled, who had transferred to a paratroop unit and
distinguished himself in a hand-to-hand struggle that had turned
the tide of an entire assault; Musa Zaritsky, the Yugoslavian,
who had lost an arm and an eye on Mount Scopus in the last
days of conflict—when the smell of ceasefire was "so thick
that it made you giddy," he had remarked in his broken Hebrew
at the time—and who came occasionally to Jerusalem from
Safed, where he lived, to seek Arie out; Micha Zalmanovich,
who had survived the Warsaw Ghetto and the Nazi plague and
the Polish forests to live and fight, as he said, the way a Jew
had to fight, and who, more violently embittered than ever,
still served as a sergeant under Arie's command; Ovadiah Malachi, the Yemenite, who had died with unspoken psalms on
his lips in the infirmary on Mount Scopus; Yankel Feldman,
from a small, out-of-the-way, long-named town in Rumania,
who had, indeed, learned to be a soldier, and in learning had
had his head blown off by an exploding tank shell outside of
El Arish in 1956. All of them and many more, too many to
count—some with names that Arie remembered clearly, as
clearly as he remembered his own; and some with names he
had known but forgotten; some with names he had never known
but remembered by their faces or only by their eyes or smiles;
some alive and some living ghosts—that walked with him
down the street that led back home.

Arie forced himself—with an effort that seemed to drain
him of his last resource of strength—to make them leave his
mind. And to make matters infinitely more difficult, a part of
him wanted to keep them with him, wanted never to banish
them from his thoughts. But he knew that he *must*—if the
peaceful flow of hearth and family were to return. It wasn't
that he would forget them—that could not possibly be; it was
simply that he wanted to relegate them, one and all, alive and
dead, to some safe and hermetically sealed vault to which he
alone had the key.

To help himself accomplish the task, he began to sing. Nothing elaborate at first, just snatches of song that had been popular in the city and in the country before he left, as well as scraps of a few perennial favorites. From these simple tunes he went on to some of the music that Ilana played: flashing melodic fragments of Beethoven and Mozart and Schubert. His body felt looser. His mind relaxed. The outpouring of song, coming from deep within him, seemed to release him from the bondage of his recent experience. At once—as if they, too, wished to stop marching for a time and rest—the ghostly steps that had echoed to each and every step that he himself took faded and were gone. Soothed and comforted, his mind turned to other thoughts and other memories.

He recalled his reunion with D'vora after she had returned to Israel from Saint-Michel and he had come down from the enclave on Mount Scopus after the final ceasefire had been signed and gone into effect. He remembered the first time he had set eyes on his infant daughter, Ilana, who had been born in Ein Kerem while he was still in the army. He thought of how the three of them had moved from the apartment on the shady street in the center of Jerusalem to the "house with the hedge," as D'vora had elected to call it from the start, and of how D'vora and he had worked, as he himself had put it, "to redress the neglect." He remembered Ilana's first piano lesson at the age of six and of how impossible it had been to get her to leave the keyboard, even though it was long past her bedtime. He recalled how D'vora had called him at the Foreign Office to say that she was going into labor and how he had arrived at the hospital—in a borrowed car, because his jeep wouldn't start—just moments before Uri was born. He thought of the first steps Uri had taken out in the backyard. . . .

Peaceful thoughts, joyous thoughts, warming thoughts that, like crystalline bubbles, rose to the placid surface of his mind. He quickened his pace. It was happening—he *knew* now with certainty that he had been transformed from Major Arnon of the Israel Defense Forces into Areleh, who lived at the end of this quiet and clear-aired Jerusalem street. His beret, with its metal emblem of sword laid across parallel sheaves of wheat; his battle jacket, with the insignia of his rank on its epaulets; his webbed belt, on which his holstered revolver was hung;

his high-lacing, dust-whitened shoes—they just *happened* to be on him at this moment, just happened to be on the body of a man named Arie who was rushing homeward to see and embrace his wife and children after a prolonged and unasked-for absence. Suddenly, he broke into a trot. Like a ribbon, the street wound backward. Everything—the cypresses, the tele-phone poles with their sagging wires, the shrubs, the driveways, the dark-roofed houses with their yellow squares of window light—looked familiar now, looked ordered and precisely in place, as if he had left them only a moment ago to go on some minor errand.

Running at a full trot, he rounded the last bend. There, on the left, some twenty or thirty meters ahead of him, at the very end of the street, was the dusk-shadowed shape of the house with the hedge. His heart swelled with warmth and excitement. He saw, in successive, overpowering visions that flashed through his mind, D'vora in the spotless, brilliantly lit kitchen—he was sure that she had returned from the hospital by now—and Ilana, her pigtails swinging, bent raptly over the piano in the living room, and Uri in his room, reading a book or putting together some intricate jigsaw puzzle. He knew it was foolish, even childish, but he was unable to restrain himself. *"I'm back,"* he cried out as he ran. *"I've come back home to my dear ones. Shalom!"*

———————

The little mud, stone, and straw house was on the northern extremity of the village in the Galilee. It was set behind a high, thick screen of broad-bladed, yellow-spined cacti, at a consid-erable distance from the rest of the village houses, as if for some reason that had long been forgotten the house had been ostracized. An old man, wrinkled and shriveled—"like a rotted fig," the rest of the villagers used to say—who survived all the other members of his family, had lived there for longer than anyone could or cared to remember. Last winter, during the heavy rains that turned the Galilee into slippery, clinging mud, he had fallen ill, and after weeks of enduring a burning fever that had slowly but relentlessly sapped the last stubborn dregs of life from his wasted body, he had died. As he had done so many times before with unctuous words and cunning manipulation, Fawzi—whom the villagers often, with wry, sardonic humor, referred to as the "chess player"—had acquired the dead man's house and the parcel of land around it. If he had been asked why he needed the miserable structure and the few neglected square meters of earth that surrounded it, Fawzi would have shrugged and, with a grim, sharp-toothed smile, answered: "In this world, one needs all one can get."

The approach to the house—still lingeringly referred to by the children of the village as the "dead man's place"—was along a narrow, twisting path whose jagged stones that clinked and popped underfoot gave clear warning that someone was on his way. Fawzi liked that: "It is a house that sounds a natural alarm," he said with a laugh. Within the forbidding, circular wall of needle-spined cacti, he set three or four vicious watchdogs who growled, as Fawzi liked to say, "at the whine of a mosquito." He gave immediate orders to his workmen to repair the house's roof—so that no matter how heavy the rain, it would no longer leak—and to seal the two windows with cinder blocks and to reinforce and strengthen the door. At a cost over which he haggled for half a day, he hired a locksmith to repair the wretched old lock that hung by no more than a hair and to install an additional new one that, as he said, "not even the Devil could pick!" The two keys—they were the only ones—were added to what he proudly called the "fat lot" on the ring that he kept religiously always on his person.

For Fawzi, the house—from which, as he was fond of putting it, the dead serf had gone to make way for the living lord—was a perfect retreat. It was high; actually, it was on the highest spot in the village, commanding a sweeping view of the terrain to all sides and of the highway in the east below; and it was isolated—not even a cockroach, Fawzi said, could come near without being spotted in advance.

Fawzi had his laborers clear the dead man's things out and then furnished the place with sparse austerity: a wooden table, several wooden chairs, two metal-framed cots, a single kerosene lamp, and a little kerosene-burning cookstove. According to his plan, the place was meant strictly and solely for business. And if one were to ask him exactly what business he meant,

he would offer the tight-lipped reply: "The business that needs
to be done."

In the Galilee, the final week of November began with a
torrential downpour. Great banks of clouds—slate-gray clouds
that looked like slabs of rock—moved in from the seething,
white-capped expanse of the sea to the west and disgorged their
rain. Skeins of lightning lit the horizons eerily, and thunder
kept up an almost constant bombardment. Trees bent in the
deluge, and some of their strained branches tore and the grass
flattened as if some giant invisible hand were pressing it down.
The water-soaked earth oozed and glistening rocks tumbled
pell-mell down the streaming slopes, and the wadis below surged
with savage floods that carried away everything in their paths.
The villagers, to the last, remained securely within their homes,
performing necessary household tasks that had been long post-
poned and taking careful note of where their roofs had sprung
new leaks and emerging only to feed their livestock and do the
most urgent chores.

At midweek the rain slackened somewhat, falling steadily
but without its former fury. Evening came—the cold, silent,
starless evening that was so often the mark of winter in the
Galilee—and Fawzi left his sprawling, many-balconied home
of hewn stone and imported timber with his eldest son, a strapping nineteen-year-old named Hussein. Fawzi led the way and
the boy followed him, almost at his heels. They wore long
khaki coats and knee-high rubber boots and walked as quickly
as they could, trying not to slip in the mud that oozed underfoot.
On the precipitous path to the house, Hussein lost his footing
and nearly fell to the ground. At the last instant, he recovered
himself and tried to pass off the near-mishap lightly, as if it
were a source of amusement. Fawzi, however, was not amused
in the least. Turning his head, he said savagely: "Clumsy oaf!
If you must stumble on a village path, what am I to expect of
you in the world outside?"

As they neared the tall, rain-slick barrier of cacti, the watchdogs, bounding forward on the long chains that tethered them
to their kennels, set up a fierce, lugubrious racket. When they
sensed it was their master who approached, their snarls turned
to fawning whines.

Muttering obscenities at the dogs, Fawzi drew out his key

ring and, fumbling among the thick array, unlocked the door of what he called wryly "the shack." Just inside the threshold, he scraped the soles of his mud-spattered boots on the rough concrete floor and shook the rain from his wet coat. Glancing over at his son, he said, "Light the lamp, Hussein—and be quick about it!"

Hussein struck a match. Through its clear glass cover, the lamp sent out a fan of yellow light. Following the direction of his father's gesture, Hussein seated himself on one of the cots. Fawzi sat at the table. With impatient twitches of his heavy fingers, he unbuttoned his coat and took out a pocket watch with a worn silver case and bent forward. "They're due," he murmured thickly. "They're due right now." In the damp silence of the room, his voice slithered like a snake from the freshly plastered walls. "Hussein!" he said gruffly. "Didn't you hear what I said?"

"Eh? Yes, Abu. I heard you very well, Abu. You said . . . that the men were due . . . right now."

Fawzi snorted. "Then why aren't they here?"

Hussein scratched his head. He had no answer to the question, but he knew that his father wanted one nevertheless. With a sigh, he said, "It must be . . . the storm, Abu. They must be delayed in the storm."

Fawzi shoved the watch into a pocket of his vest. "Rubbish!" he growled. He frowned at his son. "Don't use the storm as an excuse," he said with a sneer. "They're late in arriving because they're bumblers . . . incompetent jackasses—like you! And when they get here—assuming they ever do—I'll tell them as much to their ugly faces!"

His son stared uncomfortably at the floor.

"Did you hear me, Hussein?"

"Yes, Abu! I heard you."

Fawzi drummed on the tabletop with his fingers. Shifting the weight of his heavy body on the chair, he pulled out a tin box of cigarettes and lit one. Gray, white-veined smoke slid up through the pale-yellow lamplight. Fawzi smoked with half-closed eyes, the coarse features of his face glum and masklike. His son sat quietly and watched. On the corrugated tin sheets of the roof overhead, the rain beat a steady, mesmerizing tattoo. It spilled from the eaves and splashed to the ground, and in the paw-torn muck of the courtyard outside, it made a sucking sound. Hussein grew drowsy. He would have liked to doze, but he did not dare—his father might say something he would miss. Fawzi finished his cigarette and crushed it out in a clay ashtray and lit another. A half-hour—so Hussein reckoned—passed, and Fawzi extracted his watch once again. This time, he laid it on the table, between the tin cigarette box and the ashtray. "Thirty-five minutes," he muttered through his teeth. "They're thirty-five minutes late."

His son stirred nervously.

"Did you hear me, Hussein?"

"Yes, Abu."

Fawzi turned. "What if they don't come, Hussein?"

"If they don't come, Abu?" Hussein echoed.

"That's right! What if the pigs don't come at all! What then?"

"I——"

Suddenly, the furious barking of the dogs outside obscured the fall of the rain. Fawzi started. Inside the right-hand pocket of his greatcoat was a small snub-nosed pistol. He pulled it out and cocked it. "Hussein!" he cried, lurching to his feet. "Open the door! Quickly!"

His son sprang forward and flew across the room. He unlocked the door and yanked it open. With his head thrust forward and his gun at the ready, Fawzi went out into the rain and sloshed through the mud. "Who's there?" he shouted hoarsely. "Identify yourselves."

Two shadows, held at bay by the ferocious barks of the dogs, stood in the narrow breach of the cactus wall. One of them answered with a muffled shout.

"Louder!" screamed Fawzi. He raised the pistol. "*Louder,* I say!" he screamed. "I didn't hear you!"

The reply came again, this time more clearly.

Fawzi pressed the safety catch of his pistol and shoved it into his pocket. He whirled. "The dogs," he bellowed to his son. "Get the dogs away!"

Hussein held the collars of two of the dogs and his father held the collars of the other two while the strangers, moving unsteadily in the mud, passed into the house. When the door was shut and bolted and the strangers had been seated in chairs

at the table, Fawzi, who alone remained standing, said breathlessly: "So you're here at last." With the back of a hand, he
brushed raindrops from his nose and lips and added in a surly
tone, "It certainly took you long enough."

The taller of the two newcomers—a man with beadlike eyes
and a sharp-pointed beard—said: "We're sorry to be late, *ya*
Fawzi, but the storm held us up."

Fawzi's lips twisted with disgust. "The Jews," he snarled,
"don't allow themselves to be troubled by storms! Rain or shine,
they get where they have to get and do what they have to do—
on time!"

"But Fawzi, the wadi was a river! We had to look for a
place to cross."

Fawzi waved a hand. "Excuses," he muttered. "The Jews
don't care about excuses! They care about results."

The shorter of the newcomers looked up from wiping his
wet face with a handkerchief. "It doesn't serve any purpose to
recriminate," he said slowly in a sullen tone. "We're here
now—and let's not waste any more of our time." He put the
dripping handkerchief on the table and unfastened the collar of
his coat. "What happened in Jerusalem? Did you make an
arrangement with your brother-in-law?"

Fawzi did not reply.

"Well?" said the short man, whose name was Mustapha.
"I'm waiting for an answer—or has the Devil got your tongue?"

Fawzi's face darkened. He stiffened and haltingly, as if loath
to say what he had to, mumbled: "It . . . fell through."

"Fell through?" repeated Mustapha. "What do you mean?"

"My brother-in-law—may his house be blasted!—refused
to cooperate."

"Refused to cooperate? I don't understand."

Fawzi scowled. "Mahmoud ordered us from his home. He
is a stubborn fool——"

The tall man—his name was Gamal—shook a fist. "He is
a traitor!" he said hoarsely.

Fawzi nodded. "Exactly so," he said with a grimace. "And
he will be dealt with as such. One day——"

Mustapha cut him off. "Then the web is still asunder in Al-
Kods," he murmured.

"Mahmoud will get his due!" Fawzi persisted.

But the other raised a hand. "Never mind that now," he said. "There is always time for revenge, which does not spoil. I myself have a certain man in mind to serve our purposes in Jerusalem. It will take a while to work out all the details, but in the end, I assure you, my dear comrades, we shall have our completed web once again." He sighed and methodically, without speaking, unbuttoned his waterlogged coat. Clearing the phlegm from his throat, he said: "Let us get on to the business at hand: the attack on the kibbutz south of Ras el-Nakurah."

The tall man named Gamal nodded. He lifted a bony-fingered hand that, still covered with raindrops, shone in the lamplight. "It must be a devastating assault," he murmured. "It must result in death and mutilation, and fill the hearts of the Jews with horror."

"That it will do," assented Mustapha. "We will plan it carefully, so that it achieves the effect we desire."

"*Carefully,*" echoed Fawzi. "It has to go off like clockwork: that is the key to everything." He paused and, glancing over at the cot against the far wall, commanded: "Hussein, prepare coffee for our guests!" And then, moving to the table where the newcomers were seated, he lowered himself onto a chair. "Comrades . . . patriots . . . *fedayeen,*" he rasped. "Let us begin. . . ."

———————

The alarm clock went off— it seemed to split the air with the sound of a falling projectile—and Arie, groping blindly but with the unerring certainty born of long practice, reached out from the bed to the night table and pushed in the plunger that silenced it. Despite himself, he shivered. He had been dreaming of a full-scale battle between the Israeli enclave on the near crest of Mount Scopus and the Jordanian outpost on the wooded height of Augusta Victoria—the very battle, he realized even while he lay asleep, in which Ovadiah Malachi had met his end. He had seen, from his bunker on the southern flank, a stray projectile flying toward the house in which his family now lived. The raw, unnerving whir of the alarm clock had meshed with the dream.

For several moments, he did nothing but stare up into the darkness of the bedroom. It had rained last evening—a wild, driving rain that threw a flapping curtain of water over the rooftops and towers of Jerusalem and sheeted the sidewalks and flooded the streets. But around midnight, when he and D'vora went to bed, the downpour had tapered off and stopped and a brutal, bone-chilling cold had clutched the city in its grasp. Now, outside, one of the harsh December winds that often blew down from the north wrapped its tentacles about the house: it seemed to match the desolation in his heart and, without awareness of the fact, he lost himself in its mournful, menacing sounds.

Suddenly, he started. The luminous dial of the clock on the night table said ten minutes past five, and he realized that his wife was still asleep. Dutifully, he turned and stretched out a hand to grasp her bare shoulder and wake her. But abruptly he changed his mind and withdrew the hand. D'vora had worked late at the hospital last night. She had phoned just a few minutes to six to say that a young soldier had been gravely wounded by sniper fire and that she would be involved in the emergency surgery. She returned home well after ten, having been driven from Ein Kerem by one of her colleagues. After hastily eating the supper he had prepared, which had grown cold and, he thought gloomily, all but inedible, she had sat with Uri in his bedroom and then spent time listening to Ilana play and talking to her about the performance. By the time she finished and wished their daughter sweet dreams, it was well after eleven. Sitting in the living room side by side on the couch, with the storm drumming savagely about them, husband and wife had attempted to converse, but unsuccessfully, for stifled yawns and drooping eyelids had cut their conversation short, and, wearily, they had trudged up to their bedroom.

Arie leaned closer to his hoarsely breathing wife and stared at her shadowy, blanket-wrapped form. A powerful, glowing feeling—like the rosy heat, he thought, that rises from logs burning in a hearth—rose up in him. Men were wont to call such a feeling love, he thought, but in truth, as he suddenly realized, the definition was incomplete and inadequate. A more encompassing description of the emotion he felt would be *love arising from human kinship*. He stared at D'vora's shadow-bound figure under its cover. He heard her labored breaths and the tiny, gasping sighs that moved among them like moths. He smelled the rich yet delicate aromas that came from her woman's skin and woman's parts. He even fancied he could hear the gentle but audacious beating of her heart. And, for the first time since he had wakened from the madness of his dream of war and carnage, he smiled. And the smile, coming uncertainly and almost shyly to his lips, was at once joyous and melancholy.

Like a child—a child younger than his son, Uri, who was now ten, but he could not help himself—he wondered if D'vora were dreaming . . . and if she was, what the dream was about? Was it about how they had first met, D'vora and he, in an outdoor café in Jerusalem on a sunny spring afternoon, when the almond trees were in white, ecstatic bloom and butterflies danced spectacular minuets in the sparkling blue air? Was it about the first time they had made love, in a soft, sweet-scented haystack, in the amber-gold light of a ripe August moon that hung like a lantern in the velvet-black sky above a kibbutz in the south? Was it about their wedding, held outdoors beneath a trembling canopy, when the white-bearded rabbi had chanted impassioned blessings that seemed to remain, like indelible imprints, in the mild, gold-burnished September air? Was it about the birth of Ilana, when he was still on Mount Scopus? Or was it about the birth of his son, Uri, red-faced and flailing and unabashedly bawling out his zest for life for all to hear?

Or, Arie wondered, was D'vora's dream about some dark part of her life, something she spoke about—or even brought to conscious awareness—on rare and isolated occasions? Was it about her childhood in Germany, when the sound of Nazi boots echoed in the streets, presaging the unimaginable horror and destruction to come? Was it about the torture and death of her brother in a Nazi prison or the planned, ordered, clinical extermination of her parents in Auschwitz? Or was it about the terrible wounds, inflicted by Arab marauders who had taken up where the Nazis left off, that she saw and treated in the hospital, or about the truncated young lives that neither she nor her colleagues nor any doctor could save—despite all the medical science in the world? Was it about the Israeli soldier, barely twenty, who had undergone emergency surgery that very evening in Ein Kerem?

Arie bent over his sleeping wife and wondered. Suddenly, not like a child anymore, but like a man, he was possessed by the furious and overwhelming desire to protect the woman he loved and had bound to his life in marriage; to remove, wholly and completely and forever, her distress and pain and anguish and to confer upon her—no, to lavish upon her, as one lavishes upon an infant—infinite tenderness and solace and comfort and sublime peace, none of which was in his grasp to give. Moved to the depths of his being by the desire, he stretched out his hand once again to caress her hair and again, in mid-motion, checked himself. She was exhausted, exhausted to the point of not hearing the alarm, and he did not want to disturb her. *Let her sleep,* he thought, *let her sleep until the very last possible moment.* He would get up and prepare breakfast and eat with Ilana and Uri and wake her just in time for her to have her own breakfast and get to Ein Kerem for her shift.

Cautiously, he drew back and turned to get out of bed. But at that moment, she stirred and sighed. "It's all right, Arie," she said. "I'm up." She rolled over and faced him. "What time is it?" she murmured sleepily.

"Twenty past five."

"Twenty past five? What happened to the alarm?"

"Nothing, darling. You didn't hear it, so I thought I'd let you sleep a while longer, that's all."

D'vora sighed. "I haven't slept through the alarm in years. I guess I was really tired."

"'Tired' is hardly the word," said Arie. Moving close to her, he said, almost fiercely, "D'vora, my darling, I love you."

In the darkness, the last, trembling darkness before the coming dawn, her warm laugh seemed to burst like a flare. "I'm glad you do, Arie," she said softly. "Because I love you, too—very much."

He shifted his body to embrace her and found that her arms were open and awaiting him. Beneath the undulating blanket, their bodies made contact and struggled—hopefully but in vain, as human bodies always do—to break down the barrier of gender that separates them. Locked in each other's arms and entwined in each other's straining legs, they kissed gently and then with fervent, mounting passion. In the predawn stillness of the bedroom, their mingled murmurs crackled cozily in the hearth of awakened desire. Then, at one and the same instant, they broke apart. "Do you . . . think . . . we have time?" whispered D'vora.

For answer, Arie laughed and kissed his wife again and drew her to him. Patiently yet provocatively, with a heightening urgency that engulfed them in its stark, unwithholding fire, they made love until the first, thin, mercurial stripes of morning glinted on the shutter slats. And then they climbed out of bed.

As Arie was shaving in the bathroom, he saw his wife's image in the mirror. Her hair was uncombed and she had just slipped on a blouse, which she was buttoning. There was a look in her eyes that arrested his attention. He turned his head. "What is it, D'vora?"

His wife sighed. "I meant to bring it up last night, but there simply wasn't the time." She brushed an unruly lock of hair from her forehead. "It's about Uri . . ."

Arie put his razor down on the sink. "What about him?" he said.

"Actually," murmured D'vora, "it's about a friend of his." Her husband smiled. "Which one? He has so many."

"The one," said D'vora, "who lives in the house next door."

"The house next door?" Arie stared at her. "Do you mean . . . ?"

"Exactly! The Maleks' little girl—Layleh."

"Oh . . . *that* friend—I see."

"Precisely what do you see, Arie?"

Arie smiled again. "Well, I know, of course, that the two of them have been friends for some time—one can't help but notice them." He laughed and then, after pausing to find just the word he wanted, went on: "One cannot help but notice them *conspiring* through the hedge every now and then. And there are all sorts of other little hints and clues: Uri's rather amazing knowledge of Arabic; his constant questions about why we don't have anything to do with Mahmoud and S'ad, and his unusual interest in Arab history and customs. But why do you raise the issue, D'vora? Is there some problem that I should know about?"

"Areleh," said his wife, "our son Uri is *perennially* in the yard."

"But he loves the treehouse! He has told me a hundred times if he's told me once that it's his refuge—his *special place,* he said."

"The truth is that he seldom goes up to the treehouse. He spends most of his time at the hedge."

"And Layleh——"

"Layleh meets him there: she on one side and he on the other—by prearrangement, I suppose." D'vora cleared her throat. "I see the two of them, laughing and talking—now that I'm aware, I see them quite often, of course—from the kitchen window."

Arie looked thoughtfully back at the mirror. He saw that the shaving cream had dried on his face and mechanically picked up his brush and began to lather his cheeks and chin with forceful, even strokes.

"Well . . ." murmured D'vora.

"Well what?"

"Aren't you going to say anything?"

"Say anything about what?"

"Arie! About this . . . friendship—this relationship—between Uri and Layleh! Don't you have some feeling about it?"

Arie put his brush back in its bowl and picked up his razor.

"*Yashar—dugri,* as they say in Arabic—straightforwardly: my blessings on them both!"

"There's nothing about the relationship that . . . disturbs you?"

Arie caught his wife's eyes in the mirror. "You mean because beyond the fact that they're boy and girl, they're Jew and Arab—is that what you mean?"

"Yes."

The razor slipped smoothly down Arie's left cheek. "Why," he asked, twisting his head to the right, "should the fact that Jew and Arab are friends disturb me in any way? Isn't that what we've always hoped and prayed and worked for? Isn't that what we've always dreamed about and struggled to make real?" Arie tilted his chin upward. "How do *you* feel?" he said.

D'vora swallowed. "They live next door to each other. I guess it's natural that they be friends."

"Then why do you ask me if I'm disturbed?"

D'vora was silent for a moment. Then, with some hesitation, she said slowly: "Because there is . . . *something* . . . *something else* which disturbs me, Arie."

"Well?"

D'vora lifted a hand. "Uri and Layleh live next door to each other and have struck up a friendship. They're children. That's as it should be. But——"

"But what?"

"But you and I live next door to Mahmoud and S'ad, and we are . . ." Her voice trailed off.

"What, D'vora?"

"We are *nothing*. And that's the trouble—that's what disturbs me. In the light—or I should say, the glare—of the children's friendship, our absence—or lack—of relationship with Layleh's parents is strange."

"D'vora——"

"It pains me, Arie, and it must pain the children more so."

"D'vora, it's not our fault."

His wife shook her head. "I'm not talking about fault, Arie; I'm talking about *remedy*."

"That's just the point, D'vora—actually, you're making the point for me. You can *talk* about a remedy, or solution, to the problem for as long as you wish—but there's nothing we can *do* about it! How many times during the years we've lived in this house have we tried, only to be rebuffed? Mahmoud is an embittered man. He's built a wall around himself and his family that no one—not with the best intentions in the world—can breach." Arie gestured with the razor. "Why, virtually nobody ever visits the Maleks—neither Jew *nor* Arab! To all intents and purposes, Mahmoud has become a recluse and has drawn his family into his cave with him."

"I don't agree. I simply refuse to believe that the 'wall' is impenetrable. We've tried in the past to establish some sort of relationship, that's so. But perhaps we didn't try hard enough . . . or use the right approach. And besides—say what you like—we haven't done anything about trying for a very long time."

Arie shrugged. "Perhaps . . ." he murmured. "But still, I think it's useless. Ever since his accident, Mahmoud has seen fit, for his own reasons, to withdraw from the world—whether it be the world of Arabs or the world of Jews. I'm convinced that he isn't going to return."

D'vora parted her lips to reply, but abruptly changed her mind. Arie saw her mirrored eyes glance into the bedroom toward the clock on the night table. "I've got to finish dressing now," she said in a strained voice, "or I'll be late."

Before Arie could say another word, she went out of the bathroom. He heard her moving about the bedroom and then, as he rinsed and dried his clean-shaven face, she went down to the kitchen, and a short while later, as he was putting on a freshly ironed shirt, the sound of her voice—calling out to Ilana and Uri that breakfast was almost ready—drifted up the stairwell. Her firm but gentle voice, calling out in clearly enunciated Hebrew, seemed to be tinged with melancholy, and Arie was upset. He felt sorry that he and his wife had engaged in a discussion about the family next door *al regel achat*—"on one foot"—as it were, and even sorrier that it had ended on a somewhat sour note. Perhaps, he thought, he had been too pessimistic about Mahmoud and too harsh in expressing himself. As he drew on his trousers and went to the closet for his shoes, he resolved to raise the subject once again at the very first opportunity and attempt, if possible, to bring the discussion to a more satisfactory conclusion.

Once dressed, he opened his briefcase and made certain that the file he had brought home with him the day before was in order. Then he drew out a memorandum he had written to the director-general of the Foreign Ministry, which he wished to review before he submitted it that morning. But the discussion with D'vora in the bathroom while he was shaving nagged at him, and he found that he could not concentrate on his work. Certainly, he believed in cooperation between Arabs and Jews. In his mind—and in his heart, as well—such cooperation wasn't an idle dream or nebulous wish: he *knew* very well that it was a reality, a fact of history, since Jews and Arabs had lived side by side peacefully and to mutual advantage in the land of Israel for decades and even centuries. Some Arabs, governed by conscience and a sense of social justice, had risked their very lives to defend and protect Jewish citizens and settlers against the murderous attacks of lawless elements. There was, Arie remembered, the well-known and almost legendary story of an Arab landlord in Hebron who—during one of the riots there—had interposed his body between a band of Arab cutthroats and his Jewish tenants. He had stood defiantly in the doorway of his two-story house, before the muzzles of loaded rifles, and cried out: "Only over my dead body will you touch a hair on the heads of my Jewish friends!" And the terrorists had retreated.

Mahmoud Malek and his wife, S'ad, Arie had always firmly believed, belonged to the vast majority of Arabs who recognized, clearly and indisputably, the basic right of the Jews to live in peace and who wanted desperately—despite all political attempts to manipulate and terrorize them by power-hungry potentates—to coexist, as good neighbors, with the Jews. There was not the slightest doubt in Arie's mind or heart that the Maleks accepted and respected the Arnons and the Israeli people or that they felt anything else but loathing for the violence unleashed against the Israelis by unscrupulous Arab powers. The vacuum or gap or abyss, so Arie felt, that separated the Arnons from the Maleks was absolutely not one of human misunderstanding or conflicting political or social interests, but rather one of personal, intimate disenchantment with life and bitter, convoluted distaste for human intercourse. Mahmoud Malek was a special—a very special—case. Life had stung him, had wounded him, and he wanted nothing more to do with human society. Despite D'vora's well-meaning doubt and her guilt, the Arnons *had,* on repeated occasions through the years, tried sincerely to draw closer to their Arab neighbors; to befriend them; to establish a warm human bond with them. But no matter how vigorously or how often they tried, they had, because of Mahmoud's inflexible attitude, failed. As Arie had bluntly told his wife in the bathroom, they had failed in the past—and they always would fail. Or, Arie thought as he shoved his undigested memorandum back into its file, would they?

When he got down to the kitchen, breakfast was on the table. D'vora, in her white physician's jacket with the red Star of David on one sleeve, and Ilana, in a heavy blue pullover that her mother had finished knitting for her just a few days ago, were sitting in their places. Winter-silvery sunlight flashed in the window over the sink and lit the squares of glass in the kitchen door. The smell of newly percolated coffee was rich in the air. On the crisp checkered tablecloth, spotless utensils gleamed. Arie nodded at his wife and, seating himself, returned his daughter's cheerful salutation. Then, for a long moment into which he poured his undivided attention, he stared at her.

She was nearly seventeen now—a slender, handsome, well-shaped young girl who was, before his very eyes, crossing the threshold of womanhood. She was sensitive, but learning—with a remarkable effort of will—to control her tempestuous moods and to overcome her natural shyness. With an ever more determined sense of purpose, she was turning her asceticism into refined socialization. She was developing with an impassioned zeal the splendid qualities of her mind and her heart that found so ready and so profound expression at the keyboard. He had known his daughter Ilana, as a father knows a child, for almost seventeen years. And yet, as he gazed at her across the table this December morning, it was, he felt, with a surge of insight and affection, as if he were seeing her for the first time in his life.

She looked at him and smiled. "Is something wrong, Abba?"

He scarcely heard her question.

"Abba," she repeated.

Regaining his composure, he shook his head. "No, no," he said quickly, "there's nothing wrong, Ilana—nothing at all——" He broke off, partially because he could not—uncharacteristically, for him—collect his thoughts. There was a sudden, powerful rush of feeling in him, a torrent of mingled love and pride and sheer, untrammeled joy that overwhelmed him like a flood. Ilana was the fruit of his loving union with D'vora. She was the product of the rapport of body and soul which had conceived and nurtured and helped to shape such a child; a marvelously and mysteriously formed being; a blessing for which—if he were to start at this very moment and continue for a thousand years—he would never be able to express sufficient gratitude.

Now D'vora spoke to him. He heard her voice clearly enough, but her words seemed to him to be foreign sounds that made no sense.

She spoke again, leaning forward with a puzzled and somewhat alarmed expression on her face. Reaching into himself with all the strength of his being, he made a fierce effort to grasp her meaning.

"Arie," she was saying. "Are you all right?"

"I'm fine," he murmured. "Honestly, I'm all right! I was just..." But he let his voice trail off, for at the moment he seemed to lack the strength to explain.

His wife nodded. She picked up her cup of coffee and, sipping from it, said, "Did you see Uri on your way down?"

Arie shook his head. "No," he replied, "as a matter of fact, I didn't." He glanced toward the kitchen doorway. "Isn't he still up in his room?"

D'vora shrugged and then, with a sigh, put down her coffee cup. "Come with me for a moment," she said, pushing back her chair.

"What?"

"Don't ask questions, Arie! Just come with me."

Her husband crumpled his napkin on the tablecloth and rose obediently. Grasping his arm, D'vora led him—*k' mo g' di*, like a lamb, he thought wryly—to the kitchen door. Together they stared through the silvery, sunlit glass into the yard.

There, midway down the pale, winter-struck expanse of the grass, was Uri. He was crouching close to the bare-branched hedge, waving his arms flamboyantly and laughing and talking almost without interruption to some invisible presence on the other side.

D'vora squeezed her husband's hand. "Arie . . ." she whispered.

"What is it, D'vora?"

"Arie," she said, "if——" She hesitated.

"If what?"

"If Uri and Layleh can do it, why can't *we* be friends with Mahmoud and S'ad?"

Her husband returned the firm, urgent pressure of her fingers. He stared into her eyes intently and replied, "Perhaps . . . perhaps we can."

Mahmoud had a terrible dream.

He was young—still a teenager, he thought—and he lived in an Arab village to the east of Jerusalem. Somehow he found himself sitting in the goat shed of the village elder with a group of six or seven terrorists who were planning an attack on the Jews. The air was thick with the pungent odor of mingled hay and goat dung. In one corner of the shed, the poorly trimmed wick of a kerosene lamp that stood on the straw-littered floor sent erratic, shivering light and gray wisps of smoke upward. Through the cracks in the roof overhead, distant stars glittered. The faces of the men in whose company he sat were mottled with heavy, leadlike shadow and contorted with expressions of hatred. They gestured fiercely and rolled their eyes and showered yellow-gray barbs of spittle from their lips. With relentless malice, they heaped abuse upon those they called the "Jewish dogs" and pledged themselves—"on our blood" and "on the blood of our fathers"—to revenge themselves, and the entire army of Arab patriots, on the "infidel enemy."

Mahmoud listened with pain to the talk that he had heard all his life. To him, such "poisoned talk," as he put it, was—and always had been—anathema. He had always tried to avoid it, but like the plague, it seemed to be inescapable. He wanted to get up and leave, but somehow he had been compelled, under vague duress, to attend the gathering of conspirators and was afraid to go.

Then, suddenly, it became apparent to Mahmoud that the target of the planned attack was a Jewish family living in Jerusalem on the western fringe of no-man's land. To his horror, he realized that the *fedayeen* intended to carry out their mission against the Arnons. Though he had remained speechless all through the meeting, he felt—with a pang of anxiety that ran through him like a shaft of lightning—that he could no longer keep silent. Springing to his feet from the bale of straw on which he had been seated, he cried out: "No—this cannot be!"

The conspirators stared at him with mingled amazement and disdain. One of them—a heavyset fellow with tiny, red-rimmed eyes and a bushy black mustache who cradled a submachine gun in one arm—got to his feet as well. "Suckling!" he bellowed: *"Ya arse*—how dare you interrupt? Sit down this minute and shut your whimpering trap or I'll——"

But the elder lifted a hand. *"Sh'woyah,"* he murmured; "patience! Let the lad say his piece: perhaps he knows something that we do not."

"He is a born troublemaker," growled the man with the bushy mustache. "We never should have let him——"

"I said, *let him speak!*"

Mahmoud swallowed. "I . . . *know* . . . the Arnons," he said haltingly. "They are good people . . . peaceful people . . . people who deserve to be treated as neighbors and friends."

There was a savage uproar from the others. They raised clenched fists, and the man with the mustache shook his weapon convulsively. But the elder silenced the din with a withering look of command. "I—will not—have this," he warned in a tone of authority that allowed no opposition: "Let the lad continue. I want to see just what he has hidden in his heart."

"It is wrong to attack the Arnons," Mahmoud went on in a voice that grew stronger and more impassioned with every word he spoke. "It is wrong—no, it is shameful and criminal to attack our Jewish neighbors!"

Once again a howl went up. Two or three more of the *fedayeen* rose from their seats. The man with the mustache raised his submachine gun aloft as if it were a banner. "Silence him!" he screamed, thrusting out his purple-red face. "Shut the devil up—you hear that he speaks with the tongue of the enemy!" He waved the gun. *"Ya sidi*—muzzle the dog before I——"

The elder's countenance was grim. He riveted his venomous eyes on Mahmoud's face. "Enough," he said hoarsely. "It is clear to me where you stand and why you speak——"

"Traitor!" roared the man with the mustache, and as the others took up his cry, hurling it with repetitive force into the shifty, smoke-dulled light of the shed, he leveled his weapon at Mahmoud's chest.

Mahmoud stood motionless, facing his would-be executioner. He heard the safety catch click into firing position, and saw the black, obscene, open mouth of the blue-glinting barrel—from which, at any second, death might strike him to the dung-littered floor. For an instant he wondered why he had risen to his feet and bared his true, innermost beliefs. Why had he tried to defend the Arnon family, with whom he scarcely exchanged greetings and had, actually, nothing to do? And why he had spoken out for the Jews, who—along with all the rest of the world—were excluded from his private circle? He knew that for some compelling reason he had felt it incumbent to interrupt the meeting and make the statement he had, but he wondered why he had jeopardized his life when—so obviously—his words fell on deaf ears and ricocheted, like hail from a concrete roof, off closed, demented minds? Then, abruptly from some mysterious place where his strength waited to be summoned into use, a mighty, almost exalting sense of calm came over him. His eyes grew clear, his limbs stopped shaking, his breath slid freely from his lungs. *S'ad,* he thought tranquilly, *I love you, S'ad, and always will. Even when I am dead, I will love you, S'ad. My love is the first . . . and the last gift . . . I have to offer you. . . .*

The man with the bushy mustache tightened his finger on the trigger of his gun. "Coward!" he snarled.

"Coward!" echoed the others, waiting for the burst of bullets that would release their rage.

But the elder stood up. *"No!"* he said in a dull-bladed voice.

"Ya sidi!" cried the man with the mustache, as if in pain. "Let me get rid of this mongrel!"

The elder shook his head. "No, no," he muttered thickly. "It would just be a needless waste of bullets." He lifted a bony, blotch-skinned hand to one cheek and scratched absently. "This wretched boy is of no consequence . . . no consequence whatsoever. He is a flea . . . a louse . . . a scrap of refuse for which we have no further use." He stared at Mahmoud and with contempt said: "Get out, cur! Tuck your tail between your legs and get out of here at once! Go to the Jews, *ya chara,* and lick up their vomit!"

Amid the hoots and jeers and foul utterances of the *fedayeen,* Mahmoud hurriedly left the shed. But he did not go back to his hut. Instead, on a sudden impulse, he crouched behind a large, shadow-swathed cactus and thought about what he would do. The terrorists, he knew, would leave the goat shed soon and head for the Arnons' house. It was up to him—there was no question in his mind—to warn the Arnon family of the impending attack. To get to his destination before the attackers, he had to leave the village without delay. At once, he rose and sprinted forward into the darkness.

At the western edge of the village, the deserted, nettle-pocked ravine of no-man's land began. Bending low as he ran, he moved into it. A harsh, dry wind coming from the east tousled his hair and ruffled his clothing and seemed to push him onward. Overhead, in the murky flow of the sky, the stars tossed restlessly. Ahead, a shadow moved suddenly and his heart contracted—but it was only a jackal gliding furtively away. He kept going, running as swiftly as his legs would take him. His muscles ached and his breath came in painful, labored spurts. He could feel the sweat spreading over his face and neck and shoulders and back. But he had no time to stop.

He had not realized that the village was so distant from the Arnon house or that the terrain in no-man's land was so rough, but if he were to arrive with his warning before the terrorists got there, he could not slacken his pace. At last, before him, out of the swirling darkness, the stone wall that marked the rear of the Arnon property appeared. And then he was able to make out the amorphous shape of the house beyond the expanse of the yard.

When he got to the wall, he grasped its upper edge with both his hands and clambered up. Dust and dirt and loose bits of stone rattled down. He hauled himself—scraping his flesh and filling his mouth with musty, lichenous grime—over the top and dropped down on the other side. Utterly exhausted and gasping for breath, he opened his mouth and cried out.

But no sound emerged.

He took several, staggering steps forward and tried again.

Still, there was nothing.

He was horrified and, gathering all of his strength, tried for the third time.

This attempt, too, was in vain—not a syllable could be heard.

Then, from the treehouse in the branches of the oak tree before him, a voice cried out in Hebrew: *"Mi shamah?* Who's there?"

Mahmoud could not answer.

"Mi shamah?" the voice repeated.

Mahmoud tried desperately to recognize the voice. But he was unable to make out whether it belonged to Uri or Arie or to some unknown Jewish watchman. Red-faced and covered with sweat, he lurched forward and waved his arms furiously. As he drew nearer to the tree, he saw the barrel of a rifle protruding from a loophole of the little wooden hut in its branches. Whoever was inside *had* to understand that he had come as a friend; that he was there on a mission of life and death; that he had risked his own skin to bring a message of warning. If only he could make himself heard! But he knew—with a terrified heart—that it was impossible.

"Mi shamah?" the voice from the treehouse shouted. *"Dabayr o ani er'eh*—speak up or I'll shoot."

Suddenly, Mahmoud hit upon an idea. With a trembling hand, he fumbled in the back pocket of his pants and pulled out a white handkerchief and raised it, fluttering, aloft. Had the watchman in the oak tree seen? Mahmoud had to make sure. Waving the handkerchief from side to side, he lifted a foot to take another step forward. But even as the foot was still in the air, still in motion, a voice inside him—it was a thin, plaintive, beseeching voice that sounded like the voice of S'ad—whispered: *"Mahmoud, no—Mahmoud, you mustn't!"*

But it was too late! The momentum of his forward motion kept him going, and his foot touched the earth and the mine went off! The sound of the explosion smashed with the force of a thousand sledgehammers against his ears, and an enormous sheet of red-tongued flame enveloped his body. For a moment, he was blinded, and then he saw his legs sailing out from under him and up into the black night sky where the white-fanged stars, like sharks, rushed to devour them. His mouth—of its own spasmodic accord—jerked open and now, at last, there was the utterly useless and impotent sound of a terrible scream. . . .

"Mahmoud!"

He kept screaming.

"Mahmoud, darling!"

He wanted to stop screaming, but he couldn't.

"Mahmoud, dearest, tell me what's wrong—tell me what I can do to help you!"

He felt two warm and trembling hands on his shoulders, and he opened his eyes and saw S'ad's terror-stricken face over his. With a shudder that shook his entire frame, he said hoarsely, "I'm . . . all right, S'ad—honestly . . . I'm all right."

"Are you sure?"

He nodded slowly and forced his voice through his half-choked throat. "Yes, S'ad, I'm sure. You needn't be alarmed."

His wife's fingers slid over his cheeks. "Oh, Mahmoud..." she murmured. "I thought——"

He reached up and took one of S'ad's hands and drew it to his lips and kissed it. "I...was dreaming," he said.

His wife sighed heavily. "Do you want to——"

"No, no," he said quickly. "I would rather not talk about it."

"As you wish, Mahmoud."

Suddenly, there was a knock at the bedroom door.

S'ad started and turned. "Come in."

It was Layleh. Her bare feet padded swiftly over the floor toward the bed. "Umm!" she whispered in a disconsolate voice. And she began to weep.

S'ad gathered her daughter in her arms. "There, there, Layleh," she murmured, covering the girl's dark hair with fervid kisses.

But Layleh would not be comforted. "Umm..." she sobbed, burying her face in her mother's lap: "Abu's hurt—I heard him scream."

"No, darling," said S'ad. "Abu's all right. He's perfectly fine."

"I'm fine," said Mahmoud huskily. "I promise you I'm fine—I just had...a bad dream, that's all."

But it took a very long time to reassure Layleh and get her to go back into her room. And even then, S'ad had to sit on her daughter's bed and sing the old familiar songs to her until she was quieted enough to fall asleep.

———————

Ilana had unbraided her hair. The little lamp on the desk in the room she had grown up in spilled light in glistening wavelets down its sleek black folds. Sitting beside her on the bed, Z'ev suddenly reached out and gently began to caress it. Ilana, who had, as was so often her custom, drifted off into her own thoughts, turned and stared at him. Her lips formed a smile, but there was a sober look in her dark eyes.

Z'ev, a tall, strapping lad with cleanly chiseled features and bright, challenging eyes, said, "You were very far away, weren't you, Ilana?"

She shook her head. "No, no," she protested. "I was right here with you—very much with you. I . . . was just thinking."

"Want to tell me about what?"

"About . . . the future."

Z'ev was silent. At length, he said, "I hope . . . that your future . . . includes me."

The two of them had met at a summer camp two years ago when Ilana was almost fifteen. Z'ev was six months her senior, and they had been going together ever since. Now Ilana nodded. "It does include you, Z'ev—you know that." She moved closer to him and went on: "I was just wondering what sort of life we will have: whether we . . . and someday our children . . . will have peace."

Slowly, Z'ev let his fingers slide onto the smoothness of Ilana's cheek. "There's no point in speculating," he said softly. "We'll just have to take life as it comes. The important thing is that we really live."

Ilana stared at him and then suddenly broke into laughter.

"What's so funny?"

"It's not funny, Z'ev—it's absurd!"

"What's absurd?"

"Why, that your name is Z'ev—which means 'wolf'—and you're as gentle as a lamb!"

"I'm ferocious when I have to be."

"Are you, then?"

"Yes! And I'm loving when I'm loved."

"Then be loving," whispered Ilana, putting her arms around his sturdy neck.

After embracing Ilana one last time, Z'ev reluctantly turned and left. The sound of the screen door of the Arnon living room closing did not cause him regret. Instead, he was filled with warmth and a reassuring joy that he would one day in the future take Ilana through that door to be his wife. Buoyantly, he stepped off the porch and began with swift strides his way down the front walk. As he neared the street, a sudden noise behind him made him stop and turn his head. He craned his neck and spotted a shadowy form in the driveway and then, with a smile on his lips, called out: "Uri!"

The shadowy form slipped forward and entered the pale, bluish-white nimbus of light from the nearest streetlamp. Uri had hoped to surprise his sister's boyfriend, and when he spoke, he could not entirely hide his disappointment: "How . . . how did you know it was me?"

Z'ev laughed. "I just guessed," he said jovially. "It was a shot in the dark, no more!" Then he said: "But what are you doing out so late? Why aren't you in bed?"

Uri shrugged. "I couldn't seem to fall asleep," he said hesitantly. "And besides . . . I wanted to wait for you."

"For *me?* How come, *chabibi?*"

Uri shook his head. "Just like that," he murmured.

Z'ev nodded. "I see," he said softly. And then, taking several quick steps forward, he reached out and gently put his arm around Uri's shoulders. "How'd you like to walk me to the bus stop?" he asked. "I don't think anyone would mind, do you?"

Uri beamed. "Definitely not!"

Together, keeping step, the two of them walked up the narrow, winding street that led to the main road. Over their heads were the swarming stars and to both sides the neat, sentinellike rows of cypresses and firs through whose shadow-drenched branches the last bright arrows of light from houses soon to be dark shot out. Uri did most of the talking, speaking of his classes at school and his friends and his treehouse in the yard. Z'ev listened eagerly and encouraged the boy with frequent squeezes of his strong, warm hand. Suddenly, Uri said in an altered, serious tone: "Z'ev, do you . . . like my sister?"

"Very much, Uri."

"How much, Z'ev?"

"Very, very much."

"Enough to love her?"

Z'ev's fingers tightened about his companion's shoulder. His eyes shone. "Yes," he said softly. "Enough to love her." He smiled. "But why do you ask, Uri?"

"Because I hope that one day you'll marry Ilana—and be my brother! That's why!"

They had reached the main road and the bus stop by now and were standing beneath a canopy of silver-white eucalyptus leaves. Z'ev had to clear his throat before he could speak. Then, running a hand through Uri's tousled hair, he said huskily, "But you don't have to wait for Ilana and me to marry, *chabibi*. I already feel that you are my little brother."

At that moment, the city bus came around the bend in the road and held the pair in an embrace of blinding light.

1967

Jerusalem

EVENING.

Supper in the Arnon household was over and the dishes and utensils—washed and dried by Ilana, whose regular chore it was—had been put away, and the table cleaned and the kitchen floor swept—they were Uri's usual tasks. Arie had gone into his study for a while to finish up some work that he had not been able to get to during the day at the Foreign Office, and D'vora was alone in the living room, quietly reading the late edition of *Ma'ariv*, the evening newspaper. The March day had been an exceptionally mild one, forecasting the early and much-desired advent of spring, despite the occasional patches of pearl-gray cloud that had drifted over the rain-weary rooftops of Jerusalem. For once, D'vora had arrived home on time from the hospital. Supper, which she had heartily enjoyed preparing, had been eaten with gusto and appreciation by the family, and the atmosphere at the table had been cheerful and filled with light-hearted banter. Ilana had cut her practice session at the piano short and gone up to her room to write a letter to her boyfriend, Z'ev, who had left the city a few weeks before to begin his service in the army. And Uri—he had forgotten, as his mother noticed, to take out the garbage—had gone dutifully upstairs, without having to be reminded, and begun his homework.

Thus, D'vora had—she could scarcely believe that it had come to pass!—a free hour to herself.

But the front page of the newspaper brought her at once back to reality. As she read, her mood changed to uneasiness. There was a story about the bellicose moves of Egypt against Israel in the south; about Colonel Nasser's threats to exterminate the Jewish state; about troop deployments and political pressures. The three-column photograph that accompanied the story showed an enormous, densely packed crowd in a Cairo street. According to the caption, the Egyptians were chanting "Death to Israel!" and bearing aloft huge banners that displayed the sardonically smiling visage of their dictator and others that were emblazoned with the skull and crossbones. Lower down on the page, there was reportage on an attack against a kibbutz in the north, not far from Rosh ha-Nikrah, that had taken place the night before: a mother and child had been murdered by an exploding hand grenade thrown by Arab *fedayeen* through the nursery window. Almost reluctantly D'vora read on, and her disquiet turned to revulsion and anxiety.

A strange feeling came over her, a feeling that seemed to inject her mind with venom and cut off her breath. It was as if, she felt, she had read these same stories in the Israeli newspapers before, over and over again—the names of the victims and the geographical places involved were different, but the stories were *exactly the same*. And it was something more even than that, it was something far more disturbing and ghoulish— it was as if, she felt, with a shuddering heart and a sensation of despair, the stories she had read in the past and that she was reading this gentle March evening would appear again and again in the future, without relief and without surcease. And it seemed to her as she sat in her Jerusalem living room, in the calm, even flow of the light from the lamp, with the late edition of *Ma'ariv* open on her lap, that to read such stories time after time was the heavy and bitter burden of the Israeli: pillage and plunder; destruction and violence without respite and without consolation.

Last week's assault had been in the south—a band of *fedayeen* had ambushed a bus traveling to Beersheba and, with a hail of bullets from automatic weapons, murdered two of its passengers. Last night's assault had taken two innocent lives in the north. And, she thought as she twisted in her chair, tomorrow's assault might well be against her very own home. Arie and Ilana and Uri and she herself were alive and well and pursuing their peaceful daily tasks—but tomorrow or the day or the week after, one or all of them might be maimed or dead, struck down by a sudden attack of Arab terrorists.

The idea made her recoil, but she could not banish it from

her mind. It wasn't, when she confronted the naked truth squarely, an idea at all: it was a fact of life for every Jew whose home was in Israel. Israel, tiny Israel—no one who did not actually live in the country seemed to realize or care to realize how pitifully small a place it was—was an island . . . no, even that descriptive cliché wasn't accurate; it was a raft—in a vast Arab sea. And there was little or no sympathy with or empathy for Israel among the smugly self-satisfied nations of the world. The totalitarian nations, bound to the power-crazed fantasies of their rulers, were multiplying. The so-called western democracies, despite their pretensions to the contrary, were preoccupied with their own diversions. The Arab countries, mired in their pasts, were inflexible in their unfounded hatred. Where, then, was Israel to turn for understanding and help? To whom were the people of Israel, dedicated to peace and defying annihilation every day they lived, to go for support? And what, as an Israeli woman and wife and mother of two children, was she to do to mitigate her fear and lessen her uncertainty?

Her body doubled over and she placed her hands over her face. It was a foolish, impotent gesture, she knew—the ridiculous, almost self-mocking gesture of a little girl who goes to bed and is afraid of the dark—but, though she was a grown woman and a physician, she could not help herself. She felt alone and abandoned, and utterly exposed. She had hoped, in the gesture, to give herself some small measure of comfort, but as she sat, doubled over on the chair, with her trembling hands laid over her countenance like a mask, she only felt more deserted and more threatened. She did not mean to and she tried vainly not to, but still she thought of her parents and her brother, whose ashes were mingled with the ashes of millions of other Jews who had been murdered in the charnel house of Europe. She thought of her friends and acquaintances who had not managed to escape the Nazi purge and so had been incinerated in the death camps while the world turned its eyes and its heart away. She thought of so many of her young and vibrant and hopeful comrades, the threads of whose beginning lives were abruptly snapped off by the Arabs in Israel. And in the end, inescapably, she came to the realization that the war against the Jews, which had begun in ancient days, was still going on. *There was a war against the Jewish people: that was the truth—*

and no Jew, no matter how much he tried to deny it or how hard he tried to hide, was safe! In Israel, the Jews were defending themselves against their enemies, overtly and proudly. In other lands, they trembled and attempted to ignore the danger. But, so D'vora saw clearly, *all Jews, everywhere, were in danger*.

"D'vora?"

Pulling her hands from her face, she straightened up and saw her husband standing in the doorway.

"D'vora, aren't you feeling well?"

For a moment, she was unable to respond. The weight of what she had been thinking and feeling seemed to crush the breath from her. Then, so as not to alarm Arie, she marshaled her strength and quickly shook her head. "Don't get upset," she murmured. "I'm fine—at least physically, I'm fine."

Arie came slowly into the room and sat down on the sofa, opposite his wife. "And emotionally?" he said, staring at her.

Arie was just being kind, as usual. He knew very well that she was distraught and was simply giving her the chance to recuperate and, if possible, talk about what was disturbing her. She appreciated that. But once again, she was silent. Nodding at the newspaper which was spread, fanlike, over the floor, she said haltingly: "It's the news—I couldn't even finish reading the front page."

Her husband's eyes clouded. "Oh," he said in a tense voice, "that."

Despite herself—she had really meant to get hold of herself; had indeed thought that she had regained control—her eyes filled with tears. "Arie," she said hoarsely, "please forgive me for giving in to myself this way, but I can't seem to help it. Every time I pick up a paper or listen to the radio, there's another account of some"—she turned her eyes away and groped for the words that she did not want but had to use—"some . . . savagery," she went on, "some butchery." Her voice trailed off.

Arie fished in his back pocket for a pipe and at length drew one out. But he had forgotten to bring his tobacco pouch from the study and so was compelled to put it, unfilled, between his teeth. "D'vora," he said, "come and sit beside me."

"I——"

"Come, come," he persisted gently. "I want to be near you."

With a sigh, she rose from the chair and crossed the rug and seated herself beside her husband. But her body was stiff—it felt to her like a stringed instrument that had been drawn too tight—and even when he put an arm around her shoulders, she did not relax.

Arie gazed at her intently. Taking the pipe from his mouth, he said, "We never lie to each other; I certainly don't intend to start now." He cleared his throat. "The situation is grave, D'vora; it's reached crisis proportions. In the end..."

"In the end what, Arie?"

Her husband did not reply immediately; with restless fingers, he twisted his pipe and then, in a voice that was scarcely above a whisper, said: "In the end, D'vora dearest, we shall do...what we have to do."

D'vora's face was pale. Her taut, all but bloodless lips forced the words to emerge. "You mean...war?"

Arie squeezed her shoulder. "War is...an ugly thought," he said softly, "and an uglier reality. But sometimes there isn't any choice. The Talmud says: 'Ha-ba l'horgechah—hashkaym l'horgo. He who comes to kill you—hasten to kill him first.'"

D'vora's eyes widened. "War...again?"

"It looks that way."

"But isn't there a chance that things will...change?"

Arie shrugged. "Perhaps," he said in a lifeless voice, "but I really don't think so."

"So you believe that war is coming," said another voice.

At one and the same moment, Arie and D'vora turned their eyes toward the living room doorway where, with a schoolbook in one hand, Uri stood.

There was a moment of uneasy silence during which D'vora averted her pained glance and Arie gazed fixedly at his son. Uri was nearly thirteen now—the age at which, in the Jewish tradition, a boy becomes bar mitzvah and attains the responsibilities of manhood. He was nearly as tall as his sister, Ilana, and, though broad-shouldered, he was wiry and agile. He had his mother's well-formed facial features and her ready yet somewhat shy smile. But his coloring was his father's, and he had his father's sober, piercing eyes that, though they could express merriment and levity on occasion, never seemed to wholly give themselves over to laughter. Indeed, his classmates at school wryly characterized him, with all due respect, as *bachur she-nolad ba-tzena*—a lad born in austerity.

From his place in the doorway—his parents had no idea of how long he had been there—he met his father's gaze without flinching. And it was he who broke the strained silence. *"Nu, Abba,"* he said. "So you believe that war with the Arabs is coming."

Arie gestured with his pipe. "Hold on there, *chabibi,*" he said slowly. "I never said *it was coming.*"

Uri looked thoughtful. He shifted his textbook from one hand to the other and in a voice that he tried to make sound casual said, *"B'seder, b'seder*—okay, okay—but you did say likely."

Arie nodded.

Now D'vora regarded her son. Though her agitation had not lessened, she no longer betrayed it openly. "Uri," she said in a forceful tone, "your father's tired. Perhaps we ought to postpone this discussion until another time."

Arie's bitter smile—which, like some cruel instrument, seemed to wrench his lips apart—was even more determined. "Too tired to wonder about war?" he mused, more to himself than anyone else. "I'm afraid that is a luxury which we Israelis can ill afford." He jabbed the stem of his pipe through the air. "Uri . . ." he said in a voice that, precisely because of its quiet and measured tone, seemed all the more ominous, "things can't go on much longer the way they're going, if we are to survive." Arie paused for a moment to collect his thoughts. He twisted his pipe on his lap and added grimly: "The conclusion, therefore, is an unfortunate one."

Uri shifted his sandaled feet on the floor. He swallowed and in a voice that was just audible said, "There . . . will be . . . war."

His father gestured lamely. "Unless," he said, "a miracle occurs." He grimaced and his clear eyes filled with anguish. "But," he said in a hollow voice, "we Israelis—we Jews—have learned, at enormous cost, that miracles are few and far between."

"I'm almost thirteen now, and I was only a small child," Uri said thickly, "when the last war broke out. I don't really remember anything about it. My friends at school were small children, too. But some of them——" He could not continue.

"Go on," said his father.

Uri drew a deep breath. "Well," he murmured, "they had fathers . . . and older brothers . . . who never came back."

Arie leaned forward. His lips parted, as if he were about to speak, but he said nothing.

Uri's eyes flashed. "Why did they die, Abba?" he said hoarsely. *"Why?"*

"They died," Arie said firmly, "to defend life. And to bequeathe life to us."

"Fine words," Uri said, "but——"

Arie shook his head. "More than fine words, Uri," he declared with slow, painstaking urgency. "We are the inheritors, Uri, and only our regard for the life that was left for us will say to the dead that we appreciate the gift."

Uri hugged his textbook to his chest; his eyes clouded with puzzlement and hurt and dismay. He wet his lips nervously with little jabs of his tongue, but he did not say a word.

"Well?" said Arie, calling on his son for a reply.

Uri understood the challenge and murmured huskily: "Our gift seems to be . . ." He hesitated, as if he were afraid to finish the sentence.

"Seems to be what?" Arie pressed him.

"Seems to be . . . more war!"

"If that has to be," said Arie, "then it will be."

"But it can't be!" Uri cried out.

Slowly, as if he were compelled to exert all of his strength to do so, Arie leaned back on the sofa, his eyes fixed upon Uri with an unwavering gaze. Quietly, with a patience that seemed almost incongruous in the face of his son's impassioned outburst, he said: *"But it is."*

Suddenly, D'vora rose.

Arie glanced up at her. "Where are you going?"

His wife gestured at the front door. "Out," she said softly. "Out . . . for a little walk."

Usually, he would have asked her if she wanted some company. But this evening he sensed clearly that she wanted to be alone. And that was perfectly fine with him—he understood his wife's mood completely. With a gentle smile, he waved his pipe. "See you later, D'vora," he said and watched her go out.

When he turned his eyes to the living room archway once again, he saw that his son was gone.

———————•———————

Uri locked the door to his room with a fierce, almost violent twist of his wrist and seated himself at his desk. For several moments he did nothing except stare blankly at the wall in front of his eyes. The window to his left, over his bed, was open, and through it came the whispering of an eager yet somehow lazy breeze that blew through the newly budding branches of the oak tree in the yard and meandered on through the thinner, delicate branches of the high hedge. It was a mild breeze that carried in to him familiar and haunting scents of approaching spring. Normally, the delicious sounds and tempting smells would have gladdened his heart and, like the wind itself, made him want to wander. But this evening even the very notion of spring only made him feel sadder and more desolate than he already was. For who could say that this Israeli spring of 1967 would not be interrupted by all-out war?

The talk with his father left him shaken. He knew very well that he felt grief—terrible, frightening, inconsolable grief—but surprisingly somehow it had hardened, like concrete, into a lump in his chest that couldn't dissolve. He was certainly no stranger to sorrow—nobody in Israel, he believed, could claim such a luxury—but never before in his life had he been so completely crushed by its weight.

Like maggots, his worrisome, nagging, unproductive thoughts—the kind of thoughts that led absolutely nowhere and brought absolutely no relief—burrowed into his mind.

Abruptly, as if an electric current had shot through his body, he jerked open the center drawer of the desk and pulled out a sheet of paper. He dropped it on the desktop and reached for a pen. And then, bending forward into the bright cone of light from the lamp on his right, he tried to write carefully:

Dear Layleh,
   I know this letter will disturb you, and I beg you in advance to forgive me for upsetting you. I would like to write gentle, happy, carefree things to you because that is

*the way you always make me feel, but tonight I cannot shake
the sorrow and hurt I feel. I know . . . that you will understand.*

*Just a short while ago, my father said that Israel will
have to go to war again; that we have no other choice. I
argued—to my shame because, dear Layleh, I didn't want
to accept what he said. But I know—and actually knew all
along—that what he said is the truth. It pained me to listen
to him. It certainly must have hurt him to speak. Israel
suffers from constant attacks. The crisis is bound, one day,
to come to a head, and then the guns will begin.*

*I know that we Israelis have no choice. We want peace,
but we must put an end to the attacks. In my mind and in
my heart, I am sure that we must fight and, if necessary,
die to defend ourselves. The thing is, though, that deep
within me, so deep—perhaps in what is called the "soul"—
I feel such . . . fear! The thought of all our young soldiers—
just a few years older than I—getting wounded and dying
terrifies me, and sitting here, alone in my bedroom, I cannot
come to grips with the terror.*

*Dear Layleh, I have never before experienced anything
like this. Perhaps it is only natural and human, but even if
it is, that fact doesn't seem to be of any help at all. The
terror sits inside me like a lump of stone. Nothing makes it
go away. That's really what I'm writing to you about. It's
foolish, I suppose; there's not anything you can do to make
the feeling vanish. But still . . . I wanted to write to you.*

For a moment Uri lifted his pen from the paper and looked
around the room and gazed at the open window, beyond whose
frame the gentle wind blew idly through the darkness of the
mild almost-spring night. Not really conscious of what he had
seen, he leaned forward and continued to write:

*I am writing to you now, dear Layleh, because you are
my friend. Gradually, bit by bit over the years since first
we met at the hedge, we have built our friendship like a
nest. And it is to the nest of friendship that a person flies
when he wants to feel better. I know that you care for me,
dearest friend, and that I care for you—even when we must
sometimes bring each other pain.*

*I suppose I will end now, because I have said what I
wanted to—except for thank you. Thank you for being there
to read my letter . . . and to understand me.*

Once again, Uri paused. He had always finished his letters
to Layleh in the past with the word *b'yedidut*—"in friendship"—but this evening, somehow, that word seemed too weak.
He hesitated for a moment, trying to decide what word he
should substitute for the one that would no longer do. And
then, with determined strokes of the pen, he wrote *b'chibah*—
"affectionately"—and signed his name beneath it. When that
was done, he threw the pen down on the desktop and leaned
back in his chair.

For the very first time since he had spoken to his father
downstairs, he felt relieved. Suddenly, he was able to appreciate the sounds and smell of the wind outside and to think
with pleasure of the spring that would soon arrive and awaken
the land. Even his room was cozy and invitingly safe again.

Breathing deeply and calmly, he sat motionless for several
moments and enjoyed his newfound sense of release. Then he
picked up his letter and reread it. The contents were fine, he
decided—they could stand as they were. But his scrawl was
slovenly and imperfect. Layleh, he thought, might have a difficult time deciphering the Hebrew. With a sigh, he got another
sheet of paper out of the drawer and carefully rewrote the letter,
making certain that every word was clearly formed. When he
got to the end, he wondered for an instant if Layleh would
understand the word *chibah*. He decided that she would—but
if she didn't, she could always, under some pretext, ask her
father, who, as she had told him many times, had a fluent
command of Hebrew.

When, at length, he was done and the new, cleanly written
letter had been inserted in an envelope with Layleh's name, in
Arabic, on it and the old letter had been torn into pieces and
dumped into the wastebasket, he rose and, with the envelope
in hand, went out of his bedroom and descended the stairs. His
father was gone from the living room—Uri could hear the
steady tick-tick of Arie's battered old typewriter from behind
the closed door of the study down the hall. Ilana was back at
the piano, too deeply engrossed in her playing to notice him
passing. He went quickly into the kitchen and, to his surprise,

found his mother there. She was standing by the stove and had just turned on the burner on which the tea kettle sat. "Imma . . ." he said. "I thought you went out for a walk."

"I did go out," said D'vora, "but I'm back." She stared at him. "How about having tea with me?"

He nodded. "Sure," he replied. Feeling his cheeks grow hot, he added, "But first . . . I'm going to take the garbage out."

"Fine," said his mother. "I'll wait for you."

The night was exceptionally mild—almost balmy. The wind swayed the branches of the oak, sighing gently around the walls of the treehouse that Arie had built for him when he was a small child. Overhead, in the inky sky, a full white moon drifted majestically, throwing off a nimbus of light. Uri deposited the bag of garbage in the large trashcan by the driveway and turned. He gazed up, over the hedge, and saw the lighted window of Layleh's bedroom. Like the window of his own room, it was—he saw, to his relief and joy—open. He took several steps forward, in the direction of the hedge and, wetting his lips with his tongue, gave the prearranged signal: a well-rehearsed bird-call that the wind dutifully caught hold of. Then he sprinted across the yard and knelt at the base of the hedge and groped for the stick—over the years, it had been replaced a good many times—and found it and inserted the envelope in its fork.

Then, crouched and expectant, he waited. There wasn't too much time—he couldn't linger in the yard overlong. If Layleh had somehow missed his call or couldn't come, he would have to give her the letter the next day. But he didn't want that. He wanted her to have and read what he had written this very night. It might be silly, but still, that was what he wished.

The minutes went by; he wanted to slow them down, but they kept slipping away from him. He held his breath. There wasn't a sound from the Malek house. And there was no sign of Layleh. The water in the kettle must surely have boiled by now, and his mother would be wondering what was keeping him. He knew he ought to give up; ought to run back into his kitchen, mumbling some excuse, but he couldn't. He seemed frozen where he was. The night breeze brushed his hot face. From beyond the rear wall of the yard, an owl hooted mournfully. More precious minutes went by. His absence was becoming inexcusable—he really ought to go. What if his mother were to call him or come out into the yard and look for him? Despondently, he decided that he had to give himself a limit beyond which he would not stay at the hedge. He told himself that he would count to sixty and that if Layleh did not appear, he would pocket his letter and leave.

At once, he began to whisper: "One . . . two . . . three . . ."

Suddenly, the Maleks' kitchen door squeaked open. A slim, familiar figure, nearly a head shorter than he, slipped out of its lighted frame and flew through the darkness.

He could not restrain himself. "Layleh!"

"Uri . . ."

"Quickly, Layleh, quickly."

"I'm coming as fast as I can."

"Run faster!"

By the time she reached the hedge, Layleh was breathless. "I heard . . . your whistle, Uri . . ." she stammered, "but I couldn't . . . come right out."

"I'm glad you're here, Layleh."

She crouched. "Uri," she panted, "what is it?"

"I have something for you."

"Something for me?"

"Yes—a letter." Carefully, Uri began to twist and turn the forked stick through the hedge. "There," he cried out. "It's through! Do you have it?"

"I have it, Uri!"

"You'll . . . read it?"

"Of course, I'll read it, Uri."

"Tonight? Before you go to bed?"

"Yes, tonight. Before I go to bed."

"Promise me!"

"I promise you, Uri!"

Satisfied at long last, he rose. "I've got to go now," he murmured. "I'll see you tomorrow."

On the other side of the hedge, Layleh got to her feet. "Until tomorrow, then." Holding the envelope to her chest, she turned.

"Wait," said Uri. "Wait just a moment."

"Yes?"

Uri hesitated; then he said: *"B'chibah* . . . it means——"

Layleh's gentle but firm voice cut him off. "I know what it means," she murmured.

As he neared his back porch, a noise made Uri glance up. He halted in his tracks. There above him, silhouetted in the window of her room, was Ilana. For a moment, brother and sister stared at each other. But neither made a sign or said a word.

At length, Ilana disappeared from the window and Uri went into the kitchen. His mother served the tea. But somehow, neither of them wanted to talk and, not given to idle chatter, they drank in silence.

It was nearly midnight. Uri had gone to bed more than an hour ago but had been unable to fall asleep. He had been tired enough to sleep—that is, his body had been tired enough. He had wakened early that morning, even before the alarm had gone off, and gone through his usual routine of pushups and situps on the bedroom floor while the sun brightened the shutter over the window. Declining a ride in his father's jeep to the main road, he had trotted over to his friend Avner's house and walked with him to school. After school, he had played a hard-fought game of soccer in which he had made a major contribution to his team's triumph. Again with Avner, and with several others in his group, he had gone home on foot. When supper was over, he had completed all his chores but one and gone upstairs to do his homework. So his body, rightly, was more than willing to sleep. His mind, however, as he thought wryly, simply did not want to shut its eyes.

Lying in the soft, familiar darkness of his room, he kept thinking. Initially, it was his letter to Layleh that preoccupied him. He kept wondering what her reactions would be when she read it and trying to picture her face. At one point, he almost regretted that he had written, or at least that he had not, after putting his feelings down on paper, torn the letter up instead of rushing out to the hedge to deliver it, because he was certain that his words would disturb her. But as suddenly as the doubt had entered his mind, it left. If a person, so he concluded, could not open his heart to a friend, then what was the friendship worth? And he was certain, if Layleh needed to

share her pain with him—by the spoken or the written word—
she would not hesitate to do so.

Then his thoughts about the letter vanished. He turned from
his stomach onto his back and began thinking of the times he
had met Layleh in secret outside the confines of their divided
yards. Those meetings had been few—pitifully few, if the truth
were told—and infrequent. But he remembered each and every
encounter with clarity. They had met, by prearrangement and
after scrupulous planning, for the very first time in a quaint
little city garden on the northern extremity of their neighborhood. The day had been late in April. Golden afternoon sunlight
had, like honey, trickled down from the translucent sky. Birds
had flitted from the shrubs to the trees and back again. Bees
with plump, amber-black bodies, and scissor-winged dragon-
flies had whizzed through the flower-scented air. Side by side,
gazing at each other raptly, as if they had never before seen
each other, and then shyly averting their eyes, Uri and Layleh
had sat on a little iron-legged bench whose wooden slats had
freshly been painted forest-green. They had talked in hushed
tones and, on occasion, laughed even more mutedly, but mostly
they had just looked at each other, allowing their eyes to adjust
to the images that heretofore the hedge had screened. And when
at length they parted company, they promised faithfully to
meet—"outside the prison," as Layleh remarked soberly and
sadly—whenever they possibly could.

Uri had reserved a special place in his mind for that first
meeting. He could remember every word of conversation between Layleh and himself and each detail of Layleh's appearance, even the most minute. They had at first spoken about
the beauty of the manicured little municipal park and then of
the beauty of the city. "I love Jerusalem very much," Layleh
told him. "It always seems to be straining to fly right up into
the sky! I don't think I'd ever want to live anywhere else. I've
been to the Galilee with my mother to visit our relatives, of
course. And I've been to Haifa and Acre and to Tel Aviv and
to Jaffa. But to me, there's something special about Jerusalem."

Uri smiled. "That's the way I feel," he said. *"Yerushalaim*
is unique. No place in the world is like it." He hesitated for a
moment and then said: "But I wish the wall didn't exist!"

"My grandfather, Abdullah, owned a big house in Sheich

Jarrach," said Layleh. "Father sometimes reminisces about it and describes how beautiful it was. But I've never seen it, of course. After my mother left her village in the Galilee, she lived with her uncle, Hassan Ali, on a little street in the Old City. She often tells me how it was to grow up there as a young girl and what it was like to work in Hassan Ali's jewelry store. How wonderful it would be if the wall *were* gone and the two of us could actually go there and see those places!"

Uri's eyes gazed dreamily into the distance. "Perhaps some day," he said softly, "it will be possible."

"Perhaps . . ." murmured Layleh.

"If only there were peace," said Uri, "we could travel to Beirut . . . and to Cairo . . . and to Amman—and all over the Middle East." He twisted his body on the bench. "It's really queer, when you think about it," he continued, "that I've been to Europe already, but have never been to the neighboring countries——"

"Nor even the neighbors next door," Layleh said sadly. Then her voice became more cheerful. "But peace will come," she said. "It *has* to!"

"I agree, Layleh. It must!"

There was a silence. The two of them stared at each other. At length, Layleh said: "Are you hungry, Uri? I made sandwiches for us. I prepared them early this morning, before my parents got up."

"Really?"

"Really!"

Layleh turned and picked up the paper bag beside her on the bench and opened it excitedly, and then they both ate *baba ganoush,* or eggplant salad, stuffed into the hollows of crisp pita bread, green olives, scallions, and fresh cucumber strips. And for dessert they devoured fat yellow pears whose sweet juice dripped onto their fingers. When the remains of what Uri called their feast had been put carefully into the empty bag and deposited in the litter basket, Layleh said quietly: "Uri . . . I think that it's time to go now."

Uri frowned. "But . . . we just got here."

Layleh shook her head. "It's time to go," she repeated.

"I know—I just wish it weren't."

"So do I, Uri."

"We must . . . do this again, Layleh."

"We will, Uri."

They rose from the bench and left the park and went down a shady street and turned the corner, and then, suddenly,. Uri reached out and took Layleh's hand. The warm, firm contact of their flesh thrilled them and seemed to make further conversation unnecessary. Holding hands, they walked on in silence until they came to the place where they had agreed to separate. Uri squeezed Layleh's hand and, without hesitation, she returned the pressure. The late-afternoon sun struck tiny sparks in her dark hair, and her deep-set, sober eyes were shining. Uri moved closer to her and lightly, like a butterfly coming to rest for an instant on a leaf, he brushed his lips against her smooth cheek.

And then, without a word, they parted.

There had been several meetings after that. One in Independence Park in the fall two years later, when the wind, blustering through the city in gusts, had sent the downed, dry leaves tumbling, as Layleh excitedly observed, "head over heels" on the drab expanse of the grass. Another out near Ein Kerem in May of the next year, when the wildflowers carpeted the outlying hills of the city and butterflies circled—as if on an enormous, invisible carousel—through the glittering azure sky. And still another in November on King George Street, when a sudden burst of rainfall had sent them, hand in hand, into the shelter of a stone doorway.

Each meeting was stamped on Uri's mind like a seal. Without effort and with sharp pleasure, he remembered the expressions in Layleh's eyes and the movements of her hands and body and the subtle configurations of her lips and the softness of her skin and the colors of the dresses she wore and the nuances of her voice. And all of these impressions seemed more real—somehow, infinitely more real and alive and vibrant than they were when he met her, as he termed it in his thoughts, in the shadow of the hedge.

Now, in his room, stretched out on his back in the bed, he no longer wanted to be asleep. His memory offered him such rich rewards that even his body seemed to forget that it was weary. Thinking of Layleh and their clandestine meetings in Jerusalem made him calm; made him peaceful; made him at once sigh and smile; made him warm. With a feeling of serene anticipation, he looked forward to seeing her sometime tomorrow and making plans for their next encounter "in freedom."

Suddenly, there was a knock on his door.

"Come in," Uri called.

But though the knob twisted, the door did not open—he had neglected to unlock it. Quickly, he threw off the cover and crossed the floor. He had expected his father to be in the hallway, but it was Ilana instead. Drawing the belt of her blue robe more tightly about her waist, she said softly, "Can we talk for a bit?"

"Sure—but how did you know I'd be awake?"

"I took a chance," said Ilana. She lifted a hand. "I spoke with Abba before he went to sleep and, well . . . I rather thought you would."

Uri closed the door behind her and sat on the bed. His sister seated herself on the desk chair. She was silent for a moment and then, lacing her fingers together on her lap, said slowly: "I know that your conversation with Abba disturbed you deeply."

"It did."

"But there is, unfortunately, no way around such disturbing conversations."

Uri stiffened. "I know," he said.

"As long as the Arabs are the way they are, we have to be ready——"

"I accept that fact," Uri murmured. "It was just the sudden realization that war seems *inevitable* that got me. Somehow, I've always believed, or always wanted to believe, that we could avoid . . ." His voice trailed off.

Ilana nodded. "I know exactly what you mean, Uri," she said hoarsely. "As a matter of fact, I had much the same reaction when the realization hit me." An expression of pained recollection came into her eyes. "At the time," she said, "I went around distracted. Everyone asked me what was wrong——"

"Did you tell them?"

His sister shook her head. "No," she said, "I didn't. Perhaps it would have been better if I had. But for some reason, I kept it all to myself."

Uri thought for a moment and then said: "I suppose talking

about it brings some relief—but it doesn't change anything."

Ilana smiled softly. "No, it doesn't." Then she said: "Z'ev thought I was ill. I had a hard time persuading him I was all right."

"How is Z'ev?"

"He's fine, Uri. He just finished his basic training." Ilana cleared her throat. "He's in the paratroops, you know." She unlaced her fingers. "I wrote him a letter earlier this evening and gave him your regards."

Uri hesitated for a moment; then he said: "I'm going to join the paratroops myself!"

Ilana stared at him. "When the time comes, you'll see." She shifted her weight in the chair. "Life goes by so quickly," she mused. "I remember when we were children. It seems like only a short while ago, and now, in just a few months, I'll be wearing an army uniform."

An uneasy silence prevailed. To lessen its impact, more than anything else, Uri said, "You'll look good in anything you wear, Ilana!"

His sister did not react. Indeed, she seemed not to have heard him. For several moments she sat motionlessly and without speaking, staring fixedly at the window. Then, rousing herself from her thoughts, she said softly, "Uri—may I ask you something?"

"Go ahead."

Ilana swallowed. "What were you doing . . . in the yard tonight?"

"In the yard? When? What do you mean?"

"In the backyard, Uri—after supper."

"Oh, that . . ."

"Yes, Uri, *that!* I happened to be at the window of my room . . . and I saw you."

"Saw me?"

"What were you doing at the hedge?"

"Nothing."

"Don't tell me *nothing,* Uri Arnon!"

Uri's fingers gripped the edge of his bed. "I—I don't want to talk about it," he said gruffly.

"I think it would be better if you did."

"Better for whom?"

"Better for you, of course! Better for the Arnon family! And better for——" But she did not finish.

"That's your opinion, Ilana."

Ilana grimaced. "Come, come, Uri," she said slowly. "There's really no use pretending. Arie and D'vora and I don't exactly live in another world, you know. You can't carry on a friendship with the girl—or I should say, young lady—next door and think that nobody is aware of it. You'd be far better off facing it, Uri. We *know* what's going on between the two of you."

Uri bit his lip. "What's between Layleh and myself is not something that I want to talk about."

"For heaven's sake, Uri—stop being so defensive!"

"I said I don't want to talk about it, Ilana, and that's it!"

His sister's fingers fidgeted with the knot in her belt. She gazed around the room in silence for a time and then, with an abrupt jerk of her head, faced Uri once again and said: "You're wasting your time."

"What do you mean?"

Ilana shrugged. "You're wasting your time, Uri," she said resolutely. "Nothing can come of it."

Despite himself, Uri blurted out: "Can come of *what,* Ilana? I don't know what you're talking about! Layleh and I are friends. What has to come of it?"

His sister sighed. "You're annoyed with me—don't tell me you aren't, because I know that you are—because I won't keep quiet and you're angry with me, or maybe with yourself because you don't want to face the truth. But I'm going to tell you what I want—and have—to tell you anyway, no matter how you feel! The Maleks are kind people. Their daughter is a lovely girl. But, though they live next door to us, they are kilometers, hundreds and thousands of kilometers—no, they are light-years—apart from us. The Maleks—no matter what you, my dear brother, in your youth and innocence, want to believe— are in one world and the Arnons are in another! And those worlds, Uri, are separate!"

"Ilana——"

His sister ignored him. "We've tried," she went on, un-willing and perhaps unable to check the rapid, tumultuous flow of her speech, "to befriend the Maleks, to draw closer to them;

but our attempts have always failed. In spite of the fact that they have been anything but forthcoming, Imma has invited them and Abba has invited them, and even I—'Ilana the Aloof,' as the rest of you call me—have extended myself. But absolutely *nothing* has ever come of our efforts." Ilana drew a deep breath. "And even if it had," she continued, "even if we had been successful and managed to establish and maintain some sort of relationship, some kind of friendship . . . still, still and all, we would remain in separate worlds: the Arnons in their Jewish sphere and the Maleks in their Arab sphere." Ilana lifted her hands. "That's the way it is, Uri. Don't you understand? *That's the way it is!*"

In a trembling voice, Uri said: "Ilana, I——"

His sister rose. "Now," she said firmly, "the discussion is closed."

"Ilana——"

But his sister was already on her way out of the room.

———

It was well past midnight, Layleh knew, because in the hushed stillness of the house she had heard the chiming of the clock in the living room. She loved the clock. It had been Mahmoud's father's and had been in his house in Cairo from the time Mahmoud was a small boy. She loved its clear, delicate yet straightforward tones, which somehow, as long as she could remember, made her feel safe. Tonight, however, the sounds that drifted up to her through the hushed stairway and hall seemed more melancholy than sweet and only made her feel more vulnerable. Uri's letter, which she had read as soon as she was alone in her bedroom, had crushed her. And the chiming of the clock—proclaiming, with mournful certainty, the passage of time—reinforced her despair.

Indeed, she had reread Uri's carefully penned words a half-dozen times. Perhaps, so she thought, she had hoped to make the meaning of the letter different from what it actually was, but the meaning was undistortably clear: clear as Uri had written it and clear as she had first read it. Her vain desire to obscure it was childish, and that disappointed her. For though she was not yet twelve, Layleh did not consider herself a child. No one, she thought with a sharp pang, who grew up in Israel could be a child for very long.

She was sorry that it had been necessary for Uri to write the letter, but she was not sorry that he had written it. The letter was brutal—it spoke of the necessity for Israel to fight and of young soldiers dying—but she knew that it told the naked truth. That Uri had been able to confide his deepest feelings and fears to her was a sign of how much he trusted her. After the initial shock had worn off to some degree, she had put the letter away in a drawer among the other notes and gifts and mementos that he had, over the years, given to her and which she treasured, and tried to write an answer. But, pell-mell, a host of unruly thoughts and chaotic feelings had descended on her and she found herself unable to put them down on paper in any sort of logical order. So in the end, she had gathered up all of the crumpled sheets of letter paper from her bed and thrown them into the wastebasket.

Now, sitting up against the pillow that was propped stiffly up on her headboard, she had the letter before her once again. She had tried with all of her strength to keep from taking it out of the drawer, but had failed even at that. With bowed head, she stared at Uri's words without reading them. She knew that what she was doing was useless; that it served no constructive purpose; that it was late and she ought to put the letter away in its place and turn out her light and go to bed. But she was not able to break out of the self-induced spell.

The gentle but firm knock on her door was that of her mother's.

She started and turned and, as swiftly as she could, slipped the letter beneath her pillow. Brushing away the tears at the corners of her eyes with the back of one hand, she called out in the steadiest voice she could command: "Yes, Umm . . ."

The door swung inward, and S'ad entered the room. She was wearing a flowered kimono and had her hair wound tightly in braids that encircled her head. "I saw your light under the door," she murmured, "and so . . ."

"I was reading, Umm."

"So late?"

"Well, I couldn't sleep, you see."

"But you have school tomorrow, Layleh. How will you get up?"

Her daughter shrugged. "Don't worry," she said with conviction. "I'll get up on time, I promise you."

S'ad stood silently for a moment, staring at Layleh's pale face. Then she said softly, "May I sit down for a little while?"

Her daughter nodded. "Yes, Umm."

"Here—on the bed?"

"Of course, Umm."

S'ad lifted the skirt of her kimono and seated herself at the foot of the bed. She made an attempt to smile, but her dark eyes betrayed her concern. In a strained voice, she said, "Do you mind telling me what you were reading, Layleh?"

"Why do you ask?"

S'ad hesitated. Then she said quickly, as if she wanted to get it out before she changed her mind: "Because whatever it was, it has certainly disturbed you."

"How . . . do you know that?"

S'ad lifted a hand. "Come, come, Layleh," she said gently, "I'm your mother—and your friend. I *know*."

Her daughter looked away.

"Layleh——"

"I'm fine, Umm. I'm really fine. I'm—I'm tired. I guess I shouldn't have stayed up so late——"

"Layleh, please tell me what's bothering you. Perhaps I can help."

Layleh's head swung around again. Her eyes, brimming with tears, met her mother's gaze. "It's not just what I read that's bothering me, Umm."

"Then what is it?"

"It's—it's the world, Umm!"

"The *world?* What do you mean?"

Sincerely, with a painful urgency, Layleh wanted to explain to her mother what she meant. But again, as when earlier she had tried to write an answer to Uri's letter, a rush of disordered thoughts crowded into her mind. There was so much to say that she did not know where to begin. And what she had to say was so complicated and so snarled that the task seemed beyond her. In a hoarse, half-choked voice, she cried out—more to please her·mother than to satisfy herself: "The world,

Umm—the world of greed and hate and war!"

S'ad stretched out a hand. "Layleh!"

"Don't you understand, Umm? The world of cruelty . . . and brutality . . . and slaughter!"

"Layleh, I——"

But the dam inside Layleh—built up so frantically, with such desperate, painstaking, dogged earnestness—could no longer check the onslaught of her emotions. A wail, like that of a helpless infant, issued from her lips and she began to sob. At once, S'ad jumped up and rushed forward along the bed and, buttressing her body against the half-crushed pillow and the headboard, threw her arms around her daughter and embraced her. "Layleh," she murmured huskily, "Layleh, my darling . . ." And then, instinctively, she began to sing.

Not for the slightest instant did S'ad's daughter withhold herself. Immediately, she drew closer to her mother, as close as her shaking body could go, and, thrusting her head forward, buried it in S'ad's bosom. With unreserved surrender—as if she were yielding up everything in her there was to yield— she gave herself to the encirclement of her mother's strong arms and felt her mother's heartbeat and the warmth of S'ad's body penetrating her own, which seemed to have grown cold and numb. Through the din of her own sobs, which, strangely enough, seemed to her to be coming from elsewhere, she heard the faint snatches of her mother's voice. Gradually, it became clear to her that S'ad was singing to her, and she was able to understand the words and to realize that her mother was singing a lullaby that had been her favorite when she was a little girl. Like tender rain—there was, Layleh thought, no other image that described it so well—the lullaby-of-old, of bygone days when the world—no larger than her home or yard but nevertheless infinite in scope—had glowed anew each day like a magic-lantern slide with a brilliant intensity that no sorrow or fear or malice could dim or distort, the lullaby that she had learned and, in adoring imitation of her mother, sung to her dolls, fell upon her. It soothed and calmed and seemed to cleanse her of grief. Slowly her sobs diminished and then faded away.

At length, she found the voice to murmur: "Umm . . ."

"Yes, my dear," said her mother gently.

"Umm, I . . . love you."

"I love you too, my daughter."

"But I love you so much, Umm—so very much that I can never tell you."

"But you *do* tell me, Layleh."

"How . . . how do I tell you?"

S'ad smiled. She caressed her daughter's thick, dark hair. "Everything about you tells me, Layleh," she said softly. "Your eyes, your voice, your movements, your actions—*everything*, my dear one."

"Honestly, Umm?"

"Honestly, my precious."

Layleh sighed. She lifted her tear-stained face to her mother's and, clearing her throat, whispered: "Umm . . ."

"Yes, Layleh?"

"Umm . . ." Layleh hesitated for a moment and then went on: "Umm, I—I'm sorry that I couldn't explain things to you more clearly."

"It's all right, Layleh. It's fine. Believe me."

But Layleh shook her head. "No, no," she said stubbornly. "I *want* to explain things better to you, Umm! I want you to see . . . to know . . . to understand what's in my heart! Umm, I want—I *need* it, don't you understand?"

S'ad nodded. "Yes," she murmured, "I understand."

"Someday, Umm . . ." Layleh said hoarsely. She swallowed. "Someday I'll be able to tell you everything."

"I'm sure you will."

With a sudden shiver, Layleh hugged her mother. And then she murmured: "I'm tired now, Umm. I think I can sleep."

"Of course, you can, dear."

"Thank you, Umm, for helping me. And good night."

S'ad bent low and kissed her daughter's forehead. "Good night, my sweet girl. May you be blessed with pleasant dreams." Reaching out, she switched off the lamp above the bed and then rose. With slow, precise, practiced motions, as if the fate of the world depended on the care she took, she drew the cover over Layleh and stepped back into familiar darkness. It was only after she had closed the door to her daughter's bedroom behind her and stood alone in the hallway that she allowed her own tears to fall freely.

— ————•——

Through the darkness of their bedroom, Mahmoud said, "Well, S'ad, what was it?"

S'ad had just entered the room. With one hand still on the doorknob, she froze. "What . . . was what?"

"I heard Layleh crying."

"Perhaps you were dreaming."

Mahmoud snorted. "Dreaming, indeed!" he said scornfully. "Why, I haven't been asleep!"

S'ad's hand dropped from the knob and she made her way to the bed. When she had climbed into it and stretched herself out, she said softly, "I'm sorry, Mahmoud, for my clumsy attempt at deceit, but . . . I saw no reason to disturb you unnecessarily." She sighed. "The truth is——"

"That Layleh was crying."

"Yes."

Mahmoud's voice softened. "Why?" he murmured. "What has happened?"

"She . . . said . . ." S'ad's voice trailed off.

"What did she say?"

"She said it was . . . the *world*."

Mahmoud was silent for a moment, but his wife could hear the sharp stream of his breath sliding through his gritted teeth. "Ah . . ." he said at length, twisting his head on his pillow. "The world—so that's it." He laughed harshly. "I knew . . . have always known . . . that one day the ugliness of the world would invade her innocent life, and that the day must not be far off. The newspapers . . . the radio . . . the discussions among her classmates in school—even the half whispered conversations between ourselves here in the house."

Mahmoud paused and then, drawing a deep breath, added: "But what, exactly, touched off this rude awakening?"

"I don't know."

"Nevertheless, you must have some idea, some suspicion, S'ad."

His wife nodded. "I think it was something——" She hesitated.

"Go ahead, S'ad. Tell me what you honestly believe."

"I believe that it was something—I don't know what—from . . . from, well . . . the other side of the hedge."

"From the Arnon boy—from Uri?"

"Yes, Mahmoud, from Uri." S'ad shifted her body under the blanket and drew closer to her husband. "Layleh," she continued, "was up in her room doing homework after supper and then, suddenly, she left the house—I just happened to catch a glimpse of her going out of the kitchen door. And when I looked—I wasn't spying, you understand, I was just——"

"Go on," urged Mahmoud. "Tell me what happened, S'ad, without defending yourself."

"Well, when I looked out, I saw Layleh in the yard, at the hedge. I realized that she and the Arnon boy were meeting." S'ad sighed. "There was nothing more, Mahmoud, until I saw the light under her bedroom door—it was sometime after midnight—and knocked."

Mahmoud cleared his throat. "So," he murmured, "it's still going on—the two of them are still meeting at the hedge."

"You know it's still going on, Mahmoud. They've been meeting that way since they were children, and it's never stopped."

Her husband's breathing coursed erratically into the darkness. He was silent for several moments and then he said slowly: "How ironic."

"What is ironic, Mahmoud?"

"Why, that we should be so aloof—actually, so estranged—from the Arnons and that our daughter should be so friendly with their son." Mahmoud said. "Honestly, S'ad—doesn't it strike you as strange—even a little grotesque?"

His wife had an answer on the tip of her tongue, ready to give at once, but she withheld it until, reaching out with a hand, she touched Mahmoud's cheek. Gently but deliberately, she said: "It certainly is odd, as you yourself admit, but that is the way, my dear husband, that you have arranged matters."

"Arranged matters? What are you saying?"

"Well, aren't you the one who has insisted—despite my protests and the Arnons' repeated overtures—on the aloofness? Aren't you the one who has stubbornly kept us apart from them?"

Mahmoud grasped his wife's wrist. "Yes, yes," he exclaimed quickly, "I am, indeed, the one who has insisted that we keep exclusively to ourselves; that we have nothing to do—except for the proper amenities—with the Arnons. I admit to it openly. And, as you well know, I stand behind my reasons. I made my decision to remain aloof a long time ago. Nothing has in any way altered or transformed that initial decision—and nothing ever will. The world of the Arnons and the world of the Maleks—despite their physical contiguity—do not mesh. Like it or not, S'ad, that is a fact of life in the sad world in which we live, the world which so disturbs our Layleh." Mahmoud's powerful fingers squeezed his wife's flesh. "All of the foregoing I grant you, S'ad. All of the aforementioned I take the responsibility for, S'ad . . . but——"

"But what, Mahmoud?"

"But, my dear wife—and I am certain you will not contradict me—I have never, never once in all these years, encouraged the friendship of our daughter and the Arnon boy." Mahmoud's sudden, brittle laugh seemed, like clay, to break into pieces as it left his lips. "Why, indeed, would I? To what end or for what purpose?" He laughed again, now with naked and unrestrained bitterness. "An Arab girl and a Jewish boy—why, it's ridiculous! I would be a fool to encourage anything like that!"

Despite her resolve, S'ad felt her body tremble. "But Mahmoud," she said in a scarcely audible voice, "they're only friends."

"Friends? It sounds nice, S'ad—it sounds charming, but——"

"But what, Mahmoud?"

"But I don't think it can last, S'ad."

S'ad's outstretched hand drew back from her husband's cheek. Her fingers curled into a fist that cut into her chest. She shook her head. "No, no, Mahmoud," she said hoarsely, determined to speak her mind no matter what the cost. "The friendship between these two young people is natural . . . and good . . . and real. And it doesn't require or demand your or my—or anybody else's, for that matter—endorsement or encouragement. What Uri and Layleh have between them is theirs, and theirs alone."

"S'ad——"

"No, no," declared S'ad with forcefulness. "Let me finish, please! You have made your decision with regard to the Arnons and that is your right—no one disputes it. The shadow of that decision, rightfully or wrongfully, falls over me—I no longer contend it and yield, even if regretfully, to your will. But the friendship of Layleh and Uri is their own private affair." S'ad paused to catch her breath and then added: "Have I made myself clear?"

"S'ad——"

"Yes, Mahmoud."

"Have you said what you wished to say?"

"I have, Mahmoud."

"Then listen to me and listen well." Mahmoud steadied his voice. "In a week," he went on, "or in a month or in three months or in six—I don't know when but I do know for certain—war will come once again to this war-scarred land. War between Arab and Jew. Like an ax it has been hanging in the air, just above our heads. And, like an ax, it will split Arabs and Jews farther apart—even those who for years and decades have lived and worked together. The terrible blade will come down with shattering force, S'ad—and Layleh and Uri may very well find themselves on either side of it!"

"Mahmoud——"

"No, don't interrupt me—it's my turn now, S'ad!" Mahmoud lifted himself into a sitting position. "I know what I'm saying, S'ad, believe me, I do. I have nothing against the Arnons. They are fine people." He waved a hand. "And heaven knows, I have the deepest respect for the Jews. After all, aren't I the man who moved from his father's house in Sheich Jarrach to take his place among and beside the Jews in western Jerusalem? Am I not the fellow who envisioned the dawn of a brotherly civilization in the Middle East, in which Jew and Arab helped each other?"

"You are," murmured S'ad.

But he scarcely heard her. "I dreamed of peace," he cried out hoarsely. "I believed in peace! I wrote for peace! I labored for peace!" He gasped for breath. "But 1948," he went on, "taught me a hard lesson. Let others, I told myself, mouth pretty words and glittering phrases. Let others—well-meaning,

I don't deny, but abysmally deceived—pronounce pious wishes and high-sounding slogans! I, Mahmoud Malek, will have none of it! Better to dwell in the desert camp of reality than to set up my house on some quicksand of illusion!"

Mahmoud paused for a moment and stared down at the motionless form of his wife; a spasm of coughing seized him and he was unable to continue. When he had recovered himself, Mahmoud went on: "The more Layleh and this Uri lad care for each other, the worse it will be if there is a parting. The deeper their friendship, the harder it will be if there is a separation. War—the war that is only a matter of time on the calendar of days—will come, and it may sever once and for all every living bond that bound them to each other. Don't you see that, S'ad? Can't you understand what tragedy the future may hold?"

His wife's trembling lips parted. "Mahmoud——" she began.

But he overrode her. "And," he said huskily, "and what if the roots of their . . . friendship go deeper?"

"What do you mean, Mahmoud? What are you saying?"

"What, my dear S'ad, if their friendship is rooted in love? *What then, S'ad?*"

"Mahmoud, they are *children!*"

Mahmoud's laugh mingled bitterness and amazement. "Come, come, S'ad," he said brusquely, "you surprise me at times! Do you really insist on pretending that the seeds of love do not take hold in the soil of childhood? Are there, then, no childhood sweethearts—no innocent lovers waiting for the time when full knowledge of each other will be theirs?" He laughed once again, and this time the laugh was more like a snarl. "Especially," he added, "in this unique land, where children ripen so early."

"Mahmoud—your own suffering blinds you!"

"No, S'ad. It opens my eyes."

This time, S'ad did not answer. She realized with sudden and painful clarity that she and her husband were merely crossing swords; that their argument was futile and would lead them to no resolution or fruitful end. She was silent for several moments and then, controlling her voice, she said quietly: "And so, Mahmoud, what do you propose to do?"

"About Layleh and Uri?"

"Yes. About their friendship . . . or whatever else you choose to call it."

Mahmoud shrugged. "I haven't really thought about it until this moment," he murmured. "But——"

"But what?"

"But it seems to me that we can—and that we should—warn our daughter of what may lie in store for her if she continues to intensify this . . . this relationship."

"And what about the Arnon boy?"

"Ah, well, we can hope that his parents will warn him as well." Mahmoud reflected for a moment. "Or we can speak to Uri's parents and tell them how we feel."

"We, Mahmoud?"

"Well, that is, perhaps *you* could speak to them, S'ad."

S'ad shook her head slowly. "Not I," she murmured.

"But why not?" countered Mahmoud in a tone of genuine puzzlement. "After all, infrequently as it has been, you have had more to do with them over the years than I."

"It's not the amount of contact, Mahmoud. It's not that at all. It's simply that . . . I don't subscribe to your view! Is that direct enough?"

"But *why don't you?"*

S'ad drew a deep breath. "Because, Mahmoud," she said quietly, "I believe that friendship . . . or love, if you will . . . is stronger than war! The ax, as you put it, indeed, most probably will fall. But it can never—never—no matter how sharp or how cruel its blow—sever the ties that bind people who care for each other."

"S'ad——"

"Yes, Mahmoud?"

"S'ad, I——" But her husband could not finish the sentence. To his astonishment, he found that he had nothing to say.

———

The sun was sinking in the western sky. As he led the two men along the narrow path, now heavy with shadow, that would

bring them to the "dead man's place," Fawzi's heart pounded
with excitement that he was barely able to conceal. In a little
while evening would fall in the Galilee. The rolling hills, still
definable from each other in the ruddy glow of the sunset,
would melt into one amorphous mass. And then it would be
dark and moonless, and the mission—so painstakingly planned
and so long awaited—would begin. Was it any wonder that
Fawzi could scarcely keep himself from crying out?

Inside the mud and stone hut that reeked of stale sweat and
gunpowder, Hussein, without being told, lit the kerosene lamp.
His fingers were shaking and he needed three matches to accomplish the task, but at length it was done. A fist of sickly
yellow light that seemed as thick as wax punched into the
gloom. Fawzi installed himself at the head of the table. On his
right, the man named Mustapha sat. On his left, with his back
to the lamp, sat Hussein. There was a moment of tense, expectant silence broken only by Mustapha's harsh, wheezing
breath and the faint, dry sound of Fawzi rubbing his hands
together. Then, leaning forward, Fawzi said, "Comrades, this
is a fateful night—for us, and for our fellow *fedayeen*, and for
our cause. April is here. The weather is clear. The roads are
dry so that troops may move at an instant's notice. And everywhere, on all sides, the noose of steel is tightening around
Israel! Our web, at last, is intact again. Here, in the north and
in the south and finally, after a persistent struggle, in Jerusalem.
In a short while, the two of you will depart from this village
and make your way across the border and pass on the information our network has laboriously gathered. In due time, as
a result of your mission, a bomb will go off in the Tel Aviv
bus station . . . and so one more stick will be cast upon the pyre,
and we will be one step nearer the conflagration!" He leaned
back in his chair and carefully, as if he were performing some
solemn ritual, pulled a pack of cigarettes from an inner pocket.
Lighting one, he said: "Is everything clear? Are there any
questions about your plan? Don't hesitate, comrades—now is
the time to speak up."

The man named Mustapha grunted. "Everything is clear,
ya Fawzi," he drawled. "I have no questions."

Fawzi stared at him. "You know the route? Be certain."

Mustapha nodded. "I have studied the map you gave me,

ya Fawzi. I know the route by heart, and I know the terrain like the palm of my own hand."

"And your contacts on 'the other side'—you know them as well?"

"Assuredly, Fawzi, I do. I know the contacts as I know my own name. And I know the code words by which we are to make sure of each other." He grinned, baring stained teeth. "Why, I could repeat them in my sleep!"

Fawzi blew smoke into the sluggish light. "Excellent!" he exclaimed: "Splendid!" He turned his head and fixed his dark-ringed eyes on his son. "And you, Hussein," he murmured. "Is there any detail—even the smallest and seemingly most insignificant one—of the plan that you are not perfectly familiar with or do not understand? Do not be shy or embarrassed, my son—this is the moment to ask!"

Hussein's small, puffy-lidded eyes moved from Mustapha's coarse-skinned face to his father's. He swallowed and, almost as if it were painful for him to speak, said slowly: "No, Abu—I have . . . nothing to ask."

"And both of you have committed the information to memory? You are able to recite it—point by point, word for word, at will?"

Mustapha waved a hand. "At will, *ya* Fawzi—at will!"

Despite himself, Hussein winced. "I know it, Abu," he murmured. "I know it as well."

Fawzi drew on his cigarette. "Good!" he said. With narrowed eyes, he went on: "And your weapons—they are in order?"

"In order!" said Mustapha, twisting to one side and patting his flank. "And ready for use if needed!"

"Hussein?"

"I checked my pistol this morning, Abu."

Fawzi was silent for a moment. He glanced at his watch and said quietly: "Then you are . . . set to go."

Mustapha cleared his throat. "Set to go, *ya* Fawzi," he said crisply. "And when the mission is accomplished, to return!" He scraped back his chair.

But Fawzi reached out and caught his arm. "One last caution . . ." he said.

Mustapha remained in his seat. "Speak, Fawzi."

With precise movements of his hand, Fawzi crushed his cigarette into an ashtray. Then, in a voice that was just above a whisper, he said, "Do not be taken prisoners by the Israelis. Is that understood?"

Mustapha guffawed. "Don't worry about that!" he said scornfully.

Fawzi squeezed the other's arm. "I warn you," he said in measured words: "We cannot afford to have the information you carry fall into the hands of Israeli Intelligence. Do I make myself clear?"

"Don't worry on that score."

Fawzi dropped the burly fellow's arm and faced his son. "Hussein," he said hoarsely, "have you heard me?"

Though it was not warm in the hut, Hussein was sweating profusely. He had pulled a large handkerchief from his jacket and was passing it furiously across his pockmarked forehead and cheeks. If he had heard his father's warning, he gave no sign.

"Hussein!"

"Eh?"

"I spoke to you, Hussein!"

"I'm sorry, Abu, I——"

"Neither of you must be taken prisoner by the Israelis, Hussein! Understood?"

His son sighed and, stuffing the handkerchief back into his pocket, murmured, "Understood, Abu."

Fawzi's eyes glinted. His heavy lids fell over them, half-closing them, and for an instant, he seemed to be dozing or in a self-willed trance. But then, abruptly, they popped open and he rose from his seat with surprising agility. "Comrades," he said gruffly, *"zero hour is upon us!"*

It was dark outside; night had erased everything but itself. In the courtyard, the watchdogs—straining on their taut chain leashes—were barking viciously. Fawzi hurled foul words at their shadowy forms. Impulsively, he grasped Mustapha's rough hand and pressed it. "To a successful mission . . ." he murmured.

"To a victorious mission!" Mustapha growled.

Fawzi turned toward his son. "To your first triumph!" he called out hoarsely.

But in the racket made by the dogs, Hussein—who was already halfway across the yard—did not hear him.

------●------

For a time after the pair was gone, Fawzi stood in the paw-torn dust of the yard of dead man's place and did nothing. Aside from an occasional snarl, the watchdogs were silent and the calm, familiar sounds of night in the Galilee floated in the air: the lugubrious braying of a neglected donkey; the dull, repetitive hooting of an invisible owl; the distant laments of a roaming pack of jackals. Overhead, in the moonless sky, scattered stars shone with faint, unconvincing light, like lamps low on fuel. Fawzi pictured his two agents moving, like ghosts in the darkness, up and down the heavy-shadowed hills and through dry, stone-bottomed wadis—moving eastward, toward the border with Jordan. He sensed the obedience that drove them. He heard their thick-soled shoes slipping on the rocky hillsides and crushing the pebbles in the wadis, and saw the sweat popping from their faces and necks and leaking onto the paths they left behind. His heart raced wildly and his hands trembled. If all went well, they would be across the eastern border and safely out of the reach of the Israelis by dawn.

Suddenly, his heart contracted. It was the phrase *if all goes well*—it pierced his mind and stuck there like a thorn. Why had he thought it? What could possibly go wrong? Why should not all go well?

Abruptly, for no logical reason that he could conceive, one of the dogs in the darkness before him began barking. On impulse, he stooped and snatched up a stone from the ground and flung it at the offender. *"Ya, chara!"* he rasped. And he felt relieved when the dog—struck full in the muzzle by his rock—yelped in pain. A wind from the west had sprung up and was now blowing stiffly, slithering through the cacti and rattling the tin panels of the hut's roof. Despite his jacket, he shivered. It would not do, he thought suddenly, for him to continue standing out in the night air like a scarecrow. If he did not occupy his time somehow, his nerves—quite naturally and properly—might begin to play tricks on him.

Accordingly, he turned and reentered the hut, closing the door behind him. Usually, being in the bare-walled, sparsely furnished chamber filled him with a highly charged, almost erotic sense of pleasure. Here, in its austere confines, weapons that had been smuggled over the borders by confederates were unpacked and their parts cleaned meticulously and assembled. Ammunition was uncrated and carefully sorted out and counted. Explosives were removed from the gourds and clay vessels and baskets and sacks in which they had been cunningly concealed and stored, and land mines were painstakingly fitted together and a wide range of booby traps and other lethal devices were skillfully fashioned.

The isolated one-room house on the fringe of the village that had been secured by the natural death of an old man had, at Fawzi's behest, come to be an arsenal of death and destruction. But, as Fawzi knew well, it was more than that—far more. The unassuming, unsuspected structure, approachable by one narrow and tortuously winding path and screened by its high, needle-spined ramparts of cactus, was the center of the web which he had labored so long and with such unflagging energy to spin. Here, in the command post—the "eye of the hurricane," he named it boastfully—which he had created out of the tumbledown shack of a recluse, ordering and directing and financing the necessary repairs, the plans for his unrelenting "War against the Jews," as he called it with vicious satisfaction, were conceived and studied and rehearsed until they were ready to be put into action. Here, on unfolded maps, the routes of terrorist missions were drawn in thick, dark ink that flowed onto the waiting paper like blood. Here, the targets were designated and marked off and encircled in ragged, black strokes. The agents—the savage soldiers, as he termed them, of his campaigns—were instructed in their tasks and drilled, again and again, in the operative details required to perform them. Here, his *fedayeen* were motivated and exhorted and fired up to move out against those whom Fawzi baldly labeled the offending infidels.

This was not the first such mission of slaughter. Nor was it, most certainly, the last. But, Fawzi now began to realize with a sinking heart, there was something about this particular venture—he could not, despite his frantic efforts, guess what—

that disturbed him and dulled, even spoiled, the heady surge of power that, like molten lead, surged through him whenever he was alone.

Gloomily, he paced the concrete floor of the hut. Hearing his footsteps slap hollowly like spent bullets, he paced to and fro. Two or three times, in rapid succession, he lit cigarettes with unsteady fingers and then, after the first tasteless puff, crushed each of them out underfoot. His nerves, which like unruly threads had begun to entangle themselves in the court-yard just after Mustapha and Hussein departed, did not, as he had hoped they would, calm down now that he was inside. His muscles were tense—so tense that it seemed to him they would snap in sudden rebellion—and his mind seethed with a host of vague, disturbing thoughts.

Over and over again, as if it were being beaten out on a drum, he remembered the ugly phrase that had started it all: *If all goes well . . .*

With head thrust forward and shoulders hunched, as if with the weight of what he had so tryingly discovered, he walked toward the table. "Yes, yes . . ." he murmured hoarsely, grasping its edge and negotiating the corner with awkward, uneven steps: "Yes, yes . . . *I see it all now. I see everything clearly.*" He had realized at last, after his demanding, exhaustive travail, what had caused the disruptive phrase *if all goes well* to stick in his mind; to shatter his calm. *It was Hussein, his eldest son!*

Yes, beyond the shadow of a doubt, *it was Hussein who had brought him his pain and robbed him of his elation!* He uncoiled one fist and lifted the hand and gently passed it across his forehead. Originally, the second on the list of his most trusted agents, the man who always worked with Mustapha, was scheduled to go on the mission. But at the last moment, this man, the crafty and experienced Gamal, had fallen ill. Fawzi needed a replacement. As it turned out, none was available on such sudden notice, and Fawzi was faced with a serious problem. Everything was in readiness. His machine of violence was set to move into gear. The clock was ticking off precious moments that could never be retrieved—and he was lacking a man!

It was at that crucial point that Hussein had stepped into the picture. Quite unexpectedly and entirely out of character, he had volunteered to go with Mustapha. Mustapha had protested. Fawzi himself had hesitated. His son, he knew very well, was untested in the field; had never, in all his years, been through even a single ordeal of fire. Hussein's part in the web had been limited to serving as a closely supervised helper in the command post and to running minor errands in and around the Galilee village. On the other hand, Fawzi's son was totally loyal and had never once failed to carry out an order to the letter. Therein, Fawzi found to his consternation, lay the dilemma: whether he should send out an inexperienced youth on such a key mission or call it off altogether.

A discussion had ensued. Hussein insisted that he was entirely capable of executing the mission; that, indeed, he deserved the chance to prove himself. Mustapha objected strenuously, pointing out that even one inadvertent slip on the novice's part might cause the mission to fail and, worse still, jeopardize the web that now, after being so long in disrepair, was perfectly intact. It was up to Fawzi, as commander, to decide the issue.

Sitting in his chair in the hushed confines of the dead man's place, like a king with the eyes of his courtiers fixed upon him, Fawzi weighed the matter in his agitated mind. In the end, crushing out a half-smoked cigarette, he spoke. Staring at his son's eager face and ignoring the heavy scowl on Mustapha's coarse-featured countenance, he had declared hoarsely: "Go, Hussein! Go, my son . . . and raise the banner of your father's will!"

So the dilemma was resolved by Fawzi's uncontradictable authority. But after the pair's departure into the darkness of Galilee, while he stood in the courtyard of the mud and stone house, with the watchdogs swirling about him like restless phantoms, a stubbornly unsatisfied part of the mind had defiantly questioned the wisdom of his ruling.

He dropped his hands and laid them on the table. Resolutely, he pulled out a handkerchief and mopped his face and neck. He reached inside his jacket for his cigarettes and, finding that the pack was empty, crushed it and flung it to the floor. Slowly, he pushed back his chair and rose. Stepping carefully, as if he might detonate a mine, he crossed the room. In the food store, were a number of bottles of arak. He opened one and poured himself half a tumblerful. Within moments, the liquid's welcome warmth mounted to his head. He smacked his lips and quickly drained the glass. A feeling of buoyancy pervaded him as he felt his confidence return. Perhaps, after all, things would go properly. Maybe, when all was said and done, his judgment of his son had been wrong. He glanced at his watch and pictured the two men he had dispatched nearing the border. He felt lighthearted, even giddy and somewhat chagrined—as if his previous anxiety might well have been overstated.

Visions of what he wanted to be the future danced in his muddled brain. He saw Mustapha and his son Hussein, now redeemed in his altered estimation, reaching their appointed destination in Jordan. He pictured them passing on the information that his agents, like patient, industrious ants scurrying to and fro on their quests, had gathered, to the designated contacts. He saw the contacts move out with machinelike precision and relay the information further. At once, as if he were viewing it from some immensely lofty height, he pictured the entire vast web of intrigue he had put together, part by part, filament by filament, come alive with a furied, lethal electric current. And in the end, he envisioned the final and inexorable result of all his protracted plotting and minutely detailed planning and enormous, indefatigable work: *the thunderous explosion of the bomb in Tel Aviv, in the very heart of the infidels' territory!*

He lay down on a cot and glanced over at the lamp; its light blinded him and hurt his eyes. Willingly, now, he closed them. The darkness was comforting, seductive, soporific. He realized, to his surprise, that he was tired, that he was weary to the bone. And why not, after all his toil and travail? Relaxation was his due. A little sleep was long overdue him. He sighed and, with small effort, eased the visions from his spent and overtaxed mind. Like the white-glassed lamp on the table, only one glow remained: a new refrain excited him. *All will go well,* he thought. And then, moving his stubborn lips, he pronounced the calming words aloud: *"All will go well."* And so murmuring, he slept.

The dogs in the courtyard awakened him, their furious barking bursting into his slumber like a grenade. He started violently and opened his sleep-crusted eyes. The lamp had gone out— Hussein, in his incompetence, had failed to refill it with fuel— and the room was pitch-black. At once, he sat up and swung his stiff, cramped legs out of the cot. His head throbbed. His mouth was dry. The harsh, unrelenting barks of the dogs pained his ears. He struck a match and peered at the dial of his watch. *Four-thirty!* Who would be coming to the dead man's place at such an hour? Thieves? Someone from his household—though it was strictly forbidden? An Israeli patrol? Had something gone wrong in the village? Or . . . ? He did not want to continue the thought.

He rose. From the holster at his side, he drew his revolver and cocked it. Cautiously, he moved across the floor, hurling foul epithets at Hussein for the darkness. He knocked against a chair and, with a snarl, threw it to the concrete. At the door, finally, he fumbled with each of the locks in turn. At last, with a groan, he flung the door open. Overhead, in the clouded sky, only a handful of remote stars sputtered. Below them, the walls of cacti loomed like crags. In the courtyard, the shadowed forms of the watchdogs whirled. He stepped away from the doorway and leveled his pistol. *"Who's there?"* he cried hoarsely.

For a moment there was silence. Then a heavy voice answered him exhaustedly: "It's I . . . Mustapha."

"Who? Speak louder!"

"It's Mustapha," came the voice again—but this time it was blurred and barely able to continue. *"Ya* Fawzi . . . help me . . ." he pleaded.

Fawzi shoved the revolver into its holster and ran across the yard, kicking and striking at the charging dogs as he went. At the breach in the cactus barrier, he found Mustapha doubled up on the ground. The burly fellow's garments were in shreds. His face was covered with sweat and grime; his lungs, like punctured bellows, expelled harsh, sickly bursts of air, and his eyes, bugging wildly, were glazed and unfocused. With some last, desperate reserve of strength, he lifted a trembling hand and, wetting his parched, split lips with a yellowish tongue, stammered hoarsely: "Fawzi . . . *please . . . help . . .*"

The veins in Fawzi's temples bulged. He felt a dark tide of wrath and revulsion rise in him and had an all but irrepressible desire to smash the fallen man full in the face—but the urgent and unignorable need to find out exactly what had happened— though he knew very well, with an unbearable certainty, that the mission had come to grief—made him restrain himself. With a discipline that came from somewhere deep inside him— an old, well-tried discipline born of cunning—he said, "Can you walk, Mustapha?"

"No," whispered the fallen man. "I . . . can't . . . take . . . another step."

Struggling against his revulsion, Fawzi bent and got his hands under the other's sweat-soaked armpits. "Here . . . I'll lift you! Get up!"

"I can't, *ya* Fawzi . . . on my life!"

"But you must, Mustapha! I said I'd help you! Come on, now—try with me!"

"*Ai . . . ai . . . ai . . .*" croaked the other. "I am trying, *ya* Fawzi . . . but——"

Somehow, lurching and slipping, the two men, wrapped in each other's arms, managed to get back across the courtyard and into the mud and stone house. Fawzi struggled with his stumbling companion over to the nearer of the cots and then quickly rushed to the door and locked it securely. Bearing the lamp in one hand, he returned to the supine form of Mustapha on the cot and looked silently down. His prized agent's face was cut and bruised, and there were welts, from which blood oozed profusely onto the straw mattress, covering his hands and wrists. But then he saw the worst: the left shoulder of Mustapha's tattered jacket was marked with a large, dark, slowly spreading stain. It was clear that he had been wounded. Fawzi set the lamp on the floor and rose. Steadying his voice, he said, "Tell me what happened. Tell me everything."

Mustapha swallowed. "Water . . ." he murmured weakly.

"In time," said Fawzi.

"Please . . . a drop of water, Fawzi."

"I said, all in good time, Mustapha. First you must tell me *exactly what happened.*"

The wounded man nodded. He ran his tongue over his cracked lips. "We were two hours or so distant," he murmured thickly, "making very good time, when—when . . ." He paused and his lips quivered.

"Go on."

"When suddenly we ran into an Israeli patrol. I motioned for Hussein to get down . . . because I was certain that they . . . had not spotted us . . . but——"

"But what? Speak, *ya* Mustapha!"

"But Hussein panicked. Instead of hugging the earth, as I had signaled him, he ran——"

"He ran? *The dog ran?*"

"Yes, Fawzi, he ran blindly into the night and . . . and . . ."

"Go ahead, Mustapha."

The wounded man sighed. "And of course, the Israelis opened fire. Hussein, he—he was hit in the first burst of fire . . . and he fell." Mustapha lifted a bleeding hand. "I saw him fall with my own eyes, Fawzi. They shot him . . . like a rabbit. . . ."

Fawzi groaned. He bent forward. "Was he dead, Mustapha? Did they kill him?"

The wounded man gazed up vacantly, as if he had not understood or perhaps even heard the question.

"Did the Israelis kill Hussein?" Fawzi repeated slowly, raising his voice shrilly. "Answer me!"

Mustapha gulped. Shaking his head from side to side, he whispered: "No."

"How . . . do you know?"

"I heard . . . Hussein screaming . . . and then . . . I heard the Israelis asking questions."

"And did he answer?"

"What?"

"Did Hussein answer them, Mustapha?" shouted Fawzi.

"Yes, *ya* Fawzi . . ."

"Yes *what?*"

"Yes, he answered. He—he screamed . . . he babbled . . . he said—he said . . . all sorts of things."

"What sort of things did he say, Mustapha?"

The wounded man gasped. "I . . . don't know," he muttered hoarsely. "I . . . don't remember. It was all so sudden . . . so unreal—like a dream, *ya* Fawzi."

"And then?"

"And . . . then?"

"Yes, and then what happened! You must tell me everything!"

Mustapha nodded and, with a snort of pain, laid one hand over his grimy forehead. "And then . . ." he mumbled thickly, "they . . . came looking for me. I—I could hear their boots popping stones and snapping twigs underfoot. I—I could hear them . . . breathing." He cleared his throat and then proceeded: "I knew that I . . . had to make a break for it . . . or be lost. And so I jumped up . . . and ran! I ran with all of my strength." He licked at his lips. "The Israelis shouted after me, but I paid no heed! I just ran, *ya* Fawzi—ran with all of my strength! They fired; and . . . as you see . . . I was hit in the shoulder."

Fawzi was silent for a moment. He drew a deep breath and said: "Did . . . they follow you?"

"Follow me?"

"Yes," said Fawzi. "Did the Israelis come after you?"

Mustapha's eyes clouded. He looked stricken. "I was hit, *ya* Fawzi," he whispered. "I was hurt. But I ran—I ran like the wind itself, never stopping once to rest or look behind. I ran through nettles and through briar patches. I kept beneath the ridges and used the wadis whenever I could and doubled back on my tracks several times. I was wounded, Fawzi . . . I was losing blood all the time . . . but still I went on. I never slackened my pace. I knew that I had to tell you what happened, Fawzi—I knew that at all costs I had to get here and warn you." He forced his lips into a stiff, grotesque smile. "I *must* have eluded the Israelis, *ya* Fawzi! I took short cuts. I used all the tricks I know—they could not have followed my trail." He choked. *"Please, Fawzi,"* he gasped, *"the water . . . now . . ."*

"Yes, yes," murmured Fawzi, "the water . . ."

"Thank you, *ya* Fawzi."

With precise steps, Fawzi crossed the room and—his back to the cot on which the wounded man was stretched out—bent over a large clay vessel. But he did not draw water from it. Instead, he pulled a hunting knife from his belt. Then, cautiously, he turned his head and glanced over his shoulder. Mustapha, breathing erratically, had closed his eyes. At once, Fawzi spun around and on swift, noiseless feet recrossed the room. At the final instant, as Fawzi reached the side of the cot, Mustapha opened his eyes again and glimpsed the flashing steel of the blade above him. A look of horror exploded on his face and he parted his lips to scream. But it was already too late. The knife swooped down through the yellow lamplight and slit his throat from ear to ear.

Fawzi stepped back. "Hussein talked to the Israelis," he murmured hoarsely. "But you won't get the chance." And then, flinging the blood-sheathed knife to the floor, he ran for the door.

———— • ————

From the top of the staircase, his heavy army boots in hand, Arie called down: "D'vora . . . I just saw the postman turn into our walk. Do you want to see if he left anything?"

There was no need for him to finish the sentence. Without drying her hands, his wife, who had the day off from the hospital, rushed from the kitchen to the front door. The postman was just turning back up the street, which was lit by bright June sunlight. He called out a cheerful *"Shalom!"* to her, and, waving back with an impatient hand, she opened the mailbox and found inside the thin brown envelope for which the family had been waiting. As she reentered the house, she ripped the envelope open and called out excitedly: "Arie!"

There was no answer.

Moving forward into the living room, she shouted "Arie, there's a letter from Ilana—come quickly!"

Seconds later, Arie came padding down the stairs. He was barefoot and wearing khakis. "Read it aloud, D'vora," he said. "Let's hear what our soldier has to say."

D'vora smoothed out the fragile sheet of paper and cleared her throat. In a husky voice, she read:

> *Somewhere in Israel*
> *June 2, 1967*

Dear Family,
> *I have a little time to myself, so I'll take good advantage of it and drop you a few words.*
> *First of all, I want to set your minds at ease and tell you that I'm well. Believe it or not, I have actually gotten*

used to army food! It's not half as bad as cynics would have it. I sleep well, too—my cot doesn't bother me a bit. My duties are entirely manageable. They were somewhat strange to me at the outset, but now that I'm fully accustomed to them, they seem old-hat and I can perform without batting an eyelash. To tell the truth, basic training was difficult, and I am both grateful and relieved that that particular part of my army life is over and done with.

I had a letter from Z'ev the other day and was enormously happy to get it. He says he's fine and—in his words— "fitter than ever!" They've picked him for a noncommissioned officers' course, and he's scheduled to begin it any day now. He asked to be remembered to all of you at home— especially to Uri, whom he calls his "little brother." That brings to mind our marriage and, as I write, we are still in the process of setting the month and the exact day. Just for the record: I'm for September. Z'ev is for October—he says he likes cooler weather.

I've met a lot of new people here at the base. And— though you all know me as the eternal introvert—I've made quite a number of new friends. Abba is right: our army life binds us together, no matter what our origins or backgrounds, and in many ways we behave toward each other like the members of a family. Before I left for service, I worried a lot about the loss of my music. But—wonder of wonders!—there's a battered old piano in one corner of the dining hall. I don't know—and neither does anyone else— where it came from or who brought it here, though I bless him or her every day. It gives me the chance to play occasionally. In this austere setting, among the guns and the ammunition and barracks and barbed wire, it's strange, almost eerie, to play Mozart and Beethoven and Schubert and Chopin: but everyone, including myself, accepts it as a fact of Israeli life.

The situation is tense. All of you read the papers and listen to the radio and know very well what is going on around us. But, like all good Israelis, we have learned to take things in stride. As Abba always says, Ein breirah— *there isn't any choice! So we go about our appointed tasks, taking each new day as it comes, and try—though it's hard sometimes—not to worry about what will be in the future.*

*My chief complaint is that I miss all of you terribly—scarcely
a night goes by without my dreaming that I'm back in Jerusalem, at home—especially Uri. I regret now, very much,
that I didn't spend as much time with him as I might have,
and have made up my mind that I will behave differently
when we are together once again.*

*I think—and hope—that I will get leave soon, but in
the meantime, nobody has given me a written guarantee.
Please know that I love all of you more than I ever said . . . or
ever, for that matter, will be able to say. Keep well. Think
of me. And love me in return.*

Yours,
Ilana

Wiping her eyes, D'vora looked up. "Well," she said softly,
"that's it."

Arie said nothing. Then, drawing a deep breath, he said,
"Come here."

"What is it?"

Arie extended his arms. "Come here," he repeated.

D'vora hesitated. She shivered and then slipped into his
embrace. "Arie," she murmured, pressing her cheek against
his chest, "Arie . . ."

"D'vora . . . darling . . ."

"Arie, it's so hard . . . so terribly hard. Ilana is gone. And
now, this afternoon . . . you will go."

Her husband forced a laugh. "It's just reserve duty, dear.
The usual boring routine—why, I'll be back at home before
you know it."

"You'll be away a month."

"But it will pass in a flash. You'll see!"

"I hope so."

"What do you mean 'hope'? I *promise* you, D'vora—and
you, above all people, know I always keep my word."

His wife opened her mouth to speak, but suddenly, caught
helplessly in the storm of emotion that had been building up
since she had lifted the lid of the mailbox, she began to weep.

"There, there," Arie murmured, kissing her hair: *"Yihiyeh
tov*—everything will be all right!—you'll see." He hugged her
closer and then, in a slow, tender rhythm, began to rock her
from side to side, as one rocks a child that must be comforted.

But it took a long time for D'vora to stop crying. At last, half-relieved and half-ashamed of her outburst, she did. Drawing back, she said quietly: "See what I've done, Arie—your shirt is all stained."

Her husband nodded. "That's okay," he said with a smile that he hoped was convincing. "I'm the commanding officer, you know, and can dress as I please."

It required no small effort for D'vora to smile in return.

As Uri turned from the narrow dirt path and approached the schoolyard, a familiar voice called his name. He turned and saw just to the left of the path, standing in front of a large, scraggly-barked eucalyptus tree, the figure of Z'ev. "It's you," he cried out, "it's really you!" and broke into a run.

Tall and sunburnt and wearing his red paratrooper's beret slanted across his head, Z'ev smiled broadly and enfolded Uri in a fierce bearhug.

Uri was beside himself. "Z'ev—when did you get here? How long can you stay? Do you know that Ilana has finished basic training?"

Z'ev laughed. "One question at a time, *chabibi,*" he said warmly, ruffling Uri's hair, "and let's take the last first: of course, I know that Ilana has finished her basic training—we write to each other practically every day. As to how long I can stay, not long—but certainly until the bell for the first period rings." Z'ev reached over and adjusted the strap of the Uzi slung over his shoulder. He nodded toward the grassy highway embankment. "My command car is parked just a few meters up the road," he went on. "I was driving through the city and left it there about ten minutes ago. I figured I'd hop out and see if I could catch you on the way to school. And I did!"

"You mean you won't be coming to our house at all?"

Z'ev shook his head. "Sorry," he said. "Not this time. I've got to be off again *achad-shtaim*—one-two! But the first real leave I get, I'll be at your house for a while—don't you worry about that."

"Promise?"

Z'ev's smile flashed in his deeply tanned face, but his eyes were serious. "I promise. Now, then, tell me how everybody is."

Uri cleared his throat. "We're okay," he said. "Imma's working hard at the hospital as usual. Abba's going on maneuvers today. As for me—I'm stuck in school."

Z'ev touched Uri's chest with a finger. "Make the most of school," he said. "I wish now that I had tried harder."

But Uri scarcely heard the other's words. He clutched Z'ev's arm. For a moment he hesitated and then he said: "Z'ev—will there be war?"

"Nobody knows, Uri."

"But what do you think, Z'ev?"

The paratrooper's eyes narrowed. "I'll tell you one thing, Uri," he said slowly. "If war comes, we are ready." He saw the look that his words had brought to Uri's face and quickly grasped the boy's shoulder and pressed it. "Don't stay up at night worrying, Ureleh," he said. "You know what we Israelis always say: *Yihiyeh tov*—everything will be all right."

"But is there any way——" Uri began.

Z'ev cut him short. "How's the treehouse getting along?" he said briskly. "You and I had some great times up there, remember?" He chuckled. "Remember the time the bee sailed in and you panicked and almost fell out of the tree and I grabbed you at the last instant?"

Uri shrugged. "I never go up there much anymore," he mumbled.

From the school building, the harsh clang of a bell cut through the morning air. Z'ev glanced down at his watch. "Uri——"

"I know—you've got to leave."

"Right, *chabibi*. Now, give me a hug—a tight one!"

Uri squeezed the other's torso with all his strength and felt Z'ev's arms all but crush the breath from him. And then, at the same instant, both of them suddenly let go. Uri stepped back and Z'ev moved several steps toward the highway. "*Shalom*, Uri," he called out: "Be well. We'll see each other again before you know it."

"*Shalom*," muttered Uri, but then his throat closed and he could say no more. He stood in silence, motionless, watching the paratrooper in his crisp khaki uniform and high boots swiftly ascend the embankment. As he neared the top, Z'ev turned and shouted back: "Give my love to your parents, Uri." And he waved.

———— • ————

During the noon recess, in the dusty schoolyard, Uri's friend Avner sauntered over. Although he was several months younger than Uri, Avner was very tall for his age and for this reason jokingly called *Gamad*—"Elf"—by his classmates, a nickname he accepted with good-natured tolerance. The June sun was strong, and Avner's thickly freckled face was flushed and almost the color of his disheveled mop of brilliant red hair. As he halted in front of Uri, there was an amused gleam in his almond-shaped blue eyes and the hint of an ironic smile at the corners of his thin lips because he saw that his friend was lost in a daydream and not even aware that he had approached. Lifting a hand before Uri's face, he snapped his fingers. "Hey, Uri," he exclaimed. *"Hitorrayr*—wake up!"

Uri started. "Avner . . ." he murmured with a sheepish grin. "I'm sorry. I——"

"No need to apologize, my friend—I know you too well!" Avner laughed. *"Mah nishmah*—what's doing, Uri? I haven't seen you the last couple of days."

"We're fine. D'vora's busy at the hospital. And my father's leaving for reserves today."

"Mine left yesterday."

Uri hesitated. Clearing his throat, he said: "Things . . . don't look good, do they, Avner?"

The other grunted. "They look rotten!" he said.

"Do you think there will be a war?"

The features of Avner's long, narrow face seemed to tighten. His eyes narrowed and he shrugged. "I try not to think about it," he said gruffly.

———— / ————

When Uri returned from school sometime after four, there was a dusty jeep with a Star of David emblazoned on its hood parked in front of the house. The driver, a lanky youth with an unruly

mop of blond hair, was dozing behind the wheel. Uri stared at
him for a moment and then continued up the walk and went
through the front screen door. He found his parents in the
kitchen.

D'vora was wearing a housedress and an apron. His father
was in full army uniform, with a holstered revolver hanging
from his webbed belt and his pants tucked neatly into high,
freshly polished boots. On the spotless tiles of the floor, a
tightly packed knapsack stood. "I'm home!" Uri announced.

Arie lowered the mug of tea he was holding in his hands.
"Just in time!" he said.

Uri nodded. "I know," he murmured. "I saw the jeep outside." He swallowed. "I ran all the way, Abba—I didn't want
to miss saying good-bye."

Arie turned and put his mug down on the sink counter and
said briskly: "Well, then, let's get on with it, shall we?" Stepping forward, he enfolded D'vora in his arms. "Shalom, my
dear," he said in a crisp, businesslike tone: "I'll see you soon."

"Shalom," said his wife, attempting to maintain her composure. "Take good care of yourself."

Arie turned and put out a hand. "Uri—shalom! Keep the
home front secure."

Uri pressed his father's warm, firm fingers. "Shalom, Abba,"
he said with all the cheerful casualness he could command.
"Don't worry about anything here. I'll take charge!"

"I'm certain that you will, son. I have every confidence."
Arie bent and lifted the knapsack and swung it over a shoulder.
He smiled once—a smile that seemed to vanish almost the
very instant it was formed—and then, without another word,
he left the kitchen. A moment later, the screen door opened
and banged shut. And then, after what seemed an interminable
length of time, the motor of the jeep parked outside the house
started up and he was gone.

Mother and son stood staring at each other for several moments; it seemed that neither one wanted—or dared—to break
the deep silence. At length, D'vora cleared her throat and said,
"There's a letter from Ilana, Uri. It came just after noon."

"May I read it?"

D'vora reached into the pocket of her apron. "Here . . ." she
murmured.

Uri read the tightly formed, cramped scrawl on the brown sheet of paper slowly, as if each written word had some secret meaning. When, at length, he finished, he did not hand the letter back to his mother but laid it on the kitchen table, where it was still in plain view.

"Well," said D'vora softly, "what do you think of your sister?"

Uri swallowed and tried to conceal his emotion. "I'm proud of her," he said. "I think she has adjusted to army life." He hesitated for a moment and then added almost gruffly: "Everyone seems to be in the army—I wish *I* were too!"

D'vora's eyes filled with pain. Quickly, she turned and pretended to busy herself at the sink. When she felt that she was able to speak once again, she said, "Would you like something to eat, Uri?"

"No, thank you, Imma—I had a big lunch. I'm going up to my room now. I have loads of homework."

"Supper will be ready around six. I'll call you then."

"Good enough, Imma. See you at six!"

Through the window of his bedroom, the late-afternoon light of the brilliant June day filtered in. Carelessly, Uri tossed his schoolbooks onto the desk and seated himself in the chair. He had, indeed, a number of formidable homework assignments, but he seemed to lack the will, or even the strength, to begin even the first of them. For a time he sat in his place and fiddled with a pencil until he broke its point. He rummaged in his drawers to find a sharpener, but it was nowhere to be found—neither was another, usable pencil. At last he admitted to himself that it was useless to continue. With a sigh, he flung the pencil down and rose and went wearily over to his bed.

Stretched out full-length on his back, he half-closed his eyes. Bright little barbs of waning sunlight pricked at his eyelids. He thought of Ilana and wondered what she was doing at the moment. Then he thought of his father and tried to reckon how far the jeep was from the house and in which direction it was traveling. Where was Lieutenant-Colonel Arnon's unit posted? In the north, where the Syrian guns looked ominously down on the Galilee from the Golan Heights? In the east, where the red-kaffiyehed soldiers of Jordan's Arab Legion were? Or in the south, where Egyptian troops faced the Israelis on barren desert flats? Arie had spoken many times of the Arab "noose" that encircled Israel. Now, in his mind, Uri could envision what his father meant: on three sides, hostile Arab armies were poised for what they openly proclaimed was a "war of extermination"—and on the fourth side, to the west, where the sun was at this very moment sinking, was the sea. There were many nations on the earth, Uri realized painfully, which could *decide* whether they would fight a war or not. But Israel, surrounded by ruthless enemies and hemmed in by the ocean, had no choice: if she were to survive, *she had to fight!*

Two powerful feelings struggled for expression inside Uri. One was a feeling of fierce pride: a feeling of utter defiance in the face of overwhelming odds, an almost mystical sense that no matter what the cost and how difficult the struggle, Israel must and would prevail. The other was a feeling of crushing despair that stemmed from the knowledge of how much young life must be lost and how much suffering must be endured. Ilana's letter had casually, almost blithely, spoken of imminent "leave." But Uri did not really believe—given the steadily worsening military and political situations—that there would be any leave for his sister for a long time to come. And Arie had left the house for his "reserve duty" in a matter-of-fact and even routine fashion, with a proper, cheerful little kiss for his wife and a businesslike handshake for his son; but Uri knew quite well that it was impossible to forecast exactly when his father would return.

If full-scale conflict erupted, the entire world, as Uri had always known it since childhood, would collapse. Something else, something fearful and wholly outside the scope of his imagination, would replace it. No one—no one on earth—could promise that Ilana and his father would come back from the war well and intact or if, in fact, they would come back at all. No one could guarantee that he and his mother would emerge unscathed, or even alive. And what about Z'ev, Ilana's fiancé, and all the others who were in uniform? And what about those who were not—the civilians, the men and women and children of Jerusalem and Tel Aviv and Haifa and Safed and Tiberias and Hadera and Rehovoth and Beersheba and Eilat? Could anyone, with assurance, proclaim that they would live? When the bombs started falling and the shells began to scream and the bullets flew like leaden hornets, chaos would come.

And nobody could foretell what would come out of that chaos.

Uri shuddered. His thoughts were too dark, too painful to bear. They crushed him like enormous rocks. He wanted desperately to escape the rubble in which they had entrapped his anguished heart. He opened his eyes. His wristwatch—Arie and D'vora had given it to him on his twelfth birthday—said twenty to six. He sat up. There was just enough time, he reckoned, to talk to Layleh before supper. Swiftly, he crossed the bedroom floor. If only she would hear his signal and come to the hedge to say a few words to him, he knew he would feel better. Layleh was always an antidote for bad thoughts.

In the hallway downstairs, he heard his mother in the living room. Though the house was spotlessly clean, she was cleaning again. It was a way, he knew, for her to relieve her tension. Fresh lamb stew was cooking on the stove, its rich, appetizing odor permeating the kitchen. Noiselessly, he slipped through the rear door and went out into the yard.

Pink oleander and scarlet-purple bougainvillea were in full bloom, and at the base of the almond tree, rotting blossoms formed an ivory-brown rind. In the branches of the oak, which stood in the center of the thick green lawn, the treehouse, now weather-worn and badly in need of fresh paint, seemed to glow like some tempting but long-outgrown refuge of childhood dreams. Uri glanced nostalgically at it for a moment and then faced Layleh's window—which, disconcertingly, had its pale blue shutters closed—and then he gave the familiar signal call. He repeated it a second time and then hurried over the grass. He squatted and was about to signal once again when suddenly he noticed a small envelope tucked into the hedge. He drew a sharp breath. Layleh had left him a message.

Carefully, he reached into the tender-leafed branches and drew the envelope out and, with impatient fingers, ripped it open. He unfolded the single sheet of paper and read what Layleh had written:

Dear Friend,
    We received a letter today telling us that one of Mother's sisters is unwell. The family has asked us to come at once and help out. So Mother is packing and soon we'll be on our way to the Galilee.
    I don't have the time to tell you how much I will miss

you, dearest friend, but I am sure you can guess. Some years ago, you were away in Europe and had the same experience. Think of me as I shall think of you.

Until we meet again, I send you my fondest wishes. May they keep you well and safe!

Affectionately,
Layleh

Uri reread the note and then thrust it into a pocket. He turned. It was almost six and time for him to go into the house. But he did not want to go into the house. He did not want to go anywhere. . . .

———— · ————

That night, after Uri had gone to bed, D'vora could not seem to find a place for herself. Like a caged animal, she paced the living room from end to end, glancing repeatedly, almost obsessively, at the piano where Ilana always played and at the worn-backed chair where Arie always sat and read the late edition of *Ma'ariv*. After a time, she went into the kitchen to make herself yet another cup of tea but changed her mind abruptly and turned off the flame under the kettle before the water came to a boil. More than anything else because there was nowhere else to go, she went upstairs and into her bedroom. It was nearly midnight and her body was tired, but her mind was wide awake. Besides, she loathed the thought of getting into bed without Arie. She tried reading a medical journal, but the words seemed to jump around like frightened grasshoppers. She switched to a novel that was currently popular, but closed it almost as soon as she had flipped open the cover. At a loss, she turned on the radio, but after five minutes of the finale of the Verdi Requiem, the news came on. She had heard the news at eleven and there were no late bulletins, and so she turned it off. She was due at the hospital early and had to be up at a quarter to five. There really was no choice—she had to go to bed. Wearily, she got undressed. The sight of her naked body in the mirror on the bathroom door alarmed her in some strange way, and she hastened to slip on a nightgown.

She never had any trouble falling asleep—Arie used to say jokingly that she could doze off in the midst of an earthquake—but tonight she tossed and twisted without result. Every sound from the yard caught her attention and roused her. And, eerily, the house seemed alive with unnerving creaks. She always slept on her stomach, but now, for some inexplicable reason, the position would not do. With a groan, she turned onto her back and made a concerted effort to fill her mind with pleasant things.

Memories of her courtship came back to her. She remembered trips she had taken with Arie and conversations—almost word for word—they had had and landscapes they had seen and admired and things they had bought and which had long ago disappeared from the house. She recalled the births of her children and things they had said and done when they were small. She thought longingly of Uri's forthcoming bar mitzvah and of Ilana's impending wedding and for the dozenth time made a mental list of the guests who were to be invited to each event.

Gradually, she relaxed, the sharp edges of her mind softening as her thoughts grew blurred and incoherent. At length, with a grateful sigh, she fell asleep. For a time she slept undisturbed, and then she had a recurring dream. In the dream, she was a small child, with bright, green eyes and long, meticulously braided pigtails—much like Ilana's, only they were blond. She was alone in her little bedroom, in her parents' two-story house in Berlin. Though her windows were shut tightly, she could hear the blaring sounds of a brass band in the street, but the strident music both frightened and depressed her. She wished desperately that it would stop, but it went on and on, as if the German musicians would never tire.

Suddenly, there was a knock at her door. She started and called out agitatedly: "Who's there?"

"It's I," said her brother's voice.

"Come in, come in," she cried.

"But the door is locked!" protested her brother in an amused tone.

Quickly, she jumped out of bed and ran across the cold floorboards on bare feet—she hated how it felt—and opened the door. "Come right in," she murmured.

Her brother was ten years older than she. He was tall and
slim and good-looking, with dark, wavy hair and a very white,
unblemished complexion and keen, soulful eyes. Just above
his upper lip, the adolescent fuzz of a little mustache had begun
to sprout. "I saw your light on," he said in his resonant voice,
"and decided to pay you a visit." His smile faded and an
expression of concern came over his handsome features. "But
it's late—why aren't you sleeping?"

D'vora shrugged. "I can't . . ." she murmured.

"But why not?"

"I just can't—that's all."

"Come, come," said her brother. "There must be a reason."

She shook her head adamantly.

"D'vora . . . come on, you can tell me."

She swallowed and then, feeling her cheeks grow warm,
said haltingly: "Well, if you have to know, it's . . . the music."

Her brother looked puzzled. "What music?" he said. "What
music are you talking about?"

"There's a German brass band in the street. It's coming
closer. Don't . . . you hear it?"

Her brother shook his head in astonishment. "I don't hear
anything at all," he murmured with a frown that always, in
D'vora's estimation, made him look more charming. With quick,
graceful steps, he strode past her bed and went to one of the
windows and lifted the shade. "I don't hear anything," he said
softly. "And I don't see anything." He turned his head and
stared at his sister and, with a gentle, half-amused smile on
his beautifully curved lips, added: "Perhaps you fell asleep and
had a dream."

But in her dream—the same dream that she kept having
over and over again since first she had come to Israel—D'vora
knew that she had not dreamed of or imagined or invented the
German band, with its heavy, lugubrious, oppressive sounds,
the sounds that so crushed and terrified her. She *knew*, as she
knew that she lived and breathed, that the band was in the
street outside her parents' house and that it was coming relentlessly and doggedly closer; that behind the band were soldiers—soldiers in steel helmets and high, black boots. When
these marching, automaton-soldiers reached the door of the
house, they would enter and seize her mother and her father

and her brother and take them away. Then the band would play while her family burned in German ovens! And finally, as it always happened in the dream, she told her brother what she knew would happen—because that was exactly what came to pass—and wept as she spoke and begged her brother to listen to the truth.

But her brother, with his dark, wavy hair and shining-dark eyes and sensitive, bemused smile and lean, sinuous body, just stood by the window and shook his head. "No, no," he murmured in a tone that was at once perplexed and admonishing. "You're mistaken, dear D'vora; there's nothing outside. No band, no soldiers—absolutely nothing at all."

When D'vora opened her eyes, the gray, cobwebby light of dawn was filtering through the shutters of the bedroom window. Instinctively, she reached out for her husband, but where Arie should have been there was nothing.

———•———

On the fifth of June, the Israeli air force, almost to the last plane it could call to its command, flying under strict and unbroken radio silence, pulverized the all but completely grounded Egyptian air force, and armored units of the Israel Defense Forces plunged into the Sinai in the wake of the blow. In the north, where wildflowers ran riot over the prancing manes of the hills, Israeli forces smashed into the massed armor and artillery and infantry of the Syrians and the Iraqis. The Israeli government pleaded with Jordan to remain out of the conflict, but when shells from Hussein's army in the east began to fall on the houses and streets of western Jerusalem, a massive counterattack by Israeli units drove into the Old City and into Judea and Samaria.

A noose of steel, Uri thought— meant to crush and destroy the Jews, to choke and exterminate them—had been drawn about Israel. Now, in the first week of June, the thunder and fire of war, always and unfailingly the signs of its chaos, had enveloped that noose. Arie and Ilana were gone from the red-tile-roofed house at the end of the sleepy little winding street in Jerusalem, the "house with the hedge." They had been swallowed up—as if people with those names and those lives had never at all existed—in the chaos of war. No one could predict how or when they would come back, or if they would return at all.

D'vora was on round-the-clock duty in the hospital in Ein Kerem, the hospital to which ambulances, with red lights flashing and sirens screaming, seemed to stream in a never-ending procession and toward which helicopters, bearing the wounded in their bellies, flew like huge insects day and night. Uri had his time—his dragging, interminable, irksome time—in concrete-walled air-raid shelters beneath the same earth to which the stricken had fallen, leaking blood like sand from the shattered hourglasses of their bodies; and in which the dead, severed for all time from their loved ones and their companions, were buried.

Uri had his duties, along with his schoolmates and friends—digging trenches in the mild June sunlight under the squadrons of fighter planes that streaked ceaselessly through the azure sky, and filling sandbags and packing food and medical supplies and repairing the shelters. He was busy in mind and body, but he was busy like a machine whose well-oiled parts worked with faultless precision around the frozen core of emptiness in his heart. As if it were a sponge, he tried, desperately and stubbornly, to squeeze some feeling from it—but there was nothing to be had.

He ate with neither taste nor zest. He slept disjointedly and only for short periods of time. He did these things because he needed to do them—not to stay alive, because the war had savagely and abruptly disrupted and shattered life as he had always known it—but to keep functioning. War required him to function. Everyone seemed to tell him that and, neither believing nor disbelieving those who told him, he performed his tasks with an automatic, persevering insistence. He saw D'vora sporadically and briefly—for a time she was not his mother but someone called Dr. Arnon who tried the best she could and often failed, as he well knew, to snatch the wounded back from the magnetic shores of death. She was pale and drawn, and the familiar spark of joy was missing from her eyes, and sometimes her usually steady fingers trembled uncontrollably. When she spoke, her voice was hollow and unreal, as if she, too, were a machine of war.

Meanwhile, in the south the Israelis were pushing deep into the Sinai Peninsula, racing toward the Suez Canal; in the north, they were up on the Golan Heights, from whose emplacements the Syrians had poured down a murderous rain of shells on the valley below; and in the east, the Jordanian army was reeling in the face of Israeli armored assaults. One after another, like the shells that were flying, the radio broadcasts were interrupted by bulletins, the newspapers filled with little else but accounts of the fighting. Through the streets of Jerusalem, army convoys moved as planes roared through the skies on their never-ending missions. Everywhere, there were soldiers in battle dress— soldiers with haunted eyes and the unmistakable stamp of war on their hardened features. And although day followed day and night succeeded night, it was not time passing in the usual, human sense. It was something else—one constant, unchanging second . . . one unending year . . . ten thousand eternal years: it was no-time; *it was wartime*.

Uri never went into the yard. He moved around the house, avoiding—as D'vora had avoided, after they had left—Arie's and Ilana's favorite places, but never went into the yard. Sometimes, through the kitchen door or the window over the sink, he glimpsed it, but he never went out. The grass was there, green and tender in the warmth of the June sun, as well as the treehouse nestled in the branches of the thick-leafed oak, and the bright green wall of the hedge. On the first day that the Jordanians committed themselves to the conflict, shells had fallen in no-man's land, but the shrapnel had not touched a thing in the yard—all was intact, as it had always been ever since Uri could remember. Yet *something* was different. War had made it different, and Uri could not bring himself to go there.

Through all this, there was neither word from Arie nor Ilana, nor word or signal from the other side of the hedge. Uri tried not to think about his father or his sister—these thoughts always brought him to the blind wall of a conclusion too painful, even in imagination, to bear. Sometimes, especially at night, he thought about Layleh. But though he felt close to her as he always had, since the first day they had met, she seemed to be at a vast, unspannable distance—like the tiny image seen through the wrong end of binoculars. He wondered if he would ever see and talk to her again; if the two of them would ever, in the freshness of early morning or in the stillness of dusk, meet at the hedge and share their intimate experiences and the musings of their souls. He had no answer to his questions, none at all. *War had the answers. But war spoke in a language that human beings could not understand.*

From the sky—a great, drifting, peaceful roof over the earth—Arie, on a reconnaissance flight with fellow officers, saw the Sinai. With its cratered mountains and savage crags, it looked like the moon. But, as he and his companions well knew, it was enemy territory that had to be taken—taken at the inescapable cost of limb and life. And they, together with the men they commanded, were the ones who had to take it.

That night, in his tent, whose canvas the wind shook fitfully, Arie dreamed that he was with D'vora. They were sitting at a small, checker-clothed table in a Tel Aviv sidewalk café. Opposite them, at the curb, the delicate leaves of a ficus sapling danced to a rhythm that they alone noticed and understood. People walked slowly on the bright, sunshine-stroked pavement, seeming to drift by, like skiffs in an invisible current. Old, bearded men wearing broad-brimmed hats and long caftans and young men with muscular legs in shorts and gaily dressed women with bemused smiles on their eager lips and ebullient children with tousled hair and scraped knees and elbows. D'vora and Arie were sipping wine—red wine which the sun, probing the glasses they held uplifted in their hands, turned brilliantly and mysteriously to deep ruby-fire. For a long time, they had not uttered a word to each other. They had just sipped their wine and watched the steady parade of passers-by and stared across the table into each other's eyes. Actually, at the moment, nothing needed to be said; or, rather, everything *was* said in the glances they exchanged. Spring had come to Israel, the spring of flowing sap and kindled desire that, somehow and in some way, held, by the sheer virtue of being in existence, its own satisfaction. Peace was there—limitless, horizonless peace that stirred and fired and set free the human spirit. And, crowning everything, fitting the jumbled pieces of human striving and suffering into a meaningful mosaic, D'vora and Arie were together.

That was it! *They were together.* What more was there to say in the face of that eloquent reality? Divining—and, more than that, anticipating—each other's needs; grasping each the other's essence; understanding each other; sympathizing and empathizing with each other; strengthening each other's weaknesses and helping to repair each other's flaws; supporting and stimulating each other; adding each to the other's existence as the players in an orchestra add to the fullness and richness of the composite sound: that was the heart of their togetherness. And that was what was wholly and unequivocally understood and shared in the silence—the perfect and sanctified silence—between them.

But it ended. Perhaps it had to end. And, as so often happens, it happened suddenly. A shadow—thick and dark and ominous—fell across the sky like a slab of slate. The colors faded from the cheerful tablecloth, the leaves of the ficus becoming gray, the wine in the glasses the two lovers held growing dull. The passers-by, wary of the impending storm, scattered and disappeared from sight, leaving only the deserted slag of the sidewalk.

D'vora looked up. "But it's May," she said in a tone of astonishment. "There's no rain in May. I . . . don't understand it."

Arie shook his head. "I don't understand it either."

The sky writhed with ugly, roiling clouds that, merging to one gigantic mass, made a glacier of darkness. It grew still darker, until it was pitch-black. Thunder growled. A cold wind howled through the street, rattling the store windows and ripping at awnings and scattering scraps of paper like chaff. At the curb, the sapling bent dangerously. D'vora's eyes filled with alarm. "Arie!" she cried out. "What's happening?"

"I . . . don't know. . . . " He reached across the table to take her hand, but she was already pushing back her chair and rising.

The wind increased in violence, wailing with a ferocious, unearthly voice. The tablecloth began to lift and flap. Though Arie tried to catch them, the two glasses—only a moment ago held in calm lovers' hands—fell over, spilling the remains of their wine. Suddenly, like an enormous spear, a bolt of light-

ning flashed from the black shield of the sky and split the
buffeted ficus. D'vora screamed and, without warning, ran
from the café. "D'vora," called Arie. *"Wait—come back!"*

She was already in the street, covering her face with frantic,
struggling arms, trying to fight the force of the wind. Arie
rushed forward, but the gale held him back. "D'vora!" he
shouted.

If she answered, a clap of thunder drowned out her words.
And then, in an instant, a curtain of icy rain that turned to a
barrage of hail descended. Once again, Arie tried to leave the
café, but he was hurled back. Beyond the shattered halves of
the sapling, he had one final glimpse, in the hideous glare of
lightning, of D'vora on the far side of the street. Her dress—
the dress he had bought with her only the day before in a sleepy
little Jerusalem shop—was in shreds. Her long blond hair was
flying. Her graceful arms, as if shot through with electric current, were outstretched. Her mouth was open in an inaudible
shriek. He sensed how terrified she was and how much she
needed and wanted him to come to her. *"D'vora!"* he bellowed
in despair.

And then she was gone!

With a jerk, as if someone had touched not his flesh but his
heart with a cattle prod, Arie awoke. The wind, still prowling
across the desert flat like a restless animal, was tugging stubbornly at the canvas of his tiny tent, as it had been when he
fell asleep. Wearily, he pulled on his boots and laced them up
and strapped his holstered revolver to his waist and got into
his battle jacket. His dream had filled him with longing and
despondency. Some insidious voice that came, he thought bitterly, from behind the cobwebs in his soul, whispered that he
might never see D'vora again. Or Ilana—or Uri—or the beautiful, gracious house with the hedge—or the shining city of
Jerusalem that King David had built in ancient days.

There was a lump, a hard, choking, indissoluble knot, like
a chunk of concrete, in his throat. He was a grown man, a
husband and the father of two children; he was a soldier—a

lieutenant-colonel in the defense forces of Israel—and yet, on the very threshold of battle, he wanted to cry. Because of a silly dream in which he had been separated from D'vora and because of a fork-tongued voice within him that he could not, no matter how hard he tried, ignore or silence. But it was more than that, he realized as he bent to pick up his helmet from the earth; it was because of the life the impending battle would demand and take that his tears implored him for release. It seemed absurd that he wanted to weep in advance for the wounded and the dead. And yet—he could not deny it—it seemed only natural and right. For a moment, he wavered. He was close, so very close to sweeping away the last barrier of restraint, so close to succumbing, so close to letting the tears spill from his eyes——

Suddenly a voice from outside the tent called, "Colonel Arnon!"

At once he ducked and, carrying his helmet by its strap, pushed through the flap. Dawn was about to break. To the east, far beyond the silhouetted hulks of the tanks, the sky trembled before the onslaught of the new day's light. Lieutenant Eren, unhelmeted and carrying an Uzi submachine gun in one hand, gave him a casual salute. *"Boker tov,"* he said.

"Boker or!" said Arie. "Assemble the men."

In parade formation, in front of the waiting tanks and armored personnel carriers and dust-sheeted command cars and dwarfed jeeps, Arie stood and gazed out over the ranks of the men whom he would lead in battle, the men who would live or die under his orders. For a moment, under the desert sky which the fiery antennae of the June sun would soon probe, he stood in silence. A part of him might well have left it that way, might have left it at the silent communion of a commander with his men on the brink of combat. But, with an urgency and insistency that were even stronger, Arie donned his helmet, buckled the strap, then cleared his throat to speak. "Men," he said in a firm, even voice that shot his words from his mouth like quills, "I'd like to talk with you for a few moments before . . . we go." He set his hands on his hips. "Israel is the one place on the earth where we Jews have our sovereignty; where we can express ourselves; where we can shape our destiny; where we are a majority and exercise control over our lives.

As in the days of yore, new enemies have arisen to set the sword of extermination at our throats. As did our forefathers, we have risen to thrust the hostile forces back. As David faced the colossus Goliath, so do we now confront the Arabs.

"Behind us are the civilians of Israel. Men and women and children whose lives we protect. In Europe, not many years ago, we had no army and we were denied the right to fight. Our civilians—six million of them—were herded into death camps and burned to ash. Europe is a vast graveyard, soaked with the tears and blood and packed with the mortal remains of Jews who could not fight for themselves. Here, in Israel, it is different.

"No Israeli wants to be here today; none of us wishes to do battle; but the Arabs have called for our destruction. The Arabs have given us no choice but to repel them. We men of Israel have a heavy burden on our shoulders, but we also have the privilege of defending our lives and the lives of our loved ones. *Soldiers of Israel* . . . I call upon you to seize the opportunity and turn the tide of war to victory.

"*Acharai*—after me!"

And, so saying, Arie strode toward his jeep.

———————

That night, in his command tent, Lieutenant-Colonel Arie Arnon sat alone. Flushed with the swift and overwhelming triumph of their attack, his junior officers—those who were still among the living—had departed but moments ago. And yet to their commander, still with his helmet on and his revolver pressing heavily on his thigh, it seemed they had been gone for days or months or even years, seemed almost as if he had been alone forever and somehow always would be. The desert night, lit by stars scattered like white-hot coals across the sky, was silent, since the wind had abated. In one corner, a submachine gun of Russian make, taken from a dead Egyptian major, was propped against the sloping canvas. On the floor, where black-marked maps were scattered, a Coleman lamp blazed with fierce white light.

For a time—he could not reckon how long—Arie sat motionlessly on an empty fuel can and stared into space. The day's assault, spearheaded by his unit, had been faultlessly planned and devastatingly—to the last, minute detail—executed, and the victory had gone to T'zvah ha-Haganah l'Yisrael—the Defense Army of Israel. But Arie, who had been first into battle and last out of it, the man who had spurred and directed it, the man on whose shoulders and whose conscience the onus of command had lain, did not think of the battle. At this moment, this lonely, isolated, postvictory moment, the wounded were on their way to or in hospitals; and the dead, wrapped unceremoniously in tagged bags, were on their way to burial. But Arie, who had ordered and led them into combat, did not think of his losses. He thought of nothing—of nothing at all. His mind was as numb as his body.

It was a strange and, at first, an unrecognizable sound that roused him from his stupor. Something in him—something connected to the numbing emptiness that had him in its power—wanted to rebuff the sound; wanted to reject it; wanted to destroy it altogether. The sound was excruciatingly painful because it reminded him that he was alive—and, in his present state, he seemed to be *somewhere outside of life*.

He winced, trying to push the sound away into oblivion, *where there was no feeling*. But stealthily the sound seeped into his ears, his mind, into the essence of his being. And *something else* inside him—something connected to the fervor and fullness of life—was attracted to the persistent sound and responded. Unwillingly, he found himself listening—listening intently, as if what he heard was the first sound ever.

What was he hearing? Reluctantly but inescapably, he listened and applied himself and strained to make himself comprehend. For a while, he could not—the sound was foreign and undecipherable. And then—suddenly and with a clarity that burst in his struggling consciousness like a signal flare—*he knew!* Someone, one of the soldiers in his unit, was singing! The voice was high and clear and steady, and it pierced the canvas of his tent like the blade of a knife. Such a voice—such a warm, rich, full-throated human voice! Such a song—such a plaintive, sweet song! Where was the singer? *Everywhere*, Arie thought, *and yet—nowhere!* Where was the song? *In the midst of the camp*, Arie thought, *among the squat*,

*monstrous, shadow-thick shapes of the unmoving tanks and the
stationary armored personnel carriers and hush-muzzled guns
and exhausted, sleep-hungry men curled up like fetuses in the
snug wombs of their sleeping bags.* Arie did not know whose
voice it was. He had absolutely no idea who was singing, and
yet—and yet it seemed to belong to *everyone . . . even to himself!*

Arie shivered. Suddenly loosened, his body stirred. With
the song in his ears, flooding his mind, rolling like a river into
his heart, he reached into the inner pocket of his battle jacket
and drew out a worn leather wallet that had been emptied,
before he had left his house in Jerusalem, of everything save
for three worn photographs. One by one, he held them before
his eyes. The first was of D'vora: she was in her white physician's jacket, standing on the front lawn. The second was of
Ilana: she was sitting at the piano in the living room, about to
play. And the third was of Uri: he was squatting at the base
of the oak in the backyard, with the treehouse above him in
its branches. "My dear ones . . ." Arie murmured. "My beloved
ones . . ."

And then, understanding at long last—finally and incontrovertibly—that he would release them, Arie's pent-up tears
fell like living rain.

———————————

D'vora had come home from the hospital—just to get away,
she told Uri, just for a few scant hours, to see him and to talk
to him and, as she took pains to add, to reassure him. But she
had ended up falling asleep at the kitchen table. When the horn
of the car that had come to pick her up and return her to Ein
Kerem sounded outside the house, he had hesitated to waken
her. But he realized he had no choice and so, regretfully but
with gentle insistence, he grasped her shoulder and shook her.
She apologized profusely, saying over and over again that she
had not intended to doze off but that exhaustion and the irresistible desire to shut everything off had taken her unawares.
Uri told her that it didn't matter; that he understood. But still,
even on her way to the front door, she kept excusing her

behavior. Outside, on the porch, in the silver-haloed light of the June quarter-moon, she held him close and kissed his forehead. "I'll see you again soon," she murmured. *"Shalom."*

It seemed queer, in this time of war, to use the word, but nevertheless he did. *"Shalom,"* he said huskily. "Take care of yourself, Imma, and . . . take care of our soldiers." He stood and watched the car swing around on the narrow dead-end street and drive off. And then, uneasy in the strained and lonely immensity of the night, he went back into the house and locked the door behind him.

For a time he wandered aimlessly from room to room, like some animal, he thought wryly, that is unable to find a safe place to settle down. Then, wearily, dragging his feet like blocks of concrete, he trudged up the stairs and went into his bedroom. He had meant to read, but abruptly the desire left him, and as he lay stretched out full-length in his clothes on the bed, it occurred to him that he was utterly drained. He had spent the best part of the day digging a trench with his classmates at school, and his tired body was now giving vent to its protest. Dutifully, he closed his heavy-lidded eyes and, just as his mother had unintentionally done in the kitchen, fell asleep.

"Umm . . ." said Layleh.

Her mother did not reply.

"Umm!" she repeated, reaching out in the darkness and grasping S'ad's shoulder: "Umm . . . wake up . . . please."

S'ad opened her eyes. "Eh?" she murmured. "Who's there?"

"It's I, Umm—Layleh."

"Yes, yes—of course! Is something wrong?"

"I had . . . a terrible nightmare, Umm. I dreamed that a bomb fell on our house in Jerusalem and that Uri was killed!"

"It was just a dream, darling."

"But it was so *real,* Umm! I *saw* the bomb falling down through the sky . . . and I saw the house explode! The roof collapsed and Uri ran into the yard—his clothes were on fire— *he was burning,* Umm! He——" She shuddered and began to weep.

S'ad moved closer to her daughter and enfolded the girl in her arms. "There, there, darling . . ." she murmured. "It was only a dream—I promise you! There's no need to worry, my child. Uri is fine."

"But how can you promise me, Umm, when you really don't know? *How——?*"

"I know . . . I know . . ."

"But tell me how you know—*you must tell me how!*"

S'ad hugged her daughter tightly and kissed her hair. "My heart tells me so," she whispered. "And my heart never lies."

"Never, Umm?"

"Never, my child."

Gradually, the sobbing subsided, and Layleh lay still in her mother's arms. The one-room house, which belonged to S'ad's ailing sister, was profoundly quiet—only the pensive barking of one of the village dogs outside its mud and stone walls disturbed the silence. S'ad waited for a time and then, relaxing her hold on her daughter and drawing back on the bed, said softly, "There, my dear one, now you, too, know that it was merely a dream. The house in Jerusalem is fine. Your friend Uri is all right."

"I . . . wish . . . I could be certain, Umm."

"You can be certain, Layleh."

Layleh said nothing. Then, hesitantly, she murmured: "Umm——"

"Yes, my child."

"Umm, I don't want to stay here in the Galilee. I want to go home."

"We will go home, my dear."

"When, Umm—when will we go home?"

"When the war is over, darling."

"When will that be, Umm?"

"Soon, Layleh darling, soon."

"But how can you tell that it will be soon, Umm?"

"Because wars can't last forever—they must come to an end." S'ad patted her daughter's tear-stained cheek. "Now, close your eyes," she said gently, "and try to sleep."

Layleh did try, but her efforts were in vain. The strained silence and intense darkness of the village house—which seemed to penetrate and disturb her very being—and the persistent memory of the dream in which Uri had burned to death on the other side of the hedge kept her wide-awake. She changed her position several times and forced her eyes to close more tightly. But sleep would not come. At last, with a sigh, she said: "Umm——"

"What . . . is it, Layleh?" her mother said hoarsely.

"Umm . . . I miss . . . Uri."

"Naturally, my child—I'm sure that he misses you as well."

"I want to be with him!"

S'ad did not respond immediately. At length, when she had collected herself, she said slowly, "You care for this Uri very much, don't you, Layleh?"

"Yes, Umm, very much."

S'ad was silent.

"Well, Umm?"

"Well what?"

"Why don't you say something? I care for Uri—and he cares for me. Don't you have anything to say?"

S'ad cleared her throat. "What is there to say, Layleh? You care for someone and he returns the feeling. That's fine. Except . . ." Her voice trailed off.

"Except what, Umm?"

"Except, my child, that you are an Arab and Uri is a Jew."

"What's wrong with that, Umm?"

"In theory and in books, nothing, Layleh. But in real life——" S'ad hesitated.

"Go on, Umm. In real life, what?"

"In real life, my child, these kinds of . . . friendships . . . don't work out."

"Why not, Umm?"

"They just don't, Layleh."

"But how can you say that, Umm? How do you know?"

"My heart——"

"I know, I know!" murmured Layleh hoarsely. "Your heart tells you so! And your heart——"

"Never lies," finished her mother.

Layleh shivered and then, almost in desperation, countered: "But this time, Umm——" She did not finish.

"Go ahead, Layleh. Don't be afraid: speak."

"But this time it *does!*" Layleh blurted out.

Sa'd stared at her for a moment.

Quickly, Layleh touched her mother's arm. "Are you angry,

Umm?" she whispered. "Are you angry that I said what I did?"

Slowly, S'ad shook her head. "No," she murmured huskily, "I'm not angry, Layleh. Why should I be angry? You are young . . . and you are innocent . . . and you want what you want. I can't blame you, my child, I . . . can only warn you." Her voice dropped to a whisper. "Draw away from this Uri. Draw away from him before——"

"Before what, Umm?"

"Before it's too late, my daughter."

It's already too late, Layleh thought. But she did not dare to say it.

The war was over. The war which all the world knew as *Mil-chemet Shayshet ha-Yamim*—the Six-Day War—was done and finished with. The cannons had stopped firing and the infantry had ceased moving forward. Armored units had halted their lightning attacks, bombs had stopped falling, and the planes desisted from their punishing assaults. Best of all, ambulances and helicopters no longer streamed in unending lines to the hospitals.

But in the Arnon household, the war still lingered on. Ilana was home on leave, but, deeply depressed because Z'ev had been listed as missing in action since the second day of the outbreak of hostilities, she was no more than a physical presence in the house—a haunted-eyed body that scarcely spoke or ate or slept. And Arie was still away. He had contacted the house by telephone the day the conflict officially ended, but the connection had been broken almost at once and, aside from the fact that he was alive, the family knew nothing.

From the front lawn where he was coiling the garden hose, Uri heard the opening notes of a Mozart sonata. They drifted out through the living room window and, like luminous butterflies, whirled away into the brilliant July sunlight. Uri listened to the melody expectantly. Some months ago, almost without his consciously realizing the fact, Ilana's music had begun to interest him. But suddenly—with a crashing, cacophonous chord, the music broke off. That was the way it had been ever since his sister had returned. She would seat herself absently, almost vacantly, at the piano—as if she had no idea what she was doing—and begin to play and then, a few moments later, stop. Ever since Uri could remember, the themes which she had always called "golden" and "silver" and "crystal," attracted her with irresistible force, yet now they seemed to repel her.

Uri waited. He wished and hoped that somehow, in spite of herself, she would continue. But only the thumping, savagely final sound of the piano lid coming down issued out of the window. In the cypresses that stood in a row at the street edge of the lawn, the birds were chirping, but the song they sang—full-throated and buoyant—seemed flat to Uri's ears, and he found himself wishing foolishly that the birds would fly away. Sullenly, he set the hose down in its place and walked bare-footed across the grass and down the driveway and into the backyard.

When he got there he wondered why he had come, what it had to offer him. The yard had always been especially beautiful to him—a peaceful, magically bewitching haven; a sanctuary which harbored bountiful and boundless dreams. But today it seemed dull to him. The treehouse—endlessly a source of pleasure—looked forlorn and unappealing. The shrubs and flowers and trees somehow looked fragile and tenuous, as if at any instant they might wither. And the hedge, in full green leaf, appeared menacing.

Mahmoud was at home as he had been all throughout the days and nights of the war. Though D'vora had tried to contact him several times, he stubbornly remained alone and aloof. Layleh and her mother were still away in the Galilee village. The yard was deserted, desolate. Why, indeed, had Uri chosen to enter it?

With a sigh, he started toward the kitchen door. But just as he reached the back porch, the sound of a vehicle in the street out front arrested him. His heart contracted. *Perhaps it was Arie! Perhaps his father was coming home from battle!* In a flash he was around the house and in the driveway again. And then, running at breakneck speed, he was on the front lawn. With straining eyes and a dry mouth, he watched a dusty command car with the Star of David on its side and half-obscured

white numerals on its hood come to a halt in front of the walk.
At once, the feelings of relief and gratitude that had flooded
his mind turned to disappointment and bitterness. *Arie was not
in the car*.

Two officers got out. They took several stiff steps down the
walk and then halted. The taller of the two, a middle-aged man
with a fresh scar on his suntanned forehead, said: "Does Ilana
Arnon live here?"

"Yes, she does—I'm her brother."

"Is she at home?"

Uri nodded.

"Thank you," said the officer. He touched his companion's
arm and the two men continued up the walk.

Uri did not move from his place. His eyes followed the
officers as they mounted the front porch. He saw the taller of
the pair push the bell. Nothing happened and, after a wait that
seemed interminable to Uri, the officer pushed it again. D'vora's
voice floated out—as before Ilana's truncated sonata had—
across the lawn. "I'm coming," she called.

Uri found himself wishing that she had not answered; that
she wasn't home; that no one, in fact, was home. He wanted
desperately for the two officers to turn around and tell him they
had made a mistake and go back to their command car and get
in and drive away. *You're at the wrong address!* he wanted to
shout. *You don't belong here—you don't belong in this place
at all!* But he said nothing. He just stood there.

D'vora appeared at the door.

The taller officer said, *"Shalom.* We'd like to see Ilana
Arnon."

"Ilana . . . ?"

"Yes, *g'veret.* We should like to see her—just for a few
moments."

D'vora hesitated. Then she said, "Ilana's resting now.
Couldn't you possibly . . . ?" Her voice trailed off. A feeling
of dread took over. She knew what these official visits often
meant.

The shorter officer stirred his dust-whitened shoes on the
stone of the porch floor. "We must see her, *g'veret,"* he said.
"It's important."

D'vora nodded. "All right," she murmured hoarsely. "I'm

sorry . . . to have kept you waiting. Come in. Come in—I'll go upstairs and get her."

The door swung open and the two officers passed inside. Uri stared at the command car parked at the edge of the lawn and then back again at the silent house. Everything around him—the green-bladed grass, the cypresses lining the street, the birds on the telephone wires, the scattered puffs of cloud drifting in the sky—seemed strange, seemed unreal, about to change its deceptively assumed form. For an instant, he considered running away—running anywhere at all as long as it was away from the house into which the sober-faced, stiff-walking officers had disappeared. But he knew, even as the desire to flee formed itself, that if he were to run to the end of the world, he would never escape the consequences of their visit. He considered going inside, but as he gazed with fixed, obsessive concentration at the screen door, he realized, with a shudder that turned his body cold, that *he was afraid*.

For several moments he remained where he was. Then, moving swiftly, he went directly to the backyard and reached the oak tree and climbed the worn, crooked, weather-skewed blocks of the ladder and squeezed himself through the entrance of the little house his father had built for him what seemed an endless time ago. There was scarcely enough room for him now in the chamber. His head grazed the roof, through whose cracks and chinks quills of daylight plunged. His elbows scraped the musty-smelling walls. Hugging his knees to his chest, he sat and waited. *For what?* his mind asked himself. But the question remained unanswered because he did not dare to answer it.

Suddenly, he heard the front door creak open. A split-second later, it banged shut with a harsh finality that jarred him. He could not see them. But in his whirling mind he could picture the two neatly dressed officers, in their freshly pressed uniforms and tightly laced boots and black, precisely tipped berets, striding down the front walk and, never breaking their rhythm, getting into the waiting command car. And then, as if he, too, had somehow been synchronized to their measured pace and knew exactly when it would happen, he heard the motor of their vehicle flare up. The command car, heading for the main road, drove off. But the raucous whine of its impatient engine lingered in his ears long after it had gone.

There was silence—a queer, importunate silence that made his flesh crawl with an unnameable terror. He knew that he did not belong, had indeed no right to be, in the treehouse. But he did not want to leave. When he left for military service, his father had told him, explicitly and without any qualification, that he, Uri, was the "man of the house." He remembered Arie's words clearly, and the exact tone of his father's voice, and the solemn, trusting expression in his eyes and on the features of his face. Uri was, by strict Israeli standards, no longer a child. He was, by force of circumstance and situation, the man of the house that his father had bidden and enjoined him to be. He had, it was clear to him, no business hiding out in a childhood refuge whose shelter was no longer permitted or significant. But still—in spite of it all—he did not want to go. He wanted desperately and pathetically, like an infant who does not want to go out into the world, to remain in his womb of warped wooden boards and spongy cobwebs.

His muscles were cramped. With an involuntary groan, he released his viselike hold on his knees and, as best as he could, shifted position. Inadvertently, one of his floundering hands nudged a soft object. With astonishment, he picked it up from the splintery floor. He held it before him and peered at it incredulously. Limp and mildewed and ragtag, it was what remained of one of the pair of dolls that Layleh had fashioned years ago. He could not make out whether it was the boy or girl doll because of its state of disrepair. When he groped over the floor with agitated fingers for the mate, he could not find it. Where it had gone or what had happened to it, he would never know. Twisting his body to one side, he reached back and carefully, almost tenderly put the remains of the surviving doll in the corner where he had found it.

Somehow, in some mysterious, uncanny way, that simple, innocuous gesture was enough to stir him. It was as if, by some obscure stroke, he had managed at last to put back the childhood that clung to him and held him prisoner when he put back in its place the shapeless lump of ragdoll. With a sudden burst of pain and insight, he realized that his mother and sister were alone with the tidings the visitors might have brought. They might need him. And, like a willful child, like a coward, he had gone to hide!

Knocking a shoulder and banging his head, he thrust himself out of the treehouse. Frantically, he scrambled down the wood-block ladder and jumped to the ground; then, sprinting forward, he raced for the back door. The kitchen was deserted—an empty coffee cup stood on the table. In the silent living room, he glimpsed the dark, polished wood of Ilana's closed piano. He was about to mount the stairs when a sheet of paper caught his eye—his mother had undoubtedly dropped it on her way up. He bent and picked up the telegram and began to read the words whose significance he already knew:

WITH DEEPEST SORROW, WE MUST INFORM YOU THAT SER-GEANT Z'EV NACHMANI, FORMERLY LISTED AS MISSING IN ACTION, WAS KILLED IN THE LINE OF DUTY ON JUNE——

Uri did not read further. He could hear the crying upstairs.

———

The death on the battlefield of Ilana's fiancé, Z'ev—and the deaths in the neighboring families and in Jerusalem and throughout Israel; the deaths in battle that seemed bent on touching generation after generation in the little country, until there was scarcely a family untouched by war—threw a shadow over the Arnon household. Although there were tears in D'vora's eyes as Arie embraced her when he appeared at the door, Z'ev's death threw a shadow even over Arie's safe return from the banks of the Suez Canal, which his unit had reached before the fighting ceased. But the shadow of death, Arie told his family on the night he came back, cannot remain like a coffin lid over the house of the living. Survivors, he told them, always have a sacred duty—to the dead and to themselves—to live, and in their joy of life, to honor the memory of the fallen. Mourning, he told them, was essential in life. But it could never be a substitute for living. Though no Israeli was unscarred by death, he told them, no Israeli must be defeated by death.

The Arnons attended Z'ev's funeral, which was held in a small *moshav* in Emek ha-Sharon, the settlement where Z'ev had been born and grown up. Ilana decided to remain with the Nachmani family for a time. Arie, D'vora, and Uri drove back to the house with the hedge in Jerusalem.

Peace returned to Israel. At the cost of the lives of its soldiers, Israel, the Arnons thought, had risen up and smashed the iron ring that threatened its existence. In the north, the Syrians and Iraqis had been beaten decisively and Israeli columns had halted only scant kilometers from Damascus. In the south, the Egyptians had been routed and Israeli troops were dug in on the banks of the Suez Canal, having taken the entire Sinai Peninsula. In the east, Judea and Samaria—always, since 1948, the springboard for the launching of *fedayeen* attacks against Israeli civilians—were in the hands of the Israel Defense Forces. And Jerusalem—the ancient Hebrew capital since the dawn of recorded history; the splendorous home of David and Solomon; the legendary city where stone and spirit, earth and heaven met in a brilliant embrace—was at long last reunited and returned, the Arnons believed, to its rightful tenants. Peace had come back to Israel. And there was not an Israeli who did not hope and pray that it would remain forever...

Uri woke even earlier than usual. The tenuous darkness of his bedroom was relieved by the pale, silver-gray outline of the shuttered window. At once, he sat up. From the branches of the trees in the yard outside, the busy chattering of the birds filled his ears and touched him in a peculiar, poignant way— almost as if he had never before in his life heard the sweet, gentle sounds they made. He left the bed and on bare feet crossed the night-cooled floor tiles and reached the window to yank the shutter open.

To the east, above the dawn-softened shoulders of the distant hills, the gray sky seemed to quiver, awaiting the new day. Uri was satisfied. He was up at the right moment, in time to see the sun rise. That was exactly what he wanted; exactly what he had planned the night before. For an instant—though he knew very well it was foolish, since he was certain that S'ad and her daughter had not yet returned from the village in the Galilee—he glanced down over the gray-black hedge into the yard next door. It was empty.

He lifted his eyes and gazed once again into the distance. Over the eastern hills, the gray-white pallor of the sky was dissolving. Long fingers of scarlet and gold were now reaching up and pressing their prints onto feathery clouds. And then, suddenly, the red-orange sun—an enormous, swollen, distended sun that was squeezed out of shape like a child's rubber ball—rose from behind the hill crests and flooded the city with roseate light. Uri shivered. Jerusalem at sunrise! Hungrily, his eyes devoured the city: its tumbled pink stones and reddish earth; its swirling towers and tender trees; its onyx-hard shadows and diamond-shimmering air. *Jerusalem at peace!* How he wished that Layleh could be with him at this moment to share it.

A noise from below made him turn—it came from the kitchen. He listened for a moment and then hastily put on shorts and slipped into a shirt and wriggled his feet into his sandals. When he entered the sunlit kitchen, his father was just pouring himself coffee. There was an expression of mingled weariness and solemnity in Arie's eyes. Nevertheless, they lit up when he saw his son. Tapping the coffee pot, he said, "Want some?"

Uri shook his head. "No thanks, Abba."

"What are your plans for today, now that school's out?" said Arie.

"I'm going to see Imma at the hospital. When she called last night to say she wouldn't be home, she asked if I wanted to come over this morning."

Arie sipped his coffee. "And . . . you said you did, eh?"

"Yes," said Uri softly. "I—think she's lonely . . . if you know what I mean."

Arie's gray eyes clouded. "I know what you mean," he said. "Ever since Z'ev's funeral . . ." He fell silent. Then he said: "Uri . . . the hospital isn't going to be easy for you."

"I don't expect it to be, Abba."

"But you're going anyway, eh?"

"Abba—I have to go!"

Arie nodded but did not reply. He finished his coffee and set the empty cup in the sink and glanced at his watch. "I've got to go through a file and get some papers together," he muttered. "Grab yourself something to eat and meet me out front. I have an early meeting at the Ministry, but I'll just have enough time to drop you off at the hospital and say a few words to your mother."

"*B'seder*," said Uri.

By the time Uri drank a glass of orange juice and finished off a roll, Arie was sitting behind the wheel of the jeep. Uri locked the front door, bounded across the porch, and raced through the dew-wet grass to the driveway. Effortlessly, he swung himself into the front seat beside his father. Though he knew it was without purpose, he glanced over to Layleh's front porch. Arie's glance followed his son's, but he said nothing. Frowning slightly, he threw the jeep into gear and eased it slowly down the driveway and onto the street. Within seconds they were on their way, sliding between graceful firs and cypresses about whose sun-splotched trunks great, exclamatory snakes of purple bougainvillea wound. At the point where the twisting street intersected the main road, Arie had to stop for a time. A lumbering, groaning, dust-covered, seemingly endless convoy of army vehicles was crawling by. Uri became absorbed in watching its progress, but then, abruptly, he turned to his father and asked: "Won't this make you late for your meeting, Abba?"

Arie shrugged. "We'll have to wait and see," he said, pulling a pipe from his shirt pocket and, without filling it, setting its stem between his teeth. "If traffic is really bad, you'll have to say hello to your mother for me."

"I'm sure she'll understand," said Uri.

When the last, thick-tired command car of the convoy—its tarpaulin-hooded machine gun pointing upward and its radio antenna flexing—had rolled past them, Arie drove up onto the main road and turned in the direction of the hospital. He traveled at a brisk speed for several kilometers. But as he approached the next major intersection, he had to slow the jeep down to a crawl at the tail end of a long column of barely moving traffic. Egged and Dan buses; automobiles of every description and origin and vintage; trucks of all sizes, from tiny, beetlelike pickups to colossal eighteen-wheelers; army troop transports; motorcycles; tractors; and even donkey carts crowded the road. Up ahead, amid the blare of horns and whining of gears and rasp of overheating engines, a policewoman in a blue uniform and an MP wearing a white helmet and a white-holstered revolver strapped to his waist were doing their best to dissolve the bottleneck.

Uri's eyes shone. He had to raise his voice to make himself heard over the din. "It seems that everybody in the country wants to be in Jerusalem today!" he shouted to his father.

Arie nodded. "Why shouldn't they want to be here?" he replied. "It isn't every day that the capital of Israel is reunified!"

Uri's eyes clouded. "It never should have been divided in the first place," he said, gazing over the traffic jam into the distance. "But then, there are a lot of things that never should have been—and never should be. . . ."

Abruptly, the vehicles that were stalled in both directions began to jerk forward and then move smoothly ahead. Arie increased his speed. Without further delays, he reached the cutoff road and drove directly to the hospital. As they traveled up to the entrance of the main building, Uri said, "Well, Abba— is there time enough for you to come inside with me?"

Arie brought the jeep to a stop and looked at his watch. He shook his head regretfully. "I'm sorry, Uri," he said, "but I really can't spare the time. Tell your mother I'm fine, and give her my love."

Uri hesitated. Then he said: "Abba . . ."

Arie stared at his son. "Is something wrong, Uri?"

Uri swallowed. "May . . . I speak to you, Abba? Just for a few minutes . . ."

"What's on your mind, Uri?"

"Abba . . . it's Z'ev—I can't stop thinking about him."

"None of us can, Uri. Yet we must go on with life."

"But Z'ev's dead, Abba—he'll never live again! And I— I wasn't . . . even in the army."

Arie touched his son's shoulder gently. "You're too young for the army, Uri—you know that. You did whatever was required of you . . . whatever you could."

Uri's voice trembled. "I know . . . all that . . ." he murmured haltingly. "I know it in my mind. But my heart . . ."

Arie nodded. "The heart," he said softly, "is slow . . . to form its scars, Uri."

Uri was silent. It took some time for him to be able to speak again. At length, he said, "And there's . . . another thing, Abba. . . ." He bit his lip.

"Go on, son."

"It—it's about Layleh, the Arab girl next door."

"Yes, Uri . . . your mother and I . . . have known about your friendship with her for some time."

Uri struggled to steady his voice. "Sometimes, while the war was going on . . . and then, after we got word that Z'ev had been killed . . . I—I felt guilty."

"Guilty? What do you mean?"

"Well, I felt as if my friendship with Layleh might—might somehow have caused Z'ev to die!" Uri lifted a hand helplessly. "I know it's silly . . . that it's ridiculous . . . but still——" He could not continue.

Arie squeezed his son's shoulder. "Nothing that *you* did, Uri, caused Z'ev to be killed. The enemy killed him, as they killed thousands of our soldiers and our civilians." He sighed and after a pause went on: "As to your friendship with Layleh, that's something you will have to resolve on your own, Uri. Ideally, the two of you should be close—nothing is more natural. But I'm afraid that reality, my son, might say otherwise. The Arabs will continue to hate us for decades to come— maybe even for a century!"

Suddenly, Uri turned his head away to hide the moistness of tears forming in his eyes.

"Uri—are you all right?"

"I'm fine, Abba."

"Are you sure?"

"Honestly, Abba—I'm fine."

"I'll see you tonight, then."

Uri jumped out of the jeep. *"Shalom,* Abba," he called. "Thanks for the lift."

His father waved and drove off, but Uri did not move. For a long time, he stood on the pavement, thinking of what his father had said. Then, wiping his eyes, he turned and gazed up at the huge, curved, concrete facade of the hospital. Somehow, the sight of the mammoth, fortresslike building frightened him. A jarring thought entered his mind: *Maybe he shouldn't go in.* It wasn't too late to back out. He could still phone his mother and tell her that——

Torn by his indecision, he stood where he was and let the time slip by. At length, the guard at the gate—an older man, with gray-streaked hair and weary eyes—came up to him and tapped his shoulder. "Hey, you, *chevreman*," the guard said in a gruff, overstrained voice. "Wake up!"

Uri started. "I'm sorry . . ."

"Sorry or not, son," muttered the guard, "you can't just hang around here."

"I'm here to see my mother—Dr. D'vora Arnon."

A dusty submachine gun hung on a frayed and greasy strap over one of the guard's shoulders. It was slipping down and, with an impatient jerk, he restored it to position. "Well," he said, "if that's the case, why don't you just go over to that booth? The fellow inside will issue you a pass."

"Thanks."

The guard shrugged and turned. Uri watched the guard, in his faded and rumpled khakis that looked like they had been slept in for days, return to his post at the gate.

Suddenly, a roar filled Uri's ears as a shadow swooped across the pavement and the front of the hospital building. Uri looked up and saw an army helicopter flash by—the wounded, he realized, were still being ferried in from outlying bases. He went over to the booth and secured his pass.

Once inside the hospital, he went directly to his mother's ward. The nurse on duty at the desk looked up at him with dark-ringed eyes. "Who's the patient?" she said hoarsely, almost in a tone of routine despair, as if she had asked the question a thousand times over already that morning. "Father—brother—friend?"

Uri shook his head. "No, no," he said quickly. "I'm here to see my mother—Dr. Arnon."

The nurse managed a wan smile. "Then you must be . . . Uri."

"I am."

"My name is Dahlia," said the nurse. She cleared her throat. "Your mother's expecting you. Just a moment, and I'll call her."

D'vora, looking pale and worn, hugged her son tightly when she saw him, and then the two of them went down to one of the small, enclosed hospital gardens. From the cloudless sky, the sun shone down brightly, kindling the fine, freshly cut grass to an intense green and lighting the pale pink blossoms of the mimosa trees. Here and there, on the stone benches,

clad in faded hospital bathrobes, sat soldiers recovering from
their wounds. Uri glanced around, and D'vora followed his
glance. "These are . . . hard times," she said slowly.

Uri nodded. He could see how busy and distracted she was.

Suddenly, in a quick, impulsive movement, D'vora took
her son's hands. "Uri——"

"Yes, Imma."

"Uri, you know that I love you very much, don't you?"

"Yes, I do—and I love you very much, Imma."

"I—I'm not at home with you as much as I would like to
be, Uri, but I can't help that. It's a part of my work—a part,
actually, of my nature."

"I know that, Imma."

"It doesn't mean that I love you any less. Or that, when
she was little, I loved Ilana any less. Sometimes, through the
years, I've felt torn—almost torn in half—between the hospital
and my home. But . . . there is no resolution, I've learned, except to do the best I can in both worlds."

"I understand, Imma. And you're good in both worlds!"

D'vora turned her head away, and Uri moved closer to her
on the bench and kissed her cheek before saying goodbye.

On his way out of the hospital, Uri suddenly found that his
path was barred. Coming toward him down the corridor was
a stretcher on wheels being moved forward by two attendants
in baggy green suits and squarish green caps. Unable to keep
himself from staring at it, Uri saw, fenced in between the
sidegates, a rigid, unmoving figure whose arms, legs, and entire
face and head were swathed in bandages. Startled by the gro-
tesqueness of the mummylike wrappings and chilled by the
terrible immobility of the wounded man, Uri's instantaneous
reaction was to avert his eyes.

But a voice within him challenged his decision. *So you won't
look, eh?* it sneered. *So you don't want to see what war can
do to a man?* And, growing stronger and more insistent, it
went on: *But why should you, in particular, be exempted from
facing what must be faced? Why should you be allowed to turn
your eyes away from what nobody wants to see? What gives
you the right to indulge yourself?*

Uri trembled. He did not want to look at the bandaged man
on the approaching stretcher, but he was unable to withstand

the brutal logic of his own inner voice. With a shiver, he forced himself to look. What sort of being, he wondered, could live beneath the wide white strips of bandage that shut it off from the rest of the world? How long would this man be condemned to this kind of solitary confinement? Could the damage that had been done to him—Uri could not bring himself to imagine what the wounds under the bandages were like—ever be repaired?

The stretcher rolled by him. Now, in a complete reversal of attitude, it seemed to him that he could not take his eyes from it; that he was *compelled* to follow its noiseless passage down the hushed corridor. He suddenly had the feeling that something deep inside him was drawn to the moving stretcher; that there was some connection between himself and the "mummy man" whom he had never met and would never meet. Without warning, the stretcher rounded a bend down at the far end of the corridor, where morning sunlight poured like a waterfall through a window, and his eyes had nothing left but a fleeting glimpse of a green-coated back—and then they had nothing.

Uri turned and hurried out of the hospital. The sunshine— always, he felt, benevolent—now seemed blinding and unbearable. He shaded his eyes with a hand and, breaking into a trot, exited the main gate and turned on the light-dazzled sidewalk toward the bus stop, where a long line of people had formed. Usually, one heard cheerful banter and amusing stories and the latest, irony-laced Israeli jokes while standing in line for the bus. But this line was strangely silent, even grim, and it dawned on Uri that the people in it had, like himself, only recently come out of the hospital. Perhaps, he thought, one— or several—of them had even belonged to whoever or whatever he had seen on the stretcher beneath the hideous armored suit of bandages. And then, suddenly, it occurred to him, in a ferocious, jarring burst of insight, that not only *all* the people in line for the bus, including himself, *but all the people in the world* belonged to the mummy man inside the hospital.

On the bus, Uri considered getting off a stop earlier and going to see his friend Avner. But the desire was gone almost as soon as it had been conceived. Avner, it was true, was a loyal and close companion of long standing, but it seemed there were certain things one just could not say to him. There was really only one person with whom he wished to speak at the moment, but that person, Layleh, was gone, and he had no idea when she would return.

The bus slowed and rounded a curve in the road. Uri rose and pulled the cord and got off at his stop. Somehow, the walk down the narrow street that led to his house seemed endless, and he was relieved and grateful when he finally reached his own front lawn.

Wearily, he entered his house. The cool, dim interior made him feel a little better. Impatiently, he kicked off his sandals so that his feet could make contact with the smooth-surfaced floor tiles. In his room, he flung himself down on his unmade bed and closed his eyes. He had intended merely to rest a bit, not to sleep, but when he opened his eyes again and looked at his watch, it was after one. He had no real appetite, though. Out of a sense of duty, he ate a light lunch in the kitchen, not even bothering to seat himself at the table. Then he went back up to his room and spent the afternoon reading a novel about a kibbutz, a book he had started some weeks ago, before the war. He realized as he read, of course, that he was deliberately keeping his mind preoccupied so that he would not think of the hospital and the hushed corridor and the mummy man on the stretcher with noiseless wheels.

At ten to four the phone rang and he went down to the kitchen and picked it up. It was his father, calling from the Foreign Ministry. "Hello, there," said Arie. "How did your visit at the hospital go? How's Imma?"

"I didn't see Imma for long," Uri replied. "She was busy making her rounds."

"That's to be expected, Uri—the casualties are still coming in."

"I know, Abba," said Uri. "I saw——" But he decided not to go on.

There was a pause on the other end of the line. Then Arie said: "Are you all right, Uri?"

"Sure. Why? Do I sound as if something were wrong?"

"No, I was just asking." Arie cleared his throat. "Did your mother say what time she'd be home tonight?"

"No."

"Well, I'm going to be late myself this evening. If she happens to get home before I do, be sure to tell her I miss her very much."

"I will, Abba."

"And Uri, one more thing before I hang up."

"What is it, Abba?"

Arie hesitated. Then he said: "Was there . . . any word from Ilana today?"

"No, there wasn't."

"All right . . ." murmured Arie. "I just thought . . . there might be." He was silent for a moment and then said: "I've got to go now, Uri. Take care of yourself."

"*Shalom,* Abba!"

After he had hung up, the thought of returning to his room to read again seemed distasteful to him, and so Uri decided that he would go over to Avner's house after all. He took a shortcut and reached his destination quickly. Avner was out in the backyard, in rolled-up trousers and an undershirt, working in the flower garden. When he caught sight of Uri, he smiled and, dropping his hoe, pulled an already soaked handkerchief from a pocket and mopped the sweat from his flushed face and neck. "Well, Uri," he said warmly, "so you've arrived at last! I knew you'd show up sometime—I just didn't know when." He stepped around a patch of flaming orange zinnias and grasped Uri's hand. "How are you, Uri? How're your folks? And how . . . is Ilana doing?"

Uri shaded his eyes against the ruddy rays of the sinking sun and answered his friend's questions. It was difficult for him to speak of Ilana, but he did. And then the two boys talked at random for a while. At length, glancing at his watch, Avner said, "How about staying for supper, Uri?"

"If it's all right with your mother, I'd like that very much."

Avner grinned. "Whatever's okay with me," he said, "is okay with my mother. That's one of the basic rules in this house."

After supper—a noisy, spirited affair, with Avner's two younger sisters laughing and singing and refusing to be calmed down by their mother, who, quite obviously, did not really wish to dampen their boisterous enthusiasm—the two friends excused themselves and went out for a walk in the neighborhood. The last, clinging glow of sunset lit the sky and was reflected tenderly in the pink stones of the houses and walks. Over the shrubs and hedges and lawns, the first, faint green flashes of fireflies were beginning to be visible. From the distance came the wail of an ambulance siren.

Avner drew a deep breath. "I heard," he said slowly, "that they're going to knock down the wall tomorrow. Is it true? What does your father say?"

"It's true!" exclaimed Uri. "My father told me that tomorrow, at dawn, the bulldozers will begin work—and we'll be rid of that hideous piece of concrete forever. Jerusalem will be one city again! Uri thrust his hands into his pockets. He hesitated for a moment and then murmured in a voice that was just audible: "Maybe . . ."

Avner was puzzled and looked over at his friend. "Maybe what?" he asked.

"Maybe," Uri went on, *"just maybe* . . . when the wall comes down . . . there'll be peace. Peace from now on."

Bitter laughter leaped from Avner's mouth. "Uri," he exclaimed gruffly, "you're dreaming!"

Uri shook his head. "No," he protested. "No, I'm not."

But Avner was adamant. He took his friend's arm with surprising force. "Look, Uri," he said with conviction, "I'm afraid that no matter how much you believe there will be peace between us and the Arabs, you *are* dreaming! And you'd better wake up, because in the real world those kind of dreams are dangerous. *You* want peace, *I* want peace—*every Israeli in the country* wants peace—there isn't the slightest doubt about that. We would make peace with the Arabs today, this minute, this very second, in fact." His voice quavered. "But *they*——"

"Avner, I——"

"No," interrupted Avner, squeezing his companion's arm with all of his strength. "I haven't finished yet. The truth is that we Jews . . . we Israelis . . . have *always* wanted peace, from the very beginning. But the Arabs never wanted to let us live in peace—and they *still* don't want to. They just want to attack and destroy us! Sure, we can bring on the bulldozers and tear down the wall that divided Jerusalem, our Jerusalem, but that doesn't mean we have even *touched* the wall of hatred in their hearts."

Uri stared at his friend speechlessly.

"Well," said Avner, "what have you to say?"

Uri shrugged. "Nothing . . ."

"Come on, Uri—say something."

Uri only shook his head. "I have nothing to say," he repeated. "Nothing at all."

Avner released his friend's arm and turned. "Let's go back," he said huskily. "It's getting late."

No one was in the house when Uri got back, which most probably meant that his mother would be spending another night in the hospital—perhaps with the mummy man. Though he had napped during the afternoon, he felt exhausted and decided not to wait for his father. He fell asleep almost immediately and did not waken until a hand shook his shoulder and a warm, familiar voice kept repeating, "Uri . . . Uri . . ."

"Huh?"

"Uri, get up," said his father. "Don't you want to see them tear down the wall?"

Half an hour later, Arie brought the jeep to a halt two or three blocks before the police barricades, and he and his son jumped out and continued on foot. A dense, eager crowd pressed forward like a tide to the point where, beyond a line of uniformed soldiers and policemen, the bright yellow Caterpillar tractors, with their goggled drivers and upraised blades, were just beginning to work. In the fresh morning sunlight, the ugly wall—the gray-concrete barrier that had zigzagged through the city like a scar and split it in two; the rough-textured, forbidding wall, with its sandbagged emplacements and square-slabbed machine gun nests and redoubts from which time and again Arab sniper fire had drawn Jewish blood and claimed Jewish lives—was reeling and buckling and collapsing before the incredulous eyes of the onlookers. Gray clouds of dust and debris swirled up into the air as shards of concrete came crashing to the earth. Amid the roar of the demolition and the whine of the tractor engines, the spectators cheered and applauded wildly.

"Well," shouted Arie, bending over to his son to make sure

that he was heard, "was it worth skipping breakfast to come and see this?"

"I . . . can't . . . believe it!" Uri shouted back.

"But it's really happening!" Arie laughed, pulling out a pipe and beginning to fill it from a worn leather pouch.

Uri's eyes blazed defiantly. "Yes, Abba," he yelled. "It *is* real! I don't care what anyone else says—I *know* there will be peace now. This monster wall is coming down . . . and the barriers between Arabs and Jews will come down as well. I know it, Abba! From now on, we'll live together as neighbors and friends!"

Arie struck a match and lit his pipe. "I hope you're right, Uri."

"But I am right, Abba! I *must* be right!"

"We'll see, Uri—time will tell."

————— • ————— •

Late that afternoon, as the sun was setting, the bus that carried S'ad and Layleh ground stutteringly up the steep ascent to Jerusalem and drove on to the central terminal on Jaffa Road. The two travelers, cramped and weary from the long journey they had made from the Galilee, descended and hailed a taxi. As the car picked up speed, the driver—a grizzled Moroccan Jew with sparse white hair sprouting from beneath his multi-colored wool cap and prickly white stubble on his cheeks and chin—glanced into the rear-view mirror and said: "Have you come from far, my friends?"

"From the Galilee," replied S'ad.

"And you've just arrived?"

"Not more than five minutes ago." S'ad hesitated and then said, "But why do you ask?"

"Because you probably don't know the news——"

"What news . . . are you talking about?"

The driver grinned. *"The wall is down!"* he exclaimed.

S'ad leaned forward. "You are jesting with me," she said hoarsely.

The driver shook his head vigorously and laughed. *"On my life!"* he bellowed. "I am telling you the truth!"

S'ad wet her lips with her tongue. "When?" she murmured incredulously. "When did it happen?"

"This morning!" boomed the driver. "The bulldozers started work at dawn!"

S'ad leaned slowly back in the seat. Her eyes filled with tears and she turned to her daughter. "Did you hear," she said in a half-choked voice, "did you hear what the driver said?" She lifted a trembling hand. "Layleh, Layleh darling, the wall is down ... *the wall is really down!* Now Jerusalem is one! We can go to the Old City, to the house where I lived with Hassan Ali——" She could not continue.

Layleh's heart went out to her mother. Though S'ad had not finished expressing her thoughts and feelings, her daughter believed she knew everything that was in her mother's mind and heart. Impulsively, she took S'ad's hand and pressed her head against her mother's bosom. She closed her eyes and wished that the taxi ride were already at an end and that she and her mother were home at last. And, behind the privacy of her closed lids, she saw herself once again out in the backyard, kneeling by the green hedge, waiting for Uri. She did not open her eyes until the taxi came to a halt. Her heart pounded wildly when she saw—after the terrible absence—her house and that of the Arnon family adjoining it. But then fear swept over her and made her numb. It was dusk and the Arnon house was unlit and silent. No one could say what had happened to its occupants during the war.

Around four that afternoon, Arie phoned from the Foreign Office to say that he was leaving work early. Within the half-hour, he was honking the horn of the jeep outside the house. Uri went out to join him, and together they drove to the hospital to pick up D'vora to go out to dinner. After the three of them were seated at a table in their favorite—and crowded—restaurant on Ben-Yehuda Street, Arie proposed a toast: *"To Jerusalem reunited ... and to peace!"*

They drank red Israeli wine that glowed in its glasses, and after their meal, Arie lit a pipe and the three of them walked arm in arm down the mobbed street. Zion Square, over which multicolored lights had been strung, was thronged with Jerusalemites and with visitors from every part of the country. People laughed and sang, and some were dancing to the music of scattered instrumentalists and bands. From the direction of the Old City—freed at last, after nineteen years of its concrete barricade—green and blue and red and white flares soared high into the throbbing darkness of the sky, trailing long, dissolving ribbons of light behind them. The Arnons remained at the festivities until about ten-thirty and then made their way slowly back through the surging crowds to the jeep and drove home.

As soon as the jeep rounded the last bend in the narrow lane to their house, Uri caught sight of the lights in the front windows of the house next door, and his heart leaped exultantly. Mahmoud had kept his house in virtual darkness since the day his wife and daughter had left for the Galilee, but now the blazing windows clearly announced that Layleh and her mother might have returned. In his room, he paced the floor restlessly, waiting for his parents to retire before he made his escape into the backyard. At length—it seemed the time would never pass— the midnight radio news program was over and they went to their room. Their door was closed and the house was so quiet he could hear the crickets outside and even the erratic hum of passing cars from the main road.

Noiselessly, he opened his door and went down the stairs and through the kitchen and out the back door into the yard. From a tree, hidden in the blackness of what had formerly been but was no longer no-man's land beyond the rear wall, an owl hooted. Uri crossed the grass and, halting some meters from the heavy mass of the hedge, looked up at Layleh's window. It was dark—but it was open.

Uri crouched. He drew a deep breath and sent up his signal.

The curtains in the window stirred in the gentle breeze, but that was all.

Once again, Uri signaled.

Seconds later, a blurred, whitish shape moved the curtains apart. Like a leaf, Layleh's soft voice drifted down. *"Uri . . ."*

"Layleh!"

"Uri—it's really you!"

"Come down, Layleh!"

"I——"

"Layleh, come down!"

The shape disappeared and the curtains swung together. Uri listened breathlessly and heard the rear door of Layleh's kitchen open and close and then the sound of her footsteps following the usual route on the other side of the hedge. Then—at last—she was opposite him.

The two of them strained desperately to see each other's face. But the moon was down and it wasn't possible. Layleh tried to part the branches that separated them. "Uri," she murmured hoarsely, "Uri..." She wanted to say more, but her voice cracked and then failed.

"Layleh—how *are* you? How is your mother? And your father—we tried to contact him but——" Uri's voice, too, gave way.

There was a silence, punctuated by the hollow hooting of the invisible owl, and then, with an effort that took all of her strength, Layleh stammered: "I'm . . . fine, Uri—we're all fine. And *you?* And . . . your family?"

"We're all right, Layleh. But—but——"

"But what?"

"But . . . Ilana's fiancé was killed."

There was silence from the other side of the hedge, and then the soft sound of weeping.

"Layleh . . . Layleh . . ." Uri called out. He kept repeating her name. And then, suddenly—he did not know how or even when it had begun to happen—he realized that his eyes were moist, too. After a time, when he felt that he could control himself, he said huskily, "My father and mother say there's nothing to do . . . but go on living the best life we can. I suppose . . . they're right. But . . . it's so hard."

"I know, Uri—I *know!*" whispered Layleh. And then she said: "Oh, Uri, *I* missed you so! Sometimes I thought . . . that we would never see each other again."

Uri swallowed. "That's over, now," he said fiercely. *"It's over!* The war has ended, Layleh, and from now on there'll be peace."

"Do you really believe that, Uri?"

"Yes, Layleh, I really believe it! It—it *has to be!*" Uri drew a deep breath. "Layleh," he whispered excitedly, "did you hear that the wall has come down?"

"Yes, yes—the taxi driver told us all about it on the way from the bus station. My mother was so deeply moved—and when we got home, so was my father. I haven't seen him so excited in years!"

"And that's only the beginning," Uri said.

There was silence. Through the thick barrier of the leaves that kept them apart, Uri heard that Layleh was weeping again. "Layleh . . ." he whispered. "What's the matter? Are you all right?"

She did not answer.

"Layleh . . . please."

"I'm . . . sorry, Uri—I didn't mean to cry again. It's just that . . . there's been so much . . ."

"I understand." Uri sighed and touched the hedge, almost diffidently, with his fingertips. "Layleh," he murmured, "will you do something if I ask you to?"

"What is it, Uri? Just tell me."

"Come to the back wall with me."

Layleh nodded.

Quickly, they passed, each to one side, along the hedge until they reached the shadow-bound rear wall. Without a word, Uri began to climb over. Layleh understood and did the same. In a few seconds, freed from the barrier of the hedge and the restraint of their yards, they stood facing each other. Uri took a step toward Layleh; she came to meet him. Almost touching, they halted. Then, with a sudden, fierce movement, Uri leaned forward and grazed Layleh's cheek with his lips. And then, as suddenly, he drew back. Neither spoke, and the night was so silent it seemed to them that they could hear each other's heart pounding.

It was Uri who broke the silence. "We'd better be going now, Layleh," he said.

"Will we see each other tomorrow?"

"We'll work something out—I'm sure we can do it."

"I dreamed of you so often when I was in the Galilee, Uri— I'm certain that I shall dream of you tonight."

Uri took a step backward. "Go now, Layleh," he said.

"Good night, Uri," she said in Arabic.

"Good night," he said in Hebrew.

Hastily, they climbed back over the wall. Side by side,

though they were separated by the dense foliage of the hedge, the two friends walked slowly toward the back doors of their silent houses.

The ceremony of bar mitzvah, which, according to the Jewish tradition signified Uri's assumption of the responsibilities of manhood, was over. From their posts on the heights commanding the great square of flagstone in front of the Kotel—the remains of the Western Wall of the Second Temple—the guards with their Uzi submachine guns cradled loosely on their arms looked down as a crowd of well-wishers milled around the boy-turned-man who had been summoned to read from the Torah as Uri ben-Arie—Uri, the son of Arie. Laughing with exuberance, the relatives and friends patted his back and slapped his shoulders and warmly pressed his sweating hand.

There came a moment in the jovial, excited proceedings when Uri found himself somehow—and surprisingly—alone. He used the moment to good advantage. Quickly, he slipped through the whirling, jostling swarm of guests and dashed across the sunlit pavement to the enormous stone blocks, rough-textured and sprouting vegetation, that had been hewn and fitted into place by Jews so many centuries ago. For an instant, Uri leaned against the Kotel, pressing his cheek to its sun-warmed face of stone and putting his lips gently to this remnant of ancient days in Israel that had survived the enemies of Israel. And then, in accordance with custom, he drew from a pocket a little slip of paper on which he had written the afternoon before and rolled it up and thrust it into a crevice between the stones. At once, he felt relieved and grateful, filled with limitless hope. On the slip of paper which had gone into the Kotel to join all the others that had preceded it, he had scrawled: *She-ha-shalom yavo*—"Let peace come!"

That night, in the Arnon backyard, the bar mitzvah party took place. From the branches of the oak tree to the rear of the house and, in the other direction, all the way to the rear stone wall, colored lights had been strung. A trio of musicians—a drummer, a clarinetist, and a white-haired violinist—

played joyful and haunting tunes. People clapped and danced and sang and reminisced and partook heartily from the food- and wine-laden tables. Flushed with pride, Uri circulated among his guests. But though he was hard-put to conceal it, he kept glancing nervously at the hedge. At one point, noticing their son's obvious agitation, D'vora and Arie approached him. It was D'vora who spoke first. "Is something wrong, Uri?" she said.

Forcing a smile, Uri shook his head and murmured, "It's a wonderful party."

Arie cleared his throat. "But why do you keep staring at the hedge?" he asked.

The direct question shattered Uri's control altogether. His face grew pale. Jerking his head in the direction of the hedge, whose leaves the overhead lights had transformed into sleek rainbow surfaces of color, he blurted out: "Couldn't we have at least invited *them?*"

Arie followed his son's glance and, as he looked, a gentle, melancholy smile formed on his lips. "We did invite the Maleks to your party," he said huskily, reaching out and taking Uri's arm, "but Mahmoud politely refused the invitation."

"I—I'm sorry, Abba." Uri trembled. "I didn't realize——" His voice cracked. "I didn't mean to——"

Arie shrugged. "That's all right," he said softly. "I under-stand."

He turned to rejoin the guests, but D'vora stubbornly held her ground. "No," she said heatedly, "wait—I have something more to say. Now *is* the time to speak to our son not like a little boy, but like the man he certainly is—the man he must be in Israel!" Staring directly into Uri's eyes, she continued: "I have no negative feelings about your relationship with the Malek girl, Uri—that much you know. But I would be remiss as your mother if I did not tell you that I am afraid, afraid of what will happen if your friendship should become . . . some-thing more. Mahmoud Malek has made his stand clear. His refusal is not merely a momentary one; not just another expression of his own pain and embitterment." D'vora's eyes flashed. "It is based, though perhaps unconsciously, on hundreds of years of Arab hatred. His refusing the invitation is nothing less than a rejection of what exists between you and his daughter. And it is a warning, Uri—a clear warning of the pain that lies ahead for you if you choose to strengthen your ties to her." She swallowed. "Have you understood me, Uri?"

Uri nodded.

Then Arie put his arm around his wife's shoulders. "Come, D'vora," he murmured. "The guests are waiting."

━━━━ ·━━· ━━━━

Uri couldn't sleep.

Thoughts of the Kotel; of the crowd of well-wishers pressing about him after the ceremony; of his parents' shining eyes as they stared at him on the joyous walk home; of the party in the backyard after darkness had fallen; of his brief but significant talk with his parents aside from the guests . . . jumped every which way in his mind and kept him awake. At length, weary of tossing and turning between the rumpled sheets, he got out of bed and went to the door of his room and opened it.

Everything was dark and silent. Ilana's room was empty, as it had long been, and his mother and father were asleep. He held his breath for a moment and then went back and slipped into a pair of shorts and turned and quickly went through the door, along the hallway and down the stairs, and through the kitchen and out into the yard.

The night was hot and filled with the husky, monotonous sound of cicadas. In the soft darkness, with their cloths removed, the party-tables were littered with the debris of merry-making. Above him, beyond the crisscrossing wires from which the party lights had gleamed in varicolored brilliance earlier, the stars were shining calmly in the sky. Instinctively, he glanced up toward Layleh's window. It was dark, of course, and she was unquestionably asleep at this hour. Even if he were to repeat his signal a hundred times, he doubted that she would awaken. He wanted desperately to speak with her, but the situation was hopeless.

Suddenly, he heard a noise in the yard on the other side of the hedge. He thought that his ears were playing tricks on him, but then he saw a whitish shape move. He rushed to the hedge.

"Layleh!" he whispered hoarsely.

"Uri?"

They stood opposite each other.

"What are you doing up, Layleh?"

"I couldn't sleep."

"Neither could I."

There was a silence. With a note of hesitation in her voice, Layleh said, "How was...the bar mitzvah party, Uri?"

"It was wonderful, Layleh! I really felt—as one is supposed to—like a man!" Uri cleared his throat. "But," he continued slowly, "there was something missing."

"What...was that?"

"Don't you know, Layleh?"

She shook her head. "No, Uri."

Uri swallowed. "It was that...*you* weren't there."

Layleh was silent.

Uri touched the hedge. "Layleh...what's wrong? Why aren't you talking?"

She cleared her throat. And when, at last, her voice came through the hedge, it trembled. "And how do you think *I* felt, Uri? How do you think it was for me to hear the noise...and the music...and the laughter...and to see the lights...and to know—to know that it was your bar mitzvah party...and that I—that I——" She struggled to catch her breath and then, in a whisper, went on: "That I wasn't invited?" She coughed. "I went up to my room and closed the shutter, hoping foolishly not to see or to hear anymore—but...but still——" She was crying now. *"Oh, Uri!"*

Uri thrust his burning face against the hedge. "Layleh!" he said. "Layleh, but...you *were!*"

"I...what?"

"You *were* invited, Layleh!" repeated Uri. "In the midst of the party, I confronted my father! I actually accused him of not inviting your family——"

"And?"

"And he said that he had—that he *had invited your family to come over and be with us!*"

"Then...why?"

Uri drew a deep breath. "Your father...refused," he said slowly. "He was polite, of course—your father always is— but still, he refused the invitation."

Once again, Layleh did not speak. Then, faintly—in a voice that was cold and contained and almost unrecognizable to Uri—she said, "I see . . ."

"See what, Layleh?"

"See that my father has gone beyond isolating us from you. I see that now he has resorted to . . . lying!"

"Layleh! You can't say that!"

Layleh's laugh was bitter, and utterly alien to Uri's experience with her. "My father neglected to mention the invitation," she said. "And to me, that's the same as a lie!"

Uri did not wait for her to say anything further, nor did he say anything to her. Instead, he moved swiftly toward the rear of the yard. She saw him go and understood and did so as well. When they were both over the back wall, Uri rushed over and took her hands in his and pressed them fiercely: the warmth flowing from them coursed through him and made him shiver with pleasure. "Layleh——" he began huskily. He had intended to say so many things, but he could not seem to summon the words. So instead he kissed her lightly, his lips just touching hers. He wanted her to know that she was not alone and never would be as long as he could help it.

1971

Jerusalem

THE MOMENT URI opened his eyes, he was wide-awake.

He glanced at the alarm clock on the floor by the bed and saw that it would have given him ten minutes more to sleep. But he was glad that he was up and with a vigorous burst of energy he reached out and down and tipped the little lever that shut the clock off. In another two hours or so, he was meeting Layleh on Hillel Street and they would be off for the day to their favorite copse of firs above Jerusalem. He had often described the place, much to Layleh's delighted approval, as no more than "a stone's throw from the Garden of Eden"—and, understandably, he could scarcely contain his excitement.

At once, he jumped up and began to dress. He was sixteen and tall for his age—taller, as D'vora never tired of pointing out, than his father. He was broad-shouldered and slim and lean-muscled and agile, his hair thicker and curlier than it had been when he was a child. He had clear, unflinching, dark eyes that strongly resembled his father's and a sensitive, shy smile that—it seemed to all who knew him—came thoughtfully, perhaps even hesitantly, to his sensual lips.

As he finished dressing and went into the bathroom to wash up and brush his teeth, he thought, almost without interruption, of Layleh, the girl whom he had known since she was a winsome little child, who had crooned lullabys to her doll in the sun-mottled shade of a backyard tree and sat and sipped lemon tea and listened raptly to the tales and stories her father recited to her at the foot of his wheelchair under the broad and sun-splashed leaves of the grape arbor. She was the girl who had grown year by year into a graceful and beautiful young woman before his very eyes.

She was taller than S'ad and had jet-black hair that fell like a cascade of ebony water; darkly burning eyes under thick, curving brows; and ripe, full lips. She was narrow-waisted and sharp-breasted and had quick, delicate hands that gestured ceaselessly when she spoke; and long, sinuous legs that fell easily and naturally into the rhythm of walking or running or dancing.

As Uri descended the stairs, he thought of their friendship. It had begun long ago in the apparent innocence of childhood in the twin backyards and by the towering hedge of the two contiguous houses down at the end of the twisting, tree-lined street in Jerusalem. Over the years, it had deepened and ripened like a living vine, and had blossomed, he knew, because both he and Layleh had decided upon it and pursued it steadfastly and—above all else—had committed themselves to its consequences. As time went by, they both had become dissatisfied with their secret talks through the hedge and their hurried clandestine meetings in the neighborhood. Both of them dreamed of more. And they felt—as with one mind and heart—they had a right to more.

Now Uri was out of the house. He walked as calmly as he could up the street and nodded politely to a neighbor in passing. Once around the first bend, however, he could not contain himself and broke into a trot. The warm spring sunlight and the smell of freshly cut grass and the gentle morning shadows of the shrubs and trees brought memories of other outings with Layleh. As he ran, he remembered the hours they had spent together on green-slatted park benches that had, one after the other, become intimate haunts. He remembered long, rambling walks on the soft-hilled outskirts of the city and plays and concerts and films they had gone to together; an autumn evening when they had gone to Luna Park to ride the carousel and the silver-shafted Ferris wheel that seemed as if it might at any instant spin off through space; and that heat-drugged day in midsummer when they had boarded a bus to go to the beach in Tel Aviv.

He remembered how they had swum in the vast, blue bowl of the ocean that fanned limitlessly out to the sun-haze of the horizon; how they had sunned themselves on the shore and then built sand-castles with turrets and spires and wet-molded domes. With dry mouths and salt-crusted lips, they had eaten delicious sandwiches and had drunk endless paper-cupfuls of lemonade, and gazed at the bathers and sun-blackened revelers and sat beside each other, damp-skinned from the waves, staring into each other's eyes. Finally, Uri remembered, when afternoon had thickened to violet dusk, they had boarded the return bus for Jerusalem and dozed off rapturously on each other's trembling, tingling shoulder.

But now, almost without realizing it, Uri reached the main road. In the front yard of the corner house on the right he saw, as he stood and waited impatiently for the bus, that the *shkaydiot*—the almond trees—wore their diaphanous veils of white and, in the delicate swaying of their branches, seemed reminiscent of Layleh's limbs. Later, when at last they met and walked together away from the city toward their destination, Uri told her that she was like a *shkaydiah*.

"Waiting for the bus," Uri said, "I saw some almond trees in blossom. The wind was blowing . . . the branches were moving . . . and the petals seemed to flutter, like butterflies. The *shkaydiot* were so beautiful and so graceful that I couldn't help thinking of you."

Layleh flushed. "Thank you for the compliment, Uri," she said softly.

Uri shook his head vigorously. "No," he protested. "Don't thank me. It is really I . . . who should thank you."

"For what?"

Uri smiled. "For being as you are," he said warmly.

On all sides now, as they walked hand in hand, a tapestry of wildflowers was hung on every hillside and the hum of the insects made a pipe organ of the air. Slowly, they trekked up to the forest above the city and remained among the whispering branches of the trees, the moss-covered rocks, and the fragrant, fallen fir needles. Soon the sun sank in the west and the soft curtain of the evening fluttered gently down and wrapped them in its fine-spun folds. The time had come. Not a word was spoken between them, but both knew—precisely at the same twilight instant—that a special moment had come.

They were sitting on the forest floor, against a low, dry-barked trunk of a fallen tree. Uri turned his head and found that Layleh's face, like the reflected image in a dim-lit mirror, was waiting for him. He saw her eyes staring intently at him, and her parted, glistening lips. As if synchronized, their faces moved slowly closer, drawn by the certain knowledge that the moment had arrived and they would not—could not—let it pass. In the hushed, fragrant air of the fir woods above Jerusalem, as the gates of evening swung open to let the shadows of night pass through, they kissed. And their kiss was long and fervent and filled with indescribable sweetness and unutterable yearning. And—again in perfect unison—their arms reached out and locked gently but with resolute firmness about each other's shoulders. They pressed their bodies close, as close as it was possible to get, and felt the contours of each other's shape and the heat of each other's racing blood. Again and again—hungrily and insatiably, as if each new contact of their lips did nothing to relieve but only kindled the desire that raged within them—they kissed. Both of them shared, like two people who drink at the same time from the same crystal-clear pool, the knowledge that the moment had come and that each of them had, completely and with absolute willingness, accepted it.

Then, as in a dream, Layleh slowly and gently slid to the needle-carpeted earth. And Uri, clinging to her supple form with hands that did not falter, followed suit. Staring up into the ocean of darkness that had rolled over the land, she lay on the floor of the forest and kept breathlessly silent until his lips covered hers.

He kissed her long, thick-twisting hair and her forehead and her eyes and her cheeks and her neck. He kissed her bare forearms and her wrists and the palms of her hands and her fingers, one by one. Then, carried away on the same mighty river that held them both in its current and bore them both as it wished—or as they wished—he put his hands on her breasts, and Layleh moaned, releasing a soft cry. Uri's fingers held the flesh of young womanhood in their grasp, tightening around them and kneading their magical curves. His fingers searched and sought and implored and—with a will and sudden importunity of their own—demanded. And then, whispering into the darkness that hid their eyes and faces from each other, Layleh uttered her lover's name: *"Uri..."*

Like a stone into a deep, thick-walled well, it echoed in the silence of the night and the forest, ending what seemed like the timelessness and formlessness of a dream. The tree trunk against which they had sat and first kissed and embraced and the lush fir needle rug to which they had tumbled—all of them, together and in a frantic, scrambling rush—returned. So did the city of Jerusalem below them and the house at the end of the sleepy, twisting street. Arie and D'vora returned. So did Mahmoud and S'ad. And so did the twin, almost identical backyards, with the high barrier of hedge that ran between them.

Uri's hands soon fell away from Layleh's body as he released her from the vise of his thighs. Dizzily he struggled to get up, managing somehow to seat himself on the trunk of the fallen tree. Then slowly, as if she were lifting a burden, Layleh also rose and sat beside him.

They neither touched nor spoke. A breeze, sprung up from what direction they did not know, stirred the invisible branches and leaves above them. High above the shifting treetops, in the dark, convoluted veins of the night sky, bits of star-ore glittered, and in the distance, jackals howled a harsh-voweled song of a world without the presence of men.

Then, Layleh said his name again: "Uri . . ."

"Yes, Layleh . . ."

She shook her head. For several moments, she was silent, and then, with a sigh, she said: "Uri, we both knew—and have known for a long time—that this would happen. It was bound to happen and now, tonight, it . . . finally has. I'm . . . not sorry. I hope . . ." Her voice trailed off.

Uri drew a deep breath. "I'm not sorry either, Layleh," he said hoarsely. "The truth is that . . . I'm glad! I *wanted* it to happen!"

Layleh trembled. "So did I," she murmured. "But——"

"But what?"

"But now . . . we have somehow made a turn onto a road . . . that perhaps it would be better for us . . . not to start on."

Uri reached out and touched the back of her hand and then slipped his fingers into hers. "Layleh," he whispered, "as you yourself know, and even said before, this is a road that we started out on a long time ago."

"And . . . the end of the road, Uri?"

For answer, Uri kissed her lightly on the lips. And then he

rose and drew her up. Together, walking hand in hand as they had entered, they walked out of the woods and onto the winding dirt path that led down the hillside.

A number of months passed. Months of meetings and excursions and day-long trips around the country. A time in which the ties that bound Uri and Layleh together became stronger and tighter. There were long, almost interminable, always continued discussions about books they had read, films and plays they had seen, concerts they had heard, feelings that had elated and disturbed them, thoughts that had inspired and depressed them. They both loved nature—its seemingly infinite forms, its mysterious and awesome manifestations, its ever-varied constancies and its permanent changes—and they spent endless hours outside, observing and admiring and enjoying and speculating.

They rarely, if ever, met anymore at the hedge. They often gave it nostalgic glances, but they both believed that it was a thing of the past; that, as Layleh once said, they had outgrown it. For several months already, when they were not out together, they followed a new plan—it was Uri's idea, and Layleh had concurred wholeheartedly: to climb the stone wall at the rear of their yards and go into the territory that had once, before the Six-Day War, been known as no-man's land. Twenty or thirty meters out was a small, gnarled, terebinth that, as Uri pointed out the first time they went to the spot, had survived the ravages of time and weather and war, survived everything.

Beneath the "plucky" tree, as Layleh called it with a smile, was a boulder on which the two of them sat. Here, alone and undisturbed, they talked and whispered. Uri helped Layleh with her Hebrew lessons, and Layleh helped him with his Arabic studies. Here they sat in silence and dreamed and, more often than not, shared their dreams. And here they held hands and caressed each other and gained intimate and thrilling and unforgettable knowledge of their young bodies, kissing with passion and tenderness and the desire that blends both in ever-continued, always-rekindled ardor. Uri was right: they had begun the journey on this road a long time ago. And now they had traveled a considerable way down it. They would—they both knew, though that knowledge remained and would remain unspoken—one day reach another juncture which would, with fierce and compelling force, invite them to turn onto it. And when that day came—they both knew, as well—they would turn. Where would it end? They did not know. But that was the knowledge they could not be bothered with.

One winter's night—it was after ten—when the rain beat against the brittle tiles of the roof and the wind rapped the shutters and thunder growled in Jerusalem's sky, S'ad knocked on the door of her daughter's bedroom and, gaining Layleh's cheerful permission, entered. Her daughter was sitting cozily under a blanket in bed, with an open book on her lap. "Please sit down, Umm," Layleh said, gesturing toward the foot of the bed.

S'ad shook her head.

Layleh looked carefully at her mother's face. "Is something wrong, Umm?"

S'ad wet her dry lips with her tongue. "Your father and I have been talking recently. I decided that it might be wise to speak to you before he does."

"Speak to me about what, Umm?"

S'ad's fluttering, agitated hands suddenly seemed out of place. Hastily, she thrust them into the pockets of her robe. "Layleh," she said, "this boy—this young man—you are so fond of——"

"You mean Uri...."

"Yes, Uri."

"What about him, Umm?"

S'ad shook her head. "No," she said quickly, "it's not about him exactly—it's about...the relationship that exists between the two of you."

"The relationship?"

S'ad nodded. "It's...serious, isn't it, Layleh?"

Layleh shrugged. An amused look—as if in response to something funny her mother had said—came onto her face. When she spoke, she tried but failed to make her voice sound casual. "*Serious*, Umm? But of course it's serious! That's the kind of person I am."

S'ad dug her hands into her pockets. "Layleh...Layleh," she murmured softly. "There's no need to raise your voice to me. I'm not your enemy, and I haven't come...to attack you." She sighed and, with an effort, forced a smile onto her lips. "This relationship that you have with Uri Arnon is... *special*— isn't that the truth?"

Layleh flushed. She did not answer.

"Your father and I know that you are seeing Uri," S'ad went on. "We know that you see him quite often, as often—as a matter of fact—as you can. We know you have been doing so for quite some time." S'ad cleared her throat. "Once, many years ago," she said, "I talked to you about your...friendship with Uri. Do you remember, my daughter?"

"I remember, Umm," Layleh said in a whisper.

"At the time, the two of you really were *friends*. You played by the hedge. You told secrets. You exchanged gifts when you thought nobody was watching you and concealed them in your closets or under your beds." S'ad paused for a moment. Then she said: "But now, my daughter, you and Uri are young people—young people on the very threshold of adulthood. Your minds are rebellious. Your bodies are hungry. Your souls are adventurous—perhaps even reckless. You are, like so many young people, apt to concentrate on the present and to forget about the future."

Layleh stared at her mother. "Umm," she said huskily, "what are you saying?"

"I want you to understand," S'ad said. "I have nothing against Uri Arnon and never have had. I'm sure he's a fine young man—otherwise you would not have drawn so close to him. Layleh, what I'm objecting to is the fact that your relationship seems to have taken...another direction. Do you understand?" A bitter smile that seemed to distort her entire face appeared on S'ad's lips. "What I'm telling you—what your father and I are telling you—is harsh and cruel. But it's true." With a sudden, convulsive movement, S'ad drew her hands from the pockets of her robe and clasped them together. *"There is—no future—for you and Uri!"* she blurted out.

"Umm! Umm, I——"

With powerful, almost savage determination, S'ad's unleashed voice overrode her daughter's protest. "You are *Arab*,

Layleh! Uri Arnon is Jewish! The both of you keep forgetting
that—but the world remembers! Perhaps the two of you don't
care—but the world does! You have lives to lead, the both of
you, and those lives will be touched and handled and twisted
by the world! And some day, when you are older, you will
have children of your own, and they——"

Layleh's eyes blazed. "But the world is one!" she cried out
as much in defiance as in despair. "Jerusalem is one! Uri and
I——" Her voice cracked. Tears filled her eyes. She gestured
fiercely with a hand and knocked the book from the bed to the
floor. Gasping for breath, she stammered: "It's impossible to—
talk to you—anymore! We have the same blood in our veins.
We live together under the same roof. We speak the same
language—but it is impossible to talk to you—or to Abu—
anymore! You don't understand—you simply do not understand——" Then her voice broke and the tears rolled down
her cheeks.

S'ad took a step forward.

But Layleh shook her head violently. "No, Umm——"

"Layleh, let me comfort you."

"No, Umm! There is no comfort that you have for me."

"Layleh—dearest."

"Please go now, Umm. Please leave me alone!"

When the door closed behind her mother, Layleh bent forward and covered her eyes with her hands. She thought that
she would weep, but she did not. She thought that she would
feel desolation, but—more than anything else—she felt a kind
of relief.

———————

Mahmoud was in his study, where he had been since finishing
the supper meal. At the periphery of his consciousness, he was
aware of the rain beating steadily on the roof and slashing in
sudden spurts against the shutters. But these sounds, far from
disturbing him, only contributed to the calmness and equanim-
ity that prevailed inside him. They were natural and sponta-
neous sounds. They had a sturdy, pleasing rhythm that one
could count on. And somehow—like the layers of a cocoon—

they seemed to wrap themselves around him and protect his privacy.

He was at his desk. The lamp was shedding a friendly fan of light down. And he was—and had been—writing steadily almost since he had come into the room. On so many occasions in his life, the study had seemed to him a prison cell, even a torture chamber. But tonight it seemed cozily supportive, even—like some sheltered womb—nourishing.

The years had, to some extent, mellowed Mahmoud. In keeping with the decision made long ago—made *for* him, he used to think wryly—he had remained aloof from the company of human beings outside the intimate circle of his family. But he no longer felt, as he put it, the "naked blade of his bitterness" as keenly as once he had. He was, as he often remarked to S'ad, used to his affliction—and it, in turn, was used to him. He saw the world of men for what it was and expected little or nothing more than its dismal failure to live up to the expectations he had once, long ago, had for it. He had not—so he felt—compromised himself by even one iota, but he had learned with painstaking and repeated effort to practice rigorous isolation and thereby protect his integrity.

There was a knock at the study door.

Startled, he looked across the little room. Neither S'ad nor Layleh ever knocked when he was writing unless there was urgent cause. His heart contracted—he hoped that nothing was wrong. With an effort, he collected himself and, steadying his voice, called out: "Who's there?"

"It's I—S'ad."

"Come in. Come in."

S'ad was in her robe. She looked pale and perturbed. "I'm terribly sorry to intrude on you, Mahmoud," she murmured. "Please forgive me, but——"

He waved a hand. "Don't apologize," he said quickly. "If you knocked at my door, there must be a good reason. Besides, I've finished for the night." Almost with diffidence, he smiled. "There comes a time," he said, "when one is compelled . . . to let go."

S'ad looked somewhat relieved. Taking another step forward, she said haltingly: "I've . . . just come from Layleh's room. In the light of our recent discussions, Mahmoud, I thought it appropriate . . . to speak to her . . . about Uri."

"And?"

S'ad swallowed. "And she refused to listen. That is, she did listen to what I had to say, but she refused to understand."

Mahmoud frowned. He gripped the arms of his wheelchair. "What is there that she does not—or will not—understand?" he said hoarsely. "It's all very clear, very obvious, very comprehensible. Whatever she has with Uri Arnon, whatever exists between them, has gone too far. It never should have gotten to this point, S'ad. But since it has and there is absolutely nothing we or anyone else can do to change what is past, there is no use dwelling on that aspect. What is of importance—of paramount importance—is that it *not continue!* Did you tell our daughter that, S'ad? Did you?"

His wife nodded slowly. Squeezing the words from her mouth with both pain and reluctance, she said, "I did, Mahmoud. I told her, openly and directly, that she and the Arnon boy could have no future together."

Mahmoud banged an arm of his wheelchair with a white-knuckled fist. "They cannot!" he shouted. "None whatsoever!" He stared at S'ad. "And what did Layleh say—what did she say to that?"

His wife trembled. "She—she——"

"Go on, S'ad."

"She asked me to . . . leave her alone, Mahmoud."

"To leave her alone?" Mahmoud said incredulously.

"Yes, my husband. It—it's the first time in her life she has ever done such a thing."

Mahmoud winced. "And what . . . did you do then, S'ad?"

His wife shrugged and avoided his gaze. "I—left her bedroom," she murmured.

"You said nothing more, S'ad?"

His wife shook her head. "What else could I say?" she muttered in despair.

"Ah!" Mahmoud declared explosively. "There's much more to say—plenty more that *has* to be said!" He cleared his throat. "And *I* shall say it, S'ad! Indeed, *I shall say it!*"

The wheelchair moved forward, but S'ad blocked its way.

"S'ad!"

"Not now, Mahmoud—not now—not this minute!"

"S'ad, let me pass!"

"Mahmoud, I implore you—not while you are so angry."

"S'ad, let me——"

"Mahmoud, *please!* I beg of you: *not now!*"

There was a sudden silence that, like the blow of an ax, separated husband and wife. S'ad stood trembling, with her fingers twisting together. Mahmoud stared, red-faced and beginning to perspire, around the book-lined study. At length, he sighed and drew a deep breath and, passing a hand across his furrowed forehead, said slowly, "All right, S'ad: not now. But I will speak to Layleh."

Exhausted but relieved, S'ad turned her head and sighed, too. She knew that Mahmoud's moment of naked anger would be swallowed in the ocean of his bitterness, and that whatever else had to be said to Layleh would be said by her.

Uri waited outside the neighborhood high school for his friend Avner so that the two of them could walk home together. This afternoon—the waning part of a strange, hazy day that did not seem capable of deciding whether it belonged to fading summer or approaching autumn—Avner did not make his usual punctual appearance. Impatiently—since his friend was rarely if ever late—Uri glanced at his watch and saw that Avner was already ten minutes overdue. He was about to leave the school courtyard when a strident, familiar voice called out his name: "Arnon...*ya* Arnon, *chakeh li*—wait for me!"

Uri smiled and saw his friend bound down the front steps in a single leap and dash across the concrete. Avner brushed a lock of gleaming red hair from his freckled forehead and—pausing for an instant to catch his breath—murmured, "I'm sorry I'm late, Uri, really I am—Chaimovitz caught me in the corridor and proceeded to give me a long lecture—unasked for, you can be certain—on my shortcomings in Trig! I tried as hard as I could to get away from the old bird, but you know Chaimovitz—he's like an octopus, and once he gets hold of you he just doesn't let go."

Uri nodded. "I know Chaimovitz all right," he said appreciatively. "I barely passed his course last semester."

The two friends went out of the schoolyard gate and started up the well-trodden dirt path to the main road. They chatted, easily and discursively, about their classes, which had begun only a few weeks ago, and about their teachers and classmates. Then, as they mounted the embankment to the highway and turned left in the direction homeward, Avner—his voice suddenly taking on a serious tone—said: "Ureleh, do you realize that we're both nearly seventeen? It's hard to believe that we'll be through with high school soon and going into the army." He shook his head incredulously. "Where did the time go? Why, it seems only yesterday that we were children, playing war games in our backyards and in the woods and fields."

Uri stared at him. "And in a little while, we'll be doing it for real, eh?"

Avner nodded soberly. "There seems to be no escape from the pattern," he said. "The Arabs keep nipping away at us. After the Six-Day War, they are afraid to attack us, but they keep nipping away. And we are forced to respond."

Uri swallowed. "Maybe . . . one day," he said, "the pattern *will* change. Maybe the Arabs will see that peace is the only way."

Avner laughed bitterly. "You're still a dreamer, Uri," he said with a brusqueness which perhaps he did not intend. "You always have been one. And I'm afraid you always will be!"

Uri flushed. "Avner," he said in a lowered voice. "You know I believe in dreams."

His companion guffawed. "Believe in dreams all you want while you're asleep," he blurted out. "But look out for reality when you wake up. That's my motto."

For some moments they walked in silence. Cars and trucks whizzed by on the road, sending faint puffs of exhaust smoke into the air. The leaves of the dust-coated eucalyptuses turned like childhood tops in a mild breeze that blew from the west. In the sky, the September sun struggled to reassert its former power. Idly, with perhaps the hope of relieving his tension, Uri kicked a tin can until he lost control and it bounded away into a thicket. Avner tried vainly to whistle. Abruptly, he abandoned his half-hearted attempts and said, "What do you hear from Ilana these days?"

Uri responded at once to his friend's question. "We had a

letter from her just a few days ago, as a matter of fact," he said. "She misses Israel very much and feels, as she put it, like a fish out of water in New York. And she's terribly homesick for the family. But she writes that she had to go, and that she's totally immersed in her music, and for now, that's her life."

"Losing Z'ev was hard," murmured Avner.

"It drove her out of the country," said Uri hoarsely. "I know—and she knows—that she'll be back one day. But she'll never get over the loss."

Again, there was silence between the two friends. They did not look at each other and seemed—unaccountably and uncharacteristically—uncomfortable in each other's presence. Then, as they came in sight of the cutoff road where they had to turn again, Avner suddenly dropped his physics book. Uri stooped to retrieve it from the grass and Avner bent at the same moment. They knocked heads and ended up laughing. "Clumsy ox!" said Avner. "Oaf!" said Uri with a grin. The painful silence was broken and they felt they could talk freely once more.

Uri did not waste a moment. Clearing his throat, he said, "Avner . . ."

"What it is, *chabibi*?"

"There's something I've been wanting to discuss with you for a while."

"There's no better time than now, Uri."

Uri hesitated. He drew a deep breath and said, "It's . . . about Layleh."

"Layleh?"

"The girl who lives next door to me."

"The Arab girl, you mean?"

Uri stared at him. "I mean *the girl . . . who lives next door,*" he said slowly.

"Well, she's Arab, isn't she?" Avner insisted. "Why would you want to deny it?"

"I'm not *denying* it, Avner. I just don't think that it's relevant to anything."

Uri's friend opened his mouth to challenge the statement, but he changed his mind. "I don't want to argue," he muttered. "Tell me about her—go ahead."

Uri nodded. "Well," he said, "you know we have been

friends, Layleh and I, since childhood."

"I was aware of that fact through the years," said Avner. "With all due respect, Uri, you couldn't keep it entirely hidden——"

Uri did not seem to hear the comment. "The friendship grew stronger and stronger," he continued, staring at the ground as he walked. "It was innocent at first. We played at the hedge and sent each other presents and taught each other words in Hebrew and Arabic and missed each other when we were apart and shared each other's experiences and feelings and—and——"

"Go on."

They had reached the cutoff now and, instinctively, they both stopped. Uri dug a sandal into the soft earth. He swallowed two or three times and then said softly, "Well, Avner, during the past couple of years, something has happened to the friendship."

"It's turned sour?" said Avner quickly. "Is that it?"

Uri shook his head violently. "No, no!" he protested. "Exactly the opposite has happened!"

"What do you mean?"

Uri's eyes stared directly and unwaveringly into Avner's. "I mean," he said, with deliberate emphasis on each word, "that Layleh and I . . . have fallen in love. Or else," he went on, "we have come to the realization that . . . we have always been in love."

Avner's eyes broke their contact. They stared past Uri, down the highway.

"Well?" said Uri.

His companion did not respond.

"Well?" persisted Uri, almost truculently. "Aren't you going to say something?"

Avner sighed and turned his eyes back to Uri's face. "What is it that you want me to say, Uri?"

"Anything, Avner."

"*Anything*, Uri?"

"Yes—anything you wish!"

Like a barb, Avner's laugh shot from his lips. "I—don't—think—so!" he snapped.

"Talk—*l' azazel*—talk!"

Avner squared his shoulders. A determined, almost fierce expression fired his brown eyes. The muscles in his hard-set jaw tightened. *"B'seder,"* he said gruffly, "I'll give it to you straight. If you really want to know what I think about your relationship with Layleh—I think you're crazy. As a matter of fact, *I think you're both crazy!"*

Uri heard his companion's words with a strange calm. He seemed almost amused. "What you say doesn't really surprise me, Avner," he said. "I could sense what you were feeling . . . and, actually, I'm glad it's out in the open now. It makes . . . well, it makes things easier for me."

Avner flushed. He gestured lamely. "I don't want to hurt you, Uri," he murmured. "You know that I care for you as I care for few people in this world. As for the girl, this Layleh, I have nothing personal against her. I don't even know her, for that matter. But I do have something—very much, indeed—against the 'love' or whatever it is that you profess. It is unreal, totally impossible." Avner made a valiant attempt to smile, but he ended up grimacing. "Uri," he went on, "I, too, wish that the world was other than it is. I wish that there was peace between us and our neighbors; that we did not have to live under the constant threat of war. But— and you certainly know this as well as I do—the Arabs have not accepted us and most probably, during our entire lifetimes, will not give up their hostility toward us. 'Love' between you and Layleh is therefore out of the question. The both of you are only dreaming if you fancy it can work."

Slowly, Uri shook his head. "You're wrong, Avner."

"How—how am I wrong?"

Uri was silent for a moment. With a sigh, he said, "Listen, Avner: I am a person and Layleh is a person. We grew up together and we have grown to care for each other. *That's* what counts! That I am a Jew—an Israeli Jew—and Layleh is an Arab is irrelevant. It has nothing to do with what is between us, with what we feel for each other. I agree with you wholeheartedly when you use the word *meshugga*—crazy, but I disagree violently with the way you apply it. *I'm* not crazy . . . and *Layleh's* not crazy. *It's the world that's mad!* What have Layleh and I to do with an insane world?"

Avner winced, but his eyes remained unflinching, and

when he spoke, his voice was firm. "Never mind what you think of the world, Uri," he said. "That doesn't alter the fact that *things are as they are and will undoubtedly continue to be for as long as we live.* Like it or not, the world has erected a barrier between you and the girl you say you have chosen as your 'love.' Not the pitiful hedge that runs through your backyards and separated you as children, but a wall of suspicion and hatred so great that you will never penetrate it, let alone throw it down. Arab is Arab, Uri, and Jew is Jew! And that's the way it will be!"

"Avner——"

"What is it, Uri?"

"Avner, you're . . . mistaken. I do love Layleh, and she loves me. We have both come to realize and to accept our feelings. Our love is what matters—nothing more." Uri's lips formed a slow and melancholy but resolute smile. "The world," he went on, speaking softly but with assurance, "may mock us. But what Layleh and I have for each other will prevail."

Avner bit his lip. "Brave words, Uri . . ."

"More than words, Avner!"

His friend shrugged. "Time will tell, Uri," he said. "But remember that I warned you."

Uri reached out and grasped his companion's arm. "Thanks for your concern," he murmured, "even if it's misguided."

Side by side, the two friends started down the cutoff road. The sun was well on its way to disappearing in the west by now. Across their path, the shadows of the cypresses and blue-silver pines were lengthening. The breeze had grown stronger—more assertive, it seemed—and there was just a haunting hint of autumn chill in the September air. Avner glanced over at Uri and, clearing his throat, said hesitantly: "Have you . . . discussed Layleh . . . with your parents?"

"Not really," Uri replied. "They know, of course, that we're friends—but nothing more."

"And Layleh's parents?"

"They suspect something, but I don't think they know that our relationship is serious."

"How do you think the parents will react when they know?"

Uri tried to sound casual, but there was a tremor in his

voice. "We'll face the reaction when the time comes," he said softly. "But we really don't care. They live their lives as they see fit—and we'll live ours as we see fit. Layleh and I will make our own decisions."

Avner did not look convinced. With a toss of his head, he said, "More brave words, *chabibi!*"

"You're wrong," said Uri.

"If you say so."

"I say so!" Uri declared defiantly.

———————

It was nearly eleven and a night wind was blowing, shaking the branches of the trees in the darkness and rattling the shutters and the loose tiles on the roof. S'ad was in the living room reading some of Mahmoud's new poems. Layleh was upstairs in her bedroom. Mahmoud had wheeled himself into his study, but once there, he wondered why he had come. Somehow, the snug little chamber that was both his refuge and his bastion did not offer him its expected comfort. He was restless, strangely on edge, out of sorts. When he left off spinning the chair around and moving it to and fro aimlessly over the floor and paused to consider the source of his immediate uneasiness, he realized that, for one thing, now that he had completed his collection of poems, he felt deflated—even helpless, as if he were adrift on some dark, unfriendly ocean. For another thing, he realized that the relationship between his daughter and the young man next door was weighing upon him heavily. His wife had spoken to Layleh, forthrightly and even bluntly several times, stopping short of threats and intimidation, but to no avail. Layleh was stubborn about what she openly called her right to live as she pleased and refused to listen to reason. Her attachment to the Arnon lad—what Mahmoud had called an irrational infatuation—increased almost day by day and deepened in its intensity. Mahmoud knew—and his wife, when she was pressed to the wall, knew it as well—that something had to be done. But neither he nor S'ad knew what that something was.

As he thought about the problem—and he could not escape thinking about it—a sudden noise made him start. The wind was making all sorts of noises, but they were familiar, innocuous sounds that did not disturb or jar him. This sound, however, was different; it wasn't the wind at all. A pang of anxiety touched Mahmoud's heart, triggering a queer, disquieting presentiment of danger. He was facing the shuttered window and something compelled him to see what was behind him. Quickly, with practiced motions of his strong hands, he turned the wheelchair around. His eyes widened and, for a moment, his breathing ceased. The burly figure of a stranger wearing a long, cowled cloak and dark glasses stood in the doorway of the study.

Mahmoud's mouth opened. *"Who——?"*

The stranger stretched out a hand in a gesture plainly meant to disarm the master of the house. "Calm," muttered the intruder thickly. "Just remain calm, *ya chawaja,* and all will be well."

"Who . . . are you? How did you get into my house?"

With a sharp movement of the wrist, the stranger sent the door swinging shut behind him. He could not resist a chuckle—a phlegmy, mocking, obscene little sound that reminded Mahmoud of water moving down a clogged drain—and then he said: "Unhappily for you, my dear Mahmoud, you continue to be one of those trusting souls who do not lock their doors. And so . . ." He snapped his fingers. "I had no trouble getting into the house."

Mahmoud shuddered. He had recognized the voice of the intruder. *"Fawzi!"* he gasped.

The other burst into laughter. "How clever of you, my dear brother-in-law," he drawled, stretching out the words as if to preserve his enjoyment of their impertinence. "How awfully clever of you to penetrate the disguise that has fooled so many others!" Then, pointing a finger at the desk chair, he said, "But what are you thinking of, dear host? Where are your manners? Aren't you even going to invite me to be seated?"

"What do you want here, Fawzi?"

"All that in good time," Fawzi muttered. "You have my solemn promise that I shall answer your anxious question." He sighed. "But I have come from afar, and I am weary." He moved with slow, ponderous assurance toward the chair. "If you won't invite me to sit down, dear Mahmoud, why . . . I shall just have to invite myself."

"Fawzi——" Mahmoud began, but his voice, which he had to strain to make audible, failed him and he was compelled to watch in silence as Fawzi twisted the desk chair about and lowered his bulk onto it. Unable to speak, he watched as Fawzi unfastened his cloak and let it slip to the floor and shifted his weight until he found a comfortable position. Settling himself back with a guttural moan of relief and disdain, he crossed his dusty-trousered, high-booted legs. "That's better..." S'ad's brother murmured hoarsely. "Much better! A man thinks he can walk forever, but then his legs tell him differently."

Mahmoud stared almost with disbelief at his uninvited guest. Fawzi had grown much heavier. His body was still powerful, with its large frame and thick limbs, but it had run to fat just short of obesity and looked gross—even grotesque. His coarse-featured face, out of which two beadlike eyes stared with ill-concealed malevolence, was overrun by a thick, dark mustache and full, sharp-pronged beard. His glasses—which he now, with a languid, arrogant sweep of a hand, removed—and his fallen-away cloak completed the "disguise" that he had pridefully mentioned.

Mahmoud wet his lips with his tongue and, making a determined effort, said: "After all these years, Fawzi, why... have you come to Jerusalem... and back to my home—*back to my home*, Fawzi, when my wife and I have made our feelings about you and your... interests unmistakably clear?"

"Years, Mahmoud? Has it really been *years?*" Fawzi looked up. "Let me see," Fawzi drawled. "The last time I saw my sister and yourself was—was... let me see, now..." And, unhurriedly, as if he were reckoning some problem of no practical consequence, he began to mutter under his breath.

Mahmoud's fingers tightened on the armrests of his wheelchair. "Fawzi!" he demanded. "Answer me!"

"Questions..." murmured Mahmoud's brother-in-law. "Always questions! Do you never tire of your infernal questions?" And then, with a sudden slap of his upraised knee that seemed to echo in the quiet of the study, he said in a harsh tone: "Very well then, my dear interrogator, since you are so anxious to know, I shall tell you! I am in Jerusalem because, for the present moment, Jerusalem offers me the greatest measure of concealment. You see, my dear Mahmoud, there are those who would interrogate me—not as you do, but out of deadly enmity.

And it is within the bounds of this particular city that I can best maintain my anonymity—and, I must add, my freedom. And I am in your home, my astonished brother-in-law, because I need, to put it succinctly, your help. Does that satisfy your inquisitiveness?"

"Help?" said Mahmoud. "What help are you talking about?" His voice trembled. "What help," he said hoarsely, "could *we* possibly give *you*?"

"Our cards are on the table," said Fawzi, "so I will tell you." His eyes gleamed. "I need money," he said. "Some of the more-than-ample sum that your, shall we say, well-off father left you on his death. I need the shelter of this house for a number of days—three at the least and ten at the most. And I need you—or my sister S'ad, as the case may be—to gather certain information and make certain contacts for me." Fawzi cleared his throat. "There, my dear brother-in-law," he went on, "I have given you the list of what I require. I have spelled it out to the letter. All you have to do, Mahmoud, is to comply."

Mahmoud twisted uncomfortably on his chair. "And . . . if I . . . don't? If I refuse your requests?"

Fawzi leaned forward, a sneer disrupting the masklike features of his face. He pointed a finger at Mahmoud. "Listen," he said thickly. "You don't seem to understand our positions. I'm not *asking* you for help. I'm *telling* you that I must have it!"

Mahmoud swallowed. "And if I don't help you," he repeated stubbornly, "what then?"

Fawzi did not speak at once. Breathing heavily, he sat for a moment in silence and then, with deliberate, calculated ease, drew a revolver from a holster slung over one shoulder on a leather strap. He pointed the gun at Mahmoud and said slowly, "I have used this before and I will not hesitate to use it again. Some people understand words of warning—others require . . . harsher lessons. Do I make myself clear now?"

"You are . . . threatening to shoot me, Fawzi?" he said incredulously.

"I am telling you, Mahmoud, that I will do what is necessary! I have told you what I need. I will do anything I must to obtain it!" Fawzi lowered the pistol. "Come, come, Mahmoud," he wheedled. "Use your brains! I have no wish in the world to inflict injury on you . . . or on your lovely family. But I find myself at present in a . . . ticklish situation. If you are reasonable and do what I say, I will be gone from this house in a matter of a few days or so, and that will be that. You will oblige me by complying and I will oblige you by leaving, and no one—I assure you—will be the wiser. But if you refuse, why, then I will be compelled to resort to . . . other methods." Gently, as if it were fragile and might be harmed by the impact, Fawzi tapped the pistol against his knee. "So, Mahmoud," he drawled in almost a condescending tone, "shall I tell you exactly how much cash I will need and whom you—or Sa'd, as it may be, must get in touch with?"

Mahmoud did not reply.

"Well, brother-in-law . . . I'm waiting."

Mahmoud remained stubbornly silent.

Fawzi stared at him contemptuously. He, too, was silent for a time and, after considering another approach, he spoke with evident control. Drawing a hand across his brow, he said slowly, "I simply don't understand, Mahmoud. How can it be, husband of my sister, that you rise each morning and go to the mirror and see your reflection there and are not revolted? Don't you ever have the urge to cut your throat when you behold your image? Can it be that you have never noticed what you see—or do you deliberately, out of sloth and shame, choose to ignore it?" In a heavy, measured cadence, Fawzi shook his head from side to side and then, abruptly, stopped the motion and went on. "For years now," he said, "you have sealed yourself off in this tiny room and kept yourself apart from what goes on in the world. You do not smell the smoke; you do not see the fire; you do not hear the cries of those who perish in the flames." He jabbed a finger at the shuttered window. "Outside," he said hoarsely, "beyond that shutter, there is a struggle, a bloody struggle from which you have, by your own calculated decision, remained aloof——"

"No, no," interjected Mahmoud, thrusting his head forward. "There is no struggle out there—no real struggle between Arab and Jew! The conflict that lingers on and on, taking its terrible toll, is a conflict that you, Fawzi, and your kind invented to begin with . . . and have perpetuated and exploited." Mahmoud smiled bitterly. "There is only one real struggle, Fawzi." Savagely, he rapped his breast. "It is the struggle," he said fiercely, "in *here . . . inside a man . . .* against the evil side of his nature."

Fawzi burst into gruff laughter. "Philosophy," he snorted. "Words and more words: gibberish spoken by a self-ordained shut-in, a recluse, a cowardly hermit." He sputtered: "A mummy who has himself slammed down the lid of his sarcophagus." He drove a fist into his open palm. "Mahmoud," he rasped. "What sort of man *are* you?"

Mahmoud said nothing. He heard what the other said and yet he did not hear. There were other thoughts in his mind, thoughts which drew him away from the exchange.

"You have nothing to say, *ya* Mahmoud? Where are your precious words now?"

Mahmoud stared at him with hatred.

Fawzi's eyes narrowed to slits. "You are not a man, *ya* Mahmoud," he said with a sneer. "A man would not hide himself away as you have over the years; a man would never close his eyes and ears to the struggle." He paused, groping in his mind for precisely what he wanted to convey, and at length continued: "Actually, Mahmoud, you are some kind of blind, molelike creature which spends its time burrowing into its own offal." His eyes widened. "Mahmoud," he said in a suddenly altered voice, "you aren't listening to me, are you? What I say doesn't penetrate your skull, does it? I'm wasting my time, aren't I? There is . . . no reasonable way to reach you, after all." His face darkened. "Then, my dear brother-in-law, I shall return to the key question: will you do as I wish?"

Mahmoud bit his lip, his gaze riveted to Fawzi's lowered gun. Quickly, but with a keen eye, he calculated the distance between his wheelchair and the desk chair and—in an instant—reckoned the time he would need to reach Fawzi. It was a risky proposition: his own expertise with the wheelchair against his brother-in-law's reflex action. If only, in some way, he could throw his adversary off guard . . .

"Well, Mahmoud," repeated Fawzi. "I must have your answer. I haven't any time to lose. Speak—or our little card game will take an ugly direction."

Mahmoud forced a brittle smile onto his lips. "Fawzi," he murmured, as if genuinely taken aback, "I am and can only be a man of letters and of thought. I am isolated from the world and not given to proposals of the sort you are making." He gestured. "Just look around you at the study—at my books and my papers——"

Fawzi was plainly annoyed but, obviously in the hope of humoring his victim and attaining, without the use of open force, his desired ends, he followed with his eyes the direction of his brother-in-law's pathetic gesture.

That was the opportunity Mahmoud was seeking. It was all he had—all, indeed, that he could hope to get—and he had to use it. Instantaneously, propelled by his taut-muscled hands, the wheelchair shot forward like a projectile at enormous speed. It streaked across the small gap of floor that separated the two men by one or two meters and in a flash—given the element of surprise and its incredible velocity—reached its goal. With a groan and a violent lunge, Mahmoud grabbed for the pistol.

But Fawzi, for all his bulk and astonishment, was quicker. Not, indeed, by much—but by just enough. He snatched his weapon at the last fraction of a second from Mahmoud's clawing, desperate hands and lifted it high above the other's head and then, uncrossing his legs and spreading his feet for balance, brought the butt of the pistol down with vicious force against his brother-in-law's right temple. Mahmoud groaned and slumped forward. Bright red drops of his blood spattered the clean, speckled tiles beneath him. Fawzi jumped up, throwing over his chair. "Dog!" he growled through clenched teeth. *"Dirty, treasonous dog!"*

At that moment, S'ad threw open the study door. Seeing her unconscious husband, she rushed to the wheelchair. "Mahmoud!" she cried out. "Mahmoud, *what has happened?*"

"He ought to be dead," Fawzi snarled. "All of you ought to be dead and left out to the jackals. But killing you won't serve my purpose. Neither—it appears—will my staying here."

S'ad turned. *"Fawzi,"* she whispered hoarsely, "what have you done . . . to my husband?"

Her brother ignored her. He stooped and retrieved his cloak and swept his dark glasses from Mahmoud's desk. In the doorway, he struggled into his cloak. Waving his weapon, he said hoarsely, "I'm leaving now, S'ad. But I'll be back—I'll be back with others who believe the way I do! Then your hus-

band—and all of you—will pay the price! You'll all pay dearly,
S'ad—just like the Jews!"

———————

Again and again, Uri picked up the novel he had started the
week before and opened it. But he could not seem to find the
place where he had left off or even remember what had happened to the characters, let alone read it. He kept looking over
at the little clock on his desk. It was as faithful, he thought,
and as battered a friend as he had ever had—but tonight it did
not wish to cooperate with him because its hands did not seem
to move at all. With annoyance, he snapped the book shut and
tossed it onto his bed and got up and went to the open window
and leaned heavily on the sill.

The vast dome of Jerusalem's shimmering night sky was
moonless, but the numerous stars filled its cloudless expanse.
Uri gazed upward, trying as always to decide whether the
brilliant constellations were flashing messages that were as-
suring or indifferent—it was a game he had played ever since
his childhood days.

The night—it was the second week in September—was
exceptionally warm. There was not the faintest hint of a breeze
and not a single branch or leaf or blade of grass stirred. From
the dense black mass of the hedge and the base of the oak tree,
with its weather-warped, dilapidated wooden house, and the
shrubs and from the wilting flower garden, cicadas shrilled
their endless song. But now, instead of comforting Uri as they
usually did, the sounds grated on his nerves. He was restless,
impatient, filled with a fierce desire to see Layleh. And he was
certain that she, most probably shut away in her own bedroom
next door, was as anxious as he was to meet. *That was the
age-old, seemingly inflexible irony of their relationship*, he
thought bitterly. *The physical proximity they should have enjoyed only seemed to deepen their frustration and increase their
tension.*

Absently, Uri pulled a handkerchief out of his pocket and,
wiping the sweat from his face and neck, turned away from
the window. He had an appointment to see Layleh at exactly

eleven. Although the clock stubbornly said ten to eleven, he felt that he could not remain in his bedroom a moment longer. He went to his door and cautiously drew it open. To his right, the door to his parents' darkened bedroom was closed—he knew that his mother, weary from a hard day's work at the hospital, had gone to sleep much earlier. But from the stairwell to his left there was a fan of light that spilled onto the speckled tiles of the hallway floor, and there was the sound of a Mozart piano sonata on the phonograph—he recognized it at once as one of his sister Ilana's favorites. For a moment he hesitated—he did not want to get involved in a conversation with his father. But he realized immediately that he really had no choice, since he did not, no matter what the risk, want to keep Layleh waiting.

On bare feet, he went down the stairs. He had made up his mind to make a dash past the living room doorway, but as he approached the danger point he saw suddenly that it would not be necessary. Arie, sitting in his chair with an open newspaper across his lap, had fallen asleep. Uri's glance traveled from his father's tan, seamed face to the unfilled pipe in one hand and then to the unfolded letter lying at his feet on the floor—a letter from Ilana in New York that had arrived at noon and that he and D'vora must have read over a dozen times since supper. A sudden feeling of warmth surged over Uri. He smiled to see his father—surrounded by a golden, protective cloud of Mozart—peacefully at rest.

The brisk, marching notes of the sonata faded as Uri went through the kitchen and out the back door. He crossed the porch and hurried onto the grass. Above the meticulously trimmed top of the hedge, the roof of the house next door jutted sharply into the sky, like the prow of a ship. Suddenly, he stiffened. A noise from the other side of the hedge had caught his ear. He sprinted forward and then, through the thick screen of interlaced branches and leaves, saw the familiar blur of Layleh's figure. A cry of mingled relief and exultation rose from his heart, but his mind—disciplined by long years of caution—prevented it from shattering the lazy calm of the September air.

Separated by the living barrier of the hedge, the two figures stood directly opposite each other now, like the delicately bal-

anced plates of a scale. For a moment, as if both were governed
by the same invisible force, they maintained a perfect, unmoving equilibrium. Then, as if on a given signal, they shifted
their positions and began silently to move down the yards
toward the stone wall at the rear. Their feet made soft, scraping
sounds as they climbed. Once, a loose stone dislodged itself
and fell with a thud to the earth below, and Layleh slipped but
quickly recovered herself. But then, almost at the same instant,
they were over the wall and safely down on the starlit ground
that had once been a stretch of no-man's land between two
warring armies.

"Layleh!"

"Uri!"

Their young, supple bodies—which had so long ago learned
the harsh lessons of their relationship—came together in an
embrace that was long and fierce and hungry. Over and over,
they kissed each other and whispered to each other the words
of their own private language of endearment and, with their
eyes and hands, explored the known but unknown contours of
their bodies.

At length, breathlessly, they broke apart and looked into
each other's eyes. Uri cleared his throat. "Come," he said
huskily, reaching out and taking Layleh's trembling hand in
his own. "Let's go to the grotto and talk."

Thirty or so meters out beyond the stone wall was their
beloved "grotto": the gnarl-trunked terebinth that had survived
the ravages of time and weather and the enmity of man. Beneath
the flattened spread of its umbrellalike branches, they sat on
their porous, rain-and-wind-gnawed rock. This was their special place—the place in which they were securely away from
the reach of the world. Once, many years ago, Uri had jestingly
remarked that before there were men and women on the earth,
the "grotto" had been a favorite meeting place for angels to
talk and rest before they flew back to heaven. And, to the
surprise of both, Layleh had taken the remark with a seriousness
she refused to give up.

Side by side, hand in hand, glad of each other's nearness,
they sat silently beneath the tree on the rock, as if the further
privilege of conversation might be asking too much and might
somehow result in their banishment. Slowly, Layleh turned her

head to her companion and murmured: "Uri, you said that you wanted to talk."

"I do."

Layleh smiled. "What do you want to talk about?"

He did not return her smile. "Your father . . ." he said hesitantly. "How . . . is he?"

Layleh drew a deep breath. "He has recovered physically," she said. "But, as for his mind—or as you would say in Hebrew, his *ruach,* his spirit, well . . . that's something else entirely. He's more withdrawn, and more morose, than ever. And his volume of poems—those beautiful poems I told you about, Uri; the ones he was going to publish—he's locked them away in his files and won't suffer a word to be spoken about them!" She paused for a moment and there was a catch in her voice when she continued: "Since my mother found him unconscious in the study, Mahmoud has not been the same man. He—he seems to sit around in his wheelchair all day doing nothing, like—like a corpse!"

Uri bit his lip. "Has he . . . said anything about what happened to him that night—about how he got hurt?"

Layleh shuddered. "No, Uri."

"And your mother?"

Layleh shook her head. "My mother avoids the subject like the plague. I've tried to question her about it a hundred times, but it's futile." She hesitated for a moment and then said, "Uri, do *you* have any idea about what happened? If you do, Uri, please don't hide anything. Tell me——!"

Uri shrugged. "What does it matter," he said, "what I—or anybody else, for that matter—thinks or imagines or suspects? The fact is that somehow your father was injured, and we'd better leave it at that." He sighed and then, in a softened voice, went on: "But your father has strength, Layleh. He will recover——"

"He has recovered in the past," Layleh said. "That's true enough. But . . ." Her voice trailed off and she turned her head away.

Uri reached out and took her chin in his fingers and gently turned her face once again to his. "I respect your father, Layleh," he said. "At the core of his strength is sensitivity. And that sensitivity will keep him going." A pained smile twisted Uri's lips. "Your father," he said, "has never allowed himself to be brutalized, as men in their weakness often do. He has never permitted intimidation to deprive him of his humanity. A man like that, Layleh, *must* survive."

"Uri, if only you could know him! If only you could really know how fine a person he is!"

"But I *do* know your father, Layleh. I know him . . . through knowing *you*."

Layleh said nothing. She seemed lost in thought—perhaps about what Uri had just said or perhaps about one of the dark, oppressive fears that suddenly overwhelmed her. Uri gazed adoringly at her: at her thick mass of black hair along whose folds starlight ran like mercury; at the broad, finely chiseled features of her face; at the sinuous curves of her shoulders and breasts and thighs. But he knew that the attributes which defined her physical person did not define her essence, and he continued to gaze at her with still greater intensity, as if he wished for his eyes to somehow penetrate the shell of her lovely body and see into the most secret recesses of her being. "Layleh," he said suddenly, "I wanted you to come to the grotto with me for a special reason tonight." He swallowed and went on: "I would like . . . to discuss the future with you."

"The future, Uri?"

"*Our* future, Layleh."

A shiver ran through Layleh's body. "I see . . ." she said faintly. "Then you do . . . believe that we . . . have one?"

"Of course, I do, Layleh! And so do you!"

Layleh trembled. "Perhaps . . . that is, some of the time I *do* believe it. But there are times, Uri, when . . . when——"

"When what, Layleh? Go ahead—finish."

"When I get to thinking that it's all hopeless, Uri. When I feel that the whole world's against us and we don't stand a chance. When I'm afraid that everything—that everything we have between us will come to nothing!"

"Layleh——"

"You asked me to tell you honestly how I feel, Uri, and that's precisely what I have done. You see, Uri, though I try— and quite often manage—to push it aside or even to bury it for a while, the knowledge that you and I were born and brought up on two different sides of the hedge is always there to frighten me. We have, so far, ignored the warnings of our parents. But as for what we will do in the future you speak of . . ." Layleh's voice faded away. She was silent for several moments. Then she said: "Uri, can you understand what I'm telling you?"

Uri's eyes were clouded, but his voice was clear and level. "Yes," he said in a measured tone, "I understand what you mean, when you say we were born and brought up on two different sides of the hedge. But out of our past—the past that you and I fashioned together despite the hedge—our *future,* the future of just the two of us, must come—no matter what the future of the rest of the world may be!" Uri paused and caught his breath and continued: "Sometimes I lose my faith in the rest of the world," he said, almost vehemently. "But I never lose my faith in the two of us."

Layleh stirred. "Uri," she said softly, "what you say is very beautiful. You make it all sound as if we don't at all exist in the real world. *But we do!* We cannot, you and I—no matter how much we want to and believe we do—live in some personal Garden of Eden! How can we possibly fulfill our relationship? Even our own parents don't seem to be able to understand it—let alone approve of it. Will we have friends, you and I, who will dare to take us into their hearts and admit us into their lives?" She gestured. "Uri," she said, "there is so much bitterness, so much fear, so much hatred and violence in the world! How will we be allowed the choice we have made? How will we ever be accepted?"

Abruptly, Uri rose from the rock. His figure was tall and lean and powerfully muscled, yet in the uncertain light draining down from the moonless sky and in the empty, dreary pocket of what had been for so many long years no-man's land, he looked almost fragile—almost insubstantial—to Layleh. She gazed up at him with a lump in her throat and a tautness in her chest, and all at once a strange, irrational, dismaying fear— the likes of which she had never before experienced—took hold of her. What if Uri, her beloved Uri, decided at that instant to leave her? A terrible, anguished impulse to cry out, *"Don't go! Don't leave me, Uri! We do love each other—we've always loved each other since the time we were children!"* welled up in her, though, with the greatest of difficulty, she stifled it.

Uri walked several steps away from the grotto and then

slowly turned and faced the girl on the rock beneath the terebinth. For some moments, he stared at Layleh without saying
a word; then, in a low, tense voice, he said: "Acceptance by
others doesn't concern me, Layleh. What concerns me is that
you and I be together, as we wish and have a right to be! And
as long as you and I accept and respect and love each other,
everything else will follow."

"Uri——" Layleh burst out, but she was unable to continue.

At once, Uri retraced his steps to the grotto and gave Layleh
his outstretched hands and lifted her to her feet and tenderly,
as if his strong, flexing arms were petals, enfolded her in his
embrace. Pressed tightly to each other, the two dark shapes
fused to make a single, indivisible shadow. At every point that
the exposed flesh of their warm, young bodies touched, a fiery
current ran through them. They pressed more tightly and more
hungrily to each other and kissed with all the dizzied strength
they could muster. And then, inescapably, as if drawn by some
magnet whose force they could not withstand, they sank gently
down to the waiting earth.

Slowly and carefully, and with a patience that, curiously
enough, was not at all at odds with his desire, Uri removed
Layleh's garments and placed them on the rock. Draped in the
gauzy light of the stars, her taut, firm-nippled breasts and
rounded belly and buttocks and smooth legs shimmered in thin,
silvery fire. Without taking his eyes from her naked form, he
undressed himself and put his clothing beside hers. They were
alone, the two of them, utterly and completely by themselves.
Urgently, he gathered her in his arms and pressed her body to
him, and the warmth of their flesh seemed to fuse them unalterably together. Caressing her glowing skin, he murmured,
"I love you, Layleh."

"I love you, Uri," she whispered.

The next turn on the road of their lives—the turn they had
glimpsed some two years before in the little copse of ever-
greens on the hill above Jerusalem—was there. They both
knew it and accepted it. Uri's kisses fell upon Layleh's hair,
her eyes, her cheeks; he drank at her mouth and then, lingering
at each, he kissed her breasts. Yet stronger than his eagerness
was his restraint. He had waited too long for this moment to
have it vanish: he wanted to hold on to it, to keep it, to prolong
it forever.

Drawing his strong body to hers with all of her strength, Layleh pressed her lips to his neck and his chest and the flowing smoothness of his shoulders. And then, as she opened herself to the passionate act of womanhood, Uri entered her slowly. When he moved, Layleh moved with him; when he was still, she waited with him on the brink of the precipice—until the final moment, when the wave of their love engulfed them.

And when it was over, after their carnal-soulful pledge of love had ended, they lay peacefully in each other's arms, cradled below by a gracious bed of earth and shielded above by a lacy canopy of stars.

Then, after a time that seemed at once to be all time or no time at all, they rose and dressed and, holding hands tightly, seated themselves once again on the rock—"their" rock: the rock that Uri always said, and Layleh half-believed, had been there, in that exact spot, since the moment the world was born.

They talked again about their childhood days at the tall hedge that divided their Jerusalem yards, remembering their special signals and signs and words and phrases, known only to them, and recalling conversations and discussions and meetings in the city and excursions about the country. They gestured excitedly and laughed and sighed and interrupted the tumultuous flow of their dialogue to kiss and stroke and caress each other and to gaze silently into each other's shining eyes.

And then, for some inexplicable reason—she herself admitted that she did not know what had prompted her—Layleh began to describe a wedding that she and her mother had attended while on a trip to S'ad's village in the Galilee. "I was just a little girl at the time, perhaps three or four," she reminisced, "but that village wedding has remained clearly in my mind ever since. It took place in the spring. The almond trees were in full blossom, and I remember looking off into the distance and thinking to myself that the beautiful green mountains that encircled the village had been invited to the ceremony as well."

Uri smiled and squeezed her hand. "You're very poetic," he murmured, "like Mahmoud. And very beautiful, like your mother."

Layleh stared off into the darkness. "I used to be very comfortable with my parents," she said. "They seemed to know how to stand back and give me the room I needed to breathe.

And yet . . . they always seemed to be right there when I wanted
their help." She cleared her throat. "But things have changed
during the past couple of years—changed considerably. I would
like for us to be as close as once we were. But sometimes I
think it's not possible."

"Because of us, Layleh?"

"Yes."

"Are you sorry?"

Layleh shook her head. "Not about us, Uri. Fearful at times—
but never sorry."

"Are you sure?"

"Oh, yes, Uri—I'm certain!"

Uri was silent for a moment. Then he said: "My parents
know that there is something—something real and strong—
between us. Yet they cannot—or simply are unwilling to—
come to the logical conclusion."

Solemnly, Layleh said, "And what is . . . the 'logical conclusion'?"

Uri reflected. "I will be eighteen soon," he said. "Eighteen,
in Hebrew numerology, the equivalent of *chai*——"

Layleh broke in: "In Hebrew, *chai* means 'life.'"

Uri nodded. "Yes, Layleh, life. And I will begin my life
as an Israeli man by going into the army for three years of
service."

"And we . . . will be separated," said Layleh in a whisper.

"We will always be together, Layleh; always have each
other, no matter what the geographical distance that lies between us. We'll write to each other, and we'll see each other
whenever we can—whenever I get leave. And then, when I've
finished my service, I'll come back to Jerusalem and enter the
university."

"Have you decided what you want to study?"

"Yes," replied Uri. "That's another thing I wanted to tell
you tonight. I've finally made up my mind, Layleh. I want to
study political science." He smiled. "Eventually, if possible,
I'd like to enter government—preferably the Foreign Service,
like my father. I feel I have a contribution to make."

Layleh squeezed his hand. "You want to . . . reach across
the hedge, don't you, Uri?"

"Exactly so, Layleh! I want to bridge the hedge of thorns
that separates our peoples!"

"And you *will*, Uri!" Layleh exclaimed. "I *know* you will! Just as I know that when I'm a teacher, I will be able to reach across all the grotesque hedges that separate adults from children!"

Uri sighed and drew still closer to Layleh and put his arm around her. He wanted to speak, but for several moments no words would come. At length, when he was calmer, he said quietly: "And then, Layleh, we'll marry. And the conclusion will become a new beginning."

"So, Uri—you have it all worked out, do you?" she asked, looking into his eyes.

"Of course, I do! Any objections?"

Layleh's eyes filled with tears. "No objections, my love," she murmured huskily. "None whatsoever!"

1973

---•◆•---

Jerusalem

URI PACED THE floor of his room—the cozy, intimate, always reassuring room in the house down at the end of the tranquil Jerusalem street that had been his for as long as he could remember. Everything in the world that he possessed—the books that he loved; the mementos he had collected on hikes and excursions and trips throughout the country; some of the papers he had written in class that he felt it worthwhile keeping; letters and notes and pictures and presents given him by Layleh over the years that he treasured; his prized collections of stamps and leaves and oddly shaped seashells that he had gathered and preserved since childhood; the soccer and basketball trophies he had won in school athletic competitions; his sour-noted harmonica and worn-out guitar; his camera and his meticulously kept photograph albums; his clothing, "always in disorder," as his mother constantly reminded him—everything that materially belonged to him was in the room. And in three days' time, he would be leaving everything and taking up residence— "somewhere in Israel," as it was phrased—in an army barrack.

It was strange, he thought, as he paced from the bed to the door to the window and back once again to the bed, but he did not in the least mind leaving all his possessions behind. Somehow, he felt, they were all important in their time and place, but they had nothing to do with, were not relevant to, the new life he would be starting. It was as if he were some creature that, in the externally ordained scheme of its existence, must slough off its worn-out shell and move on to another one. As he walked with his resolute, unvarying pattern over the floor of his room, he saw everything—but it all seemed remote, as if at some unspannable distance. It didn't bother him, though.

He would, so he thought, miss nothing acutely—nothing except for the physical presence of Layleh, with whom, he felt, he shared the familiar and comforting intimacy of the room.

The little clock on the desk said six forty-five. At seven, according to the plan that his mother had given him that morning before she went off to Ein Kerem, supper would be served: a farewell supper, in his honor. He disliked the idea, but he hadn't had the heart to deny it to his parents. For their own reasons, apparently, they wanted and needed it, and so, carefully concealing his negative attitude, he had acceded to their wish. His closest aunt and uncle, whom he had always admired and loved, would be present. Avner, of course, who was also leaving for the army, and some of his other soon-to-be-soldier friends would be there. His sister Ilana, who had some weeks before returned from her stay in New York, would also be present. But Layleh—after they had both discussed the matter thoroughly and had both come to the conclusion that it was better for her not to come—would not be there. After dinner was over and the guests had departed and the house had quieted down, however, Uri and Layleh had agreed to meet each other at the hedge and go out to the "grotto."

Suddenly, Uri stopped in his tracks. There was a familiar footfall on the stairs. Arie was coming up, and somehow Uri sensed that his father would soon be at his door. He was right, of course, and seconds later, Arie knocked. "Am I disturbing you?" he asked as Uri pulled the door open.

"No, Abba, I was just about ready to come down. Is anyone here yet?"

Arie smiled. "Everyone!" he said. "One might assume that you have a few fans." He gestured. "What have you been doing with yourself?"

"Nothing much—just thinking, I guess."

"Saying good-bye to the old life, eh?"

Uri shrugged. "I suppose so."

Arie cleared his throat. "There's nothing to worry about, Uri. You'll make a good soldier."

"I'll try my best, Abba."

"I have every confidence in you, son. You know why you're going into service—why you *have to go* into service—and that's the main thing: the rest will follow on its own." Arie reached out and touched his son's shoulder. For a moment, as if it were loath to leave the young man's flesh, Arie's hand remained in contact. Then, abruptly, it dropped away. "Actually," he said with a wry half-smile, "I'm an emissary. Your mother sent me upstairs to fetch you down—just as I used to do, if you remember, when you were a child."

"I remember, Abba," Uri murmured, following his father out of the room.

The dinner, which D'vora had taken great pains to prepare, went surprisingly well. "Uncle" Mordecai—he had always been called "uncle," though, in actuality, he was a distant cousin of Arie's—was a *moshavnik*, a smallholder, with some forty years of farm life behind him. He was a hardy, strapping, grizzled man who knew literally hundreds of anecdotes about living on the land in Israel and—given his ebullient and garrulous nature—loved to tell them. Spurred on by the attention of his audience—especially the young people, who devoured his every word with enthusiasm—he waxed forth with gusto and rich, earthy eloquence, pausing just long enough between sentences to make certain that his meal was eaten. He was undeniably a master at holding his listeners spellbound, and as soon as he had finished telling one story he would immediately begin telling another. "And that reminds me," he would declare in his booming bass voice, jabbing his fork into the air with one of his enormous, hairy-backed hands and gripping the edge of the table with the other, "of something else. The year was 1922—or maybe it was in 1923, it doesn't really matter—and practically everyone in the Chuleh Valley was down with *kadachat*—malaria—and . . ." His wife, Sarah—universally called "Sureleh"—interjected her own stories, often divergent variations on her husband's. And Arie, too, dutifully added his own family reminiscences. Reserved in the face of—and perhaps intimidated by the barrage of—old-timers' tales and legends, Uri and redheaded Avner and their other friends nodded approvingly and, aside from a number of questions and observations, listened. D'vora, who did the serving, said little throughout, and Ilana, who aided her, said nothing. Although Ilana seemed, for the most part, calm, from time to time her dark-ringed eyes stared past the guests and off into some unfathomable distance.

At the conclusion of the meal, Uncle Mordecai, red-faced and perspiring, proposed a toast.

Arie assented vigorously. "Go ahead, Mordecai," he exclaimed. "Make it!"

The wineglasses were freshly filled, and the veteran *moshavnik* rose to his feet. "I toast," he boomed in his warm, resonant voice as he lifted his glass high, *"tzirei-Yisrael*—the young people of Israel: our hope and our future! May they draw *ometz*—courage—and *koach*—strength—from the well of their forefathers! And may they, through their faith and dedication, bring our people security and peace!" With a steady, work-worn hand, he brought his glass to his lips. *"L'chayyim!"* he cried out. *"To life!"*

"Omayn!" came the answering murmur.

Then, scraping their chairs back and chattering noisily, the company left the table and went into the living room. Avner asked Ilana to play the piano, and after some hesitation, she assented. With confident, knowing steps—as if she were moving toward the welcome of an old and trusted friend—she walked to the piano and seated herself on the bench from which she had absented herself for so long.

The company settled itself. There was a moment of expectant silence. And then the notes of a Beethoven sonata slid into the stillness of the room.

At length—no one could say how much time had elapsed—the glittering cascade of music stopped. No one, perhaps not even the composer himself, could say why. Ilana drew her long, white fingers from the keyboard and sat erect. No one dared to applaud. No one, not even Uncle Mordecai, said a word. But all the eyes in the Arnon living room were shining. Their souls were filled with the inexpressible dreams that Ilana's music had inspired.

Cake that D'vora had baked herself that morning and fruit and steaming coffee were served. Uri and his friends chatted animatedly amongst themselves, while the older folks renewed discussions that they had begun long ago. Ilana sat quietly for a time, then rose from her place and began removing the crumb-littered plates and empty cups. Shortly before eleven, Uncle Mordecai got up from his chair and stretched his arms. "Well," he said with an unstifled yawn, "I think it's time for Sureleh and me to be on our way. We have a long drive ahead of us, and I've got to milk at four."

"He does . . . he does," murmured his gray-haired wife with a sleepy smile.

At the door, grasping Uri's hand in his own warm and callused fingers, Mordecai said: *"Nu,* Uritchkeh—*kol tuv*— everything good! As you depended on us, so we are now depending on you." He increased the pressure of his grip: *"T'zei b'shalom, Uri, v'tachzor b'shalom*—go in peace and return in peace!"

One by one the guests took their leave. Ilana said good night and retired to her room. Arie and D'vora began to tidy up and Uri helped them. When he saw that he was of no further use, Uri said, "I'm going up to my room."

"Good night, Uri," his father said. "See you in the morning." D'vora said nothing.

Uri started up the stairs, but suddenly the walk up seemed interminable. He thought he would never reach the top. When he got to his room he noticed that he had left the lamp on his desk burning—something he rarely, if ever, did—and its light shed a soft but strangely vacant glow over his bedroom. *The cocoon,* he thought. *This room is nothing but an abandoned cocoon.*

Though the evening had passed pleasantly enough, Uri felt enervated. He had agreed to meet Layleh at midnight, and the clock said a quarter to. Wearily, he stretched himself out on the bed—in his mind, already, he called it "the" bed and not "his" bed—and closed his irritated eyes. The familiar outlines of and shapes in the room grew blurred. With annoyance, he struggled to drive off the drowsiness that came over him. But taken unawares by its stubborn strength, he dozed off. . . .

He had an eerie, deeply disturbing dream. He was in the army— stationed somewhere in the south. By order of his commander, Uri was sent out on a mission: to find a secret enemy outpost. One—two—three days passed and Uri saw nothing but the wild, barren, desolate Sinai wilderness. Nevertheless, he per-

sisted. Another three days went by, and still there was no sign
of the object of his hunt. Burnt during the hours of daylight
by the blazing sun and chilled by night in the moaning desert
winds that flung the needle-sharp sand in invisible clouds through
the darkness toward the stars, Uri grew weary and footsore,
his eyes bloodshot, his face covered with sweat-clogged stubble, and his limbs aching with exhaustion. Still, he kept on.
But at length, when he discovered that his provisions were
running out, he knew he would have to turn back.

Compelled to abort the mission, he began to retrace his
steps. Suddenly, he halted in his tracks. Ahead of him, on a
ridge, he thought he saw at last the outpost he was seeking.
Evening—cindery, purple evening—was falling, and he rushed
forward. But the outpost seemed to disappear over a distant
hill. Doggedly, Uri pursued it. He reached the hill and ascended
it. In the last, spectral light of the dying day, he stared down.
But the outpost was gone. At the bottom of the hill, there was
something—but it was not what he had been pursuing. In a
final spurt of strength, he started down the hill and, trembling
with exhaustion, reached the object....

It was a grave marker—fashioned of weather-worn pink
Jerusalem stone. Stooping low to make out what was chiseled
on its rough-textured surface, Uri read the word: *Arnon*. His
heart contracted in a spasm of pain and he felt dizzy. There
was another word—the first name of the deceased—but Uri
could not read it. Fighting the pain and the nausea, he pushed
his face closer and closer——

Uri awoke with a violent jerk. For a moment, he had no idea
where he was. Then, with a shiver, he realized that he was in
the bedroom that he would soon be leaving and—though it
seemed impossible—that he had fallen asleep. He sat up and
glanced over at the clock. It said *ten past twelve!* He had never,
so far as he could remember, failed to keep an appointment
with Layleh. And now——

In a flash, he was out of bed and out of the room and bolting
down the stairs of the silent house. He rushed through the

darkened kitchen and out into the backyard. High in the velvety
sky, a full moon flooded the landscape with quicksilver light.
He saw the stone wall at the rear, glowing eerily as if someone
had set it on fire; the tall oak, with the warped and half-
collapsed remains of the treehouse clasped in its branches; the
drooping, September-struck flowers of the garden; and the hedge.
Rushing forward across the moon-kindled grass, he cried out:
"Layleh! Layleh—I'm here!"

There was no one at the hedge. He pushed the branches
aside impatiently and peered through. There was no one in the
yard next door, either. Frantically, he moved down to the rear
wall and, grasping its crusty upper stones, peered out toward
the "grotto." In the milky moonlight, he saw the terebinth
clearly, but there was nobody under or near it. Then he retraced
his steps and gazed up over the hedge at the house next door.
Layleh's window was dark. With mingled despair and hope,
he gave the familiar signal. Nothing happened and he repeated
the call. Once—twice—three times, he repeated it. But there
was no reply—and Layleh's window remained without light.

He lifted his head and, after a moment's hesitation, sent the
signal up one last time.

Nothing. Nothing but the familiar, hollow-sounding hoots
of an owl.

At once, he turned to his right and went past his back porch
and around the side of his house and onto the front lawn. Along
the street, the row of cypresses was silhouetted against the calm
radiance of the night, and from the main road the sound of a
speeding truck cut sharply through the still air. Uri stopped and
stood uncertainly on the smooth flagstones of the front walk,
and for a moment did not know what he was doing there.

Suddenly, the moon slipped behind a cloud and a soft,
almost elastic darkness fell over the slumbering city of Jerusalem. Uri's eyes strayed to the front of the house next door.
There were bright yellow fans of light streaming out from the
living room windows. Without thinking, he moved from his
lawn to the lawn adjoining it. Then, almost automatically, he
went up the next door walk.

On the Maleks' front porch, he halted abruptly once again
and seemed to wake up and realize exactly where he was. It
gave him a queer, unreal feeling. In all the years he had lived

on the street, he had never been where he was now. He took three or four rapid steps forward and stood just scant centimeters from Layleh's front door. Was he going to ring the bell . . . or knock? His logic told him that he had better think things through carefully—and yet another part of his mind told him urgently that if he hesitated even for another moment the resolution that had, quite obviously, brought him this far would fizzle away and be lost.

Uri rapped on the weathered wood of the door. Once— twice—three times, he knocked. He heard nothing; had no answer and—beginning to regret what he had so hastily and impulsively done—was about to turn and go back home when suddenly, with a sharp creak that nearly made him jump, the door swung inward. Framed by the same warm light that spilled from the windows, S'ad stood before him.

She looked as surprised—or, perhaps, alarmed—to see him as he must have looked to see her. For a moment, there was a strained, uncomfortable silence. S'ad's hands twisted the belt of her robe, while Uri shifted his weight from one sandaled foot to the other. Then, in a fierce, nervous spurt of daring, he said: "*Salaam*, Mrs. Malek—I hope that I haven't disturbed . . . or upset you. I saw the . . . light in your windows . . . and——"

Layleh's mother shook her head. "No, no," she said quickly, anxious to put her unexpected visitor at his ease. "You haven't disturbed me—not one bit! I never go to sleep before one at the earliest." She gestured. "Won't you come inside, though? Is . . . something wrong? Can I help you in any way?"

"Nothing's wrong, ma'am. I just——"

"Come in. Please come in."

Without hesitation, Uri stepped over the threshold. He glanced uneasily around the living room for a moment and then, with more confidence, back to S'ad's face. She was a beautiful, fine-featured woman—Layleh looked very much like her—but her eyes, though they shone with a tranquil, sympathetic expression, were filled as well with painful questioning. And there were lines of care and suffering etched deeply into her face. Uri cleared his throat. "I was just . . . just wondering about Layleh. I haven't seen her about today . . . and——"

S'ad seemed to stiffen—or perhaps Uri only imagined it

so. With a sigh, she said: "As a matter of fact, Layleh is ill. She has a high fever—it came on this afternoon—and she's sleeping now."

"A fever?"

S'ad looked at him with some seriousness, but she managed a smile. "Don't worry. I'm sure it will pass and that she'll soon be well." She shrugged. "It's the season, you know. The change of weather and all that."

Uri felt his cheeks grow hot. "I wish her... a speedy recovery, Mrs. Malek," he murmured lamely.

"Thank you."

Uri swallowed. "In the morning..." he said haltingly, "when you see her, please tell her that I... inquired."

"I will—certainly I will."

Uri drew a deep breath. "Thank you, ma'am." He gestured awkwardly. "And now... I must be going. It's late... and I don't want to impose on you any longer."

"It has been a pleasure, young man—not at all an imposition." S'ad's voice trembled—or perhaps Uri only imagined it to be so. "Just a moment before you go," she said at the front door.

"Yes, ma'am."

"Your Arabic—it's excellent."

Uri flushed. "I try to speak it as often as I can," he murmured. "You see, one day I hope to go into the Foreign Service."

"And I'm sure you'll do as well as your father," said S'ad.

"I hope so." Uri moved back across the threshold. "Good night, Mrs. Malek."

"Good night, Uri."

———————

At the top of the stairs, Uri ran into his sister. "Ilana!"

Half-apologetically, Ilana said, "As so often is the case, I couldn't sleep."

"Want to talk?"

"Do you?"

"Sure—I'm not sleepy either."

"Then come into my room, Uri."

Ilana sat on her rumpled bed and Uri pulled up a chair. His eyes fell inadvertently on a photograph of Z'ev that stood on his sister's night table and then quickly—as if they had been stung—glanced back to Ilana's white, slightly hollow-cheeked face. He had truly wanted to talk to her—it was ages since the two of them had last sat together for intimate conversation—but now that the time had actually arrived, he found, to his discomfort, that he did not know how to begin or, actually, what it was that he wanted to say. He fidgeted and cleared his throat, but no words seemed willing to come forth.

Sensing his perturbation, Ilana broke the silence. "So, Uri," she said, "you'll soon be gone. How quickly life passes!"

Uri nodded. "I feel so strange, Ilana," he murmured. "It's almost as if—as if . . . *I've already gone.*"

"I know the feeling well." Ilana clasped her hands together. "You know, I'll be moving out as well next week."

"Then you've found a place?"

"I have. It's in Kiryat Moshe. I have a single room, but it's large and airy and it faces to the east. The landlord is painting it now, and when it's fixed up, it will be quite lovely."

"And when do you begin work?"

"The week after next."

"You've definitely given up the idea of concertizing, then?"

Ilana nodded slowly. "I had always dreamed of being a concert pianist," she said slowly, "but now, somehow, I would rather teach. The conservatory offered me the position, and I took it. So that's that."

"Well," said Uri. "The next three years have been decided for me. And when I'm through with the army, I'll go into political science."

"In Abba's footsteps, eh?"

"Everybody says that, Ilana. But even if he weren't in the Foreign Service, it's something I would want to do. It's just something inside me, like music is with you, I suppose."

Brother and sister were silent for a moment. They had been looking at each other, but now each of them looked away. Ilana stared thoughtfully at the window with its pale blue curtains. Uri gazed at a little white bust of Mozart she had received as a prize in a citywide competition many years ago. Then, suddenly, Ilana turned her eyes back to her brother. "Uri . . ." she said softly.

He saw that something was troubling her. "Yes?"

"Uri, what about the girl?"

"You mean—Layleh?"

Ilana nodded. "Everyone knows that there is something between the two of you." She gestured. "I have known that you were interested in each other since we were children. But I never thought . . ." Her voice trailed off.

"Thought what, Ilana?"

"That it would become . . . serious."

"How do you know that it's 'serious'?"

Ilana leaned forward. "You try—the both of you—to be discreet. But it's really quite obvious." She hesitated for a moment and then continued. "Uri," she said, with a note of urgency in her voice, "what will be the outcome? Surely, you don't think of—of——"

"Go ahead, Ilana. Finish the sentence."

Ilana drew a deep breath. "Surely, you don't entertain the notion of marrying her?"

Uri stared at his sister. "You sound like marrying Layleh would be committing suicide!" he blurted out. "I don't understand it!"

Ilana sighed. "Uri——" she began.

"Everyone sounds that way! It's ridiculous. I hate it!"

"Uri, listen to me, please. Maybe, in a way, marrying Layleh would be like committing suicide, as you put it, for the both of you. You're both from different cultures, from warring peoples. It would never work out."

Uri flushed. "Layleh and I are human beings—*individuals*—that's what counts! And the 'warring' will not—cannot—be forever; one day it must stop!"

"Uri—forgive me—but you sound like a child."

"I—we—Layleh and I sound like young people who know what they want and mean to get it—no matter what anyone else thinks!"

Ilana opened her mouth to reply, but then changed her mind. She sat quietly on the bed, rubbing her knees with her slender, tapered fingers. A sad smile formed slowly on her lips, and an expression of bitter uneasiness came into her eyes. "Ah, well,

Uri," she murmured at length, "you are young and you are passionate and headstrong, and you think things are as simple as you want them to be." She swallowed. "You are wrong, my brother," she went on. "But no one will convince you that you're wrong."

"No, they won't."

Ilana shrugged. "I'm tired, Uri," she murmured, and she rose. "I'll see you in the morning."

"Good night, Ilana."

"Good night, Uri."

The little clock said one-twenty. Uri shoved it roughly aside. Leaning back in the chair, he pulled open the drawer of the desk and took out a sheet of paper and a pen and wrote:

Dearest Layleh,

I was terribly upset to learn that you are ill. I hope that by the time you read this you are fully recovered!

Tonight was so frustrating, so maddening—so incredibly absurd! I was actually in your house, in your own living room talking to your mother . . . yet I might just as well have been a million kilometers away! I wanted so much to see you, to kiss your forehead, to stroke your cheek, to say a few words of comfort and cheer and to tell you how much I love you. And yet I had to leave when I wanted to stay. I had to absent myself when I wanted to be near you!

Your mother was surprised to see me at your front door. I thought I was dreaming when she invited me in! And yet what could have been more natural? The truth is, my darling, that our love is real . . . and that the world is a nightmare!

I know it sounds silly, but I'm comforted by the knowledge that in our dreams, at least, we are together. Someday, it will be different. It will be as it was meant to be.

There isn't much time left until I leave. I feel as though I have already gone. I have separated myself in my mind from everything in Jerusalem—everything except you! It pains me that we must part, but as things are, that is the only way toward our eventual union.

Be well, darling. Get rid of your fever and return to health! We will make some arrangement to see each other before I go. Perhaps we will be able to spend an entire day together. The weather is fine and we could go to "our" woods in the hills above the city. How wonderful that would be!

I kiss you and hold you close to me, darling! Good night. . . .

Uri

Mahmoud said, "How is Layleh?"

As she slid through the darkness of their bedroom, S'ad replied: "Her fever is still very high. If it doesn't break, we'll have to take her to the clinic in the morning."

"Agreed," said Mahmoud. "We'll be there when it opens."

S'ad sat on the bed. "Mahmoud," she said. "Have you been asleep?"

"Yes. I just woke up when you came in. Why?"

"Then you didn't hear the knocking at the front door?"

"Knocking? What are you talking about?"

S'ad leaned forward. "Mahmoud," she said tensely. "We had a visitor. He came around midnight."

Mahmoud drew a sharp breath. "Not—Fawzi?" he said hoarsely.

"No, no," said his wife quickly. She cleared her throat. "It was . . . the young man next door."

"Uri Arnon?"

"Yes, Mahmoud." S'ad was silent for a moment. Then she said, "He wanted to know how Layleh was. He said he hadn't seen her about today. But I think that, because of her illness, she missed one of their appointments, and that he was worried."

Mahmoud struggled into a sitting position. "Uri Arnon actually knocked at our front door and inquired about Layleh?"

"Yes. I invited him in and we spoke for a bit. I told him that Layleh was ill—I could see that he was terribly perturbed to hear it—and he wished her well. He was extremely polite and sincere." Despite her agitation, S'ad smiled, a smile that her husband could not see in the darkness. "He is quite a handsome lad, this Uri Arnon, and he speaks Arabic with a fluency and command that must be admired. Apparently, he had a . . . good teacher."

"Never mind all that, S'ad," said Mahmoud. "He is a Jew."

"You say that, Mahmoud!? *You, of all people?"*

Mahmoud's voice was grave. "I say it entirely without rancor or animosity, my dear wife, and you of all people know that very well. I simply state a fact—or, rather, half a fact; the other half is that our daughter is an Arab. And now this Jewish boy comes knocking at this Arab girl's door—at midnight, no less!—to inquire about her health." Mahmoud paused for an instant to catch his breath and then hurriedly went on: "The meaning is plain, my dear—as plain, actually, as all the other signs and signals and telltale clues that we have been choosing to ignore. But now, this very night, Mr. Arnon is at our door, asking if our daughter is all right. In another week or month or year, he will be at our door with a bouquet of roses for Layleh. And then, in due course, he will be at our door, asking politely—in the Arabic that our daughter has so studiously taught him—if he may have a few words with Layleh's esteemed father." Mahmoud grunted. "S'ad," he continued in a low, emotion-charged voice, "it's all painfully obvious. Perhaps, if one cares to look back, it has always been, but we simply didn't want to face it. Our gullible young daughter and her starry-eyed"—he groped for a word and then burst out— "her starry-eyed *suitor* next door stubbornly persist in a relationship that is bound to run into a stone wall! It's *madness!"*

S'ad reached out and took her husband's trembling hand. "Mahmoud," she said softly, in an attempt to soothe him, "we've been over this same ground, in one way or another, before. It doesn't do any good to rant or recriminate. For whatever reasons, we—and both of us share equally in the responsibility—have remained passive, inactive. But now——"

Mahmoud snorted. *"'But now!'"* he repeated with bitter

irony. "We *always* say that—*and leave it at that!*"

S'ad shook her head. "No," she murmured slowly, "not this time, Mahmoud." She sighed. "Ever since I answered the door tonight, I've been thinking. Uri Arnon is leaving for the army in a couple of days. He and Layleh will be parted for a number of years. This forced separation will provide the perfect opportunity for their relationship to break up." She pressed her husband's hand. "What do you think, Mahmoud? This way, you and I wouldn't have to be the ones who hurt her."

"It's possible..." Mahmoud reflected for a moment. Then he said: "If—if——"

"If what, my husband?"

"If Layleh could, in the interim—if she could meet someone else. Some fine, young Arab lad—then..."

———————

In the narrow, foul-smelling room, Fawzi paced the stone floor.

Three hollow-eyed men, sitting on stools like circus animals their master had commanded to stay in place, watched his every movement as he passed to and fro in front of the smoking lamp. They neither spoke nor moved a muscle nor—perhaps—thought, but simply sat and listened to the harsh clatter of his footsteps and watched him walk and saw the enormous black hulk of his shadow glide back and forth across the soot-smeared walls.

At length, Fawzi halted and, without haste, checked the loaded weapons laid out on the long wooden table at the far end of the room, as if he were examining the items he had brought home from some marketplace. Then, turning to his three silent and motionless subordinates, he went over—for the final time—the plans for the next morning. He spoke slowly and deliberately, letting his heavy, guttural words ricochet like rocks from the echoing stone walls. Now and then he paused to let his sentences sink in—perhaps only for effect—before describing a circle in the air with a hand or jabbing a black-nailed finger forward to press home a point in a measured, calculated way. He was patient—he had, after all, until morning for the slaughter he planned to put into action.

He waited a bit, until the silence sufficiently separated the main body of his speech from what he was to add further, and then said gruffly: "Any questions?"

There were none.

"Everybody understands his role?"

Three heads nodded as one.

Fawzi nodded, too. Then, clearing the phlegm from his throat, he said: "Then we are ready, my comrades! Tomorrow, Jews will die! And Gaza—with open arms—will shelter and hide the *fedayeen* who will have slaughtered them like sheep!"

A murmur of approval—dark as the huge shadow of the man who had addressed them—rose up from the three subordinates. They saw clearly that now their leader was relaxed, and they relaxed as well. One of them reached into his shirt pocket for a cigarette. Another pulled a bone-handled hunting knife from its sheath and peered scrupulously at its blade. The third rose from his stool and, yawning, stretched his cramped and aching limbs.

Unhurriedly, with shuffling steps, Fawzi went to the door. He unfastened the bolt, opened the door a bit, and stared intently through the crack to make certain the coast was clear. When he was satisfied, he went out.

The moon was high over Gaza. It mantled the surrounding terrain with a heavy, silver radiance and sent its shimmering rays over the rooftops of the city and filled the high-walled corridor of the street before his eyes with pale, chill, fine-spun light. With his kaffiyeh folded tightly to mask all of his face but his squinting eyes, Fawzi gazed up at it and wished that it were gone already and that the light of the new day had replaced it.

He remained outside the house, gazing upward for some time, and then, suddenly feeling the strain of the long day's preparations, turned and reentered the thick-walled room from which he had issued.

Once inside, he froze. His mouth fell open and a thin, dry sound slid from his throat.

The three men he had left were on their feet. Two were pointing weapons they had taken from the wooden table at him. The third had his hunting knife in a raised hand. An icy wave of terror ran up Fawzi's spine and seemed to crush the base of his skull. There was an instant of silence and then he murmured hoarsely: "What . . . is the meaning . . . of this?"

The man with the knife said, "Do you remember a man named Mustapha, Fawzi?"

"Of course, I remember him! He was a stalwart soldier of Islam, who died in battle——"

The other cut him off. "I am his cousin, Fawzi, and his blood is on your hands!"

Fawzi shook his head. "No," he said in a hollow whisper, "you are mistaken——"

"There is no mistake, Fawzi. Your bloody deed is uncovered!"

"On my life——" gasped Fawzi.

The man with the knife grimaced. "But you have no life left . . ." he murmured. And, hurling himself forward, he plunged his dagger into Fawzi's chest.

———————

The huge, square-nosed, army-brown troop carrier was halted in the dust-covered, drab-barracked southern military outpost that looked, in its austerity and forlornness, like some forgotten encampment at the end of the world. Around the truck, which had been halted there for some inscrutable reason more than an hour, the new recruits, in their rumpled caps and sweat-stained fatigues, milled about aimlessly or squatted in narrow, dense strips of shade along the barrack walls, or stared vacantly off into the bleak distances.

Uri remained alone in the back of the truck. The air under the rigid brown-gray tarpaulin was stale and stifling and the heat was intense. Several times since they had halted, one or another of his comrades had come forward and urged him to descend. Adamantly, he had waved them off. "It's fine," he had muttered with mingled appreciation and annoyance, "I really don't mind the heat. I'm fine."

In fact, he scarcely noticed it, so intensely was he preoccupied with the letter he was writing to Layleh. He had managed to dash off a couple of notes to her since leaving Jerusalem, but this was the first effort that was, apparently, about to develop into a complete letter. Bending forward on one of the benches deserted by his comrades, he continued to write:

> *. . . that having only a glimpse of you in your bedroom window before I left was cruel—especially when we had hoped and planned for an entire day together in "our" woods. And yet that glimpse was enough to lift my heart and cheer me!*
>
> *Dearest Layleh, I hope that by the time you read this, you are fully recovered and——*

Uri's pen stopped in midmotion. Some strange, urgent sound—a sound that he could not ignore, as he had previously shut out the laughter and exuberant conversation of his fellow soldiers—grabbed his attention. It was the voice of the lieutenant stridently calling the unit into formation. In a flash, he pocketed his unfinished letter and clipped the pen to his shirt and, snatching up his automatic rifle, sprang from the wooden bench and neatly swung himself down from the truck.

He was in the front line of the platoon, third from the right, and reached his appointed place just in time. Lieutenant Dagani, red-faced and sweating profusely, cleared his throat. "Soldiers of Israel," he cried out, squinting in the rays of the desert sun, "we have received word that Egyptian forces have managed to cross the Suez Canal! Our front-line garrisons are under heavy attack!" His face flushed to a still deeper shade of scarlet. "Men of Israel!" he shouted. *"Our country is at war!"*

He continued speaking, but in vain, for his next words were drowned out by a thunderous roar. Uri, along with every other man in the unit, lifted his eyes to the shimmering steel plate of the sky and saw—like razors ripping with savage speed through the air—a formation of Israeli fighter-bombers streaking southward.

The young fellow named Ami called out from the next foxhole: "We're not even properly soldiers . . . and yet——" He could not or, perhaps, because he was suddenly ashamed of what he was feeling, would not finish the sentence. He was no more than a month younger than Uri, but for some unfathomable reason, perhaps the incredible look of naiveté that never seemed to leave his large, dark eyes, Uri considered him to be years younger than himself, a mere child, actually, who had by some accident or unaccountable quirk or bumbling bureaucratic error been drafted into the army.

From his own foxhole, with a wry smile that unavoidably turned grim, Uri finished the sentence for him: "And yet," Uri shouted back, "they have packed us straight off into battle!" He spat the dirt from his mouth. "Is that what you were going to say?"

There was a strained silence, during which Uri almost regretted the words he had uttered, and then the other's voice drifted over: "Yes... exactly. How... did you know?"

"I assume that everyone in our unit—except for Lieutenant Dagani and the noncoms—is feeling pretty much the same thing."

Reassured by the fact that Uri did not seem to dislike him, Ami—who had informed Uri on the first day they were together that he was from Petach-Tikvah and intended to study Hebrew literature when he finished his military service—called: "We haven't even completed our basic training, you know. We're not prepared. It's—it's *terrible!*"

"So it is," replied Uri. "But apparently there was no choice. The Egyptians attacked, and our southern command needed every man it could get. So here we are...."

There was another silence. Through the darkness that enveloped the hastily formed Israeli line of defense, the wind hurled a stinging spray of sand. Then—indecipherably, because of the gusting wind—Ami's piping, childlike voice came once again.

"Louder!" shouted Uri. "I can't hear a thing you're saying!"

Ami raised his voice. "Are... you... afraid?"

"What's that?"

"I said: *are—you—afraid?*"

"I don't think about it."

"How... do you... manage that?"

"By thinking about something else—something other than war."

The wind died down and Ami's voice came across more distinctly. "Oh," he called. "Like your girlfriend, eh?"

"Yes—like my girlfriend."

"Where does she live?"

"In . . . Jerusalem."

"That's terrific! So you can see her often—whenever you like, eh?"

"Yes—whenever I like."

"Mine lives in Haifa. I've got to travel for hours to see her. I wish she lived closer."

"Maybe someday one of you will move."

"Maybe . . ." The idea seemed to amuse Ami, and Uri heard his innocent laughter glide through the darkness. And then the reedy, high-pitched voice said: "My girlfriend's name is Chavatzelet. Her family comes from Poland. What's your girl's name?"

"My girl's name?"

"Yes. Is she a sabra?"

Uri hesitated. He wanted to answer. But something—he could not say what—held him back. With mingled irritation and discomfort, he twisted his cramped body in the foxhole.

"Did you hear me, Uri?"

"Yes."

Suddenly, an unearthly scream tore the air into ribbons. Uri felt his flesh recoil. He thought he heard his next-door neighbor's voice, but he could not separate it from the nerve-shattering wail. Then came the explosion—it shook the earth, raining dirt and stones onto Uri's head and into his face—and the sky, perhaps the entire night, turned to writhing, red-white tentacles of fire. At once, Uri jammed his helmet on and crouched and held his breath. The next wail sounded and he braced himself for the explosion and when it came thrust his fingers into his ears and closed his eyes. A third shell crashed and then a fourth and then a fifth and then the earthquakelike explosions came so rapidly and so close together that one could not be distinguished from the other.

Then the answering fire came from the Israeli artillery positions on the ridge to the rear. Uri crouched, burrowing into the same sweat-soiled dirt that had, only moments before, annoyed and irritated and discomfited him. Like a mole, he twisted

himself down into the loving shelter of his foxhole, while above
him, through the shredded sky of night, the big guns dueled
with unrelenting ferocity.

He attempted to think—to think about anything but what
was actually going on—but, like fleas, his thoughts jumped
aimlessly and haphazardly about from subject to subject. So
he did nothing but squirm and shrivel and burrow. His frantic
efforts did not accomplish much, but they reminded him that
he was still among the living.

He could not have said how much time had elapsed—time,
and what little remained of the world of logic and order, had
collapsed. But at length, the artillery duel slackened off. The
enemy shells howled in one by one and burst in individual
concussions; the Israeli shells, sailing out from behind the zig-
zagging line of foxholes, responded to them in kind. Slowly,
like a foundering ship that in the very nick of time is released
from the fury of a storm, the world righted itself. Uri—completely at home in the burrow he had himself dug that very
afternoon—crouched where he was. Although his mind had
once again begun to move in its usual rational and sequential
fashion, his body did not seem willing to allow the use of even
a single muscle.

Then, as if from some incalculable distance, he heard voices
and the shrill, repetitive sounds of a whistle. With effort, he
freed his limbs from their frozen positions and, like a diver
coming uncertainly from the depths that had sealed him off
from all life on land, climbed laboriously out of his foxhole.
The acrid fumes of high explosives were in the air. A dozen
fires, eerily dotting the desert landscape like torches thrown
down by some colossal hand, were burning out of control, and
shouts and orders rang out. In the fitful, ragged light of the
flames, shadows raced this way and that. One voice penetrated
Uri's consciousness and commanded his attention: it was Lieutenant Dagani's, charged with extreme urgency and yet uncannily calm. Gripping his rifle tightly, Uri turned and moved
toward it.

Suddenly, he stumbled and almost fell. Something on the
ground, something limp and wet and broken, had tripped Uri.
Startled, he looked down, and then, sensing another human
presence, he turned. Lieutenant Dagani, helmetless and grasp-

ing a revolver in one hand, was at his side. "Are you okay, Arnon?" the lieutenant said hoarsely.

"I'm fine. But——"

Dagani looked down to where Uri's finger pointed. Slowly, like a specter in the erratic pulsing of the firelight, the lieutenant, daring to do what Uri would not, bent and examined the dark hulk on the earth. At once, Dagani rose and cried fiercely: "Medic! *Over here! Medic!*"

Uri trembled. "What?" he gasped. Then, struggling to control himself, he whispered: *"Who?"*

Lieutenant Dagani reached out and grasped Uri's arm. "It's Ami," he said.

"Ami? I . . . don't understand. . . ."

Dagani's voice said dully: "Apparently, he was frightened and left his foxhole during the shelling." The lieutenant lifted his head and bawled: *"Me-dic!"*

A thick-torsoed soldier, panting heavily, lurched out of the flame-ribbed darkness. "What—is it, Dagani?" he stammered.

"It's Gafni," said the lieutenant. "He was hit." He looked down and then quickly up again and said: "I want you to have a look."

"Right," said the medic, stooping. He held the wounded man's wrist, feeling for a pulse.

But there was none. The medic shook his head.

Uri shuddered. "He's dead? Ami's *dead?*"

Lieutenant Dagani squeezed Uri's arm with a force that made him wince. *"Mayt,"* the lieutenant said. "Dead."

Uri wrenched himself free of Dagani's grasp.

"Arnon——"

But Uri ran, stumbling blindly through the maze of gaping craters and deserted foxholes and burning fires that sent showers of sparks shooting up in the sky. He did not know where he was going or why—he just knew he had to keep going. At length, just under the black-edged ridge on which the big Israeli guns were perched, he stopped. It wasn't that he could not have gone further, though his limbs were exhausted and his breath all but gone—it was that there was nowhere he could go that would take him away from the pictures in his mind. He kept seeing the narrow, fragile-boned, freckled face of Ami Gafni. He remembered the first time he had seen Ami outside the barracks in the dusty compound of the recruits' camp, and how he had shown him how to put the parts of his rifle together properly. He recalled lending the skinny recruit a pen so that he could write home to his parents in Petach-Tikvah. He thought of the two of them—Ami and he—digging foxholes together, side by side, in the savagely glowing light of the afternoon sun. And now—just like that, as a man snaps his fingers or dusts the dirt off his pants or strikes a match—Lieutenant Dagani had simply said: *"Mayt."*

Uri turned. In the distance were the fires and shouts and scurrying shadows he had left. His head cleared and he realized that he had to get back. Moving with a determination that seemed to sap the last of his strength, he started in the direction of his unit. As he drew closer, he was able to make out the voices of the noncoms and the unmistakable, staccatolike shouts of Lieutenant Dagani, and he thought that he would be able to control himself. But suddenly his mind, like a raft, seemed to capsize and he heard, as clearly as the noises around him, the sound of Ami's reedy voice. *What's your girlfriend's name?* it said.

An icy spasm seized Uri's mind. *Why hadn't he given Ami an answer?*

At that moment, Lieutenant Dagani touched his shoulder. "Are you feeling all right, Arnon?" he said.

But Uri could not speak. He could only cover his face with his hands and try with all his might to weep.

———

Beneath the flawless blue glaze of the desert sky, the half-tracks and tanks and command cars and omnipresent jeeps were ranged like insects. In the bunkers and trenches and in the miserly parceled shade of an occasional date tree, the half-naked men, in sun-bleached forage caps and webbed steel helmets, lounged and dozed and talked endlessly and read and dreamed—awake and asleep—of a thousand places they would rather be. Everywhere, it seemed, there were dog-eared, frayed, half-shredded Israeli newspapers that had been leafed through again and again, newspapers whose banner headlines and on-the-spot stories and front-line photographs described Israel's stunning counterattacks in the north and armored thrusts across the Suez Canal and, just lately, definitive encirclement of the Egyptian Third Army in enemy territory. Now the military operations had—because of external pressure—halted, and the political war, nerve-wracking and decisive, had begun. For the soliders of Uri's unit, and for their battle-weary comrades on the southern front and in the north, the tension of waiting had replaced the chaos of combat.

In a forward emplacement, protected by thick layers of sandbags and ringed about by barbed wire, Uri handed his binoculars to his relief man and sat down to rest. His eyes, tired with the strain of observation, closed almost of their own accord and his muscles slowly relaxed. For some time he did nothing except succumb to the drowsiness that lured him into a stupor. But soon an aggressive fly, whining with brazen persistence, kept lighting on his face and roused him. At the same instant, he saw a bearded little Yemenite soldier with a dust-whitened kaffiyeh wound about his head come in through the trench. The Yemenite, still blind from the blaze of the sunlight, blinked. As his eyes grew accustomed to the dimness, he grinned and said in a squeaky voice: "Arnon, Uri?"

"I'm Uri Arnon. What is it?"

The Yemenite held out a sweat-spotted envelope. "This letter is for you, *chabibi.*"

"Thank you."

The Yemenite nodded and backed slowly away.

For some time, Uri let the letter lie on his lap. He did not make a move to open the envelope or even touch it, or even look at the handwriting to see whom it was from. For the moment, he thought, it was enough to know that he had received mail and to savor the sweet, tantalizing enjoyment of anticipation. But the pleasure of waiting could be drawn out for only so long. At length, with fingers that he could scarcely keep from trembling, he picked the letter up. A hard knot came into his throat as, at once, he recognized the meticulously formed words that made up the address: *the letter was from Layleh!*

Forgetting the intense heat and the pricking of his overstrained eyes and the anxiety that seemed to grip him, he ripped the envelope open and unfolded and smoothed out the half-crumpled sheets of paper inside and, bending forward, read:

Dearest Uri,

You have been constantly in my prayers all these inter-minably long days. Though I have wanted to write to you a thousand times, I have not—out of fear or, perhaps, cowardice—been able to do so until this moment. Then, this very morning, I received my first letter from you. And I realized, in an avalanche of guilt, that I must procrastinate no longer.

I hope and pray that you are well, my darling. The mere thought of you in danger strikes my soul with terror, and I do not know what to think or do or where to turn to bring even the slightest sense of relief. Only the letter from you this morning gave me some measure of comfort. Only the knowledge that the war cannot possibly go on for much longer affords me a little release.

I go on, of course. Everyone goes on. There is no choice. That is the lesson, you yourself told me, taught by living in the Land of Israel: that there is no choice! Before you left Jerusalem, you said that you had no choice but to go away— it was the only road that would lead you back to me. I listened to you carefully, dearest Uri, and I trusted you. And I believed you implicitly.

So, now, my darling, you must listen to me and under-stand what I say and trust me and believe in me with all your loving and generous heart. It is painful for me to write the coming sentences—fully and truly as painful as it will be for you to read them—but I am obliged to write them. I, too, dearest Uri, have no choice. I am bound to take a road that—though it seems to lead away—is, in actuality, the only road that will ultimately lead directly back to you. There is nothing that I have ever wanted to conceal from you: that has always been—and always will be—an un-failing sign of our love.

Two days ago, my parents confronted me with "the ob-vious and undeniable" fact of our relationship. They told me—flatly—that they knew it was serious, serious enough, they said, to one day lead to marriage. They were certain, they said, that I was well aware of their objections, and proposed a plan which, they believed, would "once and forever" resolve the issue—a plan which would be "objectively" fair to everyone concerned: to me, to you, to them, and to your parents. Since childhood, they contended, I had never really seen or been with anyone other than you. As the two of us are now—and will be for some time— parted by the force of external circumstances, my parents suggested that I put my feelings for and commitment to you to what they termed a "test." In short, they proposed that I meet and see someone else—someone, they said, from my own people and background and culture. If my attachment to you were to survive this test, so they said, they would give their "approval" to our relationship . . . and to our eventual union . . .

I refused, adamantly and categorically. But without the least bit of deceptiveness, they pursued their main point: if I were that sure of my love for you and my wish, eventually, to be your wife, what could I or our relationship lose by my seeing someone else? If I were not absolutely certain that my love for you would pass such a test, how could I possibly be certain that I really was in love with you?

Of course, when I heard the proposal, I knew very well there would be nothing to fear from such an absurd "test." No one in the world could ever rival or replace you, Uri. But how, in actuality, was I to accede to such a request? How could I possibly bring myself to meet or see anyone but you?

You love me, my darling . . . and so do my parents! You are concerned about my welfare, Uri . . . and so are they! You will understand, I am sure, the terrible pain and confusion I felt—and still feel. I am torn, ripped apart. I do not know which way I must turn. Thus, as harsh and as cruel as it is for the both of us, I believe that it would be better, my dearest, for us not to see each other at all until you have finished your army service. By that time, Uri darling, things will be different. They must be! I know we'll be together again! If my parents say that I must not see you for a while, so be it. But I will never see other men. I promise you. No one can ever take your place.

*So, my darling, it is written and revealed—and I am
relieved. We stand once again, soul to soul, keeping nothing
from each other. We will continue to walk the separate roads
that must one day lead us back to each other. We do not
meet these days, my dear one, by the hedge and go to our
beloved "grotto" ... but I meet you always, Uri, in my mind
everywhere I go, and I am constantly with you in the grotto
of our love.*

*Dearest Uri, my prayers are ever for you. Keep well
and safe: not only for you, but for me.*

Yours,
Layleh

In the command bunker, the Coleman lamp blazed with a blinding, unnatural light that made Uri turn his eyes away. Lieutenant Dagani's voice, strangely muted, said: "Sit down, Uri."

Uneasily, Uri seated himself on an empty food tin. "Thank
you, sir," he said. When his eyes barely grew accustomed to
the glare of the lamp, he saw that there were four or five officers
besides Dagani in the underground chamber. It was Lieutenant-
Colonel Sapir—a tall, bushy-haired man with graying hair and
a narrow, sharp-boned face—who spoke next. "Arnon..." he
began, drumming his fingers on the table at which he sat.
"Arnon, are you all right?"

"Yes sir," Uri said, still preoccupied with Layleh's letter.

Sapir, who was the commander of the entire section, seemed
to be searching for words. Slowly, he rubbed his stubble-cov-
ered chin. "You are Arie Arnon's son, aren't you?" he said at
length.

"I am, sir."

Sapir nodded. "I served with your father in 1956. I have
only the fondest memories of him."

Uri stared at the faces of the officers opposite him. They
were grim. And when his eyes met Dagani's, the lieutenant
quickly averted his gaze. Uri swallowed. A sense of helplessness—almost panic—overcame him. He made an effort to

steady his voice. "Is—is something wrong, sir?" he said: "Have I——"

Lieutenant-Colonel Sapir stiffened. "Arnon," he said dully, "there's no way to tell you what I must, except to say it." He drew a deep breath and went on: "Arnon, we have just received word that your father is dead. He was killed by a mine on the road to Damascus. I'm sorry, Uri—we're all sorry."

"My father——"

Sapir rose. "The funeral will take place tomorrow. We will fly you north in the courier plane at dawn."

"My . . . father . . . was killed. . . ." The light of the lamp seemed to explode inside Uri's skull. Heavily, as if he could no longer support it, his head fell forward. There was a raucous ringing in his ears—he thought it might be the alarm clock in his bedroom in Jerusalem. Then he felt the pressure of two warm human arms around his shoulders—he thought that somehow, perhaps, they might be his mother's. Then Lieutenant Dagani's voice whispered hoarsely: "Uri . . . Uri . . ."

Uri wanted to say something—something that, though he felt dead, would let all of them in the bunker know that he was still alive—but he did not know what to say; did not know if he remembered how to speak; did not, indeed, know for a fact that he *was* still among the living. So he sat and he—or whoever it was that had power over his body—tried to control himself, but he could not keep himself from shivering. It was cold in the bunker, suddenly cold, as if someone had shoved him into a refrigerator; the Coleman lamp sitting on the table seemed to have turned into a gleaming block of ice, and neither Lieutenant Dagani's nor his mother's nor anybody else's hugging arms could keep him warm.

"Uri . . . *Uri* . . ." Dagani kept whispering.

Then, making a supreme effort, he opened his mouth to answer the lieutenant as a soldier should answer. But if he spoke, he did not hear a single syllable of what he said. . . .

———————

The cemetery was on a mountainside overlooking Jerusalem. In the morning sunlight, the gravestones were very white and

the cypresses very dark. The mourners were huddled together
in a crowd, as if for warmth—on a day that was already too
warm for comfort. At the open grave—it looked like a mouth
that would never close—the military chaplain, in a blue-and-
white prayer shawl that half-hid his uniform, chanted the final
words of the final prayer. His dark-toned voice lifted in the
calm, bright air and flew upward and out of the hearing of
men. The last of its sternly chanted notes hovered for split
seconds and then faded into mystery and oblivion. Slowly,
amid the sound of the family's weeping, the coffin was lowered
into the freshly dug pit. Little puffs of dust floated up and then
dispersed once again to the torn earth from which they had
come. There was the sound of dirt—in little, quick-moving
rivulets—raining down on rough pinewood, the same wood
which had made the little treehouse in the branches of the oak
that stood in the yard behind the Arnon house just this side of
what was once no-man's land in Jerusalem. There was the
sound of birds and the sound of insects humming like some
ever-playing instrument of life. There was the bitter, baffled,
choking, inconsolable sound of mourning.

Gradually, as if the mourners feared the consequences of
dispersion, the crowd broke apart and straggled away: atoms
of life leaving the atoms of death. On the twisting road that
led up to the cemetery from below—and for some led back
down—a command car's motor started up with a jarring roar.
Hugging his Bible tightly to his chest, the bearded chaplain
muttered his farewells and took leave.

The last to turn from the grave was D'vora, who wouldn't
stop staring at the fresh mound of earth. Finally, supported on
one side by Uri and on the other by Ilana, D'vora was gently
led away. Behind them, with stooped shoulders, came Uncle
Mordecai and his wife, Sureleh. Slowly, with steps that sounded
as if they were falling in an echo chamber, they trudged along
the winding cemetery path to the asphalt road on which the
mourners' cars were beginning to move. Suddenly, on his right,
by a solitary silver-needled pine, Uri caught sight of a familiar
figure. Motioning to Ilana, he said, "Help Imma into the jeep.
I'll be right there."

Ilana stared at him, but did not speak.

Uri walked across the grass. "Layleh," he whispered breathlessly. *"What . . . are you doing here?"*

Layleh's eyes peered up at him from her swollen face. "I— had to come, Uri!"

Uri turned and glanced over at the jeep and then looked back at Layleh. Impulsively, he took her hand. "We're going home, now," he said. "Come, ride with us."

But Layleh shook her head. "No, no," she said hoarsely. "I wouldn't think of intruding."

"It's not an intrusion, Layleh." He pulled her hand gently. "Come . . ."

"No, Uri. I want to walk home—by myself." Her red-rimmed eyes filled with tears. "I'll see you tonight—by the hedge."

"At midnight?"

"At midnight, Uri."

He dropped her hand and left her weeping by the tree.

Uncle Mordecai and Sureleh had said their last, tearful good-byes and gone back to their *moshav*—"to mourn and to work," as Mordecai had said thickly at the front door. D'vora, under heavy sedation, was asleep in the bedroom that would never shelter Arie again. Ilana was shut away, with the door locked, in the room she had vacated after Uri's departure for the army. The house—as if it, too, were in mourning—was eerily still. Even the little clock, unwound and ignored on Uri's desk, made no sound. Through the open-shuttered window, the oppressive night air made itself felt.

Uri lay stretched out on the bed that was no longer his— and that never would be his again. He was wide-awake—the very thought of sleep was alien, almost inadmissable. Like a carousel that had gone out of control and could not be stopped, his mind whirled around and around, mechanically and unalterably, past the same images, the same faces, the same views, the same landscapes: Arie in the gnarled branches of the oak, hammer in hand, putting together the yearned-for treehouse; Arie in uniform, with his neatly packed knapsack on the freshly scrubbed tiles of the kitchen floor, getting ready with cheerful

nonchalance to set out on a month's tour of reserve duty; Arie
in a little café in Amsterdam, toasting the young family with
wine that his grandfather "did *not* make in Rishon le-Zion";
Arie at the Kotel at his son's bar mitzvah ceremony; Arie at
the seashore in Tel Aviv; Arie on a picnic in the Galilee; Arie
in the jeep, honking the horn for his son to hurry up;
Arie . . . Arie . . . *always and forever, Arie*—his father.

Uri lay on the bed. But it wasn't his house. He did not
belong in—or even to—this place anymore. He belonged to
the men in Sinai whom he had left: to the living and the dead
soldiers. As soon as he could, as soon as it was possible, he
would go back to the unit to which he now owed his first, and
perhaps his last, allegiance. And Arie, the dead father who
would go on living in his son, would go with him. There was
nothing he wanted now, at this strange and unearthly quiet
moment—nothing but to return to the ragged line of trenches
and bunkers and sandbag-and-concrete emplacements on the
bank of the Suez Canal and, so doing, to keep the faith and
the trust that his father had so lovingly and painstakingly in-
stilled in him.

Slowly—as if he were dragging it through water—he lifted
his arm and peered at his wristwatch. In the darkness—he had
not bothered to switch on the lamp—the luminous dial said
twenty minutes to twelve. At once he rose and slipped into a
pair of sandals—his heavy, Sinai-whitened army shoes were
lying on the floor where he had kicked them off—and went
out of the room. It was still too early, he knew, for his appointment with Layleh, but he felt that he could not stand being
in the house a moment longer. Swiftly, through the ghostly,
unnerving stillness, he made his way downstairs and went out
into the yard.

The sky, rising like an enormous black dome over Jerusalem, was covered with a rash of glittering stars that to Uri's
strained and smarting eyes looked like fresh scabs on old wounds.
Not the slightest breath of wind stirred. The trees and shrubs
and garden flowers were motionless. Everything—everything
once so familiar and so dearly and intimately known from the
very first of his days on earth—looked foreign, unreal. Like
the bed and the room and the house, the yard was no longer
his, and never would be so again. Like a stranger suddenly and

inexplicably set down in some remote, unheard-of place, Uri began, with automaton steps, to pace the yard that once, so long ago, had been his private and almost exclusive domain.

He walked from the back porch to the moss-covered, crumbling stone wall at the rear and turned and walked back up over the footstep-stirred blades of grass to the porch again, and then turned and began the same course once more. He passed the flower garden; the tall, broad-branched oak that still, faithfully and persistently, held the childhood treehouse in its leafy grasp; the almond tree; and the symmetrically spaced shrubs. But he did not go near the hedge that always—like a living wall—divided this yard from the other one next door. He did not even turn his eyes to so much as glance at it.

Thus, he never heard the kitchen door of the house beyond the hedge open and close, nor did he hear Layleh's figure flit wraithlike across her lawn as she called his name softly once and twice and three times. In the end, she had to raise her voice to get his startled attention.

He halted midway on his trek from the rear wall to the porch, and for the first time, as if he were just now discovering that it existed, glanced over at the hedge and saw her shape beyond its screen of branches. He turned and walked forward to his side of the hedge. By the time he got there, she was crying—crying because she felt his pain. He stood limply, silently, with his arms at his sides, listening to her sobs and then, with a shiver, said quietly: "It doesn't do any good, Layleh."

"It . . . doesn't . . . do any good," she wept. "But . . . I can't help it. . . ."

"Not helping it," he said, "doesn't do any good either." He gestured awkwardly, as if the gesture was the relic of some movement he had once, long ago, known how to perform. "My father's dead," he said dully. "Not all the weeping in the world will return him to life. Nothing that you or I or anyone in the world can do or say will return him to life. Those who knew him and cared about him and loved him can keep the memory of his life alive by honoring his faith in life."

He did not know whether she had heard him or if, having heard him, she had understood what he had said. But he did not know what else to say. He did not know how to stop her

from crying. As for himself, he had cried—shut away in the
room that once had been but was no longer his—until there
were no longer any tears left. So he stood where he was, dry-
eyed and tight-lipped, listening to the muffled, broken sounds
that came from behind the hedge. He felt desolation and loneliness and anguish. But he also felt numb, and the numbness
froze him. He wondered, even, if he were still human. And if
he were not, he wondered what he had turned into.

At length, her weeping ebbed. For some time, there was
silence. In addition to the barrier of the hedge between the two
of them, there was the fearful and impenetrable barrier of silence. Even the night, lit by old, wearily burning stars, was
silent. Then, in a voice that was just audible, Layleh said, "Did
you get . . . my letter?"

"I got it," he replied.

"I—I . . . *had* to write it, Uri."

"I know you had to write it."

"It was . . . the only fair thing . . . to do."

"I know it was fair."

Layleh hesitated. Then she said, "It is the only way—once
and for all—to silence my parents."

"I suppose so."

Layleh cleared her throat. "Uri," she said hoarsely, "I love
you. No one and nothing will ever come between us——"

"I love you, too, Layleh."

"This is simply something that I must do: another obstacle—
surmountable, of course—on the road that must in the end
bring the two of us together! Surely, you understand that?"

"I understand it, Layleh."

"Do you, Uri!? *Do you really understand it?*"

There was silence again—a curtain of strange, uncertain
silence that fell between them and kept them, like prisoners in
a divided cell, from each other. Softly, as if to himself, Uri
murmured: "I understand it, Layleh. And I also understand that
I do not belong here now. These yards . . . these houses . . . this
hedge that we have known since childhood . . . my life in Jerusalem—all of this is light-years away from me now. I belong
in Sinai. I belong with the men—living and dead—whom I
have left." He paused for a moment and then, drawing a deep
breath, continued: "I will fulfill my duty—so far as it is pos-

sible to do anything for her—to my mother . . . and then I will go back to where I belong."

"Uri——"

"We will write to each other, Layleh, just as we have agreed. And we will see."

"Uri, darling . . ."

"Good night, Layleh."

She was sobbing again, crying now from the pain of parting with Uri once more. The terrified, despairing, helpless bursts of her sobs came through the dark, inert leaves of the hedge.

But there was nothing he could do for her. There was nothing he could do for himself.

———— · ————

Avner was wearing his red beret and polished, high-laced boots. He had silver paratrooper's wings over the pocket of his khaki shirt. He was bronzed—burnt, actually—almost black by the sun and looked young, somehow younger than before he had left for the army. Only his eyes, shining with an odd, restless fire, looked older. He was sitting—unbeknownst to him—in what had once, so many light-years ago, been Arie's favorite chair in the living room of the Arnon house. With a stiff, jerky motion, he gestured. "Your mother?" he said softly.

Sitting opposite him on the couch, Uri said, "She's back at the hospital—she knows it's better for her to keep busy. Besides, as you can imagine, she's needed. Ein Kerem—all the hospitals, in fact—are overflowing with the wounded."

Avner nodded.

Uri hesitated. Then, shifting his position, he said slowly: "My mother survived Europe. She will survive this as well. She knows that Arie would want her to survive. She can't let him down."

"None of us can," said Avner. He looked around the room and then turned his restless, haunted eyes back to Uri's masklike face. "And your sister?"

"Ilana says she's going to move out of Jerusalem. She says the city's too full of 'ghosts.' She says she plans to go south— to Beersheba, perhaps. But maybe it's just a reaction to Arie's death." Uri shrugged. "We'll see."

Avner cleared his throat. "When are you going back?" he said.

"Tomorrow. And you?"

"The day after tomorrow." Avner's eyes narrowed. "I want to get back to my unit," he said. "Frankly, I'm uneasy here— I feel out of place."

"So do I," said Uri. He swallowed. "I feel . . . as if I don't belong."

Avner rose and with flat, sharp strokes of his hands dusted off his already immaculate pants. He stared at Uri for a moment and said: "What about . . . the girl next door? Do you still feel toward her as you did?"

Uri rose as well. "I love her," he said, "but——"

"But what?"

"But I can't think about that now."

The two friends walked silently across the living room. At the front door they stood awkwardly for several moments, wanting—it was obvious—to say something to each other but totally unable to speak. At length, almost as if on a given signal, they shook hands. *"L'hitraot,"* said Avner.

"See you," said Uri.

The door closed, and Avner, with swift, measured strides and swinging arms, walked down the front path and turned right on the tree-lined street. Uri watched him from the doorway until he disappeared. Then he went back into the living room and seated himself on the couch and stared at the chair in which his friend—not knowing that it had been Arie's favorite—had sat. He remained that way, in a strange, trancelike state, not moving or thinking or even feeling. When, at last, he roused himself, he saw that the sun was already sinking and that the room was half-filled with shadow. D'vora would be coming home in a short time, and he did not want her to find him that way. With enormous effort, he got to his feet and went up to the room that had once been his.

1975

Hebron

TO THE WEST, the sun was nearly below the horizon, but its afterglow was fiercely red. Great clouds with flaming underbellies stood motionless in the sky, reflecting the last raw light of the day down on the city of Hebron and on the hills surrounding it.

Layleh had left the school building where she taught more than an hour ago. Each day, the journey from the school, just off the city's main square, to the house on the outskirts of Hebron to which she and her parents had moved from Jerusalem, seemed to be longer. She tried to quicken her pace, but something seemed to drag at her feet. With a sigh, she resigned herself to the mysterious will of her body and kept trudging slowly along.

At last the houses of the town proper were behind her and she was in the outskirts, walking alone on a dirt road used chiefly by farmers and herdsmen. Sometimes, when she reached this point in her afternoon trip, she would close her eyes and imagine, as she plodded ahead in darkness, that she was back in Jerusalem, moving down the narrow street that led from the main road where the Egged buses ran to the big pink stone house with the hedge that divided the two backyards, where she and Uri Arnon had grown up and fallen in love. All sorts of memories would come rushing into her mind, memories which gave her both comfort and pain.

Looking up, she caught sight of a great, dark flock of starlings that suddenly wheeled and turned directly into the burning hearth of the western sky. And now, every once in a while, she glimpsed one of the houses on the slopes that were carefully terraced and dotted here and there with laboriously planted and tended trees which were a part of the neighborhood in which she lived.

Around the next bend, a path struck off from the dirt road and wound its way upward to the little square stone house which Mahmoud had bought upon his abrupt decision to leave Jerusalem. It was a compact, unadorned, flat-roofed house on the crest of a barren hill. There were a few neglected fruit trees and several large and somewhat forbidding clumps of wild cactus in front of it and a small, walled-in garden with flower beds and a willow tree that S'ad painstakingly looked after in the rear. It was this garden, Layleh felt, that—as inferior as it was to the spacious yard behind the house in Jerusalem—made the place at all bearable.

Ten minutes of crawling at a snail's pace along the path brought Layleh to within sight of the house. On its left, listing to one side because of the unevenness of the ground, was her father's old car, battered and spattered by successive layers of dried mud. It was used by the family infrequently, actually only in times of urgent need, and never to drive to Jerusalem or to any other of Israel's large cities. Her eyes shifted from the car to the stone front verandah, from which there was a not unpleasant view of the surrounding countryside. However, neither she nor S'ad nor Mahmoud ever sat there, preferring instead, in Mahmoud's phrase, the "shut-in" garden in back of the house.

Abruptly, Layleh lowered her eyes to the path. The dirt there was dry and hard-packed and without the relief of even a single blade of grass, for the winter rains had not yet begun to fall. Keeping her head down and her eyes on the ground, she moved forward. At once, a melody came unexpectedly into her mind. She recognized it as a song that the children in her class always sang. She loved the tune dearly; it always made her heart glad when she heard it. But now, for some strange reason, it only brought unwilling tears to her eyes, and she struggled to obliterate it and think of something else.

When she walked into the kitchen, S'ad, who was preparing the evening meal, started. "Layleh, you're late."

Her daughter said nothing.

"What took you so long?"

Layleh shrugged.

"Was . . . there some trouble in town? I was beginning to worry about you."

"There's no need to worry about me, Umm. It just takes a while to walk home."

S'ad sighed. "As long as you're safe," she murmured.

Layleh came forward and kissed her mother's cheek. "I'm safe, Umm, as you can see. Quite safe." She slipped off her sweater and took an apron from a hook on the wall. "Here, let me help you with supper, Umm."

"There's no need, Layleh——"

"But I want to, Umm."

S'ad nodded. "As you wish, my daughter."

When supper was ready and the table set in the small dining room, Layleh went out to call her father. Mahmoud was in his usual place, out beyond the willow tree, in the furthest part of the garden, seated in his wheelchair almost up against the rough stones of the rear wall. The sun was altogether down by now and the sky devoid of any red glow. A wind from the northeast had sprung up, bringing an edge of chill into the air. Moving briskly on the garden path, Layleh called to her father. "It's time for supper, Abu."

"Supper? Already?"

Layleh nodded. "Yes, Abu." She shivered. "Aren't you cold out here?"

Mahmoud shook his head. "I'm fine out here," he said gruffly, swinging his chair around and propelling it with swift motions onto the flat stones of the path.

Supper was not silent, but it was quiet, as usual. Layleh spoke about the events of the day at school, dwelling for the most part on how she had tried to help a troubled child. S'ad talked about a neighbor's illness, about the changing weather, and then about an account of a terrorist attack in the area which she had read in the newspaper. Mahmoud glanced up from his food at the speaker on occasion, but did not once choose to enter the conversation.

After they finished eating and the table was cleared and the dishes and utensils washed and put away, Mahmoud retired to his study, his "garden inside the house," as he put it. It was much smaller and more cramped than the study in Jerusalem, "not much more than a closet," as he said, but it sufficed. In the salon, S'ad worked on a tablecloth she was embroidering, and Layleh read as much as she could of a novel that a fellow teacher in Hebron had lent her. Around ten, she yawned aloud and announced that she was sleepy.

Her mother smiled thinly. "Then good night, my daughter."

"Good night, Umm."

Though Layleh had indeed been sleepy in the salon, the drowsiness seemed to vanish once she had gotten into bed. Restlessly, she turned from side to side and after a time got up to close the shutter. The risen moon, palely silver in the vast, dark sky, held her attention at the window. Her small room was at the rear of the house and she stared out into the garden. Silver-white moonlight gleamed on the encircling stone wall; it fired the mica in the garden pathway and streamed in dazzling rivulets down the curving branches of the willow. If she closed her eyes, she could imagine at once the Arnon house next door and the hedge and . . .

She closed the shutter with a bang and went back to bed. Deliberately, she paraded the happenings of the day through her mind, carefully searching for and gathering up even the tiniest scrap of solace and pleasure to mull over. Little by little, she relaxed and finally fell asleep.

———————•———•———

Layleh dreamed that she was in a kitchen, preparing supper. She had never been in that kitchen before, nor even in that house, yet somehow everything seemed familiar. It was spring. Sunshine was pouring in through the windows of the freshly whitewashed room, and the sound of the birds outside was so loud and so clear that they seemed almost to be inside the room with her. Deftly, she worked at cooking the meal. A feeling of excitement grew as she worked; as the afternoon wore on, she became almost feverish. The table in the alcove was set with a newly washed white cloth and gleaming silverware and dishes. Though it wasn't necessary, she checked it all once again, just to be sure. Yes, everything was perfect. There were two places set opposite each other and a bowl of fresh flowers in the center of the table. Two places: for herself and for Uri.

Flushed with excitement, she threw off her apron and went into the hallway to comb her long hair in the mirror. She saw her burning eyes and parted lips and scarlet cheeks and could not help smiling in anticipation. She put the comb aside and smoothed her dress, which needed no smoothing, and hurried through the charming house that somehow, though she had never been there before, she knew so intimately, and rushed out the front door to stand and wait on the rose-lined path.

Dusk was falling. Two crows, cawing harshly, vanished to the east. From the orange and lemon trees in the backyard, the scent of citrus came on a gentle breeze. She fidgeted and then changed her position, straining to see and to hear. Above her, the first star of the evening quivered in the violet-streaked sky. She felt light-headed, almost faint.

Suddenly, she heard his footsteps. She trembled, held her breath. Yes, the sound of his steps grew louder. There was no mistake—he was coming! "Uri!" she cried out hoarsely, running headlong down the path. Then she caught sight of him. "Uri, darling!" she cried, throwing herself into his arms.

He held her tightly, so tightly that she could scarcely breathe. She gazed up at him. "Come," she whispered.

He laughed. "I know that you have supper ready and waiting," he said with amusement, "but first——"

She did not allow him to go on. "No," she said hurriedly, "not to supper. Come upstairs with me. Quickly!"

In the dusk-darkened bedroom, their naked bodies shone like sinuous flames. Hungrily, fiercely, the flames merged. Over and over Uri told her how much he loved her, and Layleh wept with passionate joy to hear it. With all of her strength, her locked arms pressed Uri's body down into her own. Now that he was at last hers, she would never let him go.

1977

Army Base.
Somewhere in Israel

SUNSET.

The long, furled ribbons of cloud that traversed the sky were slowly deepening in color: they were ruby and scarlet and liquid-gold, and soon—as the sun dipped downward—they would be violet and purple and then black. Along both sides of the trampled gravel path, the freshly whitewashed stones that marked its borders gleamed in light that had not yet completely lost its power. Uri—Lieutenant Uri Arnon, as he had been called for almost a year—walked quickly forward. He had a twenty-four-hour leave that began at six, and he wanted to get going as soon as he could. At the next intersection of paths, where a huge, white-and-gray-trunked eucalyptus drooped its green-silver leaves down almost onto the heads of passersby, he turned sharply and strode the last hundred meters to his quarters.

The little room—it was the last on the left in the wooden barrack building—was, as always, in perfect order. It was furnished with a cot, a little desk, and a chair.

He closed the door behind him and, turning to his right, opened the shutter over the single window. Dusky-red light, the last light of the waning September afternoon, streamed in and flooded the spotless wooden floor. It shone on the metal frame of the cot and illuminated the single metal-framed photograph on the desk that showed D'vora and Arie arm in arm. For an instant, with narrowed eyes, he stared at the picture—it brought to mind so many other images in rapid succession that he could scarcely untangle one from the other—and then, rousing himself, he sat down on the cot and pulled the two

386

envelopes he had received earlier that day out of his shirt pocket. One—the larger—was from his mother. He opened it first and read:

*Jerusalem
September 10, 1977*

Dear Uri,

I haven't had a letter from you for quite some time— even you must admit that worry is one of a mother's time-honored prerogatives. Although I know that a lieutenant in the Israeli army is very pressured, I can't help wondering how you are and why you haven't written. It's peacetime, to be sure—though peacetime in our country seems to be different from what it is anywhere else in the world—and Sadat has come to Jerusalem, proving, I suppose, that miracles are not entirely a thing of the past. The air is filled with all sorts of emotional and euphoric phrases like "the dawn of a new era," "the breakthrough we have all been longing for and dreaming about," the "start of an epoch of amity and cooperation," and so forth: and yet the reality remains, stubbornly and inescapably, that we are still surrounded by innumerable enemies, armed to the teeth, whose avowed "holy mission" is our destruction. The undeniable facts remain that we must maintain a strong army . . . and that you have chosen the army as your "career."

I respect your choice to remain in the army, though I do not entirely understand or agree with it. Your father and I had hoped that you would attend the university and study political science. You yourself had come to the same decision. Thus, it came as a complete surprise when you announced that you had changed your mind and intended to stay in military service. We need good officers in the army, of course, but we also need good people in the Foreign Service. I hope that you will one day reconsider.

I am as well as can be expected. My work, as you know, absorbs me—almost totally. And that is the way I want it to be—that is the way it must be. Ein breirah, as we say— no choice. For our tiny country, for myself.

Ilana is fine. She has been seeing someone steadily for the last few months, and he seems to have a good, calming effect on her—she promises to introduce him to me in the near future.

There is nothing much new to report, except that my neighbors next door have changed once again. Since the Maleks moved away, this is the third time! I haven't really had a chance to meet the parents yet, but I've managed to exchange a few words with the children. They are a girl and a boy, and they remind me of Ilana and yourself when you were young.

Take care, Uri, and please write as soon as you can.

Love,
Mother

The second letter was from Layleh. Uri turned it over several times in his hands before he ripped the envelope open and read:

Hebron
September 9, 1977

Dearest Uri,

To the east of Hebron—my "exile" from Jerusalem—the sun is rising: it seems that I always waken at dawn. I dreamed of you last night and decided on wakening to write to you at once, although you haven't answered my last letter.

I am well and busy here, teaching in a local elementary school. The young, shining eyes that I see in my classes inspire me and urge me on. The world is so fiercely intent on crushing the spirit out of its children; on diluting and destroying their innocence and candor! Whenever I feel that I reach a child, I consider that I have truly won a victory.

Mother misses Jerusalem sorely. She is forever reminiscing about the house and the yard and what she calls the "heaven-embracing" city itself. She misses Yerushalaim . . . Al-Kods . . . and she always will—and yet she contents herself here with her books and her embroidery and her garden with its incredible array of flowers. And, of course, with father! Mahmoud is more alone than ever. But that, so he says, is the way he wants it. Sporadically, he writes and reads. More than anything else, he is lost in what he calls "quiet reflection."

I love you, dearest Uri, and I miss you—more than I can ever say. I know that because of the last war, and your

*father's terrible death, and your decision to remain in the
army, and because of my decision to part for a considerable
length of time, that you have kept away from me; that you
have remained on your own side of the great "hedge" of
pain and doubt and suspicion and bitterness. This separation, you surely realize, has cast a dark shadow over my
life. The only comfort, if it may be described as such, is
that I have come away from this cruel experience loving
you more than ever. Nothing could ever dull my desire for
you. Nothing could ever tarnish the memory of what we
had, or dim the hope that we can have it in the future. I
will not—and cannot—believe that your love for me has
diminished . . . or will ever cease.*

Uri, my darling, please write to me.

I await your reply. Keep well, my darling.

Yours,

Layleh

Uri let the hand that held the letter slowly fall to his lap. He
had the urge to read it once again, but the little room was quite
dark by now, and for some inexplicable reason he did not want
to get up and switch on the light. Without moving, he sat where
he was on the cot, with the open letter on his lap. He should
have been packed and ready to go by this time, but something—
some feeling he could not master or even fully understand—
held him firmly in his place. A flood of memories—memories
that went all the way back to his childhood days in his yard,
by the hedge—came flooding over him and, entirely without
resistance, he submitted to them. He felt pain—gnawing, irksome pain. And yet, surprisingly, at the same time he felt a
sort of cleansing relief. He knew he should not be sitting on
the cot in his darkened room. He knew he should be moving
around and gathering up his things. But still, he could not
extricate himself from the tide of memories that swept over
him.

There was a knock at the door. For an instant, he wasn't
aware of it. The knock came again and, dazedly, he glanced
over at the door. He shivered. "Who's there?" he muttered.

The voice outside said clearly: "Daphna."

"*Rega*—just a moment," Uri said and rose to switch on the
overhead light. He moved to the door and yanked it open.

Standing in the twilight, in a fresh, sharply creased uniform
with lieutenant's bars on its epaulets, was a tall, blond young
woman. She had a knapsack slung over one shoulder and was
smiling. "Uri Arnon not ready on time?" she said with mingled
amusement and mockery. "I don't believe it!"

"Daphna, I——"

The young woman waved a hand imperiously. "No excuses,
Lieutenant Arnon," she said. "Get your things together this
minute and let's go—otherwise, we'll miss the ride to Tel
Aviv."

Uri had met Daphna at the base several months before, and
the two of them had become good friends. As the weeks passed,
it was increasingly evident to him that she was interested in
much more than merely a friendship. Without being brazen,
she had endeavored steadily and with growing openness to
change the nature of their relationship. Though Uri could not
help being attracted to Daphna, something had been in the way
of his responding fully to her in the way she desired—something, he realized, that he *wanted* in the way.

Uri did not move from the doorway. For a moment—a
moment in which the pretty, upturned face with the freckled
nose and full, sensuous lips blurred and then returned to proper
focus—he was silent. Then, drawing a deep breath, he said
slowly: "Daphna, I'm . . . not going." He cleared his throat.
"Please forgive me, Daphna—I just can't go with you. I'll
try . . . to explain it to you . . . as well as to myself. . . ." He
paused for a moment and then went on: "I haven't been with
a woman in four years, other than casually. To share this leave
as we had planned would be to mislead you. I have first to
resolve some things. I'm sorry."

"Uri——"

But he had already walked back into his room.

———————

Uri left the army base just a few minutes after eight. He got a
ride in a jeep to the main road. The garrulous driver talked the
whole time, without getting a response and without caring in
the least, about the chances for peace now that Sadat had "come

to see the Jews in Jerusalem." Ten minutes later, Uri caught a bus to the central station in Tel Aviv. From there, he took another bus to Jerusalem. The bus was half-empty and its lights flickered on and off. The big man at the wheel, hatless and sweating and late on his schedule or anxious to be done with his day's work, drove like the wind through the soft, swirling darkness across the narrow waist of the country. Through the windows, in the distance, the lights of settlements appeared— islands of brightness in the black sea of the night.

The ascent from the coastal plain began gradually—affording only the merest suggestion of elevation—and then grew steadily steeper. The bus moaned and whined and with creaking fervor wound around the sharp bends in the road. Bearing down from the opposite direction, the white, liquescent headlights of oncoming vehicles flashed. From above, where they were set like lanterns in the coal-black sky, the stars gave off answering signals. At last, from their towering, proud perches, the first lights of Jerusalem glimmered like beacons. The bus rushed upward and then, leveling off, thrust forward into the lamp-lit warmth of the city's streets.

On the city bus he took next, Uri felt at home for the first time since he had left Jerusalem for the army. He had not intended to come to Jerusalem with Daphna—they had planned to spend their leave together in Tel Aviv—but he knew, even more strongly than at the army base, that he had made the right decision. As the last, familiar curve in the main road before the cutoff came into view, he reached up and pulled the cord. As he descended to the asphalt, he glanced at his watch: it was just minutes past ten-thirty. Adjusting the strap of his knapsack, he turned left and started slowly down the narrow, winding lane whose every tree and telephone pole and front lawn and tile-roofed house he knew by heart.

The September night was mild. A gentle, diffident, almost sluggish breeze stirred the leaves overhead. In the black sky, the stars seemed to eddy like driftwood. As he walked, the quiet neighborhood sounds of Jerusalem after dark reached his ears: the dutiful, half-hearted barking of a dog which could neither marshal the strength or the will to trot out to the street nor allow itself to ignore the passer-by entirely; the voice— high and tender—of a mother singing a lullaby to a child that

had trouble falling asleep; the sonorous strains of a symphony
issuing from some overloud radio or phonograph; the faint,
distant, tenuous, almost unreal wails of jackals drifting in on
invisible currents of air from the Judean wilderness. The scent
of newly mown grass prodded his nostrils, and the lingering
odors of cooked food reminded him that some of the evening
meals had been eaten late. He walked and stared and listened
and smelled. He walked and permitted himself for the first time
in years to be borne freely on the tide of memories that coursed
over him.

Suddenly, he was around the last bend, and the last house
on the street—the "house with the hedge"—was in front of
him. One side, the Arnon side, was completely dark—which
told him at once that D'vora was spending the night in the
hospital. The other side, where Mahmoud and S'ad and Layleh
had once lived, was all lit up. Brilliant fans of light streamed
out of the open-shuttered living room windows and spread over
the lawn. As he approached, he saw a bicycle standing on the
front porch and an overturned wagon on the stone walk. He
didn't know the name of the family that occupied that half of
the house now—D'vora had not mentioned it in her letter.

He veered to the left, to the Arnon side. He had the key to
the front door but not the slightest desire to use it. Quickly,
he crossed the lawn and reached the driveway in which, eons
ago, Arie's trusty jeep used to stand. Once there, he halted and
let his eyes grow accustomed to the dark. Within moments, he
was able to make out the star-lit, haunted, lost landscape of
his childhood and his youth: the moss-shadowed rear wall; the
petalless almond tree; the oak with the black mass of the dis-
integrating treehouse; the neglected flower garden, run to seed;
the high, dense-leaved barrier of the hedge. From the next-
door kitchen windows, he could see yellow light spilling onto
the grass. And he could hear the rattling of dishes being washed.
A woman's voice cried out shrilly: "Ya'akov . . . Ya'akov, where
are you?" And from somewhere inside the house, a man's voice
answered: "I'm coming—I'll be right there."

Uri roused himself and—as in some poignant, recurring
dream—strode the length of the yard in which he had first
known the seasons of life. He reached the rear wall and put a
hand on its ivy-laced top and then, with a soldier's ease, vaulted

over to the other side. He moved across the stony, stubble-bound terrain that had once, light-years ago, been no-man's land. In no time, he arrived at the spot he sought, and stopped in his tracks. The terebinth was still there—its branches spread out like the thin, fragile spokes of a parasol—but it seemed to have shrunk. The boulder—glowing faintly in the light of the stars—was still in its place beneath the tree, but it seemed to have grown smaller. He stood motionless and in his reverie remembered a young man and a young woman in this spot, this "grotto" that they had called their own and beautified with their whispered words and passionate caresses of love. He saw moon-fired flesh and heard unrestrained cries of desire and gratification. He recalled a thousand quicksilver images and relived innumerable embraces and remembered, almost word for word, countless conversations and discussions.

Suddenly, he started. Out of the corner of his eye, he saw something—a large, black shape—in the darkness. It was twenty or thirty meters out beyond the "grotto," out where there had never been anything but nettles and cacti. Cautiously, he moved forward toward the unknown object. When he reached it, he was both relieved and surprised: it was a giant-bladed bulldozer! He put out a hand and—as if he were patting the flank of some domestic animal—touched the metal tread. So, he thought, they were going to build here. Tomorrow or the next day or the day or week after, they would build in this forlorn, empty space in which, for so long, warring armies had faced each other and jackals has skulked at will. The house with the hedge would no longer be the last house on the street. The terebinth and the porous, "age-old" rock beneath its brittle branches—the grotto in which he and Layleh had met so many times and so often pledged their enduring love—would be gone.

He spent the night in a small, sparsely furnished, white-walled room in a tiny hotel in downtown Jerusalem. Through the open window—he did not even bother to lower the shade—the lights of the passing vehicles below flared over the pale expanse of the ceiling in an endless stream. Voices, like mysterious fish swimming to the surface of a pond, drifted up, and sometimes he could catch two or three words of a conversation. There was a movie theater directly across the street, and when the last show was over and the crowd came pouring out, a noisy uproar, like water rushing through a dry wadi bed, reached his ears. The marquee lights went out and his room was suddenly darker.

He did not sleep much. He simply lay on the narrow bed under a fresh white sheet and in his turbulent, whirling mind relived his life with Layleh—step by step and stage by stage—from the time he had first heard her singing to her doll on the other side of the hedge.

He was awake after midnight and he was up before the gray gossamer of the dawn filled the window. He heard the produce trucks lumbering into the city and the harsh clash of milk cans and wooden crates being unloaded. A little after six, he rose and washed and shaved and brushed his teeth and dressed and left the hotel.

He ate breakfast in a tumbledown little restaurant whose heavy-jowled proprietor, though he seemed still to be asleep, managed to murmur: "So, Lieutenant, so what do you think of the Egyptians? Do they really want peace, as Sadat says? Or is it just another ploy on their part? What do you think, *chabibi?*"

Uri shrugged; gulped down the remains of his coffee; collected his change and left without becoming involved. At the corner, he caught a ride in a blue-gray pickup to the outskirts of the city.

The sun was already well up in the tender blue sky, shedding the soft, golden needles of its radiance. The air was fresh, as if laved by loving fingers. The sound of birds rose like a delicate canopy. Slowly, taking in every detail around him, he started up a path that he had not walked in years. His steps were light and almost lingering. He felt—with a sense of relief that welled up from deep within him—that a terrible burden was slipping from his mind and from his heart.

He spent the morning in the little pine-tree copse that he and Layleh had called their own. Soft sunlight, strained through a net of evergreen needles, flooded down and a sharp, delicious fragrance penetrated his nostrils. Beneath his wandering feet, pine cones popped. He located a familiar fallen tree—he would have recognized it anywhere—and sat himself down on the weathered trunk. Absently, he unslung his knapsack and laid it at his feet. He loosened the collar of his shirt and removed his beret. He breathed deeply of the yet-dewy air and let his wide-open eyes roam at will.

Below him, bathed in the splendor of the new day, was Jerusalem. Its stone and tiled rooftops—pink and scarlet and white and gray-silver—gleamed in the light. Its towers of rough-textured hewn rocks seemed to sparkle, and its golden domes flashed. Its trees, standing like infallible sentinels, lined the ribbonlike streets and avenues that wound this way and that.

Sometime after the sun had passed its zenith and begun its descent, he rose and tidied himself and left the green copse that had on so many occasions sheltered him and Layleh from the rest of the world. At the bottom of the hill, he waited patiently for a city bus that would take him to Ein Kerem.

In the hospital, he caught sight of his mother before she saw him. She had aged since he had last visited her several months before—she had aged incredibly. Her hair had become heavily flecked with gray, and deep lines were etched into her face. Even her proud, erect stature had gone slack. A lump hard as a rock formed in his throat. "Imma!" he called out finally.

She turned and at once her weary face lit up. "Uri!" she exclaimed in astonishment. "When did you arrive?"

"Not long ago," he said, moving forward and gathering her limp, worn body into his embrace. "I thought I'd surprise you. I hope you don't mind."

D'vora drew back and gazed at him with affection and—still—with a measure of disbelief. "But why didn't you tell me, Uri? Why didn't you let me know in advance? I should have taken time off—heaven knows, I have enough coming!"

He forced a smile. "I didn't know I was coming to Jerusalem in advance. It was something sudden—unexpected."

"How long will you stay?"

"I don't have much time, Imma—I've got to be back at the base by six."

Her face fell, but she made an effort to conceal her disappointment. "I see . . ." she murmured. Then, collecting herself, she went on: "Well, what can't be helped . . . can't be helped." She waved a hand. "Wait here," she said. "I'll say a word to the chief nurse and be right back. We can have tea—or lunch, if you haven't already had it—in the cafeteria."

They sat at an isolated table, by a gleaming window that looked out on a garden, and ate sandwiches and drank tea and talked. Disturbed by her sharply seamed features and pallor, her troubled eyes and halting, strained voice, he scarcely understood or even heard what she had to say. Sensing his agitation, D'vora said—breaking the thread of her conversation—suddenly: "I'm tired, Uri. Very tired. But there's nothing to be done about it."

"Why don't you take a vacation, Imma?"

She sighed, and, reaching impulsively across the table, took his hand. "A vacation would just make me more tired. It's odd—but that's the truth. Can you understand what I mean?"

"I understand, Imma."

"Life must go on," she said slowly. "And my life . . . now . . . is my work." Her voice quavered. "Just as yours," she said, "is . . . the army."

He did not reply.

When he took her in his arms, he felt her body tremble. And when he kissed her on the cheek, she began—he knew it would happen—to cry. "I'm sorry . . ." she murmured helplessly. "Please forgive me."

"There's nothing to be sorry about, Imma."

She brushed the tears from her cheeks. "Take care of yourself, Uri," she said softly, hugging him. *"Shalom."*

"Shalom, Imma. I'll write to you soon; I promise."

He was back at the base at a quarter to six. At ten minutes to eleven, he was through with his duties and in his room. He switched on the light. And then, though the night was warm—one of those warm September nights that struggle to pretend that the summer has not yet flown by—he closed the shutter over the window and sat down at his desk. Drawing a sheet of paper to him, he wrote:

> *Somewhere in Israel*
> *September 14, 1977*

Dearest Layleh,
*   I want very much to see you again. In a couple of weeks,*
I'll be able to get leave. I will come to Hebron and we will
spend the day together. If my proposal is all right, let me
know at once and we'll make a definite arrangement.

He lifted his pen and hesitated for a moment and then wrote:

> *With love that has never died,*
> *   Uri*

Eight days later, he received his reply. It read:

> *Hebron*
> *September 18, 1977*

My darling,
*   I can scarcely wait. Meet me next Thursday at noon in*
front of my school—it is just off the main square.
*   With all my love and devotion,*
> *   Yours always,*
> *   Layleh*

On Wednesday night, the night before his appointment with
Layleh in Hebron, Uri could not sleep. He had gone through
a long, hard day and was thoroughly exhausted, but despite
his efforts, sleep would not come. At length, more awake than
ever, he rose and put on a shirt and a pair of trousers and went
out of his room. He did not go far—just a few steps on the
gravel path in front of the barrack building. There was a full
moon in the sky—as silver-white as frost—and the whitewashed stones that marked the path shone in the cold fire of
its light. He gazed up at it and, stretching his weary limbs,
wished that it was gone and that dawn had come and that he
was on his way to Hebron and to Layleh.

"Uri——"

He turned and at once recognized Daphna coming up the

path. "Daphna!" he called out, waving a hand.

She halted. "So, Uri," she murmured. "It seems that we both have insomnia."

"So it seems."

She stared at him. "You . . . were going to explain things . . . more fully. If you feel up to it, now is as good a time as any."

He nodded. "It's simple, actually," he said softly. "I thought that . . . perhaps something had passed. But . . . it hasn't." He paused for a moment and then, drawing a deep breath, went on: "Apparently, Daphna, it is my present . . . and will be my future."

Despite what she was really feeling, Daphna smiled—a smile that curved her full lips gracefully and lit her eyes. "Another woman," she said. "Actually, *the* woman. . . ."

Uri nodded once again.

"Your childhood sweetheart?"

"Yes, my childhood sweetheart."

Daphna extended her hand, attempting to hide her disappointment with a magnanimous gesture. "I'm sure that you know I wish you well, Uri."

Uri took the outstretched hand and pressed it. "I know you do, Daphna."

"*Kol tuv*, Uri—everything good!"

He watched her walk slowly down the path and disappear. Where she had been, there were only bright, quivering rays of moonlight. Relieved that his conversation with her had been easier than he had expected, and now suddenly sleepy, he turned and went back to his room.

The moonlight brushed down over the branches of the willow tree that stood—"like a mourner," Mahmoud always said—in the center of the ivy-walled garden. Layleh could scarcely make it out because of the tears—the tears of joy and expectation—that filled her eyes. She had tried, all that afternoon and all through supper and all through the interminable evening that followed the meal, to control her excitement and had succeeded, though she did not know how. But now, in the hush of the night-blanketed garden at the rear of the little house they had moved to in Hebron, her discipline broke down and she gave herself over to the sweet, jubilant release of her tears. On bare feet, she left the rough stone path and crossed the cool grass and lowered herself onto a small, mossy-legged bench and covered her face with her hands and wept joyously.

When she looked up, her mother was standing in front of her. "Umm..." she murmured softly, brushing the tears from her flushed cheeks. "How long have you been here?"

"Not long," said S'ad.

"Come, dear Umm—sit by me. There's plenty of room."

S'ad shook her head. "No, Layleh, I'd rather stand." She stared in silence for a moment and then said, "Why are you crying?"

Layleh met her mother's glance directly. "Umm, I'm not crying now. I was...but it has passed." She smiled. "Don't worry," she said. "It doesn't mean anything, Umm. A few tears now and then don't really matter...and sometimes they even bring relief."

S'ad took a step closer to her daughter. "You have cried too much these last years, Layleh," she said slowly. "First in Jerusalem...and then here in Hebron. No, Layleh, you have cried too much—out of too much pain—and for what?"

"Umm——"

"No, Layleh, let me finish." S'ad paused to catch her breath and went on: "Perhaps..." she said with a little shrug of her shoulders, "perhaps you did love this Uri and he did love you. But the love was love between children. She sighed and, struggling to steady her voice, continued: "You have not seen this young man in a long while, my daughter. Time is passing. You have not fulfilled your womanhood in marriage. How long do you think that you can go on in this fashion, tying your life to some fantasy? How long can you stay aloof...and alone...and isolated?"

"Umm," said Layleh in a trembling voice, "Umm, you don't understand. You simply don't understand! Uri was wounded. Wounded by his father's death...and by the war...and by the fact—the undeniable fact, Umm—that I was willing to agree to this forced separation."

S'ad's eyes filled with a puzzled expression. "What are you saying, my daughter? Now, I truly don't understand."

"Your *own husband* was wounded, Umm! Have you given up your love for him? Have you written him off? Have you abandoned my father, Umm?"

"Layleh. Layleh, please——"

But S'ad's daughter shook her head. "No," she said firmly. "You can say what you wish—you can talk from this moment until the world ends—and it won't matter! It's *what I feel for Uri . . . and what he feels for me that count! And nothing else!*"

Now there were tears in S'ad's eyes. Her body seemed to shrivel. Her voice, when she was finally able to utter a sound, was hoarse and broken. "Layleh, my daughter . . ." she murmured. But she could say no more.

Layleh rose from the stone bench and put her arms around her weeping mother. "Enough, Umm," she whispered tenderly. *"Enough."*

When, at length, S'ad became calm, the two women drew apart. Drawing a deep breath and wiping her tears on her sleeve, S'ad said softly: "Come, my daughter, let's go into the house now. There's a pot of fresh tea on the stove—we can drink . . . and then go to bed."

"Thank you, Umm, but I'd rather be out here by myself for a while longer."

S'ad nodded acquiescently. "Then . . . good night, my dear one."

"Good night, Umm."

After the back door had closed, the garden was still once again. From its lofty station in the sky, the silver-white moon shone down, kindling the last remains of the long-ago faded and dead roses on the trellises and soft humps of the oleander bushes and the drooping branches of the willow tree. Layleh, standing by the stone bench where her mother had left her, gazed upward. Her heart throbbed with joy and ached with longing.

———————

Uri was up and out of bed at the crack of dawn. He slipped into a bathrobe and snatched up his towel and toilet articles

and ran all the way along the dew-damp gravel paths to the
shower room and showered and shaved and brushed his teeth
and, taking a little more time than usual—not much, but still
a little more—to comb his hair. He then hurried back to his
room and put on a freshly laundered and ironed uniform and
strapped his holstered revolver around his waist and donned
his beret and—without bothering to eat breakfast or to so much
as take a sip of coffee—strode swiftly to the front gate of the
army base and showed his pass to the guard on duty.

The day was fine. Pale-gold sunlight streamed down from
the azure, lightly clouded sky and birds were singing from their
perches. The Star of David, the shepherd-king of Israel, framed
by two horizontal bars of blue, danced from the top of a flagpole
in the gentle westerly breeze that was blowing.

A dust-whitened command car, with its motor idling impatiently, stood in front of the checkpost. Uri vaulted over the
tailgate and seated himself on one of the parallel benches. The
driver—who looked as if he might just as well have been in
some high school classroom as in the army—kept twisting his
head and looking past the high barbed-wire fence into the grounds
of the base. Two other soldiers—a pudgy major with a reddish-
brown handlebar mustache and a tall, gangling first-sergeant
with a mop of red hair that seemed intent on escaping from his
slanted beret—came out through the gate and climbed into the
waiting vehicle. The major sat up front, next to the driver.
Lifting his arm with a sudden, choppy movement, he checked
his wristwatch and, with a tight smile, glanced back over his
shoulder at Uri and the first-sergeant sitting opposite him and
then swiveled his doll-like head to the front and—almost with
a flourish—nodded to the driver that it was time to move. The
command car jerked forward and roared down the empty road,
sending up spumes of fine white dust behind it.

After a time, the major turned his head again. Staring at
Uri, he said: "Going far, Lieutenant?"

"To Hebron," Uri replied.

The major cleared his throat. "Things have been tense there
for the past couple of weeks. Watch yourself, Lieutenant."

Uri raised his voice over the whine of the engine. "I will,"
he said: "Thanks for the advice."

The command car came to a screeching halt at the Hebron
cutoff, and Uri jumped out. His watch told him that it was just

eleven-thirty: he knew he would be at Layleh's school in advance of his appointment, but he didn't mind being early. Briskly, he began the walk down the road that led directly toward town. Moments later, he heard the sound of a vehicle behind him and turned. An army jeep with a single occupant was coming his way. With a wave of his hand, he flagged it down. "Thanks for the lift," he said as he hopped into the dusty front seat.

The driver, a craggy-faced artillery captain wearing an old, open-necked khaki sweater with the sleeves rolled sloppily up above his elbows, nodded unceremoniously. With a glance at Uri, he shouted above the whine of the motor: "You're undoubtedly here on business, Lieutenant. Nobody in his right mind would come to this place for pleasure."

Uri shrugged.

The captain grimaced. "Where do you want me to drop you, *chabibi?*"

"At the main square, if it's no trouble."

"No trouble at all," said the captain with an unexpected smile that somehow seemed to take his weather-worn face by complete surprise.

But as soon as the jeep entered the town proper, the captain's smile faded and was replaced by a scowl.

"What's the matter?" said Uri.

"Something . . . is wrong . . ." muttered the captain, shifting gears. With a grunt, he jerked his head. "Look," he said hoarsely. "Over there——"

To his right, Uri caught sight of three or four Arabs as they disappeared hurriedly into a narrow alleyway between stone houses. An instant later, from the center of the city ahead of them, there was a thunderous, concussive explosion, and before Uri's eyes a dark, ragged cloud of smoke drifted up into the quivering blue brightness of the sky. Shrill, unearthly cries rang out in the terrible stillness that followed the crash. And then automatic weapon fire ripped through the air. The jeep shot forward and rounded a corner. Uri spotted a pair of young Israeli soldiers running. *"What is it?"* he cried out.

"Don't . . . know," answered one in a voice that could barely be heard.

Suddenly, without warning, a donkey cart emerged at breakneck speed from a cross street and surged directly into the path of the oncoming jeep. The captain swerved sharply to avoid hitting it and ran up over the curb full-tilt into the facade of an iron-shuttered house. *"Dammit! Dammit to hell!"* screamed the shaken, red-faced, sweating captain at the terrified cart driver.

Leaving the captain behind, Uri leaped out and, drawing his revolver, joined the soldiers. At full speed, the three of them ran and turned into a street that led directly to the main square. From the direction of Military Headquarters, a siren began to wail. Ahead, scattered across the sunlit flagstones of the square, bodies lay crumpled. To the left, down a side street that led out of the square, crouching Israeli soldiers with Uzis opened fire.

There were two or three soldiers beside the fallen Jews. Catching sight of Uri, one of them ran up. He was ashen-faced and sweating profusely, and there was blood on his hands and on the sleeves of his shirt. "Lieutenant," he mumbled hoarsely, fighting for breath and straining to form his words coherently, "they seemed to come out of nowhere, the Arabs—it happened so quickly." He winced and flecks of white spittle showed at the corners of his mouth. "They tossed a grenade and then they opened up with automatic weapons," he said, pointing to the left side of the square, "from over there——" He blinked and fell silent for a moment, and when he spoke again his voice was no more than a wisp of sound: "The settlers—were hit in the first burst of fire. And the Arab woman lying there, who was standing in front of the school building, was cut down by the grenade. . . ."

Fear gripped Uri's heart. He ran toward the fallen woman.

From the blood-spattered stones of the square where she lay, Layleh gazed upward. Above her, glittering through a vast distance, was the sky she had always turned to in time of sorrow and in time of joy alike. It looked like a flowing river and then it looked like a lake and then it looked like the bottom of an immensely deep well, and then her vision blurred and it looked like nothing she had ever seen or imagined before.

When her sight cleared, Layleh saw a familiar figure—the figure that haunted her dreams and her waking hours alike—running toward her. Her gaze lifted and, through the waves of pain that swept over her body and made her mind seem to shudder, she saw the beloved features of her Uri. A violent longing, stronger than any she had ever in her life felt, seized her. She strained desperately to raise herself and to call out to him, but she had not the strength to command the slightest movement of her head or limbs and could not force a sound from the ragged fire that surged from her chest through her throat. Yet she saw his eyes, she saw his eloquent, loving eyes clearly, and she knew—knew beyond any doubt or uncertainty—that he saw and recognized her! Through her agony, she felt joy and even comfort, and though her lips were stiff and alien she smiled in her mind and in her heart. He was coming closer and closer. And then an avalanche of nausea washed over her and her vision failed. . . .

Uri knelt beside her, and her eyes fluttered open. "Uri . . ."

"Layleh . . . Layleh . . ." he cried, the tears streaming from his eyes.

He wanted—he wanted desperately—to enfold her in his arms and crush her to him. But he dared not do it. Over her breast, the dress—the same dress she had worn in "their" woods above Jerusalem—was heavy with welling blood. Her dark eyes, made restless by pain, stared into his; gazed into his; searched into his. Kneeling in the stone dust of the square, with the sound of the sirens screaming closer and the percussive bursts of the Uzis and the indecipherable shouts ringing in his ears, he bent closer and put his lips to her forehead and kissed her gently.

"Uri . . ." she whispered hoarsely. "Uri . . . am I . . . dreaming? Uri . . . is it . . . really *you?*"

"I'm here, my darling."

"Here . . . to stay . . . with me?"

"Yes, my darling . . . here to stay with you."

"Forever . . . Uri?"

"Forever, darling."

Then, with the light dying in her eyes, she smiled. "So . . ." she whispered faintly, with the last flow of breath that she was ever to have. "So . . . you *are* here, Uri." She gasped. "So . . . I . . . am . . . awake, after all."

"Yes, yes, my darling!" he sobbed.

But she was not awake. She was no longer alive.